# HYGIENE for MANAGEMENT

***A text for food hygiene courses***

**Richard A. Sprenger, B.Sc.(Hons.), D.M.S., F.C.I.E.H., M.R.E.H.I.S., F.S.O.F.H.T.**

Published by

**HIGHFIELD PUBLICATIONS**

"VUE POINTE", SPINNEY HILL, SPROTBROUGH,
DONCASTER, SOUTH YORKSHIRE, DN5 7LY U.K.
Telephone: Doncaster (01302)850007
Facsimile: (01302)311112

**TO JAYNE, JASON, CHRISTIAN AND BECKY**

First published 1983
Second edition 1985
Third edition 1988
Fourth edition 1989
Fifth edition 1991
Sixth edition 1993
Seventh edition 1995
Reprinted January 1997



ISBN 1 871912 60 1



*Printed by Garnett Dickinson Print Limited, Rotherham and London*

# Contents

# *Acknowledgements*

During the compilation of this book I have discussed the content with, and received guidance from, several experts in the field of food hygiene and many persons employed throughout the food industry. I am grateful for their comments and assistance. I am indebted to Angela Hunter for applying her skills to correcting errors and making the English more readily understandable. I record sincere thanks to the following people for their contributions and support: Mark Du Val (LACOTS), John Frater and Graham Walker (REHIS), Ned Kingcott and John Barnes (DH), Dr. Philip Barlow, Phil Cassidy and John Birkett (University of Humberside), Dr J. D. Selman and David Timperley (Campden & Chorleywood Food Research Association), Dr W. J. Reilly (The Scottish Centre for Infection and Environmental Health), Patrick Wall (PHLS Communicable Disease Surveillance Centre), Perry Donaldson (Northern Group PHC), Dr. Diane Roberts (PHLS), David Edwards (Hull C. C.), Mike Sheard (Leeds Metropolitan University), Yvonne Garraway and Clare Batty (Doncaster M.B.C.), Roger Armstrong (Bradford M.D.C.), Julia Mottishaw (University of Huddersfield), Peter Bird (Lever Industrial), Steve Bagshaw (Holchem Laboratories Ltd.), Peter Bateman (Rentokil Ltd.), John Kay (Killgerm Chemicals), Bill Woodley (Northern Foods), Tony Saunders, Simon Barrett, Clive Wadey, Mike Glarvey and last but not least I acknowledge with gratitude the inspiration and constructive comments from Richard North.

I would also like to thank the following companies for providing photographs to illustrate many of the points covered in the text:

| | |
|---|---|
| Altro Floors Ltd., | 7 Caxton Hill, Hertford SG13 7NB<br>Tel: Hertford (01992) 584212 |
| Digitron Instrumentation Ltd., | Technology House, Mead Lane, Hertford SG13 7AW<br>Tel: Hertford (01992) 587441 |
| Foster Refrigerator (U.K.) Ltd., | Oldmedow Road, King's Lynn, Norfolk PE30 4JU<br>Tel: King's Lynn (01553) 691122 |
| Hygienius Ltd., | Cotterhill Farm, Bug Hill, Woldingham, Surrey CR3 7LB<br>Tel: (01883) 652598 |
| Lever Industrial Ltd., | P.O. Box 100, Runcorn, Cheshire WA7 3JZ<br>Tel: Runcorn (01928) 719000 |
| Rentokil Ltd., | Felcourt, East Grinstead, West Sussex RH19 2JY<br>Tel: Lingfield (01342) 833022 |

# *Preface*

All organizations work towards achieving objectives and the primary objectives of commercial food businesses are to produce, distribute, store, handle, prepare or sell food at a profit. To ensure a profitable operation, managers must implement policies and documented systems relating to all their activities. One of the most important of these policies is maintaining cost-effective hygiene by way of a planned hygiene programme based on hazard analysis and controls at points critical to food safety. To formulate such a programme, managers will require an understanding of basic microbiology and food legislation. In large organizations, information of a more technical nature will be required and this is normally provided by specialists, such as microbiologists or hygiene officers. High standards of hygiene are imperative to prevent food poisoning, food spoilage, loss of productivity, pest infestation and prosecutions for contraventions of legislation. However, these standards of hygiene must be achieved at a reasonable cost to ensure that the business remains profitable.

One of the most successful and cheapest methods of reducing the risk of food poisoning is to ensure that all staff receive comprehensive training in the aspects of hygiene relating to their work. A trained, informed supervisory staff is essential in every food establishment and all personnel must be motivated to work towards the objectives of the organization. Suitable persons need to be employed and they must be given repeated instruction on correct food handling methods. Staff should be required to attend a nationally recognized hygiene course of an appropriate level or comparable in-house training sessions.

Management commitment is essential to achieve hygienically operated premises. Managers must lead by example and demonstrate a belief in the necessity for hygienic practices.

The correct handling of food is essential to profitable operation. Food which is stored at incorrect temperatures may result in food poisoning or spoilage, and failure to carry out stock rotation will result in waste food and pest infestations. Supervision of food throughout processing is essential to avoid contamination, and suitable packaging, storage facilities and distribution vehicles must be provided.

To ensure hygienic and efficient operation, premises must be planned, designed and constructed in accordance with certain basic principles. The correct materials must be selected for surface finishes and equipment. Cleaning, disinfection and maintenance costs must be considered at the planning stage, as a modest increase in capital expenditure may reduce considerably the day-to-day operational costs.

Infestations of insects, rodents or birds are likely to result in food contamination, food wastage, prosecutions and even closure of food premises. Managers must be aware of the basic principles of pest control and the action to take in the event of invasion by pests. Guidance is given on environmental controls, selection and use of contractors and common eradication techniques.

One of the most important and frequently neglected functions of management is to monitor and control operations in order to facilitate any necessary adjustments to ensure achievement of objectives. The actual operation or standard should be compared with that which was planned. Regular hygiene inspections of food premises should be carried out by trained personnel, and food should be sampled at all appropriate stages of production and sale. Quality Assurance is essential, not only in food factories but also catering premises and retail outlets. A reduction in customer complaints can be an important indicator of improved food hygiene.

## Management responsibilities

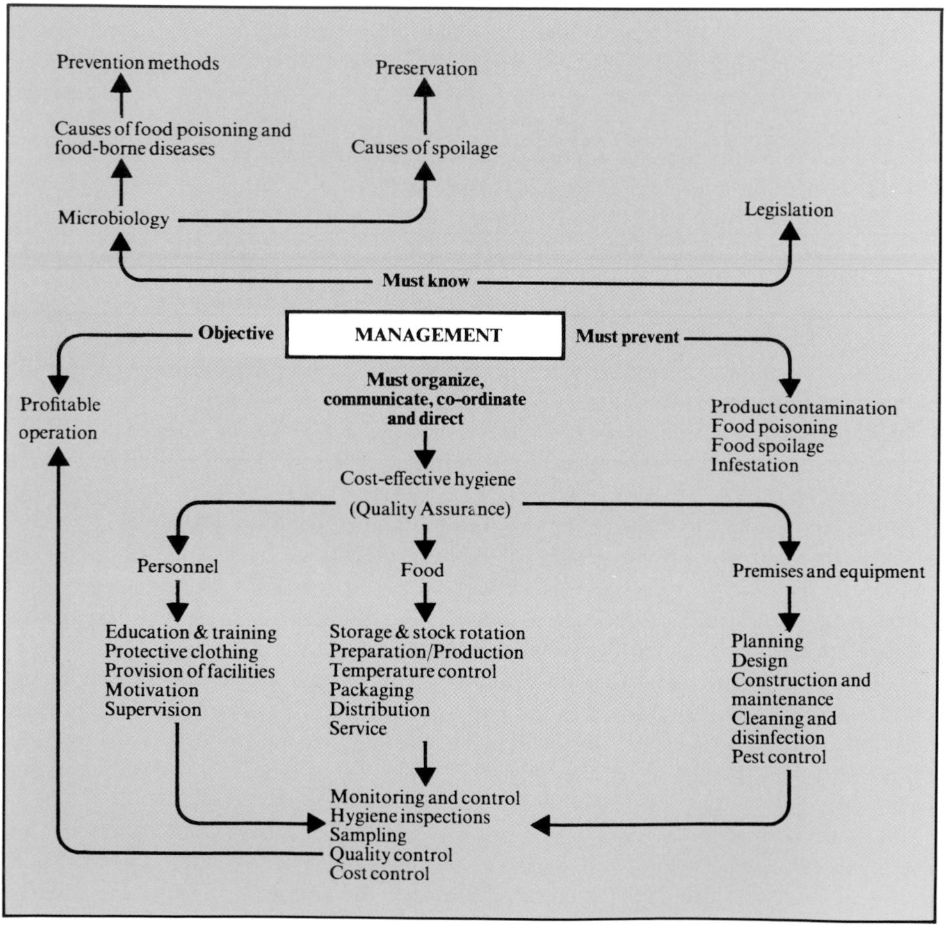

CHAPTER 1

# An introduction to food hygiene and food poisoning

Hygiene is the science of preserving health. A hygienic operation presents no risk of illness from the operations carried out therein. Food hygiene is much more than cleanliness, it involves all measures necessary to ensure the safety and wholesomeness of food during preparation, processing, manufacturing, packaging, storage, distribution handling and offering for sale or supply to the consumer. This will involve:

(1) protecting food from risk of contamination of any kind and this includes the effective cleaning and disinfection of food premises and equipment, and requires high standards of personal hygiene and training of staff;
(2) preventing any organisms multiplying to an extent which would expose consumers to risk, or result in premature decomposition of food; and
(3) destroying any harmful bacteria in the food by thorough cooking, processing or irradiation.

**The cost of food poisoning and poor hygiene**

Persons carrying on a food business have legal, commercial and moral obligations to provide safe food. The costs resulting from food poisoning can be very high, as are those from poor hygiene. These costs, both financial and social, fall on employers and employees as well as those persons who are ill. Costs for employers include:

(1) the loss of working days, and productivity, from illness caused by employees eating contaminated food. Even minor infections increase costs for employers through absence of employees;
(2) the closure of food premises by local authority action;
(3) a loss of business and reputation, either from bad publicity or from public reaction to poor standards, food poisoning outbreaks and even deaths;
(4) fines and costs of legal action taken because of contraventions of hygiene legislation or because of the sale of unfit or unsatisfactory food;
(5) civil action taken by food poisoning sufferers;
(6) food losses due to premature spoilage or damage, because of poor stock rotation, incorrect storage temperature or pest infestations;
(7) higher staff turnover, with attendant costs and inefficiencies from staff unwilling or unable to tolerate poor standards;

(8) food complaints and costs of internal investigation;
(9) loss of production; and
(10) decontamination, cleaning and replacement of equipment.

Food employees may suffer by:

(1) losing their jobs because of closure, loss of business or because they become long term carriers of food poisoning organisms especially salmonella; and
(2) losing overtime or bonuses.

**Cost-effective hygiene**

Cost-effective hygiene involves the identification of hygiene priorities and the allocation of available resources to these priorities. To achieve this objective it is imperative to implement hazard analysis, risk assessment and monitoring and control procedures to ensure the safety and wholesomeness of all food products, especially high-risk foods.

**High-risk foods**

High-risk foods are ready-to-eat foods which, under favourable conditions, support the multiplication of pathogenic bacteria and are intended for consumption without treatment which would destroy such organisms. These foods are usually high in protein, requiring refrigerated storage and protection. They include:

(1) all cooked meat and poultry;
(2) cooked meat products including gravy and stock;
(3) milk, cream, artificial cream, custards and dairy produce;
(4) cooked eggs and products made with eggs, for example, mayonnaise, but excluding pastry, bread and similar baked goods;
(5) shellfish and other seafoods, for example, oysters; and
(6) cooked rice.

**Bacteria**

Bacteria are essential to life. They are minute organisms, often referred to as germs, which are found everywhere, including on and in man and food. Bacteria on the body are usually confined to a particular site, and are known as commensals (part of the normal flora). For example, some species of staphylococcus are found on the skin and in the mouth and nose, other species are transient and may cause skin infections, such as boils. If harmful (pathogenic) species of staphylococcus, especially those which cause skin infections, are transferred to food they may cause illness. Most bacteria are harmless, some being necessary, for example, in yogurt and cheese manufacture. However, two types of bacteria create major problems within the food industry:

(1) *Spoilage bacteria* - responsible for the decomposition of food.
(2) *Pathogenic bacteria* - responsible for causing illness such as dysentery, typhoid and food poisoning.

**Food poisoning**

Food poisoning is an acute illness, usually of sudden onset, brought about by eating contaminated or poisonous food. The symptoms normally include one or more of the following; abdominal pain, diarrhoea, vomiting and nausea.

Food poisoning may be caused by:

(1) bacteria or their toxins;
(2) chemicals including metals;
(3) plants or fish;
(4) viruses;
(5) mycotoxins.

**Bacterial food poisoning**

Bacterial food poisoning may be defined as, "an acute disturbance of the gastrointestinal tract resulting in abdominal pain, with or without diarrhoea and vomiting, due to eating food contaminated by specific pathogenic bacteria or their toxins". The incubation period is normally short (between one and 48 hours). The number of bacteria required to cause illness in the healthy adult is usually large and multiplication of bacteria normally occurs within the food.

Patients usually recover in a few days but where body defences are low, illness may be prolonged and lead to complications. Botulism is more serious, often results in death, and survivors can take many months to recover.

**Carriers**

Carriers are people who show no symptoms of illness but excrete food poisoning or food borne pathogens which may contaminate food, for example, salmonellae or shigellae. Organisms may be excreted intermittently.

*Convalescent carriers* are people who have recovered from an illness but still harbour the organism. The convalescent state may be quite prolonged and salmonellae are sometimes excreted for several months.

*Healthy carriers* are people who have displayed no symptoms but harbour the causal organism. Healthy carriers may have become infected with pathogenic bacteria from contact with raw food with which they work, particularly poultry or meat.

Symptomless carriers can only be confirmed by bacteriological or, in some cases, serological screening, i.e. examination of faecal specimens or blood. However, routine screening of food handlers to detect carriers is not cost-effective. Intermittent excretors may be missed and a person may become a carrier the week after screening.

Medical questionnaires/interviews of new starters (important to identify persons with a history of gastrointestinal illness), induction training, effective communication and supervision of company rules, counselling, bacteriological testing of persons returning to work after illness involving diarrhoea or vomiting or illness whilst on holidays abroad and contacts of persons suffering from food poisoning are all useful to assist in the detection of carriers.

**Allergy**

An identifiable immunological response to food or food additives may be described as an allergy. The allergen is usually a protein and several systems within the body may be affected, for example, the respiratory system, the gastrointestinal tract, the skin and the central nervous system. Symptoms vary considerably and may include bronchitis, vomiting, diarrhoea, urticaria (rash) and migraine.

The first exposure to the specific food, for example, peanuts, does not produce symptoms, however, subsequent exposure results in a typical allergic response. Reactions may be mild or extremely severe and may occur immediately the food is consumed, or up to 48 hours later. An allergic response should not be confused with food poisoning.

## THE INCIDENCE OF BACTERIAL FOOD POISONING

Because high standards of food hygiene should prevent the contamination and multiplication of food poisoning bacteria in food, trends of food poisoning statistics are often used as a measure of hygiene standards or as an indication of the success or failure of control systems or enforcement procedures. In the late 1980's the increase in the reported number of salmonella cases, and the consequential public concern, was one of the main reasons for the enactment of the Food Safety Act, 1990.

Unfortunately, national statistics on the reported number of confirmed food poisoning cases are unavailable. Furthermore, trends in reported food poisoning statistics can be seriously distorted by factors which may have nothing to do with hygiene standards, such as the inclusion of a new "food poisoning" organism which may or may not be transmitted by food, for example, campylobacter. The number of ill persons seeking medical help and the number of faecal specimens submitted will also affect the statistics, for example, because of new legislation or increased publicity.

Furthermore, the vast majority of persons suffering from diarrhoea and vomiting are not reported and the Department of Health is currently undertaking studies to ascertain the actual levels of food poisoning in the community.

*Notifications of food poisoning*

Doctors attending a case of suspected food poisoning, (any disease of an infectious or toxic nature caused, or thought to be caused, by the consumption of food or water) are legally required to notify the Proper Officer of the local authority. Each week the Proper Officer sends details of notified infections to the Office of Population, Censuses and Surveys (OPCS), which collates this data for England and Wales. This notification scheme is intended to facilitate the rapid identification and investigation of suspected cases of food-borne illness by Environmental Health Officers and enables implicated food premises to be identified as quickly as possible.

As the OPCS statistics include a large number of persons suffering from diarrhoea and/or vomiting which are not proven to be food-borne, they could more accurately be described as "notified cases of gastroenteritis," and should not be used to indicate trends in food poisoning. In fact current trends are more likely to be affected by such things as viral gastroenteritis, campylobacter enteritis, including non food-borne, and the willingness of doctors to notify suspect cases of food poisoning.

In the absence of information on the number of confirmed food poisoning cases, alternative statistics should be used by persons interested in trends of food poisoning. Arguably, the most representative statistics of actual trends of food poisoning are those relating to specific organisms known to cause food poisoning, such as salmonella.

*Food poisoning statistics*

A **case** of bacterial food poisoning is a person with symptoms who has become ill as a result of eating contaminated food. This can only be confirmed by isolating food poisoning organisms or toxin from faecal or vomitus specimens. Statistics relating to isolates and suspect cases should not be confused with confirmed cases.

Figure 1 shows the annual totals of salmonellosis based on laboratory isolations from faecal specimens. Although the vast majority of isolates will be cases of salmonella food poisoning these statistics also include symptomless excreters, persons who may have non food-borne salmonellosis and persons who acquired the illness abroad. Nevertheless, at the present time, these statistics are the most accurate representation of salmonella food poisoning trends over the last ten years.

A survey in Yorkshire and Humberside between June and August 1986 showed that 27.4% of reported cases of salmonella food poisoning in that period originated abroad, although the national percentage is usually considered to be much lower.

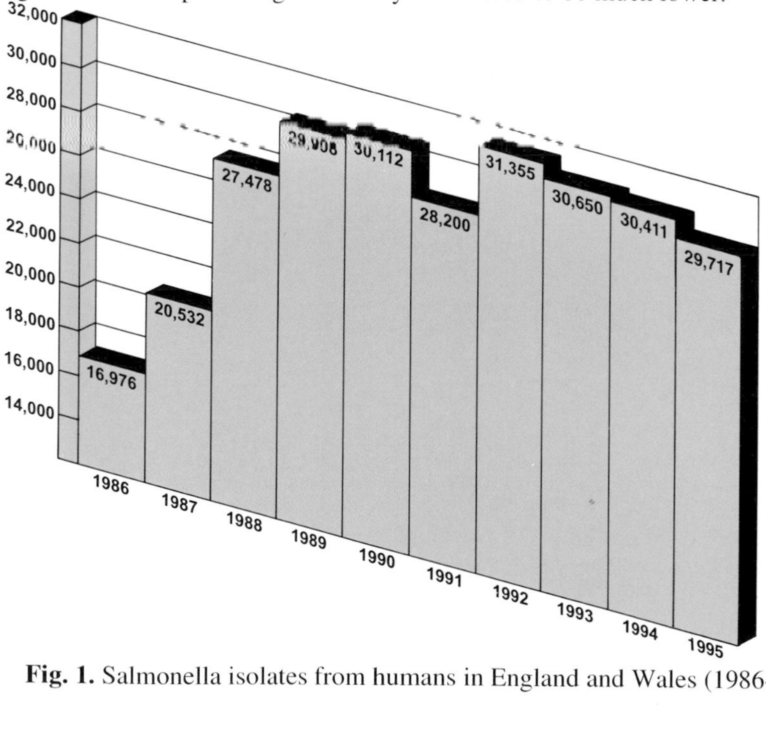


**Fig. 1.** Salmonella isolates from humans in England and Wales (1986-1995).

**TABLE I** LABORATORY REPORTS OF OUTBREAKS OF BACTERIAL FOOD POISONING AND SALMONELLOSIS IN ENGLAND AND WALES(1986-1995)*

| **Outbreak** | **1986** | **1987** | **1988** | **1989** | **1990** | **1991** | **1992** | **1993** | **1994** | **1995** |
|---|---|---|---|---|---|---|---|---|---|---|
| General outbreaks | 169 | 169 | 213 | 205 | 197 | 210 | 213 | 160 | 137 | 148 |
| Family outbreaks | 275 | 288 | 294 | **820 | 793 | 792 | 1545 | 1455 | 1249 | 1095 |

*All statistics relating to England and Wales (excluding acquired abroad) are provided courtesy of the P.H.L.S. Communicable Disease Surveillance Centre.

**Changes in the analysis of individual cases have improved the identification of family outbreaks, resulting in a large increase in this category (1989 onwards).

*General outbreaks* - two or more cases in different households.

*Family outbreaks* - two or more cases confined to the same household.

**TABLE II** CASES OF *BACILLUS SPP., STAPHYLOCOCCUS AUREUS* AND *CLOSTRIDIUM PERFRINGENS* FOOD POISONING (1986-95)

| | **1986** | **1987** | **1988** | **1989** | **1990** | **1991** | **1992** | **1993** | **1994** | **1995** |
|---|---|---|---|---|---|---|---|---|---|---|
| *Bacillus spp.* | 65 | 137 | 418 | 164 | 162 | 95 | 182 | 31 | 87 | 87 |
| *S. aureus* | 76 | 178 | 111 | 104 | 55 | 61 | 109 | 28 | 74 | 59 |
| *Cl. perfringens* | 896 | 1266 | 1312 | 901 | 1442 | 733 | 805 | 562 | 449 | 342 |

**TABLE III** COMMON LOCATIONS OF OUTBREAKS OF FOOD POISONING (1984-1993)

| **Location** | **1984** | **1985** | **1986** | **1987** | **1988** | **1989** | **1990** | **1991** | **1992** | **1993** |
|---|---|---|---|---|---|---|---|---|---|---|
| Private houses* | 367 | 259 | 326 | 324 | 320 | 820 | 793 | 792 | N/A | N/A |
| Restaurants/hotels/ receptions | 94 | 64 | 71 | 92 | 90 | 102 | 102 | 101 | 121 | 120 |
| Hospitals | 37 | 36 | 33 | 26 | 21 | 16 | 10 | 15 | 6 | 11 |
| Institutions** | 13 | 19 | 19 | 13 | 29 | 22 | 40 | 27 | 23 | 37 |
| Canteens | 16 | 10 | 9 | 4 | 14 | 6 | 8 | 8 | 13 | 14 |
| Schools | 7 | 8 | 8 | 3 | 6 | 7 | 4 | 7 | 12 | 10 |
| Farms | 9 | 3 | 2 | - | 3 | - | 2 | 1 | 1 | 1 |
| Shops | 10 | 5 | 4 | 13 | 11 | 12 | 6 | 17 | 18 | 10 |

*Outbreaks originating in private houses are general outbreaks (involving members of more than one private residence), for example, dinner parties but mostly food prepared in a domestic kitchen and served at receptions, functions in marquees, village halls etc. From 1992 the latter has been included with "receptions". In most investigations of family outbreaks the suspect food is not identified.

**Institutions include nursing homes, residential homes, prisons and army camps.

**TABLE IV** SUSPECTED FOODS INVOLVED IN BACTERIAL FOOD POISONING OUTBREAKS (1983-1991)

| Food vehicle | % Outbreaks 1983 | 1984 | 1985 | 1986 | 1987 | 1988 | 1989 | 1990 | 1991 |
|---|---|---|---|---|---|---|---|---|---|
| Chicken/poultry | 26.0 | 12.1 | 16.8 | 19.9 | 21.1 | 13.8 | 10.6 | 12.5 | 8.3 |
| Turkey | 9.0 | 10.6 | 11.5 | 7.4 | 12.0 | 8.8 | 5.6 | 7.8 | 7.5 |
| Beef | 12.5 | 13.6 | 6.7 | 8.1 | 7.7 | 5.6 | 9.2 | 6.3 | 6.0 |
| Pork/ham | 5.7 | 5.5 | 7.2 | 16.2 | 4.2 | 8.1 | 9.2 | 2.3 | 3.0 |
| Lamb | 2.0 | 0.5 | 2.8 | 1.4 | 0.7 | 0.6 | 0.7 | 2.3 | 3.7 |
| Other meats/pies | 17.0 | 25.5 | 22.5 | 21.3 | 21.9 | 12.5 | 20.4 | 10.2 | 13.4 |
| Gravy/sauces | 0.5 | 1.5 | 0.0 | 0.0 | 0.7 | 1.3 | 0.0 | 0.8 | 0.7 |
| Milk/dairy | 6.7 | 10.0 | 5.7 | 3.7 | 1.4 | 1.9 | 0.7 | 1.6 | 2.2 |
| Rice | 4.6 | 2.0 | 1.4 | 3.7 | 3.5 | 2.5 | 6.3 | 6.2 | 2.2 |
| Fish/shellfish | 1.6 | 3.5 | 1.0 | 1.4 | 3.5 | 1.9 | 0.7 | 0.0 | 0.0 |
| Eggs/egg products | 1.0 | 0.0 | 4.3 | 2.9 | 5.6 | 22.5 | 10.6 | 13.3 | 14.9 |
| Other foods | 13.4 | 15.2 | 20.1 | 14.0 | 17.6 | 20.6 | 26.0 | 36.7 | 38.1 |

The food implicated in food poisoning outbreaks due to *Salmonella,* is only identified in around 20% of outbreaks.

**TABLE V** FACTORS CONTRIBUTING TO 1479 OUTBREAKS OF FOOD POISONING IN ENGLAND AND WALES (1970-1982)*

| | Contributing factor | Total number of outbreaks in which factor recorded (%)** |
|---|---|---|
| 1 | Preparation too far in advance | 844 (57) |
| 2 | Storage at ambient temperature | 566 (38) |
| 3 | Inadequate cooling | 468 (30) |
| 4 | Inadequate reheating | 391 (26) |
| 5 | Contaminated processed food | 246 (17) |
| 6 | Undercooking | 223 (15) |
| 7 | Contaminated canned food | 104 (7) |
| 8 | Inadequate thawing | 95 (6) |
| 9 | Cross-contamination | 94 (6) |
| 10 | Raw food consumed | 93 (6) |
| 11 | Improper warm holding | 77 (5) |
| 12 | Infected food handlers | 65 (4) |
| 13 | Use of left-overs | 62 (4) |
| 14 | Extra large quantities prepared | 48 (3) |

*Roberts D. 6th Edition of Food Poisoning and Food Hygiene.
**In some outbreaks more than one factor was involved.

**TABLE VI** FOOD-BORNE DISEASE IN NORTHERN IRELAND (1989-1995)

| **ORGANISM** | **1989** | **1990** | **1991** | **1992** | **1993** | **1994** | **1995** |
|---|---|---|---|---|---|---|---|
| *Salmonella spp.* | 203 | 260 | 160 | 224 | 178 | 276 | 446 |
| *Clostridium perfringens* | 0 | 0 | 0 | 1 | 0 | 0 | 0 |
| *Staphylococcus aureus* | 0 | 0 | 0 | 0 | 0 | 0 | 0 |
| *Bacillus cereus* | 0 | 0 | 2 | 0 | 0 | 0 | 1 |
| *Yersinia enterocolitica* | 1 | 1 | 4 | 9 | 9 | 7 | 9 |
| *Campylobacter spp.* | 192 | 244 | 306 | 419 | 353 | 440 | 557 |
| *Escherichia coli (total)* | 128 | 120 | 142 | 98 | 83 | 81 | 99 |
| *Escherichia coli 0157* | 1 | 1 | 2 | 1 | 2 | 3 | 7 |
| *Shigella sonnei* | 258 | 17 | 43 | 98 | 104 | 102 | 253 |
| *Giardia lamblia* cysts | 47 | 69 | 49 | 63 | 58 | 40 | 49 |
| Cryptosporidial oocysts | 13 | 204 | 149 | 58 | 177 | 89 | 81 |
| Food poisoning* | 501 | 819 | 636 | 915 | 954 | 1005 | 1266 |
| Rotavirus | 173 | 220 | 272 | 297 | 580 | 176 | 442 |
| SRSV | 2 | 8 | 23 | 35 | 17 | 28 | 31 |
| Adenovirus | N/A | N/A | 181 | 188 | 181 | 189 | 209 |

*Notifications to Health Boards. (All the remaining statistics are obtained from laboratory reports, notified to the DHSS (NI).

## THE INCIDENCE OF FOOD-BORNE DISEASE IN SCOTLAND

There are approximately 3,000 reported cases of food-borne disease in Scotland each year, the majority being caused by the common food poisoning bacteria.

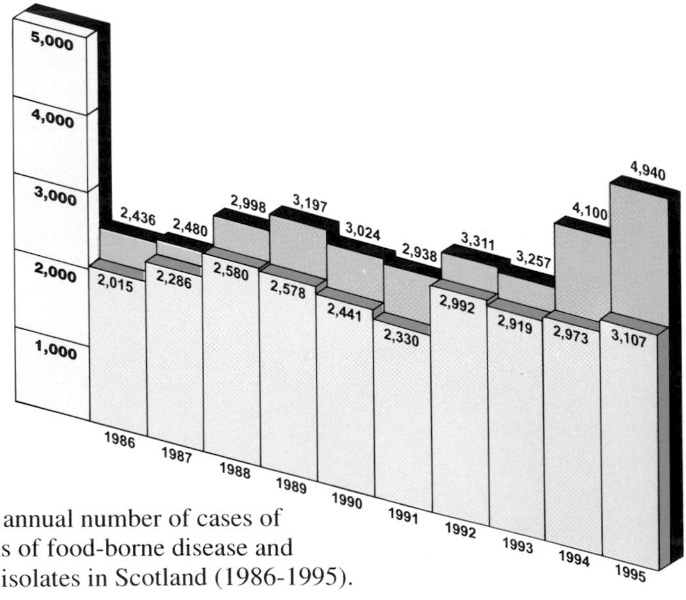


**Fig. 2.** The annual number of cases of notifications of food-borne disease and salmonella isolates in Scotland (1986-1995).

**TABLE VII**

OUTBREAKS OF FOOD-BORNE DISEASE IN SCOTLAND (1985-1994)*

| | **1985** | **1986** | **1987** | **1988** | **1989** | **1990** | **1991** | **1992** | **1993** | **1994** |
|---|---|---|---|---|---|---|---|---|---|---|
| General outbreaks | 50 | 51 | 58 | 72 | 50 | 51 | 35 | 30 | 47 | 39 |
| (persons involved) | 1105 | 626 | 1372 | 1235 | 745 | 1083 | 755 | 356 | 706 | 652 |
| Household outbreaks | 135 | 133 | 176 | 147 | 146 | 124 | 115 | 157 | 156 | 121 |
| (persons involved) | 380 | 361 | 453 | 411 | 397 | 336 | 302 | 424 | 386 | 335 |
| Number of deaths | 5 | 4 | 2 | 2 | 0 | 3 | 0 | 0 | 1 | 0 |

*Food-borne disease* - any disease of an infectious or toxic nature caused by, or thought to be caused by, the consumption of food or water.

*Household outbreak* - involves two or more persons resident in the same private household not apparently connected with another case or outbreak.

*General outbreak* - involves two or more persons not confined to one private household.

**TABLE VIII** OUTBREAKS OF FOOD-BORNE DISEASE IN SCOTLAND (1985-1994) (PLACE WHERE FOOD MISHANDLED)*

| **Location** | **1985** | **1986** | **1987** | **1988** | **1989** | **1990** | **1991** | **1992** | **1993** | **1994** |
|---|---|---|---|---|---|---|---|---|---|---|
| Commercial catering ** | 6 | 13 | 38 | 32 | 26 | 32 | 20 | 16 | 40 | 22 |
| Hospital | 3 | 1 | 3 | 5 | 1 | 2 | 1 | 0 | 0 | 0 |
| Private residence | 2 | 13 | 30 | 38 | 24 | 28 | 17 | 30 | 23 | 25 |
| Residential home | 3 | 4 | 2 | 1 | 1 | 2 | 3 | 0 | 0 | 1 |
| Oil Rig | 1 | 0 | 0 | 2 | 3 | 1 | 0 | 0 | 1 | 0 |
| Farm | 4 | 2 | 4 | 2 | 2 | 3 | 4 | 2 | 0 | 0 |
| Non-Commercial catering | 1 | 1 | 2 | 1 | 0 | 0 | 0 | 1 | 0 | 0 |
| Factory canteen | 1 | 2 | 2 | 0 | 3 | 0 | 0 | 1 | 0 | 1 |
| Schools | 1 | 0 | 1 | 1 | 1 | 1 | 0 | 1 | 1 | 0 |
| H.M. Prison | 0 | 0 | 0 | 2 | 1 | 0 | 0 | 0 | 0 | 0 |
| Military catering | 3 | 0 | 1 | 1 | 3 | 0 | 0 | 1 | 2 | 0 |
| Processing plant | 1 | 1 | 2 | 1 | 2 | 3 | 0 | 0 | 0 | 3 |
| Retail outlet | 0 | 3 | 13 | 8 | 4 | 2 | 3 | 9 | 4 | 2 |
| Others/unknown | 24 | ♣144 | 136 | 125 | 125 | 101 | 102 | 126 | 132 | 106 |

*All statistics relating to Scotland courtesy of the Scottish Centre for Infection and Environmental Health. The statistics provided for 1994 are provisional.

**Includes hotels and restaurants.

♣From 1986 this figure includes general and family outbreaks whereas earlier years exclude family outbreaks.

**TABLE IX** FOOD VEHICLES INVOLVED IN FOOD-BORNE DISEASE OUTBREAKS IN SCOTLAND (1985-1994)

| Food vehicle | 1985 | 1986 | 1987 | 1988 | 1989 | 1990 | 1991 | 1992 | 1993 | 1994 |
|---|---|---|---|---|---|---|---|---|---|---|
| Chicken | 23 | 25 | 40 | 44 | 25 | 18 | 15 | 25 | 19 | 11 |
| Meat/meat products | 25 | 25 | 24 | 24 | 15 | 14 | 10 | 5 | 11 | 5 |
| Turkey | 3 | 1 | 2 | 2 | 2 | 1 | 0 | 1 | 4 | 0 |
| Milk and cream | 9 | 3 | 5 | 1 | 1 | 7 | 6 | 3 | 2 | 3 |
| Rice | 2 | 2 | 3 | 4 | 2 | 1 | 1 | 0 | 0 | 2 |
| Shellfish/fish | 1 | 2 | 5 | 12 | 5 | 1 | 1 | 1 | 5 | 12 |
| Eggs/egg products | 0 | 2 | 2 | 8 | 10 | 2 | 3 | 4 | 10 | 10 |
| Others | 7 | *6 | 7 | 6 | 6 | 4 | 5 | 5 | 3 | 10 |
| Not Known | 116 | 121 | 153 | 122 | 130 | 95 | 109 | 143 | 149 | 107 |

*Includes one outbreak of hepatitis A involving ice-cream.

**TABLE X** FACTORS CONTRIBUTING TO OUTBREAKS OF FOOD-BORNE DISEASE IN SCOTLAND (1985-1994)

| Contributing factor | 1985 | 1986 | 1987 | 1988 | 1989 | 1990 | 1991 | 1992 | 1993 | 1994 |
|---|---|---|---|---|---|---|---|---|---|---|
| Cross-contamination/ contaminated equipment | 6 | 6 | 9 | 11 | 7 | 12 | 6 | 8 | 10 | 4 |
| Inadequate cooking | 5 | 11 | 4 | 7 | 15 | 9 | 7 | 5 | 13 | 3 |
| Inadequate cooling | 9 | 8 | 7 | 4 | 4 | 7 | 5 | 3 | 2 | 3 |
| Inadequate refrigeration | 5 | 11 | 8 | 18 | 9 | 4 | 2 | 2 | 5 | 1 |
| Inadequate reheating | 8 | 8 | 2 | 10 | 4 | 6 | 7 | 2 | 5 | 0 |
| Inadequate thawing | 4 | 1 | 5 | 7 | 1 | 5 | 1 | 3 | 2 | 0 |
| Infected handler | 0 | 3 | 1 | 3 | 4 | 3 | 3 | 4 | 4 | 2 |
| Raw foods/unsafe source | 0 | 0 | 0 | 0 | 0 | 3 | 4 | 10 | 10 | 14 |

## THE PREVENTION OF BACTERIAL FOOD POISONING

Management must provide a satisfactory environment, competent and properly trained personnel, suitable equipment and facilities and adequate temperature control to ensure that food at all stages of production, storage, distribution and sale is as safe as reasonably practicable.

### The food poisoning chain

The chain of events associated with an outbreak of food poisoning consists of:

(1) contamination of high-risk food with food poisoning bacteria;

(2) multiplication of these bacteria; and

(3) consumption of the food.

In order to prevent illness this chain must be broken and it is essential that care be taken to ensure that:

**(1) The contamination of food is kept to an absolute minimum:**

This may be achieved by:

(i) separating raw and cooked food at all stages of preparation, storage and distribution. The same equipment or working surface must not be used to handle raw and high-risk foods, or ready-to-eat foods such as lettuce, unless disinfected between uses. The liquid from thawed, frozen meat and poultry must not come into contact with high-risk or ready-to-eat foods;

(ii) not using unsuitable, defective or dirty equipment;

(iii) not using dirty wiping cloths. Disposable cloths are preferable;

(iv) only handling food when unavoidable. Tongs, plates and trays should be used in preference to hands;

(v) maintaining the highest standards of personal hygiene at all times. Hand washing, particularly after handling raw meat or using the W.C., is essential. Suitable protective clothing must be worn;

(vi) keeping food covered wherever possible;

(vii) preventing insects, animals and birds from entering food rooms or coming into contact with food;

(viii) storing food in rodent-proof containers and ensuring that the lids are tightly replaced after use;

(ix) using the correct cleaning procedures. Premises, work surfaces and equipment must be kept clean and, where necessary, disinfected;

(x) not handling parts of crockery or cutlery which come into contact with food, for example, knife blades or inside glasses and cups;

(xi) removing unfit or waste food and refuse promptly and keeping them apart from other foods;

(xii) keeping food and equipment off the floor;

(xiii) not using wash-hand basins for washing food or food equipment and not using food sinks for hand washing.

**Fig. 3.** Failure to separate raw and cooked food in a meat factory.

**(2) Bacteria already in food are prevented from multiplying by:**

(i) storing food out of the danger zone. Food should be kept below 5°C, for example in a refrigerator, or kept above 63°C, for example , in a bain marie;
(ii) ensuring that refrigerators are maintained at the correct temperature;
(iii) ensuring that when food is removed from chilled storage for preparation this work is carried out as quickly as practicable. High-risk food must not be left in the ambient temperatures of kitchens or serving areas.
(iv) cooling food as rapidly as possible;
(v) not allowing dried foods to absorb moisture;
(vi) using suitable preservatives.

**(3) Those bacteria within food are destroyed by:**

(i) thorough cooking;
(ii) heat processing such as pasteurization, sterilization or canning.

**Fig. 4.** Badly stored meat.

A combination of a suitable temperature and sufficient time is always required to destroy bacteria. The time and the temperature required will depend on the particular organism. For example, spores of *Clostridium perfringens* are much more heat resistant than salmonellae. Furthermore, a time/temperature process only destroys a percentage of vegetative bacteria and the greater the numbers that are present the more likely it is that some will survive. Practical work carried out in Hull indicated that under certain circumstances large joints of ham had to be cooked to a centre temperature of 70°C for one hour to ensure the destruction of *Salmonella give.*

## Cooking

Cooking not only renders food palatable but also ensures a measure of preservation. Improper cooking of poultry and other meat is extremely hazardous. Frozen poultry requires special attention including adequate thawing followed by sufficient cooking to secure the necessary centre temperature to destroy pathogens. Management must introduce effective control procedures to ensure that correct temperatures of cooking and storing food are achieved. The time between removal from the refrigerator and cooking, between cooking and eating or between cooking and returning to the refrigerator must be kept as short as possible.

# CHAPTER 2 Microbiology

Bacteria are single-celled organisms found everywhere; in soil, air, water, on people, animals and food. Bacteria are measured in micrometres (µm) and 1µm = 1/1000mm. Staphylococci have a diameter of around 0.75µm and salmonellae are about 3µm in length. The naked eye can see to approximately 75µm and consequently bacteria are only visible in large numbers when they form colonies or occasionally as a slime on the surface of food. Bacteria may be examined at a magnification of 1000 times using a powerful microscope. (A housefly similarly magnified would be nine metres long.)

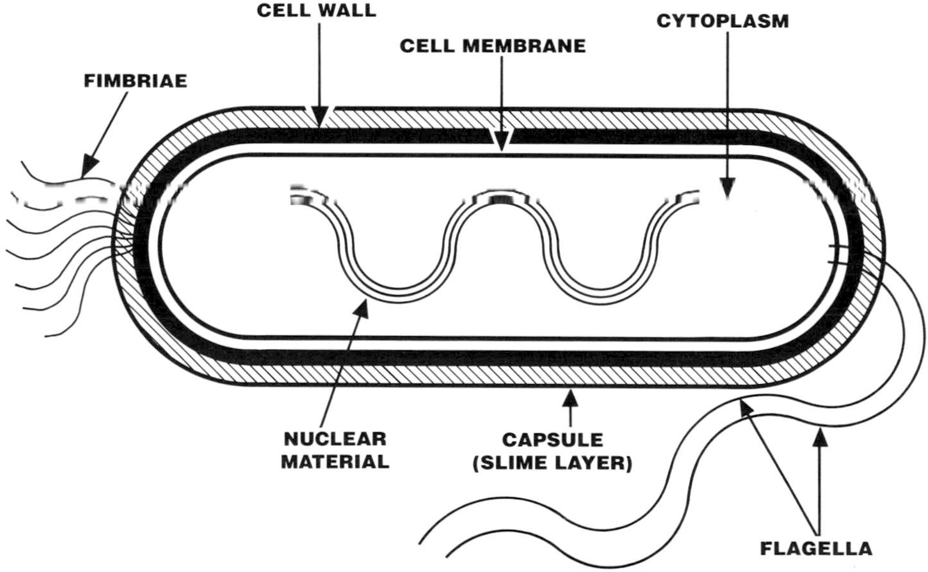


**Fig. 5.** The structure of a typical bacterium.

| | |
|---|---|
| capsule | a gel-like secretion which surrounds many bacteria and protects them against desiccation and harmful chemicals. |
| cell wall | a rigid, permeable structure which surrounds the bacterium and gives the cell its shape and strength. |

| | |
|---|---|
| cell membrane | a semi-permeable membrane which controls the passage of nutrients and waste products both into and out of the cell. |
| cytoplasm | the major part of the cell and the medium within which the metabolic reactions occur. |
| flagella | present in some bacteria for locomotion. |
| fimbriae | thought to aid adhesion. |
| nuclear material | determines the genetic characteristics of the bacterium. |

## Appearance of bacteria

Bacteria vary considerably in shape:

*Cocci* are spherical; some form chains, for example, streptococci. Others form clusters, for example, staphylococci.

*Bacilli* are rod-shaped, for example, salmonellae, *Escherichia coli.*

*Spirochaetes* are spiral.

*Vibrios* are comma-shaped.

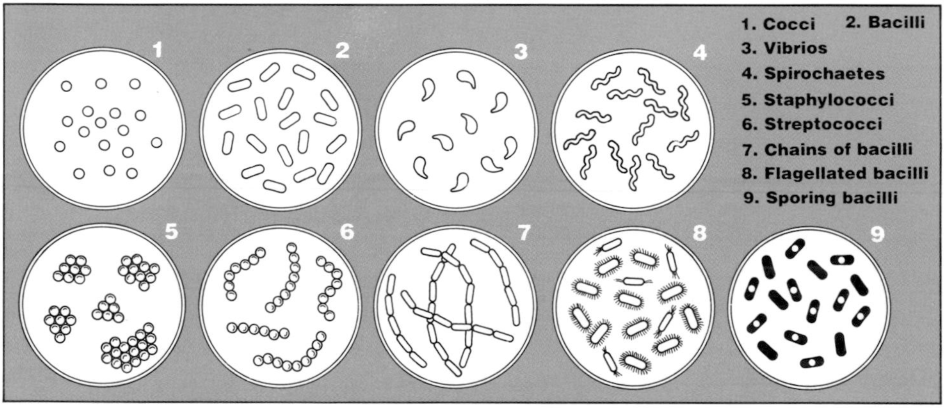


**Fig. 6.** Appearance of bacteria under a microscope.

## Spore formation

With minor exceptions only two bacterial genera, *Bacillus* and *Clostridium*, are able to form spores which are capable of surviving adverse conditions, such as lack of nutrients. Temperatures achieved in normal cooking may destroy the vegetative bacteria but any spores present will probably survive. Furthermore, these temperatures trigger the spore into germination and as the food cools down, providing the environment is suitable, a new mature vegetative cell capable of reproduction is formed.

Spores may be resistant to desiccation, disinfectants and heat. Very high temperatures in excess of 100°C are often required, for long periods, to ensure their destruction. The time and temperature used in the canning of low-acid foods is based on the destruction of *Clostridium botulinum* spores (121°C for three minutes).

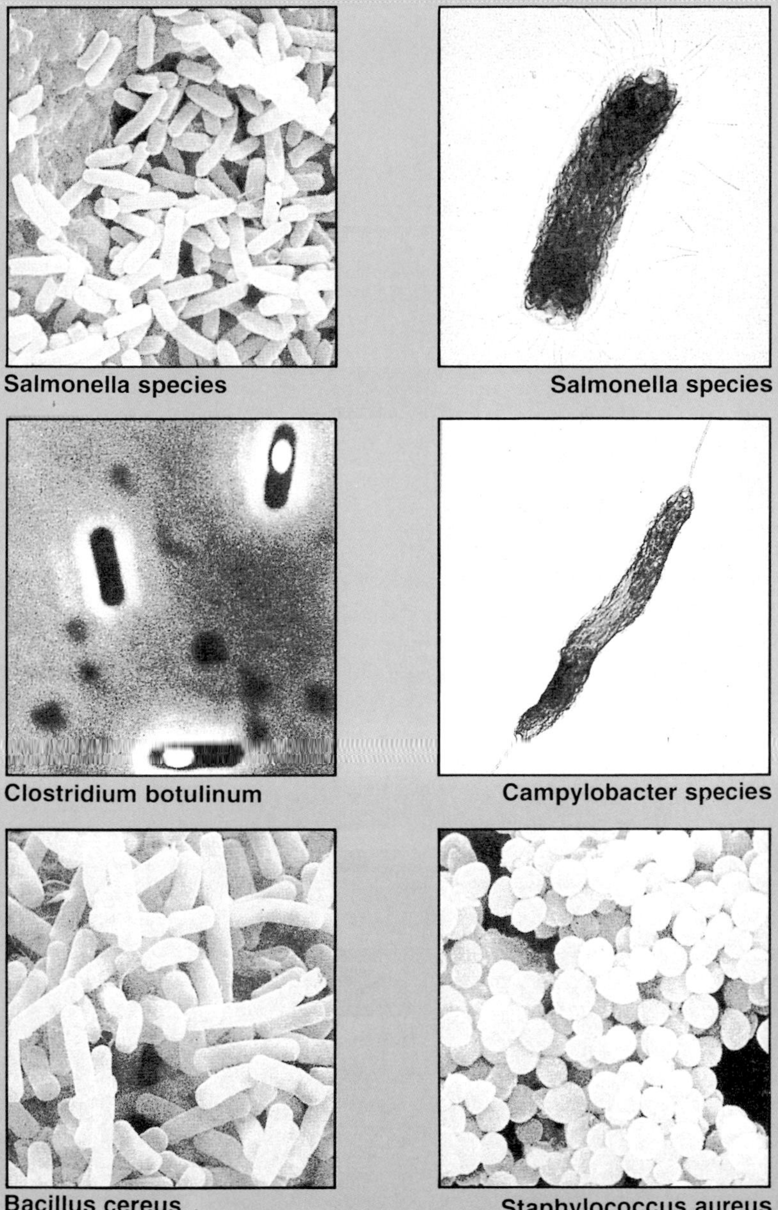


**Fig. 7.** Examples of pathogenic bacteria as viewed under an electron microscope. (Not to scale) (Courtesy of Unilever PLC.)

**Toxin production**

Certain bacteria release poisons known as toxins. Some toxins such as those produced by *Clostridium botulinum* are often the cause of death of persons consuming food contaminated by this organism.

*Exotoxins*

These are highly toxic proteins usually produced during the multiplication, or sporulation, of some Gram +ve bacteria, for example, *Staphylococcus aureus* and *Bacillus cereus*. Quite often these toxins are produced in food and occasionally are heat-resistant so that, although cooking may destroy the bacteria, the toxin is unaffected and can still cause problems if the food is eaten. Botulinum exotoxin is not heat-resistant.

*Endotoxins*

These form part of the cell wall and are released on the death of the bacteria (usually Gram –ve). They are commonly produced in the intestines of persons consuming food contaminated by such organisms as salmonella.

*Enterotoxins*

Is a general term relating to exotoxins which affect the gastrointestinal tract.

**The identification of bacteria**

As individual bacteria are so minute it is not practical to work with a single cell and the first stage in identification is to obtain a pure culture containing millions of organisms. This involves spreading the bacterial mixture onto the surface of a solid culture medium in a petri dish using a sterile wire loop. The usual medium is nutrient agar which consists of beef extract, peptone, water and agar to solidify the medium. Blood, serum or other protein matter may be added to enrich the medium and promote rapid growth.

Selective media, and atmospheres, are used to encourage the growth of specific bacteria whilst suppressing the growth of competitors. For example, the addition of crystal violet inhibits the growth of Gram +ve bacteria. MacConkey agar, which contains bile salt to inhibit the growth of non-intestinal bacteria, is used to grow some enteric bacteria. Selective atmospheres are used in a similar manner, for example, strict anaerobes such as *Clostridium perfringens* will not grow in air.

The inoculated medium is then incubated at a constant temperature for an appropriate length of time, for example, 24 hours. The temperature is often critical in promoting or precluding growth. Most of the common food poisoning organisms prefer a temperature of 37°C whereas 44°C is used to isolate *Escherichia coli*. During incubation each bacterium can become a pure culture of millions of bacteria which appear as small discrete spots on the agar and are known as colonies.

The shape, size, colour and consistency of a colony can be of great value to identification. However, other methods will probably need to be used, including staining reactions, microscopical examination and biochemical reactions. In order to identify individual members of bacterial groups it may be necessary to use more complex tests such as serotyping, phage typing and plasmid typing.

*The Gram stain*

Bacteria can be divided into two major groups, the Gram positive and Gram negative types, depending on whether or not they retain a violet/iodine dye after treatment with alcohol. Gram +ve bacteria retain the dye and are blue-purple whereas Gram –ve are pink. Staining is carried out after a suspension of the bacteria is applied to a microscope slide using a sterile wire loop. The slide must be heated to fix the bacteria before the application of the stain.

| CHEMICAL ADDED | COLOUR CHANGE | |
|---|---|---|
| | GRAM +VE | GRAM –VE |
| Crystal violet | Blue | Blue |
| Iodine | Blue-black | Blue-black |
| Alcohol | Blue | Colourless |
| Safranin | Blue-purple | Pink |

*Microscopical examination*

High powered or electron microscopes can be used to observe staining reactions, cell shape, the presence of spores and the motility of a particular bacterium.

*Biochemical reactions*

Bacteria that cannot be identified by morphology (shape and size) and cultural characteristics may be distinguished by their biochemical reactions. For example, some bacteria will ferment sugars to produce an acid, which changes the colour of a liquid medium, and gas which can be collected in a small inverted test tube immersed in the medium. Other biochemical properties of bacteria which may be utilized include the ability to digest gelatin, egg and serum; to split fats; reduce dyes such as methylene blue; and produce ammonia and hydrogen sulphide.

*Serological typing*

This test is used to distinguish different members of the same group of bacteria. It involves observing the reaction between the antigens of the particular bacteria and the antibodies produced in the blood serum (antisera) of human beings or animals infected with the same bacteria. Examples include *Salmonella enteritidis* and *Salmonella typhi.*

*Phage typing*

Phage typing enables even finer differentiation of bacteria. Bacteriophages are viruses parasitic on bacteria. Each virus is host specific and will only attack one particular type of bacteria. The bacteriophages are inoculated onto the bacteria culture. Susceptibility of the bacteria to the virus enables positive identification of the phage type. Phage typing is particularly useful for identifying salmonellae and staphylococci. Examples include *Salmonella enteritidis PT4* and *Salmonella enteritidis PT2*.

## THE MULTIPLICATION OF BACTERIA

Bacteria reproduce vegetatively (non-sexually) by the process of binary fission (dividing into two). After cell division each daughter cell grows to maturity and itself divides. The time between each division (known as the generation time) varies between species but, given the right conditions, is commonly around 20 minutes. However, under optimum conditions *Clostridium perfringens* and *Vibrio parahaemolyticus* are both capable of division in ten minutes or less.

**Fig. 8.** Binary fission in bacteria. Times are typical for some food poisoning species.

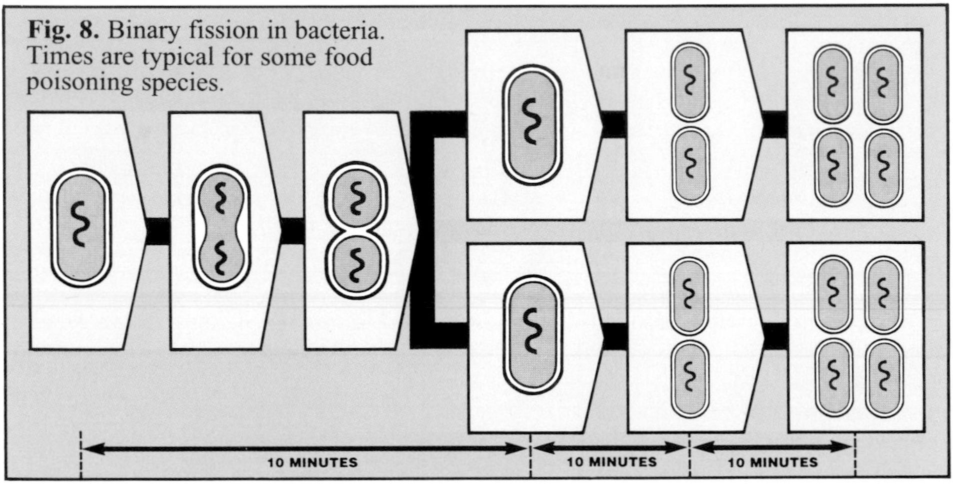


Given a generation time of ten minutes 1,000 bacteria could become 1,000,000 in one hour 40 minutes. (1,000,000 bacteria per gram of food may cause food poisoning and 1,000 bacteria per gram is not an uncommon level of contamination.)

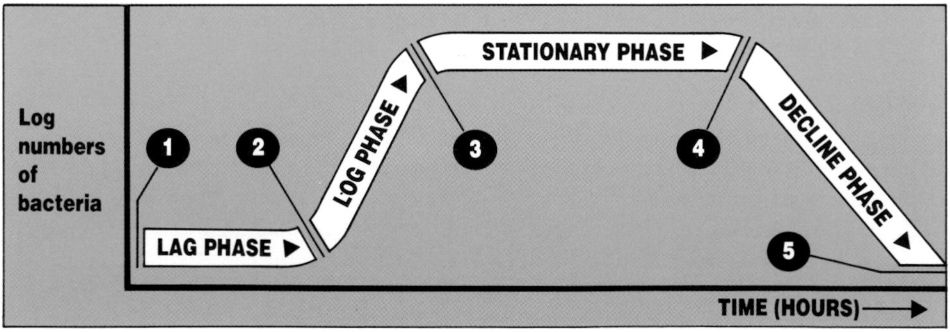


**Fig. 9.** Bacterial population growth curve.

When bacteria contaminate food and conditions are favourable, they begin to multiply. The increase in numbers does not occur at a uniform rate but passes through a succession of phases. These phases are described as follows:

1 to 2 the lag phase - no multiplication.

2 to 3 the logarithmic phase - rapid multiplication.

3 to 4 the stationary phase - numbers of bacteria remain constant as the number produced is equal to the number dying.

4 to 5 the decline phase - numbers decrease as numbers dying exceeds those produced.

It is important to ensure that bacteria growing in food are kept in the lag phase for as long as possible by ensuring unfavourable conditions, such as low or high temperatures and low moisture, are maintained. The lag phase is short if there are large numbers of young bacteria in optimum conditions.

## Factors influencing bacterial multiplication

*Nutrients*

Bacteria require carbon, hydrogen, oxygen and nitrogen with smaller amounts of sulphur and phosphorus, together with trace elements such as sodium, potassium, magnesium, iron and manganese. All nutrients must be in solution (dissolved in water) before they can enter the bacterium. The elements are converted into the constituents of cytoplasm by a process described as a metabolic reaction. Certain vitamins may be required to facilitate these reactions.

Most pathogenic and spoilage bacteria obtain the essential basic elements from sugar, amino acids, fats and minerals. The types of food favoured include high protein food such as milk, eggs, meat and fish. Foods with high sugar or salt content are unsuitable for the growth of most bacteria and are therefore potentially safe. *S. aureus* and *Listeria spp*. are exceptions.

*Hydrogen-ion concentration (pH)*

The pH of a solution is measured on a scale of 0 to 14. Acid foods have pH values below 7 and alkaline foods above 7. A pH value of 7 being neutral.

All bacteria have their own optimal, minimal and maximal pH for growth with most preferring a pH near neutrality. Most bacteria will not grow in food with a pH below 4.5 and this allows lower processing temperatures to be used in preservation techniques, such as canning, to render food safe and free of spoilage organisms. However, a large number of pathogens introduced into an acid food will not die off immediately and may still cause illness. *S. typhimurium* has survived in fruit juices (pH 3.2 at 22°C) for 4/5 days*. A food poisoning outbreak occurred in New Jersey, USA, following the consumption of apple juice (pH 3.6) contaminated with *S. typhimurium.*

Generally, moulds and yeasts are less sensitive to the pH of food than bacteria.

---

*Long Ashton Report 1976 p. 136.

*Moisture*

All life requires water which is used to transport nutrients into the cell and take away waste products. Dry products are poor media for the multiplication of bacteria, for example, flour, biscuits and bread. However, some bacteria, especially spore formers, are able to survive dehydration and when dried egg or milk powder is reconstituted by the addition of liquid, the food once again becomes potentially hazardous. Most other foods contain sufficient moisture to promote bacterial growth.

*Water activity* ($a_w$)

The amount of moisture in any food available to bacteria is normally considered in terms of water activity. The $a_w$ of pure water is 1.00 (a saturated salt solution 0.75). Bacteria prefer an $a_w$ around 0.99 and many will not grow below 0.95 $a_w$. However, *Staphylococcus aureus* will grow at an $a_w$ of 0.89 and some bacteria can exist below 0.75. Yeasts and moulds tolerate lower levels of $a_w$, some as low as 0.62. Fresh meat has an $a_w$ of 0.95 to 1.00, bread 0.94 to 0.97, cured meat 0.87 to 0.95, jam 0.75 to 0.80, flour 0.67 to 0.87 and sugar 0.19.

*Temperature*

Bacteria have a maximum and minimum temperature for growth between which there is an optimum temperature when multiplication is the most rapid. Usually bacteria are separated into four groups:

| | Optimum | Range | Importance |
|---|---|---|---|
| *Psychrophiles* | < 20°C | –8° to 25°C | Include bacteria which cause spoilage in refrigerators and cold stores. |
| *Psychrotrophs* | >20°C | –5° to 40°C | Include *Cl. botulinum* type E, *Yersinia enterocolitica, Listeria monocytogenes* and *Aeromonas hydrophila.* |
| *Mesophiles* | 20° to 45°C | 10° to 56°C | Include most common pathogens which cause food poisoning. |
| *Thermophiles* | > 45°C | 35° to 80°C | Important in canning - some are very heat resistant and if not destroyed will cause spoilage if cans are stored at high temperatures. |

*Presence of oxygen*

Some bacteria require oxygen to grow and these are known as obligate aerobes. Others flourish in the absence of oxygen (obligate anaerobes). Bacteria which grow either with or without free oxygen are known as facultative. Some food poisoning bacteria are anaerobic, such as clostridia, others are facultative anaerobes, such as salmonellae and staphylococci. Microaerobic bacteria grow in the presence of minute quantities of free oxygen, for example, campylobacter.

Free oxygen is normally present in food, except those foods with a high liquid content which have been thoroughly boiled, roast joints and vacuum-packed foods.

*Competition*

When there are many different bacteria present, they will compete for the same food. Fortunately most food poisoning bacteria are not as competitive as the normal flora found on food and, unless present in high numbers, will usually die. Modified atmospheres will favour anaerobes.

**Moulds**

Moulds are aerobic, or facultative anaerobes, multinucleate, chlorophyll-free fungi which produce threadlike filaments (hyphae) and form a branched network of mycelium. Moulds, which may be black, white or of various colours, will grow on most foods, whether moist or dry, acid or alkaline and high in salt or sugar concentrations. The optimum growth temperature is usually 20°C to 30°C, although they will grow well over a wide range of temperatures and may cause problems in refrigerators. Growth has been recorded as low as −10°C. High humidities and fluctuating temperatures accelerate mould growth.

Microscopic mould spores are inseparable from atmospheric dust and large numbers may be present in food premises. Moulds commonly affect bread and other bakery products, and although spores are usually destroyed in baking, subsequent contamination is difficult to avoid. Rapid cooling of bread and wrapping below 27°C will reduce mould problems. Also important is the removal of dampness and mould growth in factories and the thorough cleaning and disinfection of plant and equipment.

Food must always be stored in accordance with the manufacturer's instructions and never sold outside its use-by date. Mishandling of vacuum packs of cheese may result in punctures and consequential mould growth. As the mycelium grows over the food, hyphae penetrate the substance and consequently mould soon returns if scraped off the surface. Regular checking of stock is imperative to avoid customer complaints. The presence of mould on food is usually considered to render it unfit for human consumption. Cheeses produced with specific moulds are an exception.

Certain species of mould, for example, *Aspergillus flavus*, are capable of producing poisonous metabolites, known as mycotoxins, which may affect animals and humans. Even toxins produced by some species of *Penicillium* have induced carcinogenic effects in animals including marked damage to the liver and kidneys and may, in large doses, constitute a hazard to man. Both aspergilli and penicillia are common in nuts and cereals, especially rice. Incidents of poisoning by mycotoxins in the UK over the last 50 years have been extremely rare: a few cases of ergotism were recorded in Manchester in 1927. However, constant vigilance is required by Environmental Health Officers employed at ports to prevent the import of mouldy food or animal feed. In 1984 several tons of peanuts intended for human consumption were found to be contaminated by small amounts of aspergilli and were condemned.

**Fig.10.** Mouldy food complaints may result in prosecutions.

## Yeasts

Yeasts are microscopic unicellular fungi which reproduce by budding. They vary in size from around 5μm diameter to 100μm in length. Most yeasts grow best in the presence of oxygen, although fermentative types grow slowly anaerobically. The majority of yeasts prefer acid foods (pH 4 to 4.5) with a reasonable level of available moisture ($a_w$ above 0.88). However, many yeasts will grow in high concentrations of sugar and salt with an $a_w$ as low as 0.62. The optimum growth temperature for yeast is around 25°C to 30°C with a maximum of around 47°C. Some yeasts can grow at 0°C and below.

Yeasts are used in the manufacture of foods such as bread, beer and vinegar. However, they cause spoilage of many foods including jam, fruit juice, honey, meats and wines.

# CHAPTER 3 Food poisoning

Bacteria are responsible for most food poisoning cases, followed by virus particles with poisonous plants, chemicals or metals occasionally causing problems. Because food poisoning organisms are found everywhere it is impossible to operate a food business without them being present in either small or large numbers. Which is why good hygiene practices are so important to minimize risk of illness from consuming contaminated food.

## BACTERIAL FOOD POISONING

There are at least ten types of bacteria known to be responsible for causing food poisoning outbreaks in the United Kingdom:

*Salmonella spp.*
*Clostridium perfringens*
*Staphylococcus aureus*
*Bacillus cereus* and other *Bacillus spp*
*Streptococcus spp.*
*Clostridium botulinum*
*Vibrio parahaemolyticus*
*Escherichia coli*
*Yersinia enterocolitica*
*Aeromonas hydrophila*

**TABLE XI** TYPES OF FOOD POISONING

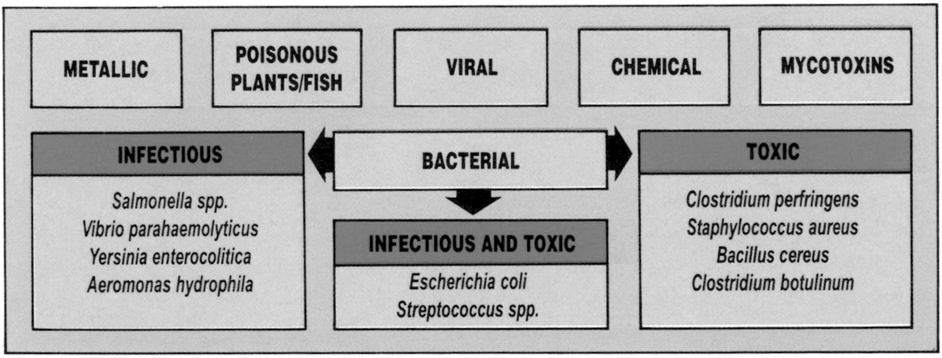


### Salmonella

Salmonellae are Gram –ve, facultative anaerobic rods. There are approximately 2,200 serotypes of salmonella, the commonest being *S. enteritidis* and *S. typhimurium.*

The growth range of these bacteria is from 7°C to 45°C with a generation time of ten hours at 10°C. If present in sufficient numbers in consumed food (normally 100,000 + per gram), the digestion process may not destroy them. The bacteria multiply in the intestine and diarrhoea results after penetration of the intestinal wall. The endotoxin released on the death of the cell probably produces the fever associated with salmonellosis. Salmonellae are able to survive in soil for several months.

The primary sources of salmonella are the intestinal tracts of animals and birds. Animals may become infected from the consumption of contaminated feed or contact with carriers or infected animals. Ill animals should always be isolated and animal feed treated to ensure it is free of salmonellae.

Transport of animals and poultry in overcrowded, dirty vehicles and poor hygiene in the slaughterhouse, which results in the spread of infection and an increase in the contamination of carcases by faecal material and intestinal matter, are problems which must be overcome to reduce the incidence of salmonellosis. Raw meat, especially poultry, is the main source of salmonellae in food premises. In 1994, a survey by the Public Health Laboratory Service found salmonella contamination levels of 41% in frozen and 33% in chilled chickens, compared with 54% and 41% in 1990 and 64% and 54% in 1987.

**TABLE XII** ROUTES OF SALMONELLA FOOD POISONING

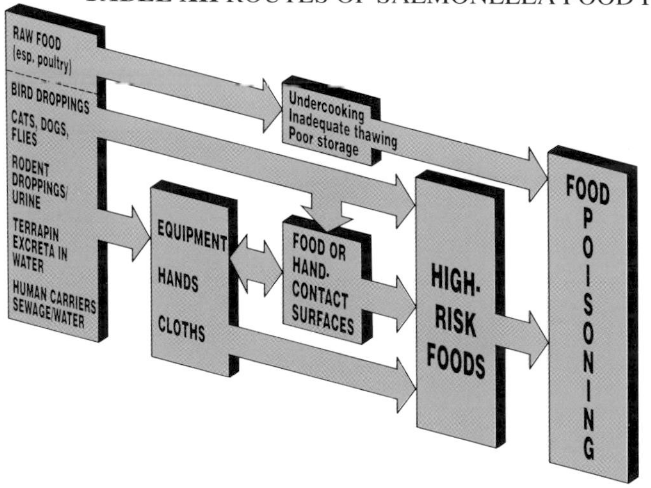


In 1982, *S. napoli* in imported Italian chocolate bars resulted in an unusual outbreak affecting 272 people. The chocolate was at least seven months old, the incubation period was up to ten days and the infective dose was commonly less than 100 organisms. In 1984 in Canada, *S. typhimurium* in cheddar cheese (< 10 organisms per gram) resulted in 2,000+ cases. An outbreak of *S. typhimurium* at Stanley Royd Hospital, Wakefield in 1984 involved 450 cases and 19 deaths. In 1985 an outbreak involving dried baby milk contaminated with *S. ealing* resulted in 60 cases and one death. The adverse publicity resulted in the closure of the factory responsible. Since

1988 raw eggs have been considered to be the source of a large number of salmonella outbreaks, most involving *S. enteritidis.*

An egg sandwich shared by two women at Manchester Airport in 1988, resulted in compensation of £183,500 for food poisoning and other subsequent conditions, including irritable bowel syndrome, constipation and heartburn. In 1991 a sandwich bar in Colchester had to pay approximately £25,000 in legal fees and £100,000 in compensation to 76 victims. The sandwiches, which contained home-made mayonnaise (raw egg), had been stored in a car boot at temperatures exceeding 30°C. The tangible costs of salmonella infection in 1992 were estimated at £350/500 million.

## Clostridium perfringens

These bacteria are Gram +ve, anaerobic rods which form spores under adverse conditions such as exposure to free oxygen. The normal growth range is between 15°C and 50°C and there is no division at 10°C. *Clostridium perfringens* can reproduce every ten minutes at its optimum growth temperature of 43°C to 47°C. Growth in meat was shown to be preceded by a lag of two to four hours at 35°C but no lag at 46°C*. Spores may survive boiling for several hours.

**TABLE XIII** ROUTES OF CLOSTRIDIUM PERFRINGENS FOOD POISONING

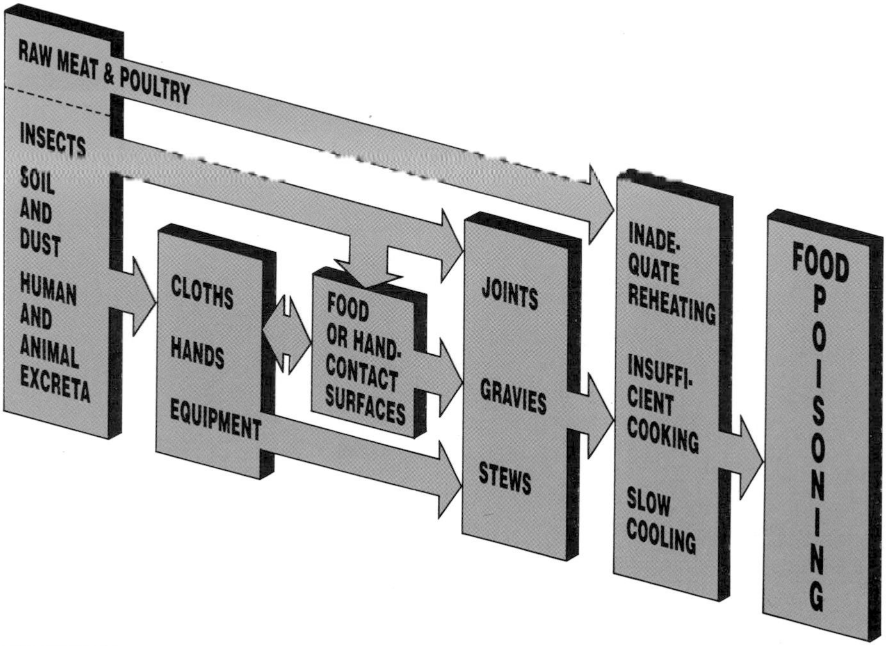


*Hall H. and Angelotti R. (1965). "*Clostridium perfringens* in meat and meat products." Appl. Microbiol., 13:352-357.

Illness is caused when large numbers of ingested organisms sporulate in the intestine and in so doing release an enterotoxin. The infective dose for adults is around 1,000,000 per gram of food.

*Clostridium perfringens* food poisoning usually occurs as a result of food handling malpractices in large kitchens. On cooking, oxygen is driven from the food creating anaerobic conditions ideal for the growth of the heat activated spores. Stews, gravies and large joints of meat allowed to cool slowly in warm kitchens are most commonly associated with outbreaks of *Cl. perfringens* food poisoning.

*Clostridium perfringens* has been shown to sporulate in meat products and produce enterotoxin in the food. Although not common, this explains why the incubation period for this type of food poisoning has been reduced to as little as two hours.

### Cooking and simmering bulk fluids

Temperature distribution within bulk liquids during cooking is not uniform. Variations can be extreme and under certain conditions cool spots can form. Because of the nature of heat transference in liquids, stable convection currents are set up and liquid outside these currents may remain stationary at a low temperature.

Where a number of adverse factors combine, parts of a bulk liquid may be visibly boiling, whilst other areas of the liquid may be at a temperature which allows the multiplication of *Clostridium perfringens*. The most dangerous combination is when a large volume of a viscous liquid, such as gravy or stock, is boiled and then simmered in an open pan on a solid type cooker, especially when the pan has no lid, the kitchen is cool and the pan contents are left unstirred. The initial boiling activates *Clostridium perfringens* spores from which the vegetative bacteria grow. Furthermore, the boiling destroys other organisms, thereby reducing competition. *Clostridia* within the cool spot survive and multiply under virtually ideal conditions.*

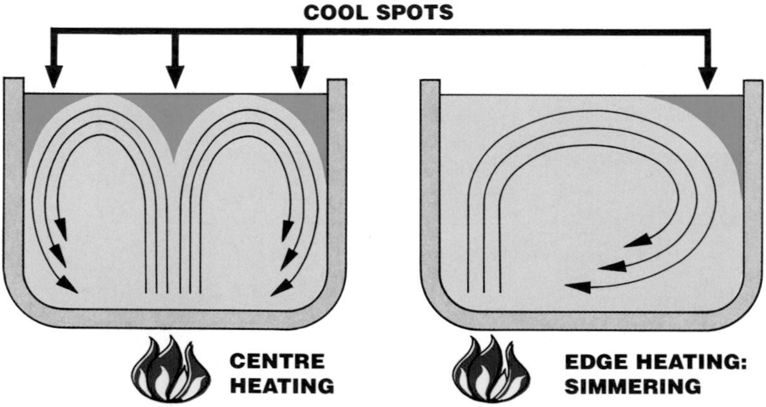


**Fig. 11.** Circulation currents and the formation of cool spots.

---

*North R. A. E.: Unpublished information.

**TABLE XIV** THE FORMATION AND PREVENTION OF COOL SPOTS

| Problem | Remedy |
|---|---|
| Volume of liquid, especially greater than 25 litres | Cook in smaller volumes: use several small pans in preference to one large pan |
| Intensity of heat, especially low edge heating | Use heat source equal in diameter to pan base |
| Large tall pans | Use wide low pans |
| Failure to stir | Stir frequently, at least every ten minutes using a clean utensil |
| Cool draughts and absence of lids | Keep excessive cold air draughts away from cooking area. Keep lids on pans between stirring |

It is preferable to use alternative equipment such as jacketed kettles or bratt pans.

**Clostridium botulinum**

*Clostridium botulinum* is a Gram +ve, anaerobic, spore-forming, gas-producing rod. There are several types of *Cl. botulinum* that produce neurotoxins in food which, if consumed, often cause fatalities. Types A, B, E and F are associated with food poisoning. Types A and B are commonly found in the soil and are usually associated with vegetables and meats. Psychrotrophic type E is found in mud, streams, oceans and fish. The optimum growth temperature is 20°C to 30°C but toxin production is possible down to a temperature of 3°C. Spoilage of fresh fish usually occurs long before the production of dangerous levels of exotoxin. Furthermore, the toxin is heat labile (sensitive to heat) and is destroyed by boiling.

Unfortunately, the spores of *Cl. botulinum* are very heat resistant, for example, a temperature of 121°C for three minutes is used as a basis for ensuring their destruction in canned low-acid foods. Strict canning controls are essential. Toxin production does not occur below a pH of 4.5. If consumed, spores are usually harmless as they are unable to grow and produce toxin in man's intestinal tract. However, there have been five cases of infant botulism reported in the U.K. between 1978 and 1994 where spores have apparently germinated in the infant gut and toxin has subsequently been produced. Infant botulism was first described in the USA and since 1976 over 900 cases have been recorded. Some cases have implicated honey contaminated with *Cl. botulinum* spores. In 1991, 100 + cases of botulism in Egypt resulted from the consumption of contaminated raw salted fish

Outbreaks of botulism are most frequently associated with low-acid canned foods or smoked products, especially fish. If contaminated, fish products may become toxic before they become unacceptable through spoilage. It is preferable, therefore, to store such products below 5°C to ensure their safety. Nitrates and nitrites are often added to cooked meats, bacon and ham to prevent the germination of spores in vacuum packs.

Although gas may be produced which causes cans contaminated with *Cl. botulinum* to blow, this does not always occur and cannot be relied on as a method to detect suspect cans. In 1978, four elderly people in Birmingham developed botulism after eating a contaminated can of Alaskan salmon. Two of them died. In 1989, 27 cases of botulism type B occurred following the consumption of hazelnut yogurt and one person died. Underprocessing of canned hazelnut puree, used in the yogurt production, was stated to be the cause, and a change from sugar to saccharin increased the $a_W$ and allowed germination of the spores.

**Staphylococcus aureus**

This organism is a Gram +ve, facultative anaerobe which is salt-tolerant and can, therefore, survive in some cured products. Approximately 40% of adults carry *Staphylococcus aureus* in the nose and throat and 15% on their skin, especially the hands. Around half of these strains are enterotoxigenic.

If present in food, *Staphylococcus aureus* will, under ideal conditions, produce an exotoxin which may survive boiling for 30 minutes or more. The growth range for *Staphylococcus aureus* is between 7°C and 45°C and the generation time at 10°C is 30 hours.

**TABLE XV** ROUTES OF STAPHYLOCOCCAL FOOD POISONING

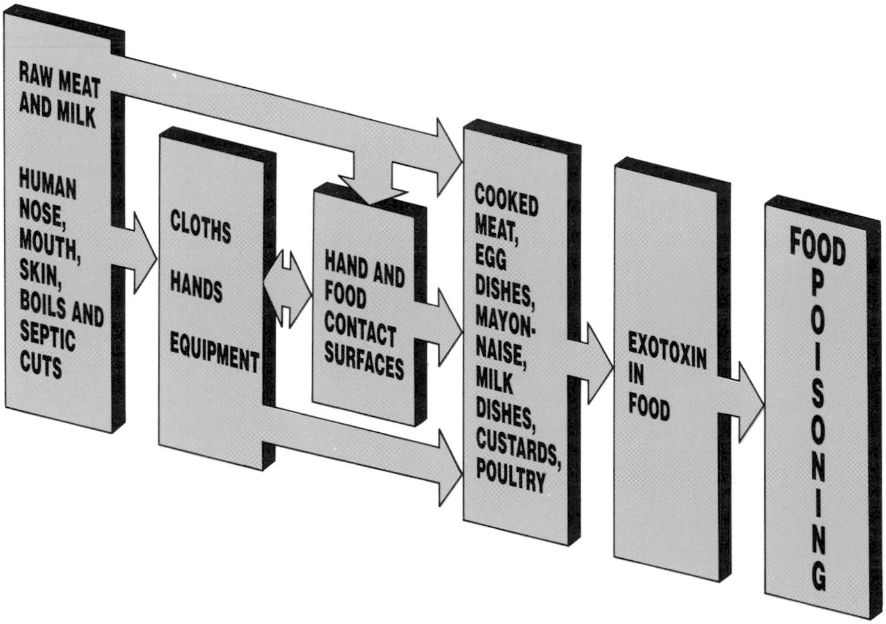


The majority of outbreaks are caused by the direct contamination of cooked foodstuffs by hands soiled with secretions from the nose, mouth and skin lesions.

Frequently, the cooked food has been handled while warm and storage conditions have encouraged the organism to produce its toxin.

In 1985, 47 cases of *Staphylococcus aureus* were caused by the consumption of imported Italian lasagne.

**Bacillus cereus**

*Bacillus cereus* is an aerobic, Gram +ve, spore-forming bacterium which is capable of causing two distinct forms of food poisoning. The more common type in this country is characterized by nausea and vomiting one to five hours after ingestion of contaminated food, usually rice dishes, although cornflour and vanilla slices have also been implicated. The spores survive normal cooking, and rapid growth and exotoxin production will occur if the food is not cooled quickly and refrigerated. One of the exotoxins produced is very heat resistant and can survive a temperature of 126°C for 90 minutes. Consequently, once the toxin is produced subsequent reheating is of little value. The second type of *Bacillus cereus* food poisoning is rare in the UK and has an onset period of eight to 16 hours. Toxins are produced in the intestine and symptoms are usually diarrhoea and abdominal pain.

*Bacillus cereus* grows between 7°C and 48°C with an optimum between 28°C and 35 °C. It is distributed throughout the environment but is particularly common in soil, vegetation, cereals and spices. It also causes spoilage of cream - referred to as bitty cream.

*Bacillus cereus* is often isolated in low numbers in many types of food. However, large numbers (100,000 + per gram) must be isolated to prove that a contaminated food has caused food poisoning. It is recommended that faecal specimens are sent to the laboratory under refrigeration to avoid other organisms multiplying.

**Bacillus subtilis and Bacillus licheniformis**

*Bacillus subtilis* and *Bacillus licheniformis* are aerobic spore-forming bacteria which have occasionally been implicated in food poisoning incidents. The main symptoms are nausea and vomiting, usually within one hour of consuming contaminated food. Diarrhoea is less common but may occur after approximately 12 hours. In 1994 an outbreak of *Bacillus subtilis* involved meat pasties seasoned with contaminated black pepper. The spores had survived the cooking process.

**Vibrio parahaemolyticus**

*Vibrio parahaemolyticus* is a Gram –ve, marine facultative anaerobe which grows between 8°C and 44°C, with an optimum of 35°C to 37°C. Given ideal conditions the generation time may be as short as five to seven minutes*. Rapid growth may occur in seafoods or the human intestine.

---

*Barrow G. I. and Miller D. C. 1974 International Symposium on *Vibrio parahaemolyticus*, Tokyo: Saikon Publishing Co.

**TABLE XVI** FOOD POISONING BACTERIA

| Bacteria | Source | Onset period (hours) | Symptoms and duration of illness | Control |
|---|---|---|---|---|
| *Salmonella* (Infection) | Raw meat, milk, eggs, poultry, carriers, pets, rodents, terrapins, sewage/water | 6 to 72 usually 12 to 36 | Abdominal pain, diarrhoea, vomiting and fever (1 to 7 days) | Sterilization and strict control of animal foodstuff. Slaughterhouse hygiene. Safe sewage disposal and chlorination of water. Screening of carriers or suspects. Refrigerated storage of high-risk foods. Thorough thawing and cooking of frozen poultry. Excluding pets, rodents and insects from food. High standards of personal and food hygiene. Avoid raw milk, use pasteurized or sterilized. Separate raw and high-risk foods |
| *Clostridium perfringens* (Toxin in intestine) | Animal and human excreta, soil, dust, insects and raw meat | 8 to 22 usually 12 to 18 | Abdominal pain and diarrhoea. Vomiting is rare (12 to 48 hours) | Separate raw and cooked foods. High standards of hygiene. Thorough cooking. Rapid cooling and refrigeration within 1.5 hours of reaching 63°C. Joints should not exceed a size of 2.5kg |
| *S. aureus* (Toxin in food) | Human nose, mouth, skin, boils and cuts. Raw milk from cows or goats with mastitis | 1 to 6 | Abdominal pain, vomiting, prostration and subnormal temperatures (6 to 24 hours) | Avoid handling food, use utensils. Good personal hygiene, especially regarding hand washing. Exclude handlers with respiratory infections involving coughing or sneezing. Cover cuts with waterproof dressings. Exclude persons with boils or septic cuts. Avoid cross-contamination. Avoid the use of raw milk. Rapid cooling and refrigeration of high-risk foods |
| *Vibrio para-haemolyticus* (Infection) | Seafoods | 2 to 48 usually 12 to 18 | Diarrhoea, vomiting, fever, abdominal pain and dehydration (1 to 7 days) | Avoid cross-contamination. Cook well. Avoid raw shellfish |

| Bacteria | Source | Onset period (hours) | Symptoms and duration of illness | Control |
|---|---|---|---|---|
| *Clostridium botulinum* (Toxin in food) | Soil, fish, meat and vegetables | 2 hours, to 8 days usually 12 to 36 hours | Difficulties in swallowing, talking and breathing, double vision and paralysis of the cranial nerves. Fatalities are common and the recovery of survivors may take several months | Strict control over processing low-acid canned foods. Discard blown cans or those with holes or defective seams. Strict control over smoking and handling of smoked fish. Store smoked fish in a freezer. Avoid cross-contamination. Care in gutting and preparing raw fish. Ensure adequate cooking temperatures |
| *Bacillus cereus* (i) (Toxin in food) | Cereals, especially rice, dust and soil | 1 to 5 | Vomiting, abdominal pains and some diarrhoea (12 to 24 hours) | Thorough cooking and rapid cooling. Storing at correct temperatures. Avoid re-warming. Avoid cross-contamination |
| (ii) (Toxin in intestine) | As above | 8 to 16 | Abdominal pain, diarrhoea and some vomiting (1 to 2 days) | As above |
| *Escherichia coli* (Infection and toxin) | Human sewage, water and raw meat | 10 to 72 usually 12 to 24 | Abdominal pain, fever, diarrhoea and vomiting (1 to 5 days) | High standards of hygiene. Thorough cooking. Avoid cross-contamination. Storage at correct temperature. Safe sewage disposal and chlorination of water used for drinking or food production |

Outbreaks of *Vibrio parahaemolyticus* food poisoning in the UK are infrequent and usually caused by the consumption of imported seafood, such as cooked prawns and dressed crab from the Far East. In 1995, 17 faecal isolates were reported to CDSC. The organism is sensitive to heat and outbreaks are normally caused by contamination after cooking and multiplication due to unrefrigerated storage. *Vibrio parahaemolyticus* is one of the commonest causes of food poisoning in Japan as it prefers the warmer coastal waters, and seafoods form a high percentage of the staple diet. However, it is occasionally isolated from the UK coastal waters, especially in the South.

### Escherichia coli

*Escherichia coli* is a Gram –ve, aerobic rod which is a normal part of the intestinal flora of man and animals. It is usually used as an indicator of faecal contamination of food or water. However, certain strains are known to be pathogenic and produce an enterotoxin in the intestine which results in symptoms of abdominal pain and diarrhoea. One group of pathogenic *E. coli* is responsible for severe infantile diarrhoea and another group causes travellers' diarrhoea. A major outbreak in the USA was traced to the consumption of soft, fermented cheese. Growth of *E. coli* has been recorded as low as 4°C.*

### Yersinia enterocolitica

*Yersinia enterocolitica* is a psychrotrophic, Gram –ve, facultative anaerobic rod which is quite widespread in nature, particularly in wild and domestic animals. Not all strains of *Yersinia enterocolitica* are pathogenic for humans. Faecal-oral transmission involving infected animals or persons or the consumption of contaminated food and water are the usual ways of spread and it is not heat resistant. Yersinia has been incriminated in several major outbreaks of food poisoning in the USA and is commonly isolated as a cause of diarrhoea in Sweden, Norway and Germany. Foods involved are usually of animal origin and outbreaks have involved chocolate milk, reconstituted powdered milk, turkey and chow mein. Epidemiological evidence from Belgium suggests raw pork as a food vehicle. In 1995, 229 faecal isolates of *Yersinia enterocolitica* were reported in the UK, although few cases could be traced to the consumption of food.

Symptoms include diarrhoea, abdominal pain, fever, headache, pharyngitis, occasionally vomiting, acute mesenteric lymphadenitis, pseudo appendicitis (especially in children) and arthritis. The incubation period is usually one to 14 days and bacteria may persist in the stools for several months. Yersinia has been isolated from raw milk, shellfish, raw and cooked meat, particularly pork, poultry, liquid egg, salami, dairy products, salads and vegetables. Of particular concern is the ability of *Y. enterocolitica* to grow on food during refrigerated storage, despite the normal microflora. This is in contrast to the majority of pathogens which are usually not able to grow competitively.

### Streptococcus

Certain streptococci, for example, *Streptococcus faecalis* and *Streptococcus viridans* have occasionally been implicated in food poisoning outbreaks in the UK. However, irrefutable evidence has been difficult to obtain and is usually circumstantial. Large numbers of streptococci have been found in food suspected of causing illness within three to 22 hours of consumption.

### Aeromonas hydrophila

*Aeromonas hydrophila* is a Gram –ve, facultative anaerobic, rod-shaped bacterium. It is a pathogen of fish and frogs and is common in nature, particularly in water. It is able to grow at temperatures as low as 1°C. Symptoms include diarrhoea.

---

*Olsvik O. and Kapperud G., 1982. Enterotoxin production in milk at 22°C and 4°C by *E. coli* and *Y. enterocolitica:* Appl. Environ. Microbiol. 43:997-1000.

*A. hydrophila* has been implicated as a food-borne illness in several countries including the USA. It is capable of growth in many foods at low temperatures despite the presence of competing microflora. Incidents in the UK are rare.

## CHEMICAL AND METALLIC POISONING (See Chapter 6)

Residues of drugs, pesticides and fertilizers may be present in deliveries of raw materials. Pesticides sprayed onto fruit and vegetables just prior to harvesting may result in cumulative toxic effects and should be strictly controlled. In 1988 a warning was issued by the DH regarding the levels of dieldrin residues in eels taken from rivers and lakes in the UK. Two outbreaks of chemical food poisoning in 1991 resulted from the contamination of watermelons (USA) and cucumbers (UK) with the pesticide aldicarb. In 1995, warnings were issued regarding the need to peel carrots.

Chemicals can enter foodstuffs by leakage, spillage, or other accidents during processing or preparation. Unacceptable levels of benzene migration from plastic packaging has been known to occur. However, acute chemical poisoning from food premises is rare and is usually caused by negligence, for example, storing weedkiller, pesticide or cleaning chemicals in unlabelled food containers.

Chemical additives of food have to undergo rigorous tests before they are allowed and are usually harmless. However, some may cause problems if ingested in large amounts, for example, monosodium glutamate*. The onset of symptoms usually occurs in less than one hour and may include burning sensations in the chest, neck and abdomen. Nitrates and nitrites are added to ham and bacon to inhibit the growth of *Cl. botulinum* and *Cl. perfringens* and to produce a desirable red colour. However, the maximum amounts allowable have been reduced because of the carcinogenic effect on animals. The use of antibiotics in food production is usually prohibited because of the dangers of developing resistant bacteria which could prove harmful to the populace.

Some chemicals are extremely poisonous and if ingested may result in severe vomiting within a few minutes and in some cases fatalities. Other chemicals may cause cancer or other serious chronic disease. Environmental contaminants such as dioxins may, for example end up in cow's milk as a result of contaminating grazing land.

Problems may occasionally be caused by naturally occurring toxicants, for example, the processing contaminant ethyl carbamate formed during the fermentation of alcohol and other fermented food.

Chemical poisoning may also occur because of waste, such as mercury compounds, polluting river water used for drinking or food production. Poisons may be taken up by fish which may cause illness in humans if consumed. In 1984 a large outbreak of gastrointestinal illness in the North-West of England and North Wales was caused by drinking mains water contaminated by phenol.** From May 1981 to December 1982 approximately 20,000 Spanish people became ill after using olive oil sold by street vendors which allegedly contained industrial waste oil. At least 350 people died.

---

*Schaumburg H. H. (1969) Science, 163: 826-828.
**Jarvis S. N. *et al.* Br. Med. J. 1985; 290:1800-02.

Several metals are toxic and if ingested in sufficient quantities can give rise to food poisoning. The symptoms, mainly vomiting and abdominal pain, usually develop within an hour. Diarrhoea may also occur. Metals may be absorbed by growing crops or contaminate food during processing. Acid foods (pH $< 7$) should not be cooked or stored in equipment containing any of the following metals:

*Antimony*

Antimony is used in the enamel coating of equipment. Under certain conditions antimony poisoning can occur. Vessels with chipped enamel should not be used.

*Cadmium*

Cadmium is used extensively for plating utensils and fittings for electric cookers and refrigeration apparatus. It is readily attacked by some acids including fruit and wines. Foods, such as meat, placed directly on refrigerator shelves containing cadmium may become poisonous. Earthenware from some countries may contain acid-extractable cadmium which may be hazardous if used with acid food.

*Copper*

Copper poisoning has been caused by a worn copper dispensing outlet on a soft-drink machine. Copper is also an initiator of rancidity development in fats and oils. Copper, and bronze fittings, must be avoided when processing foods such as milk.

*Lead*

Lead is a very poisonous metal and if ingested may cause acute poisoning. Consumption of food and drink is the main exposure route of people to lead, especially fruit, leafy vegetables, cereals (air-borne lead from petrol and incinerators), kidneys, wine and shellfish (industrial effluent or geological sources). Lead is also released from containers made of ceramics and lead crystal. The glazing of earthenware vessels is compounded with lead oxide and the storage of acid products in such vessels should be avoided. Chronic poisoning from lead absorbed by soft water passing through lead pipes is not classed as food poisoning. The Lead in Food Regulations provide a maximum general limit for lead of 1ppm in most foods. Some imported cans may have lead seams and must be carefully examined.

*Tin and iron*

Most cans used for the storage of food are constructed of tin-plated iron sheet. Occasionally, due to prolonged storage, certain acid foods such as pineapple, rhubarb, strawberries, citrus fruits and tomatoes react with the tin-plate and hydrogen gas is produced. Iron and tin are absorbed by the food which may become unfit for human consumption. The Tin in Food Regulations, 1992 impose a statutory limit of 200 ppm for the amount of tin permitted in food.

*Zinc*

Zinc is used in the galvanizing of metals. Galvanized equipment should not be used in direct contact with food, particularly acid foods.

*Aluminium*

Although concern has been expressed about aluminium being a factor in some cases of pre-senile dementia, contaminated food is unlikely to play a significant part.

## POISONOUS PLANTS AND FISH

Poisonous plants are rarely the cause of food poisoning in food premises. Plants responsible for causing acute poisoning include deadly nightshade, death cap (which may be mistaken for edible mushroom) and rhubarb leaves. In 1981 apricot kernels containing enzymatically produced hydrogen cyanide caused the poisoning of 24 children and four deaths in Israel. In 1983 several people became ill after drinking herbal tea contaminated with deadly nightshade. MAFF has advised consumers to avoid drinking comfrey preparations containing a high level of pyrrolizidine alkaloids (a large group of natural toxicants which occur in some plants, such as comfrey and ragwort [Senecio species] ).

The gonads, liver and intestines of some fish are highly toxic. For example, the puffer fish, which is considered a delicacy by the Japanese, has caused fatalities because of the failure to remove the toxic organs during preparation.

Six incidents of red whelk poisoning have been recorded in the UK since 1970, the latest in 1991 in the North of England. Symptoms include tingling of the fingers, disturbance of vision, paralysis, nausea, vomiting, diarrhoea and prostration. Recovery is usually within 24 hours. Intoxication is due to poisoning by tetramine which is present in the salivary glands of these whelks.

### Red kidney beans

Between 1976 and 1982 there were 26 reported incidents of food poisoning, affecting at least 118 persons, associated with the consumption of raw or undercooked red kidney beans *(Phaseolus vulgaris).*

The onset period is short, one to six hours, and recovery normally rapid. Symptoms may develop after eating only four raw beans and include nausea, vomiting and abdominal pain followed by diarrhoea. Recovery is usually around three hours but may be up to two days.

A naturally occurring haemagglutin, which can be destroyed by boiling for ten minutes, is responsible for the illness. The temperatures achieved by "slow cookers" are usually insufficient to destroy the haemagglutin.

In 1986, a number of people became ill after eating vegetable burgers containing haricot beans. The symptoms resembled those caused by red kidney beans and it is likely that undercooking resulted in a failure to destroy the high levels of haemagglutin in the raw beans. In 1994 there was one suspected outbreak involving red kidney beans.

**Scombrotoxic fish poisoning**

Scombrotoxic fish poisoning is caused by toxins which accumulate in the body of some fish during storage, especially above 4°C. The onset period is between ten minutes and three hours. Symptoms last up to eight hours and include headache, nausea, vomiting, abdominal pain, a burning sensation in the mouth, diarrhoea and urticaria. Scombrotoxic poisoning results from the conversion of histidine, an amino acid found in dark-fleshed fish, to histamine by the action of spoilage bacteria. Histamine, alone or in combination, is thought to be responsible for the illness and is normally found in high levels in the fish causing food poisoning.

The illness is usually caused by consuming spoilt fish, although toxic canned fish may look and taste acceptable. Problems arise in canning fish as, once formed, the toxin is very heat resistant and will not be destroyed during processing. Refrigerated storage of fish should prevent toxin formation.

From 1979 to 1990 there were 434 suspected incidents of scombrotoxic fish poisoning involving 943 people, 164 incidents were confirmed by histamine analysis (levels greater than 5mg per 100g of flesh). Fish involved included smoked, canned and soused mackerel, canned tuna, canned sardines, pilchards and raw tuna. In 1994, 12 outbreaks were reported involving 50 persons.

**Ciguatera poisoning**

Approximately 300 species of fish caught in the Pacific and Caribbean may give rise to ciguatera poisoning and could cause problems if imported into the UK. The fish involved are usually large shore or reef species, such as barracuda, sea bass, groupers and eels, which feed on smaller fish that have eaten toxin producing dinoflagellates (single-celled algae eaten by fish and shellfish). A few species produce toxin which is not destroyed by cooking and is present in the flesh and viscera, especially the liver. The fish look, smell and taste normal. The onset period is usually one to six hours and symptoms include malaise, disturbed vision, alternating feelings of hot and cold, respiratory paralysis, numbness or burning of the mouth, throat and tongue, weakness, abdominal pain, vomiting and diarrhoea. Occasional deaths are recorded. In 1990, three people suffered ciguatera poisoning after eating a home-cooked red snapper imported from Oman. No outbreaks were reported in the UK in 1993 or 1994

**Paralytic shellfish poisoning (PSP) and diarrhetic shellfish poisoning (DSP)**

Paralytic and diarrhetic shellfish poisoning may result from the consumption of mussels and other bivalves which have fed on poisonous plankton (various species of dinoflagellates). The aquatic biotoxins causing PSP and DSP may withstand cooking. Symptoms for PSP include a tingling or numbness of the mouth almost immediately and this spreads to the neck, arms and legs within four to six hours. Death, when it does occur, is usually caused by respiratory paralysis within two to 12 hours.

In 1968 an outbreak of PSP affected 78 people in the North East of England and in May 1990 the DH issued a public warning not to eat shellfish and crustaceans caught off the North East coast because of high levels of toxin. Action is taken to prevent the consumption of bivalves if tests are positive for the presence of DSP toxin or if levels of PSP toxin exceed 80μg/100g shellfish flesh In 1994, 9% of 233 mussel samples exceeded the regulatory limit for PSP and 1% of 225 mussel samples for DSP. Most of the unsatisfactory samples were from the North East coast where there is no commercial mussel fishing. Hazard warning notices were erected to advise the public.

In May 1994 the first case of DSP was reported in the UK. Two people developed chills, nausea, abdominal pain, vomiting and diarrhoea one to two hours after consuming imported mussels. Symptoms persisted for 36 hours.

## MYCOTOXINS

Mycotoxins are metabolites of some moulds which cause illness, and sometimes death, for example, aflatoxin and ochratoxin A. Symptoms vary depending on the particular mould. They are often carcinogenic but some may cause gastrointestinal disturbances, for example, *Aspergillus ustus.*

Aflatoxin M1 has been detected in milk and milk powder and there is increasing interest in the presence of patulin, a mutagenic mycotoxin produced by certain species of *Penicillium* and *Aspergillus* moulds which infect apples and pears. Because of migration, cutting out the visible mould may not remove the risk. Patulin is not destroyed by pasteurization. In 1996 the DH issued guidance on patulin, following concern over high levels in apple juice sold in the UK. Juice containing levels of patulin in excess of 50ppb should not be used. In 1992, 26% of MAFF samples of juices from pressed apples (cloudy juices) exceeded 50 ppb, however, in 1994 only four per cent of MAFF samples of juices from pressed apples exceeded this limit.

### Aflatoxicosis

Aflatoxicosis is a food borne illness caused by the consumption of aflatoxin produced by the common moulds, *Aspergillus flavus* and *Aspergillus parasiticus*. The illness may be either acute or chronic but the effects include liver cirrhosis and the induction of tumours. Foods usually implicated include cereals and nuts. Most illnesses caused by aflatoxins occur in underdeveloped countries where considerable amounts of mouldy cereals are consumed over prolonged periods. The Aflatoxins in Nuts, Nut Products, Dried Figs and Dried Fig Products Regulations, 1992 (SI. 3236) prohibit sales of the above products if levels of aflatoxin exceed 4μg/kg. In 1994 two samples of peanut butter and one sample of peanuts from a major retailer had a mean aflatoxin concentration of 20μg/kg for the peanut butter and 23μg/kg for the peanuts. Voluntary withdrawal was undertaken. A MAFF survey of herbs and spices in 1994 found five per cent had levels of aflatoxin above 10μg/kg, but none above 50μg/kg which is the action level. Domestic cooking will not destroy aflatoxin.

## VIRUSES

Outbreaks of food poisoning are increasingly being attributed to microscopic virus particles. As these organisms only multiply in living tissue the breakdown in hygiene, particularly in relation to temperature control, which normally precedes bacterial food poisoning, is not an essential prerequisite to the outbreak. The infective dose is thought to be small.

Viruses can be destroyed by the heat of normal cooking and incidents usually involve raw food, especially shellfish such as oysters and cockles, or food contaminated after cooking. Bivalve molluscs are "filter feeders" (mussels, oysters, clams, cockles and scallops) and are known to concentrate viruses from sewage polluted water and, therefore, shellfish grown in such water must be regarded with suspicion. The normal depuration process (relaying in clean water) removes bacterial contamination but may not remove viruses. Shellfish must be obtained from reputable sources and have been cultivated in sea water free of contamination.

The attack rate is normally high and a large proportion of persons consuming the contaminated food are likely to be affected. The incubation period is usually longer than bacterial food poisoning, around 24 to 48 hours. Secondary cases among close family contacts are common. Symptoms include diarrhoea, abdominal pain, fever, nausea and vomiting and the illness usually lasts for around 24 hours. The onset is often explosive and vomiting may be "projectile". Virus particles may be detected in the faecal specimens of ill persons by using an electron microscope, but specimens should be examined within 48 hours of first symptoms as the number of viruses in faeces declines rapidly after 24 hours. The first time that similar virus particles were detected in both oysters and the faecal specimens of ill persons who had consumed the oysters was in Kingston-upon-Hull (1980).

In 1995 there were 21,091 cases of gastrointestinal viral infection reported to laboratories, including 17,149 rotavirus, 1,155 adenovirus, 2,369 small round structured viruses, 278 astrovirus and 140 calicivirus. Spread is usually by the faecal-oral route, some being food borne, and possibly by the respiratory route. Over 80% of cases involved children under five and outbreaks have occurred in hospitals, old people's homes, holiday camps and at wedding receptions.

The first recorded outbreak of food-borne viral gastroenteritis was identified in an American school in the town of Norwalk, Ohio in 1968.

## THE INVESTIGATION OF FOOD POISONING OUTBREAKS

The effective investigation of food poisoning outbreaks, by all disciplines involved, is essential to limit the spread and to obtain accurate information on causal factors, vehicles and sources of infection. This information can then be disseminated to food businesses and enforcement officers to assist in a risk-based approach to production and control and make a major contribution to preventing food-borne illness.

The objectives of the investigation of an outbreak are to:

(1) contain the spread of the outbreak;
(2) identify the focus of infection (place where food prepared or served);
(3) identify the food vehicle involved (the food eaten which gave rise to illness);
(4) identify the epidemic organism or chemical responsible;
(5) trace cases and carriers, especially food handlers;
(6) trace the source of infection (the reservoir from which the bacteria originated);

(7) determine causal factors, i.e., how the food vehicle became contaminated and what stage of food preparation allowed bacterial multiplication; and
(8) recommend how food should be prepared in the future to prevent recurrence.

The isolation of the epidemic organism in food remains provides the best evidence to confirm the food vehicle in the event of a food poisoning outbreak. Consequently, the retention of samples of high-risk foods served by catering businesses throughout the day can prove very useful. However, it is often impracticable to save all meals because of the expense and refrigerated space required. (Samples needed for up to five days).

**The role of management**

A manager will become involved in food poisoning investigations when:
(1) a food handler reports that he or she is suffering from diarrhoea and/or vomiting;
(2) persons purchasing food from, or eating at, the premises complain that they have subsequently been ill. The complainants may contact the local Environmental Health Officer who will inform the manager;
(3) persons attending a function begin to vomit whilst on the premises.

If a manager is notified of a suspected case of food poisoning, he or she should immediately contact the Environmental Health Department (EHD) and then make enquiries to find out:
(1) whether any staff have been ill;
(2) which food or meals were implicated and how they were handled or prepared; and
(3) whether or not any other persons were affected.

It is advisable not to serve further meals or suspect food until the Environmental Health Officer has carried out a full investigation. It is essential to co-operate fully with the investigating officer and to provide required information as soon as possible.

Immediately upon becoming aware of an outbreak of food-borne infection associated with the premises the person in charge should:
(1) stop serving any more food and stop any more food being eaten;
(2) telephone a doctor or ambulance if necessary (if people are ill on the premises);
(3) retain any remaining food, cans, cartons or other forms of food packaging which may be needed to trace suspect food consignments;
(4) telephone the EHD to arrange for an investigation by an Environmental Health Officer (an out of hours emergency number should be available);
(5) telephone the owner of the business;
(6) not clean up until bacteriological investigations have been carried out;
(7) prepare a relevant menu list and, as far as possible, details of food preparation, when purchased, storage temperature, method of cooking, cooling or reheating;
(8) if possible, make a complete list of persons consuming the suspect meal, including their addresses;
(9) prepare a complete list of all food handlers and other staff, especially those involved with the suspect meal. Absent staff should be included, the reason for the absence should be given;
(10) prepare a list of suppliers;

(11) remain available on the premises to give the necessary information to the investigating officer, for example, when the meal was served, the number of people known to be affected, etc.; and
(12) when the investigation has been completed, thoroughly clean and disinfect the premises. Advice should be obtained from the Environmental Health Officer.

**The role of the Environmental Health Officer in food poisoning investigations**

The circumstances of an outbreak investigation may vary considerably. Notifications require different levels of response, however, all activities must be carefully coordinated and structured. There are six key stages:

(1) *Preliminaries*: reviewing notifications; formulating an initial hypothesis of the nature of the disease; determination of case definition, population at risk and general case search area; deciding on resources needed; defining responsibilities and reporting systems; setting up communication channels; briefing investigators; and issuing documents/forms etc.
(2) *Case finding*: searching for cases, carriers and contacts; recording detailed case histories of sufferers, food consumption details, symptoms, times of onset, personal and occupational details, obtaining specimens; assembling data to formulate a hypothesis as to focus of infection, meals/foods eaten, the location(s) and approximate time of preparation.
(3) *Site investigation*: secure assistance of managers, collect menus, details of food and suppliers; identification of all food production staff and their functions, staff records and sickness returns; locating production areas, food and waste stores and meal remains; seizing or detaining suspect food; postponing cleaning and disinfection; terminating or modifying food production, if necessary, to prevent spread of disease; collecting food and other relevant samples and swabbing surfaces; inspecting and recording site conditions; interviewing managers and staff; arranging for collection of specimens from staff. (Food handlers with symptoms must be excluded from food handling duties). Officers should not allow the sale of food from the premises to be resumed until they have, as far as is reasonably practicable, satisfied themselves that food can be produced safely with no identifiable risk to the consumer. Site investigations are the most important part of the investigation to ascertain the cause of the outbreak and require the special skills of an officer experienced in inspecting food premises and interviewing techniques.
(4) *Intermediate review:* assemble all available data; assess control measures needed; formulate a provisional hypothesis as to vehicle(s) of infection, causal factors and sources; review investigation progress and determine need for further investigations; prepare an interim report and if appropriate issue public warnings.
(5) *Source tracing:* sample ingredients used to identify contamination levels; assess possibility of organisms surviving processing; analysis of food sample results, swabs and specimens; trace the distribution chain of suspect ingredients or other foods; investigate primary produce/animals or birds.

(6) *Consolidation:* collation and processing all data to test the hypothesis; carry out, as necessary, further detailed investigations of critical factors in the outbreak; discussion of a draft final report with investigators, agreeing final hypothesis and formulation of remedial and control measures; publishing the final report.

The investigation should be carried out bearing in mind that a criminal offence may have occurred and legal action may have to be taken. Statements from staff are preferably taken under the Criminal Justice Act, 1967, as amended and interviews of persons likely to face prosecution should be carried out under the Police and Criminal Evidence Act, 1984.

# CHAPTER 4 Food-borne infections

Food-borne diseases may be considered to differ from food poisoning in that:

(1) the incubation period is normally longer;
(2) a relatively small number of organisms is capable of causing the illness;
(3) the food acts purely as a vehicle and the multiplication of the organism within the food is not an important feature of the illness;
(4) infection may also be spread by non-food items;
(5) the infective organism enters the blood stream; and
(6) symptoms may or may not include diarrhoea and vomiting.

## Typhoid and paratyphoid fever

Sometimes known as enteric fever, typhoid is caused by the bacterium *Salmonella typhi* and paratyphoid by the bacterium *Salmonella paratyphi*. The incubation period is normally between one and three weeks. Symptoms include fever, malaise, slow pulse, spleen enlargement, rose spots on the trunk and constipation or severe diarrhoea. The fatality rate for typhoid is between two and ten per cent. Paratyphoid is generally much less severe and symptoms may be similar to salmonella food poisoning.

The organism is excreted in the faeces and urine of patients and carriers. Up to five per cent of persons affected become permanent carriers. In 1995, 435 cases of enteric fever were reported in England and Wales, although most of these were visitors from endemic areas abroad. Enteric fever may be water-borne, due to contamination by sewage, or food-borne, for example, milk or cooked meat contaminated by polluted water or by carriers who are food handlers. Laboratory confirmation is by bacteriological examination of blood, faeces or urine. In 1993 an outbreak of *S. paratyphi B* in France resulted from eating cheese made from raw goat's milk.

*Prevention*

(1) Ensuring the safety of all water supplies. Water used for food preparation or drinking should be chlorinated.
(2) Ensuring the satisfactory disposal of sewage.
(3) Ensuring the heat treatment of milk and milk products, including ice-cream.
(4) Preventing the sale of raw shellfish, especially if harvested from sewage polluted waters, without appropriate treatment.

(5) Identifying carriers and ensuring that they are not employed within the food industry. Medical questionnaires should be used as an aid to recruitment.
(6) Maintaining high standards of personal hygiene amongst food handlers, especially with regard to thorough hand washing after visiting the W.C.
(7) Ensuring high standards of hygiene in food production and distribution.

## Dysentery

*Bacillary dysentery*

In the UK *bacillary* dysentery is usually caused by the bacterium *Shigella sonnei* and less frequently by *Shigella flexneri*. It is an acute disease of the intestine characterized by diarrhoea, fever, stomach cramps and often vomiting. Stools may contain blood, mucus and pus. Fatality is normally less than one per cent and the severity of illness depends on the type of *Shigella* causing the infection. The incubation period is normally around four days, although it varies between one and seven days. Dysentery is spread through faecal-oral transmission from an infected person or by the consumption of contaminated foods, including water or milk. In 1994 imported iceberg lettuce was implicated in several cases and outbreaks of *Shigella sonnei*. There were approximately 4,600 reported cases of dysentery in England and Wales in 1995, many involving young children. Preventive measures are similar to those used for typhoid, with the emphasis on personal hygiene.

*Amoebic dysentery*

This form of dysentery is rare in Europe apart from persons becoming infected whilst visiting tropical and sub-tropical countries where it is endemic. The causative organism is *Entamoeba histolytica,* a microscopic single-celled protozoan. Symptoms include abdominal pain and mild or severe diarrhoea alternating with constipation.

## Campylobacter enteritis

Campylobacter has been implicated as a cause of acute enteritis since 1977, and it is now the most frequently reported reason for acute bacterial diarrhoea. In 1995 approximately 43,900 campylobacters were isolated from faecal specimens submitted in England and Wales, and 5,000 in Scotland. However, high-risk food was only proven to be a vehicle for a few of these. The main vehicle has yet to be identified.

Campylobacters are spirally curved rods and most species are microaerobic; oxygen at normal atmospheric pressure prevents growth and numbers decline. They are thermophillic and grow well between 37°C and 43°C but not at 25°C. At 48°C they are inactivated.

The causal species of human enteritis are *Campylobacter jejuni* (approximately 90%) and *Campylobacter coli* (approximately 10%). Symptoms vary in severity and include headache, fever, diarrhoea (often blood stained), persistent colicky abdominal pain (may mimic acute appendicitis) and nausea (vomiting is rare). The incubation period is usually between two and five days and the normal duration of illness is one to seven days. A second "dose" of symptoms may occur three weeks after the first.

Illness can be caused by less than 500 organisms and multiplication within foods below 30°C does not occur. Most reported cases are sporadic and peak in the late spring. Mortality is minimal and complications are rare. Campylobacters disappear from the stools within a few weeks of illness and long-term carriers have not been detected. Because of the low transmissibility and inability of campylobacter to multiply at room temperatures, infected food handlers should usually be allowed to resume normal duties when their stools are firm. The contamination of food by human excreters has not been proven.

Animals and wild birds are the main reservoirs of infection and as campylobacters can survive in water for several weeks at low temperatures, untreated natural water is a potential source. Furthermore, water storage tanks could be contaminated by birds or small animals.

Campylobacters are commonly found on raw poultry, in raw milk and sewage and on carcase meat and offal. Between 30% and 100% of raw poultry may be contaminated by as many as $10^7$ organisms per bird. Cross-contamination from raw poultry is extremely likely and hands can carry campylobacters for up to an hour.

Transmission is thought to be from raw and undercooked poultry, and meat, raw milk, bottled milk pecked by birds, especially magpies, and infected animals such as dogs and cats. Person to person spread is rare as are secondary cases.

Freezing reduces the number of campylobacters but once frozen they can survive for several months. The organisms may be destroyed by heating food to 60°C for 15 minutes and are sensitive to drying,* chlorination and salt in excess of two per cent.

Control measures include reducing the numbers of campylobacters in raw meat and the food chain, hygiene training of food handlers, especially on the dangers of cross-contamination and the importance of thorough cooking, and raising the hygiene awareness of consumers.

## Listeriosis

Although food is not the only means of transmission, and in the majority of cases a source of infection is not identified, listeriosis may be considered as a food-borne illness and is caused by *Listeria monocytogenes,* a Gram +ve, psychrotrophic bacillus which is widely distributed in the environment. The bacteria may be excreted by human or animal carriers, and many cases of cross-infection have been recorded. Symptoms include fever, septicaemia, meningitis and abortion; neonates, pregnant women, immuno-suppressed persons and the elderly are most at risk. The incubation period is one to 70 days.

Prior to 1977 an average of 50 cases of listeriosis were reported annually. Since then numbers have increased with a peak of 291 cases and 63 deaths in 1988. In 1995, 91 cases of listeriosis were reported. The death rate is usually around 30% but mainly involves persons with other serious illness.

---

*Svedhem A. et al., (1981) Journal of Hygiene, Cambridge, 87, 421.

The organism, which is described as a low temperature pathogen, is salt tolerant and is reported to be able to multiply between 0°C and 42°C, although growth at 3°C is very slow. Under refrigeration small numbers of listeria can soon dominate competing organisms and may also become more infective due to the production of a toxin (listeriolysin O).

Thermal death time is widely disputed: the bacteria may have a greater ability than normal to recover from heat damage. Under certain conditions, core temperatures in solid foods may have to be as high as 91°C to ensure destruction, if the product is subsequently intended for chilled storage. However, most reports state listeria is not especially heat resistant. An outbreak in France in 1992, probably due to the consumption of pork tongue in aspic, resulted in 279 cases, 63 deaths (including seven neonates) and 22 abortions. In 1987 Switzerland banned the production of Vacherin Mont d'or cheese following 60+ deaths over a period of around four years. Sporadic cases have implicated turkey frankfurters, dried mushrooms, salami, veg rennet and undercooked chicken.

Surveys in the UK have shown that soft cheese (10%+) and pâté (10%) often contain high levels of listeria with lower levels frequently being isolated in raw meat/poultry/fish/vegetables/milk (up to 60%), fried rice, salads, ice-cream and retail processed-chilled food (up to 24%). In 1989 the Government issued a warning to risk-groups to avoid soft cheeses, reheated meals and pâté.

**Streptococcus zooepidemicus**

This bacterium may cause a serious flu-like illness together with septicaemia, meningitis and bacterial endocarditis. *Streptococcus zooepidemicus* is found in a variety of animals including horses and cows, when it may cause mastitis.

In 1984 twelve persons in West Yorkshire, ten over 70 years of age, were hospitalized after being infected with *Streptococcus zooepidemicus*. Eight of these subsequently died, including a day-old premature baby. All eleven adults drank raw milk. The organism was isolated from a bottle of milk and three cows from the supplier's herd. In 1994 two persons drinking raw milk were infected by *Streptococcus zooepidemicus* and one of them subsequently died. The organism was isolated from a sample of the milk from the herd.

## Hepatitis

Hepatitis is caused by a virus and the two main types are hepatitis A and hepatitis B. Type A is the more common. In 1994 there were 2,341 laboratory notifications of infectious jaundice, some of these being food-borne and associated with shellfish.

*Hepatitis A*

The onset is abrupt and symptoms include fever, malaise, nausea, abdominal pain and later jaundice. The duration of the illness varies from one week to several months. Man is the reservoir for the virus and transmission is often by the faecal-oral route. Faeces, blood and urine may all be infected and can contaminate food, especially water, shellfish and milk. The incubation period is from 15 to 50 days. The fatality rate is less than one per cent. Preventive measures are similar to those used for typhoid. A temperature of 90°C for 90 seconds will inactivate hepatitis A virus.

**Brucellosis (undulant fever)**

A systemic disease caused by the bacteria *Brucella abortus* and *Brucella melitensis*. Symptoms include intermittent fever, extended depression, headache, weakness and generalized aching. The illness may last from a few days to several months. Fatality is less than two per cent. The incubation period is usually five to 21 days. Transmission is normally by contact with an infected cow or by the consumption of raw milk or milk products. The brucellosis eradication scheme which involved slaughtering all infected animals, and the heat treatment of milk have largely eliminated this disease. In 1995, 19 cases of brucellosis were reported in England and Wales (Some of these being contracted abroad).

**Tuberculosis**

A chronic bacterial disease caused by *Mycobacterium tuberculosis,* the human tubercle bacillus, and *Mycobacterium bovis* in cattle. The bovine type also affects man and can result in extra-pulmonary tuberculosis involving the bones, lymph nodes, kidneys, intestines and skin. The incubation period is four to six weeks but development of the later stages may take years. Airborne transmission and contact with infected sputum occur, although bovine tuberculosis is primarily spread by the consumption of raw milk or dairy products. Tuberculosis used to be a very common disease of bovines but is now rare due to the slaughter of all infected animals. Heat treatment of milk was introduced primarily to combat this disease.

**Verocytotoxin (VTEC) producing E. coli 0157**

Since the 1970's *E. coli* strains producing verocytotoxin have been associated with severe illness typified by acute abdominal pain and watery diarrhoea that becomes bloody. Fever is absent and failure to isolate a pathogen may result in misdiagnosis. The illness lasts six to eight days and faecal specimens should be examined within six days of the onset of symptoms. Up to 20% of cases may be hospitalized, 4% (especially children under five) may develop haemolytic uraemic syndrome resulting in kidney failure (HUS) and around 2% may die. Person to person spread may occur.

Outbreaks of *E. coli* in parts of North America are common where it is known as "the barbecue disease". *E. coli 0157* (the most common serogroup of VTEC) outbreaks have implicated raw milk, undercooked beefburgers, contaminated water, yogurt and freshly-pressed apple cider. The organism has also been isolated in lamb, chicken, turkey and pork. In 1991 the first UK outbreak of *E. coli 0157* involving beefburgers was reported from Preston. In 1993 an outbreak in Sheffield implicated raw milk, and undercooked beefburgers were suspected in an outbreak in Gwent. The organism is heat sensitive and control involves thorough cooking and preventing contamination. There were 792 laboratory reports of *E. coli* 0157 in England and Wales in 1995.

**Giardiasis**

Giardiasis is a type of gastroenteritis caused by the parasitic protozoan *Giardia lamblia (Giardia intestinalis)*, which is a common inhabitant of the intestinal tract. The incubation period is six to 22 days and symptoms include watery diarrhoea, flatulence, abdominal pain and distension. Alternatively, there may be less acute diarrhoea with fatty stools, lassitude and weight loss. The infective dose is very low and may only require one viable cyst. The main sources of infection are human cases and carriers. Transmission is by the faecal-oral route. Cases involving food are rarely proven. Water-borne outbreaks occasionally occur and chlorination without filtration is ineffective. There were 6,186 laboratory reports of giardiasis in the UK in 1995, mainly affecting children. However, many of these probably originated abroad.

**Cryptosporidiosis**

Cryptosporidiosis is a gastrointestinal infection caused by parasitic protozoa, *Cryptosporidium spp.* Symptoms include diarrhoea, vomiting, anorexia and abdominal pain. The incubation period is probably around ten days. The sources of infection are cattle and other domestic and wild animals. The protozoa cling to the surface of the intestine and produce oocysts which pass out in the faeces. The oocysts (4 to 6 μm in diameter) are unaffected by the chlorine levels in tap water. Transmission is by the faecal-oral route, although it is believed that close contact with infected animals is more significant than contaminated food or water. In 1995, 5,705 incidents of cryptosporidiosis were reported in England and Wales.

## PARASITES AFFECTING FOOD AND/OR MAN

A parasite is a plant or animal that has the ability to live on another plant or animal known as the host. The parasite obtains its nourishment from the host. Parasites may pass through complicated life cycles which depend on intermediate hosts for the cystic stage of their life. For example:

*Taenia saginata* - the adult tapeworm attaches itself to the intestine of man (adult host), eggs are passed out in faeces and may eventually reach grazing land where they are eaten by cattle (intermediate host). The eggs hatch in the gut and the resultant cysts migrate to the muscle via the blood. If infected, undercooked meat is eaten the cysts become adult tapeworms;

*Trichinella spiralis* - adult worms live in the gut of the host, for example, rats. Larvae are produced and are carried to the muscles, via the blood, and encyst. If infected meat is eaten, for example, by a pig, the life cycle begins again;

*Fasciola hepatica* - the adult fluke lives in the bile duct of the host, for example, cattle. Eggs are passed out in faeces and hatch on wet land. If the cysts find a mud snail (intermediate host), further development occurs before they end up on vegetation waiting to be eaten by sheep or cattle. They infect persons who eat watercress grown in contaminated water.

**TABLE XVII** PARASITES AFFECTING FOOD

| Name | Cystic stage | Intermediate host | Adult host (intestine) |
|---|---|---|---|
| *Taenia saginata* (Beef tapeworm) | *Cysticercus bovis* | Bovine muscle especially cheek, heart, tongue, shoulder and diaphragm | Man (occurs as a result of consuming affected flesh). 44 cases in 1995 (most imported) |
| *Taenia solium* (Pork tapeworm) | *Cysticercus cellulosae* | Normally the pig (occasionally, dog, cat, rat & man) - embedded in muscles, especially the heart, diaphragm, tongue and shoulder | Man (rare in the UK). 1975-1989, 31 cases (all imported) |
| *Diphyllobothrium latum* (Fish tapeworm) | Plerocercoid | Freshwater fish especially fatty tissue. (Affected fish should be condemned) | Man and other fish-eating mammals (rare in the UK) |
| *Trichinella spiralis* | Trichinella cyst | A small worm that may encyst in the musculature of pigs, especially the diaphragm, the tongue, larynx and abdominal muscles. In the UK rats are the most affected animal | Same as the intermediate host. Infection in man is due to the consumption of raw or undercooked pork. 1976-85, 23 cases (all imported) |
| *Fasciola hepatica* | Fasciola cercariae | Mudsnail (*Limnaea truncatula)* | Mainly sheep and cattle. It is common in the UK but rare in man. 1976-85, 24 cases (23 imported) |
| *Echinococcus granulosus* | Hydatid cyst | Cattle, sheep, horses & pigs, normally the liver & lungs. Man may become affected by eating food contaminated by ova and also by dogs licking the hand or face (known as hydatid disease) | Normally dog. 1995, 11 cases |
| *Taenia hydatigena* | *Cysticercus tenuicollis* | Cattle, sheep and pigs, normally in the liver | Dog |

# CHAPTER 5 Food contamination and its prevention

Contamination of food may be considered as the transference of any objectionable matter into or on the food. Thus, carcases may be contaminated with faecal material, high-risk food may be contaminated with spoilage or food poisoning bacteria and flour may be contaminated with rodent hairs. To prevent the consumption of unacceptable or unsafe food, contamination must be kept to a minimum.

There are three types of contamination:

(1) *Contamination by bacteria, moulds or viruses (microorganisms)*
Usually occurs in food premises because of ignorance, inadequate space, poor design or because of food handlers taking short cuts. In the early stages it will not be detectable. Contamination of this sort is the most serious and may result in food spoilage, food poisoning or even death.

(2) *Physical contamination by foreign bodies including insects*
Physical contamination may render food unfit or unsafe but often involve pieces of paper, plastic, metal or string and is usually unpleasant or a nuisance.

(3) *Chemical contamination*
Examples include pesticides on fruit and detergent residues from cleaning

The Food Safety (General Food Hygiene) Regulations, 1995, require that food shall not be exposed to risk of contamination. However, for an offence to have been committed it must usually be proved that there is a risk to the health of people consuming the food and regard must be had to the nature of the food, any further treatment, such as cooking, that the food may receive before sale and the manner in which it is packed. It is unfortunate that the terms "contamination" and "cross-contamination" are not defined in current legislation. Clear definitions would assist uniform enforcement and avoid the unnecessary expense involved in some court cases.

In the USA the Food Service Sanitation Manual of the Food and Drug Administration states that:

"at all times, including storage, preparation, display, service and distribution, food shall be protected from potential contamination including dust, insects, rodents, dirty equipment, unnecessary handling, coughs and sneezes, flooding, drainage and overhead leakage or condensation".

## CONTAMINATION BY MICROORGANISMS

Mould spores will be present in the atmosphere, on surfaces, especially damp surfaces, and on mouldy food. Food should always be covered and mouldy food must be segregated. Furthermore, mould must not be allowed to grow on walls, ceilings and window frames. Mould growth often occurs if food is stored at the wrong temperature, at high humidity and in excess of the recommended shelf-life. It may also affect cheese stored in vacuum packs which are pierced. Canned goods which are removed from cases opened with unguarded craft knives may become punctured, thus giving rise to mould growth inside the can.

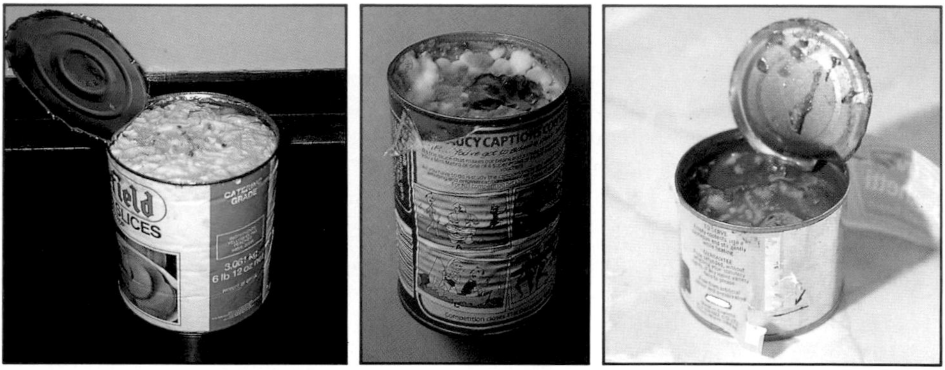

**Fig. 12.** Mould growth on food due to can punctures.

Viruses are usually brought into food premises by food handlers who are carriers, or on raw food such as shellfish which have been grown in sewage polluted water.

Bacterial contamination is the most significant as it results in large amounts of spoilt food and unacceptable numbers of food poisoning cases. Food poisoning bacteria may be brought into food premises by the following sources:

(1) man;
(2) raw foods and water;
(3) insects, rodents, animals and birds; and
(4) from the environment, including soil and dust.

### Man

People commonly harbour food poisoning organisms in the nose, mouth, intestine and also on the skin. The hands are never free of bacteria and the soiled hands of food handlers are likely to harbour large numbers of moulds, yeasts and bacteria, some of which may be pathogenic, for example, *Staphylococcus aureus*. The presence of boils and septic cuts usually guarantees the presence of staphylococci and food handlers suffering with these conditions should be excluded from working in food premises.

Carelessness, ignorance of, or disregard for, hygienic food handling may result in contamination and possibly food poisoning. All food handlers must have high standards of personal hygiene, wear suitable protective clothing and, as far as possible, avoid handling food directly; tongs and other equipment should be used. The importance of thorough and regular handwashing cannot be overstressed.

## Raw food

Foods such as raw meat, milk, shellfish and eggs are all likely to be contaminated with large numbers of bacteria, which may include food poisoning bacteria. Even when produced under hygienic conditions raw foods must be considered a hazard.

## Raw meat and poultry

The contamination of meat starts on the farm and poultry meat is the most common food implicated in outbreaks of food poisoning, especially salmonellosis. Eggs from infected breeding stock may result in the introduction of chickens which are already excreting salmonellae. The younger the chicken the more susceptible it is to becoming infected and becoming an excreter. Other possible sources include man, dogs, cats, rodents, insects and wild birds. Overcrowded and badly constructed sheds, which cannot be cleaned and disinfected, encourage the spread of infection throughout flocks.

Animals which are ill should be segregated and infections treated as soon as possible. Stress, excitement, fatigue and overcrowding increase the likelihood of animals excreting salmonellae. Symptomless excreters remain a major problem.

Animals and birds should be transported to slaughterhouses in clean and disinfected vehicles. Slaughtering should be carried out in slaughterhouses which comply with the appropriate regulations. Animals should be kept as clean as possible before and after slaughtering. The flesh of healthy, live animals is virtually free of microorganisms. However, on slaughtering, the walls of the intestine lose the ability to resist bacterial penetration. Consequently, evisceration must be carried out as quickly as possible.

The hide is a possible source of food poisoning organisms, although most contamination of the carcase is likely when the stomach and intestines are removed. All dressing must take place clear of the floor. Areas and procedures which may result in contamination should be eliminated. Poor hygiene amongst slaughterhouse operatives, dirty equipment and unsatisfactory practices will undoubtedly contribute to the amount of contaminated raw meat or poultry leaving the slaughterhouse.

The skin of poultry is usually heavily contaminated with bacteria. Bruises also harbour many bacteria, a large number of which may be staphylococci. Many birds in the slaughterhouse become contaminated by processes such as scalding, mechanical defeathering and evisceration. Scald tanks operating at 52°C are a much greater risk than those operated at 60°C, as fewer organisms will be destroyed at the lower temperature. Thorough spraying of poultry, with clean water, after evisceration is essential to reduce bacterial loads.

Physical inspection of animals, meat and offal will not detect food poisoning organisms.

## Fish and shellfish

Apart from *Vibrio parahaemolyticus* and *Clostridium botulinum,* which rarely cause problems in this country, most pathogenic bacteria are introduced into fish by poor handling. As fish spoil rapidly they should be gutted and stored under hygienic conditions on ice, in refrigerators or freezers, as soon as possible after removal from the water.

Shellfish are often contaminated with food poisoning organisms, especially bivalves such as cockles, oysters and mussels grown in sewage polluted water. The amount of heat used to remove the meat from the shells is usually inadequate to destroy the pathogens and recontamination is always likely. A significant number of cases of viral food poisoning and hepatitis are attributed to the consumption of shellfish. Even shellfish which have been relaid in clean water, subject to UV treatment, may still contain viruses. Between 1981 and 1990, 42 outbreaks of illness were associated with eating crustacean species, mainly prawns and 151 outbreaks associated with molluscs. Of these, confirmatory microbiological or epidemiological evidence was obtained in seven and 107 outbreaks respectively.

**Eggs**

Although the shell of eggs, especially if dirty, may be contaminated with salmonellae, it is considered that infected reproductive tissues are the main route of internal contamination, usually of the albumen. Other than cracked eggs, numbers of salmonellae are likely to be low and the bacteriostatic properties of the albumen should prevent significant growth for at least 21 days if temperatures remain below 20°C.

In 1994 a report of a 1992/1993 PHLS survey indicated that 17 out of 7,730 six-egg samples were contaminated with salmonellae, either on the shell surface (nine samples) or internally (eight samples). The eggs were obtained from high street outlets and stored for at least five weeks at 21°C before testing. A PHLS survey of 94,050 eggs in 1991 indicated that one out of 650 UK eggs and one out of 370 EC imported eggs were contaminated with salmonellae.

Most of the food poisoning outbreaks associated with hens' eggs have in fact involved dishes containing raw egg, for example, home-made mayonnaise or lightly cooked egg white, for example, meringue and are more likely to have been caused by incorrect food handling and failures in temperature control, notwithstanding the source being contaminated eggs. The use of pasteurized egg is recommended for dishes which will not be cooked sufficiently to destroy salmonellae. Food handlers must always wash their hands after handling eggs and never take risks with egg products. Cross-contamination must be avoided.

**Milk**

Milk is an ideal medium for the growth of microorganisms which may be introduced from:

(1) the animal itself, especially if ill or very dirty;
(2) the person carrying out the milking; and
(3) unhygienic equipment or storage tanks.

In an effort to reduce the problems from milk, government schemes have been carried out to ensure that all herds are tuberculin tested (accredited) and free from brucellosis. Milk from cows or goats suffering from mastitis must not be used for human consumption as it may be infected with staphylococci and streptococci.

Raw or underprocessed milk has been implicated in several large food poisoning outbreaks involving *Salmonella spp.* and *Staphylococcus aureus,* in addition to several outbreaks of campylobacter enteritis.

**Water supplies and drainage**

Although not an ideal medium for the multiplication of bacteria, water can nevertheless transport certain pathogenic organisms considerable distances, for example, salmonellae. Furthermore, bacterial spores may survive for several months in water. Pollution of water is usually caused by human sewage or faecal contamination from animals. The Aberdeen typhoid outbreak (1964) was associated with cans of Argentinean corned beef which had been cooled in sewage-polluted water.

Cold water supplies used for washing food or equipment require suitable treatment and must be of potable quality. Pipework must be properly installed and maintained. Potable and non-potable supplies must never be connected or confused. Regular bacteriological and chemical checks of water used in food production are essential.

Satisfactory drains must be installed to carry away waste water. Flooding, leakage, back-siphonage and blockages must, as far as practicable, be prevented. Food, including canned or packaged food, which has been in contact with sewage-polluted water must be regarded as unfit.

**Vegetables and fruit**

Vegetable crops, cereals and fruit must be grown on land which is free from toxic materials and must only be sprayed with insecticide and other such chemicals in accordance with manufacturer's instructions. Irrigation must not be carried out with sewage-polluted water which may contain pathogens, tapeworm eggs or other parasites.

After harvesting, vegetables must be stored under conditions which do not expose them to risk of contamination, for example, from poisonous chemicals or rodents. Animals and birds must be kept away from storage areas.

Sorting and packing of fruit, and raw vegetables used in salads, may introduce pathogens from food-handlers, especially via the hands. All such foods must be thoroughly washed before use. Particular care must be exercised to avoid contaminating vegetables to be eaten raw. An outbreak of salmonellosis in the USA involving coleslaw and onions was traced back to contamination of the vegetables prepared on the same work surface used for cutting up raw chickens.

**Animals and birds**

Both domestic and wild animals are known to carry pathogens on their bodies and in their intestines. Large numbers of *Staphylococcus aureus* are commonly found on the skin and noses of cats and dogs. Salmonellae are often present in the intestines. Consequently, pets must always be kept out of food rooms. Persons handling animals should always change their clothing and wash their hands before touching food. Pet food may be contaminated and should be kept out of food rooms. Terrapins are occasionally implicated in food poisoning cases through contact with infected water. Wild birds have been responsible for an outbreak of salmonellosis in a hospital kitchen.

**Insects**

Insects are capable of contaminating food by defecation, feeding, walking on or dying in the food. Insects of particular concern, with regard to bacterial contamination, are flies, cockroaches and pharaoh's ants.

**Rodents**

Rodents, including both rats and mice, commonly excrete organisms such as salmonellae. Contamination of food may occur from gnawing, defecating, urinating or walking over food or food-contact surfaces.

**Dust**

There are always large numbers of bacteria and spores in dust and moisture droplets floating about in the air. Open food should always be removed or covered during cleaning. The ventilation of premises should always be from high-risk areas to low-risk areas unless each area is independently ventilated. All air drawn into food premises should be filtered and intakes of ventilation ducts must be positioned to avoid introducing contaminated air. The ventilation system should not produce turbulence within the premises.

**Soil**

Soil harbours a considerable number of pathogens such as *Clostridium perfringens* and care must be taken when bringing raw vegetables such as potatoes, carrots and lettuce into food rooms.

## VEHICLES AND ROUTES OF BACTERIAL CONTAMINATION

Sometimes bacteria pass directly from the source to high-risk food, but as bacteria are largely static and as the sources are not always in direct contact with food, the bacteria have to rely on other things to transfer them to food. These things are known as **vehicles** and the main ones are:

(1) hands;
(2) cloths and equipment;
(3) hand-contact surfaces; and
(4) food-contact surfaces.

Indirect contamination using an intermediate vehicle is by far the commonest, for example, the passage of bacteria from the intestine of a food handler to food via the hands, after using the toilet. Where contamination is passed from raw food to high-risk food via, for example, a worktop, this is known as **cross-contamination.** The path along which bacteria are transferred from the source to the food is known as the **route**. Knowledge of sources, vehicles and routes is vital to food poisoning prevention, as different controls apply to each. It must be assumed that all sources are contaminated, i.e. every worker is a carrier and all raw meat, animals, insects and the surrounding environment are contaminated.

**TABLE XVIII** SOURCES, VEHICLES AND ROUTES OF CONTAMINATION

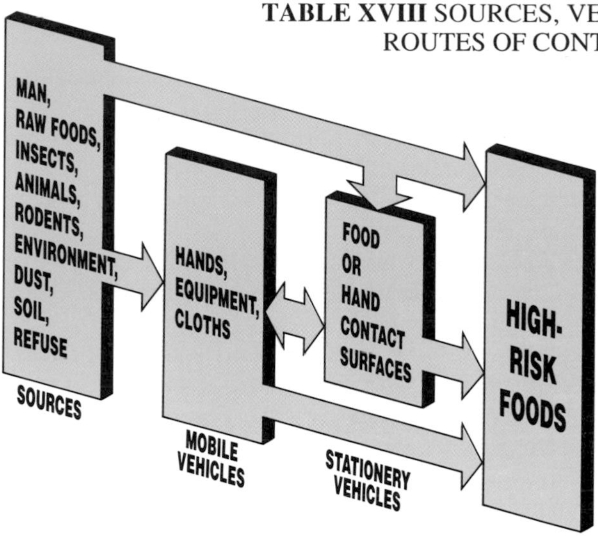


Prevention of contamination depends on either removing the sources, or putting barriers between them and the vehicles or between them and food. Thus human access to food must be restricted, raw foods handled in separate areas, vermin excluded and work areas enclosed in suitably constructed and ventilated rooms. Similarly, vehicles must, where possible, be excluded. Handling should be minimized, wiping cloths used sparingly or destroyed after each use, hand-contact surfaces, such as tap handles, replaced with knee-operated taps, and the number of surfaces with which the food comes into contact limited.

In the nature of food preparation, however, routes between sources and vehicles survive, giving rise to contaminated vehicles. Consequently, routes must be disrupted by cleaning and disinfection. For example, should a work surface come into contact with a contaminated source, raw meat for instance, the surface must be cleaned and disinfected before it is used for cooked meat.

The interrelation between sources, vehicles and food can be complex with many diverse routes being taken by the contaminants.

## CHECK LIST FOR CONTAMINATION CONTROL

(1) Purchase food and raw materials from known, reliable and hygienic suppliers. Test for quality and inspect suppliers' premises if appropriate.

(2) Accept deliveries only if transported in clean, properly equipped vehicles, with clean drivers wearing satisfactory protective clothing. Refrigerated vehicles may be necessary.

(3) Inspect deliveries immediately on arrival. Reject or segregate any damaged, unfit or contaminated material. Where relevant, check temperature, codes and date markings and reject out-of-date food.
(4) After checking, remove deliveries immediately to appropriate storage, refrigerator or cold store.
(5) Keep any unfit food, chemicals and refuse away from stored food. Use only food containers for storing food.
(6) Keep high-risk foods apart from raw foods at all times, in separate areas with separate utensils and equipment. Colour coding is useful.
(7) Maintain scrupulous personal hygiene at all times and handle food as little as possible. Exclude potential carriers.
(8) Keep food covered or otherwise protected unless it is actually being processed or prepared, in which case bring food out only when needed. Do not leave food lying around.
(9) Keep premises, equipment and utensils clean and in good condition and repair. Report or remedy defects with the minimum of delay. Disinfect food-contact surfaces, hand-contact surfaces and, where appropriate, hands.
(10) Ensure that all empty containers are clean and disinfected prior to filling with food, for example, empty cans or milk bottles.
(11) Control cleaning materials, particularly wiping cloths. Keep cleaning materials away from food. Remove food and food containers before cleaning. Care must be taken to ensure that all cleaning residues, including water, are drained from food equipment and pipes.
(12) Remove waste food and refuse from food areas as soon as practicable. Store in appropriate conditions, away from food.
(13) Maintain an active pest control programme (see Chapter 14).
(14) Control visitors and maintenance workers in high-risk areas. Ensure hygiene disciplines apply to all personnel, including management.
(15) Inspect food areas and processes frequently, act on any defects or unhygienic practices. Train staff and monitor performance. Food handlers and engineers must be aware of the bacteriological and physical contamination they may introduce.
(16) Ensure adequate thawing of foods, separate from other foods.
(17) Make suitable provisions for cooling food prior to refrigeration.

## PHYSICAL CONTAMINATION

Foreign bodies found in food may be brought into food premises with the raw materials or introduced during storage, preparation, service or display. It is essential that managers are aware of the types of foreign bodies commonly found in their particular sector of the food industry and that they take all reasonable precautions and exercise all due diligence to secure their removal or prevent their introduction. A record should be kept of all customer complaints and steps should be taken to identify the source of the contaminant.

Reported complaints involving foreign bodies (undesirable contaminants which are usually solid matter) are at an unacceptable high level and may pose a threat to consumer health and leave manufacturers and retailers vulnerable to prosecution and lost sales.

Examination of consumer complaints reveals a high incidence of problems associated with processed foods and in particular:

(1) milk and milk products;
(2) cakes and confectionery;
(3) fruit and vegetables (canned, bottled, dried and jams); and
(4) meat, poultry and fish products.

Contamination of food by extraneous matter will cause customer dissatisfaction and may result in bad publicity. If press and media coverage results, the impact on the business can be disastrous leading, in the worst possible case, to loss of product confidence and even company viability. It is therefore in the interests of the manufacturer to minimize the risk of foreign body contamination.

Foreign bodies, such as bone in chicken meat or stalks in vegetables, are intrinsic and should be minimized by care in harvesting and processing, although foreign body detection and removal systems, such as the use of inspection belts, will also be necessary. The presence of extrinsic foreign bodies in food, such as glass or rodent droppings, is usually of greater concern as this indicates a breakdown in hygiene and will not be tolerated by the consumer.

Extrinsic foreign bodies may be considered as those which:

(1) are present in deliveries of raw materials;
(2) originate from the structure of the building, installations or equipment. Contamination may occur at any step from storage through to service but is most likely during processing;
(3) originate from food handlers;
(4) originate from the activities of maintenance operatives;
(5) originate from packaging;
(6) originate from pests or unsatisfactory pest control
(7) originate from cleaning activities; or
(8) are a result of post-process contamination including sabotage by disgruntled employees, blackmail attempts or from the kitchens or equipment of consumers.

Although in the minority, some foreign bodies may be considered as a serious health hazard such as glass, stones, wire or rodent droppings, which may result in cut mouths, dental damage, choking or illness.

However, all foreign bodies are, at the very least, a nuisance and manufacturers in particular must implement appropriate systems to prevent or remove such contamination. The hazard analysis and critical control point system (HACCP) provides the most effective preventative approach, especially for manufacturers, and will be extremely useful if the company wishes to avail itself of the due diligence defence in the event of a prosecution.

**The use of HACCP to control foreign body contamination**

Conduct an analysis of all possible hazards associated with product: Prepare a flow diagram of the steps in the process, from harvesting through to filling of a closed container or to the consumption of the food by the customer. Identify and list the hazards and specify the control measures. Set target levels and tolerances and establish a monitoring system to ensure control. Establish appropriate corrective action and effective record keeping.

Having defined the terms of reference as outlined above, a team should be selected which, if possible, includes those with experience in production, Quality Assurance, engineering, purchasing of packaging and raw ingredients, hygiene and transport. Extraneous matter may result from poor control in any of these areas and a broad base of experience is vital if HACCP is to be effective. The first task of the team is to clearly define the products under consideration and then construct and verify a flow diagram. The team should consider which foreign body hazards exist and the risk of contamination and then use this risk assessment to identify critical control points. The consequences of a particular hazard (serious health risk or nuisance value) will need to be considered when determining controls and critical control points. Account must also be taken of good manufacturing practices and any Industry Guides to Good Hygiene Practice.

**Preventative systems**

When identifying preventative systems it will be necessary to consider:

(1) the training of staff. Training programmes including the identification of training needs, induction training, reinforcement and refresher training. Records of training should be kept on personal files;
(2) the design, structure, layout and maintenance of food rooms and the implementation of a clearly defined policy relating to use of glass;
(3) the design, construction and maintenance of equipment and especially deterioration with age;
(4) personal hygiene and practices, including protective clothing;
(5) cleaning and disinfection procedures;
(6) instruction and training of maintenance and pest control operatives; and
(7) instructions relating to deboxing and packaging.

**Foreign body detection and removal**

No system can guarantee to remove every contaminant and the effectiveness of a particular machine or system will depend on the type of foreign body, the initial level of contamination and the maintenance of the equipment. The performance of most machines will deteriorate with age and use and constant testing is essential. There are many contaminant detection and removal systems available including:

Metal detection systems
X-Ray systems
Sieves and filtration

Optical systems
Magnets
Air or liquid separation systems
The use of operatives, for example, as spotters, on bottle lines or illuminated inspection belts.

## IDENTIFYING HAZARDS AND SPECIFYING CONTROL MEASURES

### Raw ingredients

The variable nature of raw material quality is one of the main sources of problems in food processing. Raw materials have traditionally been a major source of extraneous matter and food manufacturers use a range of cleaning, sorting and grading operations to separate out the offending material. In the manufacture of frozen peas for example, stones, metal screws, cigarette ends, stalks, sticks, caterpillars and dirt often accompany the vined peas as they arrive at the factory.

Control measures should include specifications to detail maximum permissible levels of contaminants in incoming materials. By agreeing specifications with suppliers and monitoring and evaluating the supplier performance in meeting the specifications, the company has an effective tool in minimizing the risk posed by extraneous matter. Measurements of cleaning and sorting efficiencies in the initial handling of raw materials is a necessary control measure.

Before using raw materials, cleaning or washing and inspection may need to be carried out. For example, vegetables used in food factories must have stones and less-dense material removed. The vegetables should then be conveyed on an illuminated inspection belt of an appropriate colour. The speed of the belt and number of operatives involved in the detection and removal of foreign bodies will depend on the product and the original amount of contamination. Belts should be illuminated to at least 540 lux. Conveyor belts should be designed to eliminate crevices and to allow access to facilitate cleaning and repair. They must be kept clean and inspected frequently for signs of wear or damage. Plastic coated and woven belts should be repaired or replaced if frayed. Wooden sides and rubber strips should not be used and tracking control is recommended to prevent wear. Where practicable, conveyor systems after inspection (and metal detection if present) should be completely enclosed. Food conveyors should be above waist height, as should the tops of boxes, cans and bottles.

Liquids used in food production should be filtered and powders sieved. Filters, screens and sieves should be as fine as possible and must be cleaned and checked regularly. Worn equipment must be replaced. Wooden-framed sieves are unacceptable.

### Packaging materials

Packaging may be a source of extraneous matter in the form of warehouse and transport dirt/dust, wood from the pallets, paper and polythene strips from over-wraps and a variety of insects and even rodents. Containers (cans, jars, bottles and plastic pots) may be used directly for filling with minimal cleaning, and any rogue material in the container (metal splinters, glass, dirt, insects, etc.) may end up in the final product.

*Staples, cardboard, string, fibres, cloth, rubber, plastic and polythene*

Food may be delivered in various containers including paper sacks, cardboard boxes and polythene bags. Particular care is necessary when emptying containers to avoid contamination of food. As far as practicable, all unpacking and packing should be carried out in areas separate from food production or preparation if open food is exposed to risk of contamination.

String removed from hessian sacks and ties removed from bags should immediately be placed in suitable containers provided specifically for the purpose. As an extra precaution, coloured string may be specified to aid detection should it end up in the product. Paper sacks should be cut open, although care must be exercised to ensure pieces of paper do not finish up in the food. It is preferable for raw materials to be emptied into suitable lidded containers and not dispensed direct from paper sacks.

Particular care is needed to ensure that staples, which tend to fly considerable distances when boxes are prised open, do not contaminate food. Suppliers should be requested to use adhesive tape to fasten boxes, instead of staples. Many products are delivered in black polythene bags and small pieces of polythene often end up in the product.

Effective measures in terms of good manufacturing practice should be adopted within the HACCP scheme to minimize the risk of contamination. An example would be the use of secondary packaging which is removed prior to primary packaging material entering a high-risk area.

## The building, installations and equipment

*Wood splinters*

As far as possible the use of wood should be eliminated from food production areas. Wooden containers used for transporting raw materials should be phased out. Pallets should not be double stacked over open food.

*Bolts, nuts and other pieces of metal*

As far as practicable nuts should be self-locking. Bolts, nuts and screws should be non-corroding and positioned to ensure that, should they fall off equipment, they do not drop into the food.

*Flaking paint or rust*

Ceiling structure, pipes or equipment, should be non-flaking and rust-free. This is especially important when such fixtures are positioned directly above open products. In some older factories this problem is very difficult to overcome and consequently additional protection is necessary, for example, enclosed systems for conveying food and empty containers, such as cans. New factories should be designed so that fixtures, ducts and pipes are not suspended over working areas or food if the product is exposed to risk of contamination.

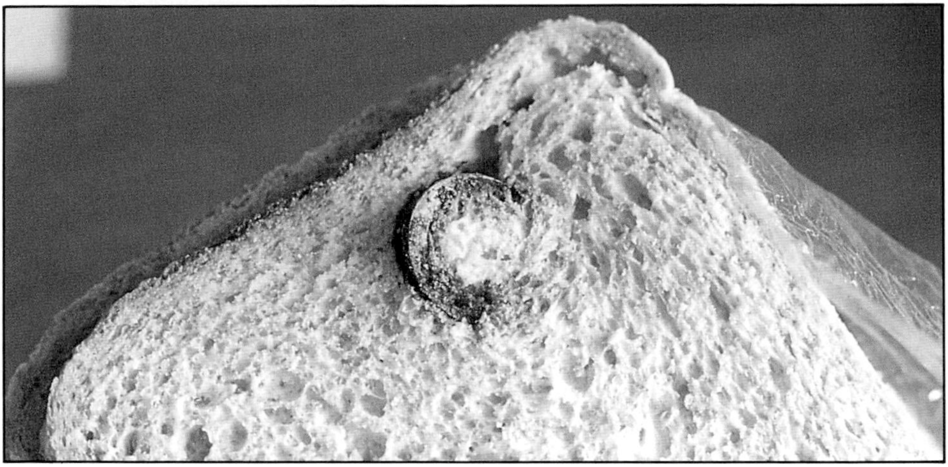

**Fig. 13.** Metal washer baked in breadloaf.

*Grease and oil*

Wherever necessary, food-grade grease and lubricants should be used. It is important that engineers use the minimum amount necessary to lubricate moving parts and that grease is not left on the machine. Careful control will ensure the absence of complaints relating to grease in food. It is preferable for motors not to be positioned above open food. When this occurs, suitable non corroding, cleansable drip-trays should be fixed underneath to catch oil spillages.

*Glass*

The use of ordinary glass, porcelain and enamelware in food factories should be avoided. Perspex or wired glass windows should be used. Diffusers should be fitted to all fluorescent tubes. All beakers, funnels, etc. used by the quality control staff in production areas should be unbreakable. Glass containers, other than those used for the final product, drinking cups, glass mirrors and gauge covers must all be eliminated from food production areas. Scales coated in vitreous enamel should be replaced, preferably by stainless steel. Particular care is necessary with glass containers used for product as any line breakages may result in glass contaminating other products.

In the event of any glass breakage it is important to ensure that:

(1) the supervisor is notified;
(2) production and preparation ceases where contamination is likely;
(3) the glass is cleaned up using a vacuum cleaner and/or brush; and
(4) all products adjacent to the breakage are examined and in the event of possible contamination are discarded.

All filling hoppers, elevators and belts conveying open food should be protected against overhead contamination. Guards must be easy to remove to facilitate cleaning. Hoppers, silos and tanks containing food must be checked and cleaned before use and protected from contamination with close-fitting lids or covers which must always be used correctly.

Regular checks should be made of conveyor belts, rubber seals, gaskets, brushes, etc. as deterioration can result in small pieces of rubber or bristles ending up in the food.

### Notices

Notices used for warnings, advice or instructions should be properly fixed and permanent. Sheets of paper sellotaped to equipment or close to open food are unacceptable. Recipe instructions should be enclosed in sealed polythene bags.

Notice boards should be kept out of areas where open food is handled and should be covered in perspex or similar sheeting.

### Processing or reworking of product

The manufacturing process is a major source of extraneous material which may find its way into the product during processing as a result of the following:

(1) cross-contamination resulting from poor layout, unsatisfactory cleaning or inadequate removal of waste material from the processing area;
(2) inadequate consideration of hygienic design principles when purchasing and installing plant and equipment and subsequently poor maintenance;
(3) premises not suitable for hygienic food production or poor maintenance of the fabric of the building;
(4) problems with conveying packaging materials, filling and sealing; and
(5) delays/breakdowns in processing.

### Maintenance operatives

Engineers must be trained to take extra care when working with food equipment to ensure that they do not leave loose nuts, swarf and pieces of wire in food rooms on completion of maintenance. Temporary repairs with string should be avoided. It is good practice for managers to check areas where engineers, builders or contractors have been working before food handling commences.

During production, areas which are being decorated or where repair or maintenance work is being carried out, must be suitably segregated by screens such as heavy duty polythene, to avoid exposing product to risk of contamination. Maintenance workers should not wear grossly soiled overalls and should not stand on or climb over machinery or open food if there is the slightest risk of introducing contamination. If necessary all food should be removed or protected with clean polythene sheeting. The use of ladders over open food or hoppers can result in dirt falling off shoes or rungs and ending up in the final product. After the work has been completed all tools, screws, swarf, grease, etc. must be removed and the area cleaned and, if necessary, disinfected before use. Whenever possible, equipment should be removed from food areas for repair.

**Cleaning activities**

Care must be taken during cleaning and all staff involved should be trained to ensure they do not expose product to risk of contamination by using worn equipment, especially brushes which are likely to lose their bristles, or by using inappropriate methods such as high pressure spraying during the production of open food. Particular care must be exercised when using paper towels or cloths to ensure small pieces of paper or cloth do not end up in the product.

**Food handlers**

Contaminants originating from personnel include earrings, hair, fingernails, buttons, combs and pen tops. Protective clothing, including head covering, must be of a suitable type and worn correctly. The personal hygiene of food handlers must be beyond reproach, and earrings and jewellery other than wedding rings should not be worn. Pencils, pens and pieces of chalk must not be used in situations which expose food to risk of contamination, for example, near filling hoppers and mixing vessels.

Sweet papers, cigarette ends and matches are common contaminants and staff should not eat sweets, chew gum or smoke in food rooms. Regular training and reinforcement such as posters should be used together with strict supervision and enforcement of company rules.

**Post-process contamination**

Contamination of the product may occur during warehousing or distribution. Furthermore, malicious tampering of products in supermarkets continues to pose a threat to manufacturers and retailers. Finally, contamination of the product may occur in the consumer's home and this should always be considered when investigating a complaint.

*Control measures*

Tamper-evident packaging is now widely applied in the food industry as a result of sabotage and blackmail by unscrupulous individuals. Most notably, the case of Rodney Witchelo who was convicted in December 1990 for 17 years after being found guilty on charges of a £3.75 million blackmail plot after contaminating food products and threatening to kill customers. The food industry acknowledges that tamper-proof packaging is difficult to achieve but tamper-evident packaging is now widely used and examples include:

(1) roll-on aluminium pilfer-proof enclosures;
(2) heat shrunk plastic sleeves;
(3) adhesive labels or strips on the side of the cap and jar;
(4) vacuum sealed containers with audible click feature; or
(5) a combination of the above.

**Pests and pest control**

Rodents, rodent hairs and droppings may be brought into food premises with the raw materials or introduced during the preparation or storage of food in infested premises. Food showing evidence of rodent contamination is unfit and should be rejected.

Insects, larvae and eggs may also be present in raw materials, although some may find their way into food rooms via openings. Several insects multiply rapidly and infestations can soon spread throughout food premises. Infested food should be discarded and appropriate control measures introduced (see Chapter 14).

A reputable pest control contractor, experienced at working with food businesses, should be employed to lay rodent bait or traps and control pest infestations should they arise. Bad pest control is likely to result in food contamination. For example, electronic fly killers positioned above open food, work surfaces or containers will probably result in dead insects in the food, as will the use of insecticides to destroy flying insects, for example dichlorvos strips or sprays, in the presence of open food.

Cleaners and other staff must be instructed not to touch bait trays, unless authorized to do so, and never to put bait trays on shelves above open products whilst cleaning is being undertaken.

**Fig. 14.** a) Rat in frozen sweetcorn. b) Mouse in canned green beans. c) Snail in jam. ( Courtesy of Doncaster M.B.C. )

**All reasonable precautions and all due diligence**

A food company facing a prosecution as a result of selling a contaminated product will need to demonstrate that they have installed and used an effective, documented detection and rejection system which is checked regularly if they are to successfully use the due diligence defence provided in the Food Safety Act, 1990. It will be up to the courts to decide what is "reasonable" having regard to good trade practice, Industry Hygiene Guides and the risk and consequences in relation to cost.

All complaints should be fully investigated. In order to identify the contaminant, and its origin, all relevant details must be recorded. If the complainant will not release the object a photograph may be beneficial.

The presence of the foreign object indicates a breakdown in procedures and relevant systems will need auditing, preferably using the HACCP approach, and modifications made to prevent a recurrence.

If the defence of due diligence is to succeed, appropriate records will be needed including:

(1) number and type of specific complaints and action taken to prevent recurrence;
(2) documentation relating to the HACCP system including working procedures, monitoring/checks and reviews;
(3) details of staff training/qualifications;
(4) details of pest control; and
(5) recall procedure.

If practicable, records should be retained for three years.

## Metal detection

Metal detection systems should be provided on production lines after visual inspection of the food just prior to packaging or preferably just after packaging. Metal detection is also useful to screen raw ingredients to avoid damaging processing equipment. Systems must be installed in accordance with manufacturers' instructions and routine maintenance checks are important. Regular checks on performance must be carried out, as must checks on the efficiency of metal detectors and rejection systems. Appropriately sized rods or balls made from different metals should be used, for example, stainless steel, copper and aluminium (1mm to 3mm). Sensitivity is affected by the ratio of the aperture size to product size, the orientation of the metal contaminant, by salt, moisture, vibration, moving metal, the proximity of other detectors, the cleaning methods and by changes in temperature and humidity. The use of a metal detector will only assist a defence of due diligence if there is a controlled system for its operation. If a metal detector is found to be defective during routine testing, all product passing through since the earlier satisfactory check must be retested. All reject product must be examined to identify the reason for the rejection and to trace sources of contamination within the factory.

The latest detectors provide automated self-checking and adjustment, automated compensation for product effect, confirmation that reject product has been deposited in the reject bin and warn of low air pressure which may prevent effective rejection.

Although products in aluminium foil can be checked for ferrous contamination, non-ferrous metals and non-magnetic stainless steels, commonly used for food equipment, will not be detected. Research is continuing to develop a detection system which is capable of removing all forms of physical contamination, whatever the packaging material; microwaves, lasers and ultrasound are being considered.

In 1995, on appeal from Crown Court, a company had its fine reduced to £7,000 with costs of £7,834 for selling chocolate confectionery containing a Stanley knife blade. Although many steps had been taken to avoid contamination, metal detection was not provided at the end of the processing line. The Lord Chief Justice stated that even though this was a first offence the seriousness warranted a large fine. Furthermore, the costs should stand because the company had elected for jury trial.

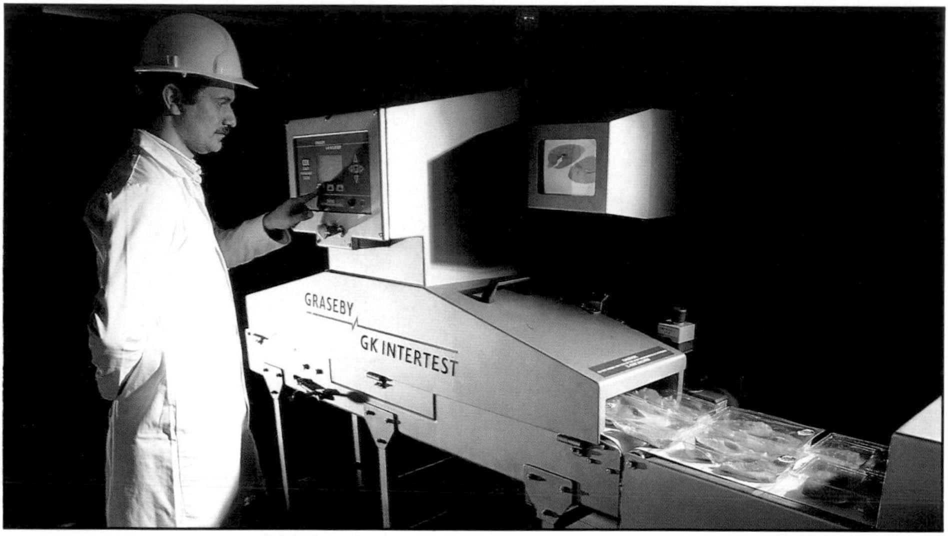


**Fig. 15.** Contaminant management system using X-ray inspection. (Courtesy of Graseby GK Intertest Ltd.)

*X-ray inspection systems*

Several companies are now using X-ray inspection as a central feature of their contaminant management system. (A documented system which includes comprehensive detection and rejection equipment which is regularly tested, with records being kept.)

Detection levels of under 1mm can be achieved depending on product speed and presentation. Pipeline systems are claimed to inspect up to 1.5 tonnes per minute and still achieve a 2mm resolution. Product presented in a uniform way facilitates the most accurate detection of contaminants.

Current applications include the detection of bone in meat products, stone and glass in fruit and vegetables, and steel, plastics and natural rubber from processing machinery. Usually the greater the density of the contaminant the easier it is to detect. Contaminants can be identified in plastic, card or glass packaging and even in sealed cans. Because foreign bodies are precisely located and rejected there is a reduction in wastage of non-contaminated product which may be rejected, by metal detection.

X-ray systems can simultaneously be used to inspect the size and shape of product which enables packages with missing product, or underfills, to be rejected.

## REMOVING DIRTY CANS AND BOTTLES

Single-use containers such as cans should be inverted and cleaned immediately before use. Canwashers are preferable but compressed air may also be used. If practicable, some form of inspection of empty containers, for example, using highly polished metal mirrors, should be employed.

Returnable bottles which are washed and disinfected before refilling pose much greater problems. Unacceptable dirty or cracked bottles should be removed prior to washing. The bottlewasher should be well maintained and always operated at the correct temperature, using suitable types and quantities of detergents and disinfectants in accordance with the manufacturer's instructions.

Spotters should be employed to remove dirty bottles which pass through the bottlewasher. The number of spotters required will depend on the speed of the line and the number of unsatisfactory bottles leaving the bottlewasher. Lines operating at speeds greater than 300 per minute may require two or more spotters. Black and white backgrounds for empty bottles, and suitable mirrors positioned behind filled bottles assist in the detection of those which are unsatisfactory. Spotters should be changed at regular and frequent intervals, for example, every 30 minutes.

Dirty bottle bases are almost impossible to detect by personnel, and side and base-scanners are essential. These devices consist of several beams of light which travel through the glass and onto a photo-electric cell. If one of the beams of light is broken, for example, by a piece of dirt, the bottle is rejected automatically. Quality control staff should carry out regular checks to establish the number of dirty bottles escaping detection and how the effectiveness of any of the above measures can be improved.

## CHEMICAL CONTAMINATION

Unwanted chemicals can enter foodstuffs during:

(1) growth, for example, veterinary drugs, fertilizers, pesticides and environmental contaminants such as lead or dioxins;
(2) processing, for example, oil, cleaning chemicals or insecticides;
(3) transport as a result of spillage or leakage; and
(4) sale, for example, cleaning chemicals, insecticides and leaking of such things as plasticizers from packaging. Chemicals may cause acute poisoning or cause long term illnesses such as cancer (see Chapter 3).

### Cleaning chemicals

To avoid taint, some cleaning chemicals, such as phenols and perfumed soap, must not be used in food premises, especially by those handling dairy/fatty foods. All cleaning materials must be kept in properly labelled containers and stored in a manner which obviates any risk of contamination.

CHAPTER 6

# *Nutritional safety and food quality*

*by Dr P. J. Barlow* *Associate Dean, University of Humberside*

Nutrition is the science of nourishment and involves looking at the nutrients in a foodstuff and how these are broken down (by digestion), absorbed and utilized by the body. Virtually all foods are made of the same components, but they are present in quite different proportions. Foods may contain: **proteins, lipids (or fats), available carbohydrates, vitamins, minerals, indigestible material (roughage), water, contaminants (by accident) and additives (by design).**

Some foods are important in the diet because they are rich sources of a particular nutrient, for example, meat and fish are high in protein, double cream is rich in fat, and bran is high in indigestible material. However, for fitness and health it is necessary to have a **balanced diet** that includes a range of foods that give us all the nutrients in the quantities that are required to maintain the body and supply us with our energy.

The actual requirements for the various nutrients differ from person to person, and at different stages of life for the same individual. Thus, a highly active teenager will require a different balance of nutrients compared with an elderly person or pregnant female.

Standards in the form of Recommended Intakes for different nutrients and Recommended Daily Amounts of food energy and nutrients have existed for some time. However, the understanding and use of these standards has always caused problems. In 1991 the Government set up a special Committee called the COMA Committee (Committee on the Medical Aspects of Food) to look at the problems and provide some clear advice that people could easily understand. The Committee recommended the consumumption of less fat, sugar and salt and more roughage, starch and vitamin C.

## PROTEINS

Protein is an essential part of the diet and forms part of every cell within the body. Proteins are composed of carbon, hydrogen, oxygen and nitrogen. In addition, sulphur may also be present. These simple elements join together to form **amino acids**, which in turn join together to form the protein.

There are 22 amino acids commonly found in food proteins, and these amino acids are in a constant state of flux as the proteins are broken down by digestion and recombined to perform essential bodily functions. These functions include repairing the body, building new tissue, defending against infection and regulating body chemistry.

Some of the proteins are very complex and may contain many thousands of amino acids. The human body can also manufacture most of the amino acids from other dietary constituents but there are eight amino acids that cannot be made and must be included in the diet. Thus a **complete protein** refers to foods that contain the correct balance of all the necessary amino acids. Complete proteins include foods such as meat, fish, milk and eggs, but also certain vegetable proteins such as Meso and textured vegetable protein. Peas and beans are also good sources of protein but are not complete. People who are vegetarians need to include a wide range of vegetable foods in their diet in order to obtain all the required amino acids.

## LIPIDS

The term lipid refers to fats and oils and also includes fat related substances such as sterols (for example, cholesterol) phospholipids and fat soluble vitamins (A, D, E and K). The distinction between fats and oils is only that fats are solid at room temperature and oils are liquid under the same conditions. Fats and oils consist of carbon, hydrogen and oxygen, but **not** nitrogen.

The form in which most fats occur in foods are as triglycerides. These consist of glycerol with three fatty acids attached and it is the type of fatty acid present that decides the properties of the fat. All fatty acids consist of long chains of carbon atoms joined together.

Fatty acids may be classified into three groups: saturated, monosaturated and polyunsaturated.

**Saturated fatty acids**, mainly associated with animal fats, are the ones which contain the maximum amount of hydrogen. They are solid at room temperature, for example, lard and butter, but there is some evidence that high intakes may be linked with heart disease as they seem to increase the amount of cholesterol in the blood. One of the suggestions from the COMA Committee was that most people should aim to reduce their intake of saturated fatty acids.

**Monosaturated fatty acids**, are soft or liquid at room temperature and the best example is olive oil which is high in the fatty acid, oleic acid. Monosaturated fatty acids are long chain fatty acids which have two missing hydrogen atoms. Current nutritional advice is that a high proportion of monosaturates in the diet is desirable from a health point of view.

**Polyunsaturated fatty acids (PUFAs)**, are long chain fatty acids with more than two hydrogen atoms missing, for example, fish oils. They are liquid at room temperature. The big problem with PUFAs is that they are very susceptible to the development of rancidity.

The body is unable to manufacture certain fatty acids and thus two fatty acids (linoleic and alpha-linolenic acid) are necessary in the diet and are referred to as essential fatty acids or EFAs. Lipids have a number of roles in the body and are involved in forming cell membranes as well as providing an energy source. On a weight for weight basis, lipids deliver more than twice as much energy as carbohydrates, thus on any slimming diet it is necessary to reduce lipid intake but **not** eliminate it completely which will lead to a deficiency in EFAs and the lipid soluble vitamins.

**TABLE XIX** NUTRIENTS

| **Nutrient** | **Function** | **Source** |
|---|---|---|
| Carbohydrates (starch & sugar) | To provide energy and heat, to utilize fat | Sugar, treacle, honey, fruit, potatoes, bread, rice |
| Fats (animal or vegetable) | Warmth, energy and protection of some organs | Milk, butter, oils, nuts, margarine |
| *Minerals* Calcium | Bone and teeth development | Milk, cheese, butter, eggs, greens, nuts |
| Phosphorus | Maintenance of normal acid-base balance of the body and bone development | Milk, eggs, liver |
| Potassium | Cell membrane activity | Most foods, especially fresh orange juice |
| Iron | Red blood cell development | Beef, liver, spinach, raisins, prunes, flour |
| Proteins (vegetable or animal) | Growth and repair of body cells. Synthesis of enzymes | Milk, meat, fish, eggs, cheese, peas, beans and flour |
| Water | Vital to form essential solutions for metabolism, and to carry substances around the body | |

## HARDENING OF FATS AND OILS

In order to make products such as margarine from vegetable oils, it is necessary to make the oils more solid at room temperature. This can be done by adding back some or all of the missing hydrogen in unsaturated fatty acids. This process is known as **hydrogenation** or fat hardening.

One possible problem that occurs during this process is that some of the fatty acids are converted to a type known as **trans** fatty acids. There is some evidence that the intake of these fatty acids might increase the blood cholesterol and actually be detrimental to health.

One other factor that may cause fats and oils to become detrimental to health is if they are heated repeatedly. This causes the oil to become dark in colour and to develop the taste and odour of rancidity. Oil used in processing needs to be changed at regular intervals. It should never be topped up with new oil but should be completely changed.

In a general move to reduce the fat content of foods, **fat substitutes** have been developed. These are substances that have the characteristics of fat in a food but are not digested and thus reduce the energy (or calories) provided by the food.

## CARBOHYDRATES

Carbohydrates are compounds that are also composed of carbon, hydrogen and oxygen. When used as an energy source in the body they are converted, like fats, to carbon dioxide ($CO_2$) and water ($H_2O$).

Carbohydrates may be divided into two main categories: **available carbohydrates** (sugars and starches) and the **unavailable carbohydrates** (roughage).

There are a large number of sugars found in food but in the body the most important is glucose. This sugar is always present in the blood at a level of around 1mg/100ml. It is also used as the body store of energy in muscles and the liver and awaits use as the water soluble polymer, glycogen.

Perhaps the best known type of sugar is sucrose which is obtained from sugar cane and sugar beet. This is the product that many people have in their tea or coffee and is incorporated into many food products. Sucrose consists of a molecule of glucose and a molecule of fructose (the main sugar found in fruits) combined.

Sucrose, when used as an ingredient in foods, provides "empty calories", in that it only provides energy and no other nutrients. Sucrose is a highly refined product which contributes nothing but energy. If consumed as a large fraction of the total diet it may well displace other energy sources which would have been better nutritionally balanced and thus in excess, its consumption lowers the overall quality of the diet.

One final sugar to mention is lactose. This is the sweet component in milk and provides the medium for the Lactobacilli bacteria to ferment and produce lactic acid which causes the souring of milk

Starches are large chain-like molecules made up of sugars. They are referred to as **polysaccharides** which just means many sugars. Good sources of starch include root vegetables such as potatoes and yams, pulses such as peas and beans, and cereals such as wheat and corn. Starches are broken down in the digestive tract to the sugars (especially glucose), which are then absorbed and used by the body for energy.

One of the COMA Committee recommendations was for most people to cut down on their sugar intake as excess sugar is linked with dental decay and being overweight. A number of food products now have their sugar replaced by artificial sweeteners, for example, diet coke. The most common artificial sweetening agent is aspartame which is composed of amino acids.

Unavailable carbohydrate is fibre which is not digested to any extent and does not provide any significant amount of nourishment. Most of the fibre we take in is excreted in the faeces. It is present in foods of plant origin and comprises the structural tissue of plants, for example, the husk of wheat, skin of apples and "string" of celery.

It is now recognized that fibre is an important part of the diet and may be particularly important in the prevention of certain disease conditions, for example, constipation, appendicitis, bowel cancer and diabetes.

The fibre in our diet is of two types: soluble and insoluble. Insoluble fibre is mainly found in cereal bran and fibrous fruits, for example, oranges. It helps food pass through the gut more quickly and provides a bulking agent for the faeces. Fibre swells in the stomach and creates a feeling of fullness - thus it is especially important as part of a diet to stop people feeling hungry. As the fibre collects in the lower bowel ready for excretion it absorbs toxins, contributing to good health. This insoluble fibre improves regularity of bowel movements and reduces constipation.

Soluble fibre is present in most fruits and vegetables and many grains, it forms a gel in the digestive tract which delays the absorption of sugars from the intestine to the blood stream. This is especially important in people prone to diabetes. Soluble fibre also appears to be helpful in the elimination of cholesterol from the body.

A recommendation of the COMA Committee is that most people need to increase their intake of fibre. However, if very high levels of fibre (especially insoluble fibre) are consumed this may interfere with the absorption of certain minerals.

Malnutrition is a term that is used to describe diets that are not properly balanced. Most people associate the term with problems of the developing countries where there is insufficient total food, but strictly speaking the term merely describes "bad nutrition". Thus, any diet that is lacking in any group of nutrients be it protein, EFAs, vitamins or minerals may be described as malnutrition. Two groups of nutrients that may be lacking in the diet of some people in the UK are **vitamins** and **minerals.**

## MINERALS

The average person contains about 4kg of minerals. Of this about 1.5kg is **calcium** which makes up the major part of the skeleton and teeth. Other minerals, for example, potassium, sodium, iron, zinc, manganese and chromium are found in the body and are necessary for good health. We obtain minerals from a whole range of foods, but some foods are especially rich in certain minerals, as shown in table XIX.

It is much more difficult to affect the minerals during processing than it is the vitamins. Thus, what finishes up in the product will normally reflect what was in the food to start with. The original mineral content will reflect where the product was grown, for example, what was in the soil. This means that similar products might have quite different levels of some of the minor trace minerals such as selenium, chromium, manganese and cobalt.

Sometimes, even if a mineral is present in the food it cannot be absorbed and utilized by the body. The availability of a mineral from the food we eat is called its **bioavailability.**

An example of a poorly bioavailable mineral is the iron in wholemeal bread. The reason for this is that wholewheat contains a substance in the bran called **phytic acid.** This combines chemically with minerals such as iron to form phytate salts (i.e. iron phytate in our example) and this compound passes straight through the gut and is excreted in the faeces.

**TABLE XX** VITAMINS

| **Vitamin** | **Function** | **Source** |
|---|---|---|
| **(a) Fat soluble** Vitamin A (retinol) | To prevent eye disease and to promote growth. To build up body resistance to disease. Daily requirement approximately 750μg for adults. Children and pregnant women require more. Deficiency results in night blindness and skin eruptions | Animal fats, fish, liver oils, dairy produce, green vegetables and carrots. Exists in plants as carotene (a yellow colouring matter) |
| Vitamin D | Controls the uptake of phosphorus and calcium for strong bones and teeth. Very important for young children. Deficiency results in rickets and brittle bones. Can be produced by the fatty tissues of the skin. (If produced synthetically - is known as calciferol.) Excess vitamin D causes hardening of the arteries and calculi may be formed in the kidneys. Daily requirement 7.5g for babies and up to 10g for adults | Halibut and cod liver oils, butter, eggs, milk and oily fish |
| Vitamin E | An antioxidant reported to be needed for a healthy neuromuscular system. Like vitamin A it is readily stored in the body and deficiency is unlikely. (Also claimed to aid fertility and prevent miscarriage) | Milk, egg yolk, peanuts, oil contained in seeds, green leaves and wheatgerm |
| Vitamin K | Blood clotting | Meat and green vegetables |
| **(b) Water soluble** Vitamin B1 (thiamine) | Deficiencies result in neuritis, poor appetite, sore tongue and mouth, limb stiffness and possible muscle atrophy. In some countries, for example. Japan, China, India, deficiency results in beriberi (inflammation of the nerves) | Wholemeal flour, bacon, liver, egg yolk, yeast and pulses |
| Vitamin $B_2$ (riboflavin) | Daily requirement 1.5 to 3mg, more in pregnancy. Relatively heat-resistant. Essential for tissue maintenance. Deficiency causes mouth sores and dermatitis | Wheat, whole grain flour, milk, liver, fish, eggs, yeast and spinach |
| Vitamin $B_6$ (pyridoxine) | Necessary for metabolizing amino acids. Deficiency results in peripheral neuritis, loss of weight, hypochromic anaemia (daily requirement 2mg) | Wheat, whole grain flour, liver, fish, eggs, yeast, nuts and spinach |

| Vitamin | Function | Source |
|---|---|---|
| Pantothenic acid | Essential constituent of the diet (requirement 6-8mg) | Kidney, liver, yeast and fresh vegetables |
| Nicotinic acid (niacin) | Deficiency of nicotinic acid and protein results in pellagra (a disease affecting the skin, nervous and digestive system). Daily requirement 10mg | Meat, liver and yeast |
| Biotin | Deficiency results in skin disturbances and lassitude | Vegetables, nuts, liver, eggs, yeast and kidney |
| Folic acid | Helps in blood cell formation. Deficiency causes anaemia | Kidney, liver, yeast and green vegetables |
| Vitamin C (ascorbic acid) | Needed for healthy capillary walls. Aids healing of wounds and repair of damaged tissue. Daily requirement 30mg for adults, 60mg for children. Quickly destroyed by high temperatures as in canning of low-acid foods. Also lost by oxidation during prolonged storage. Deficiency results in sore, bleeding gums, loosening of teeth, slow wound healing, haemorrhages under the skin and in severe cases scurvy | Fresh fruit, green vegetables, especially tomatoes, oranges, lemons, grapefruit, blackcurrants and potatoes |

## VITAMINS

Vitamins are organic substances that are essential to life, needed in only small amounts but cannot be synthesized, in the main, by the body. Vitamins generally serve regulatory functions in the body and often act as triggers for the actions of enzymes. Vitamins divide into two groups: **fat soluble (A, D, E, K)** and **water soluble (B, C)**.

Unfortunately, a number of vitamins are susceptible to loss or damage by heat and/or exposure to light. This means that as food is processed the vitamin content may well be reduced. Vitamins C and A are especially susceptible to these processing losses. If products have to be reworked or reprocessed this loss increases. Thus, if milk does not reach the correct temperature of processing and has to pass through the pasteurizing plant for a second time, its nutritional quality may well be impaired.

## CONTAMINANTS IN FOOD

Most people now recognize that we live in a polluted environment and that we are exposed to a whole range of contaminants, many of which can be found in foodstuffs. Some of these toxic substances act as **anti-nutrients** and thus we not only need a well-balanced diet to counteract this activity, but in order for the body's own defence and detoxification system to work, an adequate supply of many specific nutrients is necessary.

An appropriate supply of proteins, minerals, vitamins and essential fatty acids all help to build an effective immune system to deal with the exposure to toxic compounds.

Thus, man is subjected to a whole range of "non-biological chemicals" including products of combustion, toxic metals and pesticides. These and other pollutants add to the burdens that many people already have to cope with from potentially harmful substances such as alcohol, cigarettes, various stimulatory drugs and a host of naturally occurring toxins present in small amounts, even in natural healthy food.

Although the body is well-designed and equipped with detoxifying mechanisms for many of these harmful substances that are ingested, inhaled or absorbed through the skin, the body's self-defence mechanisms are increasingly becoming overloaded. When the total body burden exceeds our ability to cope with these poisonous substances they are not broken down and excreted, but may be incorporated into the bone, fat, nervous tissue, etc. in the body and may well interfere with normal body functions and produce abnormal states of body and/or mind.

Interestingly, these effects may not be immediate but can be delayed for days, months and even years after exposure. This process can happen, for example, with toxic metals such as lead and mercury. Often excess toxic metals are deposited in bones of the body and will cause no immediate problem. However, in times of stress, when perhaps more calcium is required by the body, this will be released from bone stores together with toxic metals.

Many common disease conditions do seem to be associated with raised body levels of pollutants or deficiency of an essential nutrient. Usually, the effect of this imbalance is not **acute**. Indeed, the pollutants or deficiency that gives rise to acute symptoms including death, or some other obvious effect, are easily dealt with as cause and effect are clearly related. More often, the effect is **chronic,** giving rise to a whole range of minor symptoms such as poor concentration, increased allergic response, an increased susceptibility to infection, etc. In such cases the cause and effect relationship is much less easy to confirm. All these minor symptoms can occur for a variety of reasons and a specific disease will thus be difficult to positively associate with a particular pollutant.

Furthermore, the combined effect of pollutants in the body may be greater than the sum of individual toxicities - a phenomenon referred to as **synergism.**

The toxicity of many compounds taken into the body is increased in people who are inadequately nourished. The reason for this is that many pollutants are anti-nutrients and they do their damage by competing and interfering with the absorption and/or utilization of nutrients or possibly by reducing excretion rates.

One nutrient considered to be of particular benefit with regard to pollution problems is Vitamin E (tocopherol). A number of environmental pollutants and toxins are thought to initiate the formation of free radicals (highly reactive compounds), potentially giving rise to tissue injury. The administration of Vitamin E to animals has reduced the damage from a variety of these pollutants including ozone, lead, various nitrosamines and methyl mercury. In addition, Vitamin E may also have a protective effect against radiation injury (also related to the production of free radicals). Thus, it is postulated that Vitamin E might well protect against the deleterious consequences of air pollution, exposure to UV radiation and chemical contaminants in the environment such as pesticides. Alternatively, one might consider that people who have a deficiency of this vitamin are most susceptible to the toxic effects of these pollutants. Vitamin E may also enhance the immune function, along with other nutrients such as Vitamins A and C.

## PESTICIDES AS FOOD CONTAMINANTS

The widespread use of pesticides in agriculture has led to concern about their effects on food safety. The term pesticide comprises a whole range of substances designed to kill specific organisms. Included are insecticides, herbicides, ascaricides, fungicides and soil sterilants. Some of the substances used are natural products such as pyrethrum, but most are synthetic compounds developed in research laboratories and produced commercially.

Pesticides are thus designed to be toxic and whilst they may be especially toxic to one group of organisms, there is a good chance that many will show some degree of toxicity to others, including **man.** Pesticides are often referred to as **beneficial poisons**, but it is important to balance their benefit against the possible dangers to man. As regards wheat, it has been estimated that about 30% of the global crop is lost annually through pest and mould contamination. If no pesticides were used, it is suggested that the figure could rise to 60%. On economic grounds therefore, the use of pesticides might well be justified.

When members of the public buy foods, they require them to be free from mould or evidence of pest damage. If food is infested with pests, not only is it unattractive but it could also be contaminated with bacteria, parasites or moulds which could be harmful to health. So pesticides can play an important role in food hygiene but they do need adequate control. It is estimated that something like 26,000,000kgs of pesticides are used each year in the UK. They may be used in food supply, in the streets, in parks, workplaces and in the home. They affect everyone to some degree. Pesticides may thus contaminate our food, the air we breathe and the water we drink (run off from treated crops). However, there is little doubt that over the years pesticides have contributed greatly to the improvement of human and animal health.

There are many thousands of compounds that are used as pesticides and these days it is not uncommon for a particular crop to be treated more than once and some products are sprayed many times during their growth cycle. The possible toxic effects of these combinations have not been fully investigated and it is more than likely that synergistic effects do occur. Many of the pesticides are highly persistent in the environment and once released just pass through the food chain to concentrate in the dominant species which in many cases is **man.**

There are now available techniques that are accurate at detecting residues from a wide variety of pesticides, even at extremely low levels, for example one part in $10^{12}$.

After application of the pesticide, some fraction will be broken down by the action of light, water or microbiological action. The breakdown products may be inert substances or may themselves be toxic. If the pesticide is actually absorbed by the plant, it may be metabolized by the plant to produce some very different compounds which may in turn be inert or even more toxic to the animal (including man) who consumes the plant. Sometimes it is not the main pesticide that causes the real problem, but trace contaminants of the pesticide, for example, small amounts of dioxin in the herbicide 2:4:5:T (trichlorophenyoxyacetic acid).

In the UK, before any new pesticide can be used it must be officially approved. In addition to toxicological testing, evidence regarding the fate of the pesticide in the environment is sought. Under the Food and Environment Protection Act, 1985 (FEPA) pesticides must be shown to be capable of being used in a safe manner. Under the Control of Pesticide Regulations, 1986 the use of a particular pesticide is restricted to its "approved use". This may limit the use of the pesticide to a particular crop.

Most farmers/growers will fully accept the information provided and will try to use the pesticide in the prescribed manner. However, some pesticides are not diluted to the correct strength before use and some people still consider that if one spraying of a crop is good, then two or three must be better! Also, more than one type of pesticide may be used. Thus, some crops are wrongly treated and the "safe pesticide" becomes a problem because of its incorrect use.

With regard to the use of pesticides, the concept of maximum residue level (MRL) has arisen. The MRL is simply the maximum amount of residue to be expected on a crop if the pesticide is used in accordance with the product approval. Thus, the concept of MRL is not related to potential risk to health but to agricultural practices. Nor does the use of an MRL take into account combinations of particular pesticides which can in some circumstances increase potential toxicity considerably.

The other term used in relation to pesticides - and indeed to many other potentially toxic material - is **acceptable daily intake (ADI).** This is the actual amount of a substance which current scientific information suggests can be consumed daily over a lifetime and should not result in harm to the individual.

Thus, it is necessary for any concerned food manufacturer to check that the raw materials he uses are free from such contaminants. There are now Regulations that set the maximum levels of certain pesticides that can be present in specific foods. (The Pesticides (Maximum Levels in Food) Regulation, 1988.) However, it is better to try and use raw products that are not contaminated with such chemicals.

Currently, there are just over 400 pesticides approved for use on crops in the UK. Residues of these may be found in many products such as stored potatoes, fumigated nuts and bran from stored wheat. It is impossible to know by looking at a product how much residue might be present. The level will depend on the type and amount of pesticide applied, where the food was stored and many other factors.

However, it is possible to significantly reduce levels by adherence to strict kitchen hygiene and by selecting an appropriate method of preparing the food. The Consumers Association reported in "Which" (October 1990) the result of some tests they had carried out on potatoes and apples. They found that washing the apples and potatoes had little effect on the residues examined, even though they were mainly on the skin. This is not too surprising as many residues will not readily dissolve in water. Peeling, as might be expected, was much more effective in removing residues. Peeling removed about 85% of the residue in apples and 75-90% in potatoes. It should be remembered that peeling removes 12-14% of the apple/potato along with many nutrients and some fibre.

## FOOD ADDITIVES

Many modern day foods do contain additives. They are needed to produce the types of food we have now come to expect. For example, margarine could not be produced without emulsifiers and stabilizers to keep the water and fat together. If there were no additives present many foods would have much reduced shelf-lives and some foods may become hazardous. Most responsible food companies have a policy as regards the use of food additives to only make use of them when they are technically necessary, and in the main to always use natural additives, for example, vitamin E as an antioxidant, in preference to man-made additives. The term additive is a broad one and covers such products as: preservatives (see Chapter 7), antioxidants, colours, emulsifiers and stabilizers and artificial sweeteners.

All of the compounds allowed in food are tabulated on permitted lists, and often the maximum amount of the additive allowed is also specified. They have all had a good deal of research carried out on their safety and many continue to be studied to make sure that they are safe. A few people are allergic to some food additives, for example, some children are allergic to the colour tartrazine, but in the main the amount of additive used in a product causes no problem. Perhaps the potential problems lie in the effects of combined additives. If a person consumes a variety of foods, they may take in a whole range of different additives and the long term effects of this is less well understood. This is one of the reasons that many manufacturers have decided to limit the use of additives.

Approved food additives usually have a special number. Any number that also has an E designation means that the additive has been approved by the European Community. The purity of the additive is also described in EC legislation.

Perhaps the group of food additives we come across most are the preservatives. These compounds can help reduce food wastage, give wider choice of foods and help to keep food safe.

If an additive is present in food it must be declared on the label of the packaged product. The additive may be properly named, for example, ascorbic acid (vitamin C) or may be listed by its code number E300.

## HEALTH FOODS AND HEALTHY DIETS

Over recent years there has been a large increase in the number of health food shops. These shops claim to sell foods that are healthy which, by inference, suggests that other shops sell unhealthy food.

The matter is, however, not as simple as it might seem. As we have seen earlier, a healthy diet is a balanced diet, including a whole range of foods to ensure that we obtain all the necessary nutrients. Obviously, we do not want to consume contaminated food, but modern day foods are produced under strict hygiene conditions to prevent all types of contamination (bacterial, chemical and physical). Thus, there is little chance of obtaining seriously contaminated food from a reputable source. The other argument often put forward is that highly processed foods have many of their nutrients removed during the manufacturing process. This may well be true for certain foods, for example, wholemeal bread versus white bread. In this case, a number of vitamins and minerals are lost during the milling process. However, the inclusion of some such foods causes no problem when part of a balanced diet.

Problems only occur when a person has a limited selection of foods and then regardless of whether the food is processed food or a "health food", deficiencies of particular nutrients or toxic excesses may occur. (There are reports of people dying because they lived exclusively on carrots!)

## THE COMA REPORT AND NUTRITIONAL LABELLING

In view of the growing interest in links between diet and health, the findings of the report are difficult to ignore. A reputable food company would be very remiss if it did not try and implement some of the COMA report recommendations.

Diet plays a key role in the prevention of some of the major life-threatening diseases of middle and latter life, for example, the link between saturated fat consumption, blood cholesterol and coronary heart diseases is now reasonably well established.

For a consumer to construct a healthy and balanced diet there is a need for a meaningful declaration of nutritional information to be provided with the product. Currently the nutritional labelling of foods is voluntary, but if such information is given it **must** be given in a particular manner. If nutritional information is provided it can only be given in one of the following groups:

Group 1: energy, protein, fat and carbohydrate.

Group 2: energy, protein, carbohydrate, sugars, fat, saturates, sodium and fibre.

The information is given per 100g or per 100ml with an option for per serving size. The per 100g is given to allow comparison between products. Most major manufacturers now use the Group 2 format.

## DIGESTION

Most of the foods we consume must be broken down by the body into a simpler form which can be used or stored. The process for achieving usable products is known as digestion. On entering the mouth, solid food is cut and torn by the teeth and at the same time moistened with saliva to aid swallowing. In addition, saliva contains an enzyme, salivary amylase, which converts starch to sugars. Food is passed to the stomach by contraction and dilation of the muscular walls of the oesophagus; a process known as peristalsis.

The stomach is a muscular bag which churns the food and also secretes gastric juices from glands in its mucous membrane lining. These juices contain hydrochloric acid and also pepsin, an enzyme which breaks down proteins into peptides. The acid destroys some microorganisms and stops others from multiplying. The food normally remains in the stomach for three to five hours when it is gradually released via the pyloric valve into the first part of the small intestine, the duodenum. The second and third part of the small intestine are known as the jejunum and ileum respectively.

Food in the small intestine is further broken down by digestive juices produced by the mucous membrane of the small intestine, bile and pancreatic juice. Trypsin, an enzyme produced by the pancreas, and erepsin, produced in the small intestine, complete the breakdown of proteins and peptones into amino acids. Bile salts from the gall bladder emulsify fats which are acted on by another pancreatic enzyme, lipase, to form fatty acids and glycerol. The carbohydrates are finally converted into single sugars such as glucose, by the action of the enzymes, amylase and sucrase.
These basic food components are absorbed through the small intestine and into the capillaries. They eventually end up in the portal vein and are transported to the liver.

The remains of the food, consisting of fibre, cellulose, dead bacteria and cells, pass into the large intestine which is divided into three: the caecum, the colon and the rectum. Water is absorbed from the contents of the large intestine along with sodium chloride. The remaining mixture is expelled as faeces.

Should food containing large numbers of food poisoning organisms or toxins be consumed, the normal body defences will be unable to cope. The body will react by attempting to expel these poisons by vomiting or diarrhoea. Diarrhoea results when the food has been hurried through the intestines because of the food poisoning irritants and consequently, there is insufficient time to extract the water which passes out with the faeces. Excessive water loss may cause dehydration.

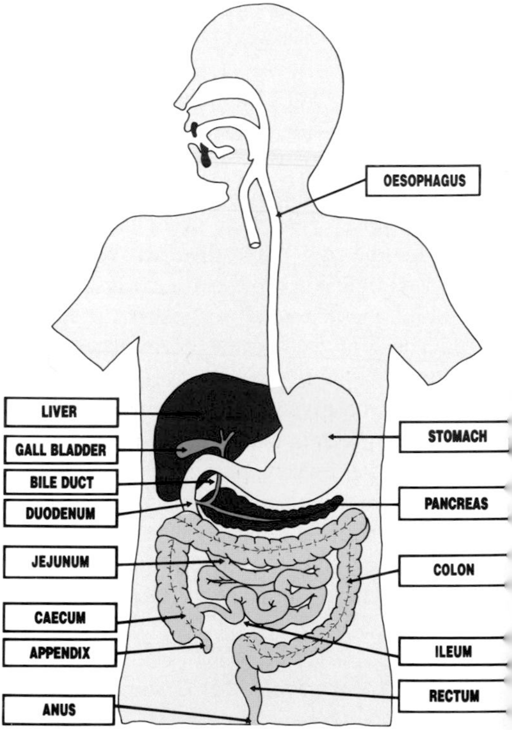


**Fig. 16.** The human body

CHAPTER 7

# The storage and temperature control of food

The storage of foods is important to ensure adequate provision throughout the year and to overcome fluctuations in supply. Furthermore, bulk purchasing is normally cheaper and more convenient. However, it is preferable for fresh produce, particularly perishables, to be supplied daily. All suppliers should be approved and deliveries monitored as part of the hazard analysis and control system.

Correct storage of food is fundamental to the hygienic and profitable operation of any food business. Failure to ensure satisfactory conditions of temperature, humidity, stock rotation and the integrity of packaging can result in problems of unfit or spoiled food but will, at the very least, result in a considerable reduction in shelf-life. The product may become unmarketable because of staleness or changes in texture or colour. More serious problems may be caused by mould growth, infestations of stored product insects, rancidity, slime and off-odours. If the food contained pathogens and storage conditions allowed multiplication of these organisms, then consumers would be exposed to an unacceptable and unnecessary risk. Furthermore, these problems may spread to other areas within the premises, and the cost of discarding or sorting contaminated and waste food can be quite considerable.

Food begins to decompose as soon as it is taken from the plant, the ground, the animal or the sea. Storage conditions should reduce the rate of decomposition as much as possible to ensure that the nutritional value, appearance, taste and fitness of food is of the highest standard. During storage, food should not be exposed to risk of contamination or taint. Cleanliness and a satisfactory environment are important to prevent physical contamination or damage which may render food unsaleable or unfit.

### Raw materials

Food premises must have adequate and suitable storage facilities to keep all raw materials satisfactorily. The quality and bacteriological condition of raw materials has a significant influence on the finished product. Furthermore, unsatisfactory deliveries may introduce problems such as insects, rodents or mould into the storage area.

To demonstrate due diligence and to ensure that deliveries meet the agreed specification an effective, documented checking system must be implemented. The inspection required will depend on the type of product and the condition of other deliveries from the same source. Checks may include: quantity, temperature, date code and quality. Damaged or discoloured packaging must be regarded with suspicion and the consignment thoroughly examined by trained staff, preferably before unloading from the delivery vehicle. Leaking cartons, rusty cans and old stock should all be rejected. A documented system detailing reason for rejection should be maintained.

Perishable food must be checked quickly and removed to cold stores, freezers or refrigerators without delay. Unloading of vehicles should take place, as far as practicable, in covered bays screened from adverse weather. Raw food and high-risk food should be completely segregated to avoid risk of contamination. Non-food items and strong-smelling foods which may cause taint problems should normally be delivered separately.

Once unloaded, batches of food should be clearly marked to ensure they are used in strict rotation and to identify the date of delivery in the event of subsequent complaints, for example, mould growth.

**Raw meat and poultry**

Raw meat joints should be stored between −1°C and +1°C, with a relative humidity of approximately 90%. Humidities above 95% encourage unacceptable microbial growth and humidities below 85% result in excessive evaporation and subsequent weight loss. Air speeds should be low, around 0.3 metres per second, as it should only be necessary to remove heat coming through the insulated wall, or introduced when opening the door, provided that only cooled food is placed in the refrigerator/cold store. Meat should not touch the wall surface.

Given the correct temperature and humidity the shelf-life of meat depends on the initial bacterial loading. For example, meat with a total viable count of less than 100 organisms per gram will have a shelf-life of at least double that of meat with a count of approximately 1,000,000 organisms per gram. This fact clearly illustrates the need for the hygienic handling of meat in the slaughterhouse. The avoidance of contamination and multiplication during distribution is also important to maintain low counts of microorganisms. Joints of beef packed in a temperature controlled atmosphere and stored at −1°C to +1°C should keep for up to a week. Beef usually has a longer shelf-life than pork, lamb, poultry and fish. Processed raw meats, offals and such products as sausages have the shortest life.

**Eggs**

As soon as possible after lay, eggs should be stored in a clean, dry place, at a constant temperature below 20°C (ideally between 10°C and 15°C ). Fluctuations in temperature result in condensation and must be avoided. They should not be stored near heat sources such as fridge motors or in direct sunlight. After delivery to consumers and caterers, eggs should be stored below 8°C under refrigeration and should be used within three weeks of lay. Stock rotation is essential and cracked or dirty eggs should not be sold. Hands must always be washed after handling raw eggs.

### Meat pies, pasties and sausage rolls

These products must be obtained from a reliable source and should preferably be stored under refrigeration. Temperatures of around 7°C, with good air movement, are recommended so that the pastry remains crisp. As these foods are cooked to temperatures as high as 90°C very few bacteria survive and consequently, they remain bacteriologically safe at this higher than normal temperature of refrigeration. However, stock rotation is important and such products should be sold on the day of production or the following day. Pies or pasties to which something has been added after baking should be stored at or below 5°C. Fluctuations in temperature result in condensation and mould growth.

As these products may be consumed without further cooking they must never be stored with raw meat or vegetables. Strong smelling foods such as cheese may introduce taint or mould problems. Price tickets must not be stuck into pies or any other food. If pies are to be sold hot from retail outlets they must be cooked thoroughly and if stored, maintained above 63°C. Alternatively, pies may be microwaved as required. They must never be rewarmed.

### Fruit and vegetables

The quality and shelf-life of fresh fruit and vegetables depend on the way in which they are handled, transported and stored. Deterioration may be physical, physiological, chemical or pathological. Storage conditions should reduce the rates of respiration and transpiration (loss of water by evaporation) to ensure the maximum shelf life. Although each fruit and vegetable has its own optimal storage conditions, a general guide is to keep them refrigerated (0°C to 2°C) at a relative humidity of 90%. However, tropical fruits such as pineapples and bananas should be stored around 10°C to 13°C to avoid "chill injury". Rapid turnover and practical difficulties such as lack of separate refrigerators usually results in catering premises storing fruit and vegetables in cool rooms without undue problems.

Care must be taken to avoid warm moist conditions and condensation which will encourage bacterial spoilage and mould growth. Low humidities and excessive ventilation result in dehydration and must also be avoided. Fruit should be examined regularly and mouldy items removed to avoid rapid mould spread. Transit wrappings may need to be removed to avoid condensation.

### Ice-cream

Ice-cream is an ideal food for bacterial growth and must be handled with care. Ice-cream should be kept in a clean freezer, preferably by itself, and open ice-cream must never be stored with raw products. It should always be kept frozen and if defrosted must be discarded. One tub of a particular variety should be used completely before opening a fresh one and nothing should be placed on top of an open tub. Lids should normally be kept on. The texture of ice-cream is more temperature sensitive than other frozen foods and it is often held at −12°C or slightly higher. However, it should only be stored for one week at this temperature.

Clean scoops should be used for serving ice-cream and these should be rinsed in clean, running water after each use and wiped dry using disposable paper. After service the scoop must be cleaned, disinfected, allowed to dry and stored in a protected place.

**Milk and cream**

Milk used to be a major source of disease and even now raw or inadequately heat-treated milk continues to cause problems. Milk and cream should be stored under refrigeration (below 5°C) and should be placed in the refrigerator or cold store as soon as received. Imitation cream should also be stored under refrigeration. Raw milk comes in bottles with green-coloured caps or in cartons labelled untreated and should not be used by any food business. Crates of milk should not be stored below raw meat.

**Flour and cereals**

Flour and cereals should preferably be stored in mobile stainless steel containers. Lids must be tight-fitting. Large stocks of flour kept in original sacks must be stored clear of the ground and free from damp. Condensation may result in mould growth on wet flour and must be prevented. Regular cleaning of containers used for flour storage must not be overlooked. Frequent inspections, at least weekly, should be carried out for rodents or insects. Permanent bait points, laid by trained operatives, are recommended.

**Canned foods**

The risk from canned foods is very small compared with the number produced and the excellent safety record of cans filled in this country will be maintained if:

(1) blown cans are not used;
(2) badly-dented, seam-damaged, holed or rusty cans are not used; and
(3) stock rotation of cans is carried out. Stocks should be marked with the date of delivery to ensure older cans are used first.

Canned goods should be examined regularly and blown or leaking cans must be rejected. Cans from the same batch should not be used until clearance has been received from the manufacturer or the local Environmental Health Department.

*The shelf-life of canned foods*

High-acid cans of fruit such as prunes, rhubarb, tomatoes and strawberries are quite likely to blow if kept longer than recommended by the manufacturer. The acid nature of these foods enables them to attack the tin and iron of the can, especially at the seams, and hydrogen gas is released causing the can to blow. An unacceptable amount of tin and iron may be present in the food and even if the can is not blown, high levels of these metals, with or without a metallic taint, will render the food unfit for human consumption. Fortunately, the development of new lacquers for these products has increased their shelf-life.

Some large cans of meat, especially ham, may only have been pasteurized and therefore need to be stored under refrigeration. If this is the case, the can should be labelled to this effect.

Once the can is opened the contents should be placed in a suitable plastic or stainless steel container, if the food is not for immediate use. If the food is discoloured or has an unusual smell or texture, it must be rejected. The inside of the can should be inspected and if there is any rust or discolouration, the food must not be used. Provided that cans are stored in a cool, dry place canned food will remain at its best for the following times:

| | Months |
|---|---|
| rhubarb, pasteurized solid meat packs (refrigerated) | 9 |
| fruit juice, prunes, milk products | 12 |
| new potatoes, blackberries, raspberries, plums | 18 |
| vegetables, baked beans, soups, ready-meals | 24 |
| solid-pack cold meat products and fish in oil | 60 |

After the above times the food will not present a health risk but there may be changes in colour, texture and flavour.

**Wrapping and packaging**

Packaging of food is important not only to assist marketing but also to:

(1) prevent chemical, physical and bacteriological contamination;
(2) retain quality and nutritional values;
(3) prolong shelf-life; and
(4) provide a water vapour and gas barrier.

Packaging materials must be economic, non-toxic and easy to remove. Chemicals from packaging materials must not leach into the food or expose the food to risk of contamination when opened or removed. Materials must be capable of withstanding the storage conditions to which they could be exposed, for example, freezing. The integrity of seams is particularly important and seams must withstand the pressures, handling and distribution systems which they are likely to experience.

The use of laminates and plastics is increasing whilst the more traditional materials such as wood are declining in popularity. Laminates may consist of several materials including duplex board, polyethylene and aluminium. Plastics include polyethylenes, polypropylene, polystyrene and polyvinyl chloride (PVC). Grease-proof paper or aluminium foil can also be used.

Packaging and wrapping materials must be stored in clean areas where they are not exposed to risk of contamination. Wrapping of food must be carried out under hygienic conditions by staff who observe the same high standards as employees involved in food preparation. Suitable hand-washing facilities should be available close to wrapping and packaging areas.

*Cling film*

Cling film is useful for preventing the dehydration of food and protecting it against contamination (special breathing films are available for raw meats). Under certain conditions, however, it can speed up spoilage and mould growth by trapping moisture against the surface. It is important therefore that:

(1) raw meat or wet food is unwrapped when removed from the refrigerator; and

(2) food wrapped in cling film is not left in bright light or sunlight.

In 1995 the Ministry of Agriculture, Fisheries and Food advised that because of the risk of chemical migration, cling films should not be used where they could melt into food such as in conventional or microwave ovens or for wrapping foods with a high fat content such as cheese, meats with a layer of fat, fried meats, pastry products and cakes with butter icing or chocolate coatings, unless the manufacturer's advice indicated their suitability for this purpose.

*Vacuum packing*

Vacuum packing is being used for an increasing number of foods, particularly fresh meat, bacon, poultry, cooked meat and cheese. The use of a vacuum pack for fresh meat was pioneered by the Cryovac Division of W. R. Grace Limited in the USA in the 1950s. (Cryovac is a registered trade mark of W. R. Grace & Co.)

Materials such as nylon/polyethylene laminate, which are used in vacuum packing, prevent the entry of oxygen and moisture, thus reducing spoilage of food by bacteria, moulds and rancidity. Furthermore, the food is protected against contamination, excessive drip and weight loss due to dehydration. The storage life of food is prolonged considerably, often being doubled or more. Immediately after opening the vacuum pack the contents should be removed. The slightly darker colour of meat and the acid odour will disappear shortly after being removed.

Vacuum packing will not improve the quality of a poor product and strict observance of hygiene and temperature control throughout the operation is essential. After the air is removed closure may be effected by heat sealing or the application of a metal clip.

Vacuum packs may allow the growth of anaerobic food poisoning organisms and if not stored under refrigeration there is a possibility of consuming unspoiled but unsafe products. Cooked meat which is contaminated with food poisoning organisms just prior to vacuum packing is particularly hazardous. The absence of competition from other organisms will, if temperatures permit, enable the rapid growth of these pathogens.

Vacuum packing of fish, especially smoked salmon and trout, is a worrying development as conditions are ideal for the multiplication of *Cl. botulinum* which is commonly isolated from the intestines of these fish. Storage of these products should always be below 3°C.

Care must be taken to avoid puncturing packs, for example, with sharp bones or rough handling. Defective seams commonly result in the loss of pack integrity. However, air-tight vacuum packaging may blow because of the presence of fermentative lactobacilli. Semi-permeable films favour the growth of aerobic bacteria which produce slime and off-flavours.

It is advisable to purchase branded vacuum packs from reputable suppliers to avoid receiving low grade meat of dubious origin. Unmarked packs without "use by" dates should always be regarded with suspicion.

*Controlled atmosphere packing*

Controlled atmosphere packing is being used increasingly for products such as raw meat and fish, to reduce spoilage rates and maintain a more attractive colour. Gases used include carbon dioxide, nitrogen and oxygen which must each be at the correct concentration depending on the product. Storage under refrigeration remains essential to retain product quality, safety and shelf-life.

**Damaged stock**

All damaged stock should be segregated and thoroughly examined before use. If there is any doubt regarding the fitness of food it should be discarded, or the local Environmental Health Department may be asked for advice.

**The greenhouse effect**

Food, especially high-risk food, should not be stored in windows or in glass display cabinets which are exposed to direct sunlight. The heat within the cabinet will build up in the same way that it does in a greenhouse, with the result that ideal temperatures for bacterial multiplication are provided. The greenhouse effect may even occur in chill cabinets without proper chilled air circulation, and fluorescent tubes may exaggerate the problem.

**Storage systems and equipment**

Safe food storage and stock rotation are facilitated by the use of systems and associated equipment:

*Mobile Racks* - wheel mounted stainless steel shelving on adjustable supports allow free standing storage, shelf spacing to be set for specific stores and easy inspection of contents.

*Slotted Trays* - available in high-density coloured plastics, frequently used by bakeries for bread deliveries. They enable stacks to be set up to store a variety of different items. They can be dismantled and stacked in space saving nests when not in use.

*Bins* - bulk dry-foods may be stored in mobile plastic or stainless steel bins and wheeled from the store to the point of use.

*Mobile Silos* - as above but larger, with a gravity fed hopper discharge allowing substances such as flour to be stored in safety and transported to the site of use.

*Pallets* - large quantities of bulk goods can be stored on pallets and moved around with fork-lift trucks or hand-operated pallet trucks.

**Stock rotation**

Satisfactory rotation of stock, to ensure that older food is used first, is essential to avoid spoilage. Stock rotation applies to all types of food. Daily checks should be made on short-life perishable food stored in refrigerators whereas weekly examination of other foods may suffice.

Stock which is undisturbed for long periods will encourage pest infestations. Good stock rotation has the added advantage of assisting in the maintenance of the correct levels of stock. Remember the rule: **"First in, first out."**

### Codes

Stock rotation has been much easier since the advent of open-date coding but some products do not require a "use-by" date and, in these cases, retailers should adopt their own code to identify the date of delivery. A colour code system is one of the easiest to use; a blue line for Monday, a red line for Tuesday etc. The practice of selling old stock cheaply is not recommended and it is an offence to sell foods bearing an expired "use-by" date or to change this date (see the food labelling regulations, Chapter 17).

### Dry-food stores

Rooms used for the storage of dried and canned foods should be dry (R.H. of 60 to 65%), cool, well-lit, well-ventilated and large enough to facilitate the tidy packing and rotation of stock. They must be kept clean and spillages should be cleared away promptly. Internal walls should be free of cavities. External walls should be north-facing. Wall surfaces should be smooth and impervious. Joints and cracks harbour dust, prevent efficient cleaning and encourage pest infestations. Floors should be impervious, jointless and capable of being kept clean. Sufficient strength is required to support loads and any vehicles used in the store. The method of cleaning must be considered when selecting finishes. Where practicable, wall/floor joints should be coved. Ceilings should be easily cleaned but should not assist condensation if this is likely to be a problem. Ledges collect dust and should be avoided. Wooden pallets should be replaced, for example, by reinforced plastic pallets, as they allow a build-up of dirt and dust which provides ideal conditions for mites and insects.

Stores should be rodent and bird-proof; doors should be provided with metal kick-plates, and airbricks, if present, fitted with wire gauze. Holes around pipes passing through walls should be effectively sealed. As far as possible food should be kept in rodent-proof containers. All goods should be stored clear of the wall and floor to allow cleaning and pest control. Stores should be close to the areas in which it is intended to use the food and also be readily accessible to delivery men who should not have to pass through food preparation areas. Natural ventilation will assist in keeping the temperature of the room low, but in the summer, mechanical ventilation and circulation will probably be necessary. The absence of windows will prevent solar heat gain. Temperatures of around 10°C to 15°C should be maintained for the best storage conditions and stores should not be situated next to a source of heat, for example, adjacent to the boiler room.

Shelves should have a non-absorbent, cleansable finish. Tubular mobile racking made of non-corroding metal is recommended. Cupboards should be avoided. Non-food items including cleaning equipment and chemicals, and strong smelling foods, should not be stored in dry-food stores.

**The storage of perishable foods**

High-risk perishable foods may be contaminated by pathogenic organisms which can multiply to dangerous levels without altering the appearance or taste of the food concerned. For this reason all premises should have adequate cooling and cold storage facilities to keep perishable food not intended for immediate consumption.

## REFRIGERATORS

Refrigeration must be considered as a means of delaying and not preventing food spoilage by bacteria and moulds. Furthermore, although the common food poisoning organisms are incapable of multiplication or toxin production below 5°C, there is increasing concern regarding certain psychrotrophic pathogens capable of growth below 5°C, including *Yersinia enterocolitica* (1°C), *Listeria monocytogenes* (0°C), *Aeromonas hydrophila* (1°C) and *Clostridium botulinum* type E (3°C). Fortunately, growth and toxin production at temperatures just above 0°C takes several days or weeks and should not usually cause problems during short term refrigerated storage. The consequences for prolonged refrigerated storage of food, even in vacuum packs, are of more significance. The nearer the refrigerator operates to 1°C the safer it will be.

**Siting**

Refrigerators should be readily accessible and should not be positioned near any heat source. Ideally they should be in well-ventilated areas away from the direct rays of the sun. Multi deck cabinets may be affected by drafts from doorways, high room temperatures and ventilation and heating grills fitted in ceilings, which may result in significant increase in temperatures. High humidities will eventually result in problems of condensation and sweating. The siting of the unit should allow the cleaning of the surrounding area as well as the cooling coils.

**Construction and design**

Refrigerators should be constructed to facilitate easy cleaning. Large motors are best positioned outside as they generate heat and collect dust. (This also ensures a good circulation of air.) The inner skin and shelves should be impervious, non-corrosive and easy to clean. The number, position and size of shelving are critical in ensuring the effective distribution of cold air to all parts of multi-deck units. Lighting inside cabinets can raise temperatures and, if used, should be of the cold cathode type. Floors should preferably be jointless, laid to a suitable fall and coved for ease of cleaning. Door seals should be checked regularly as they can become perished and difficult to clean. Large chill stores should be fitted with self-closing doors and protected by air-locks, air-curtains or plastic screens. Storage capacity must be adequate to cope with peak demands. Damage to the external or internal cladding of units which enables moisture to penetrate the insulation will reduce the effectiveness of the refrigerator by creating a "warm bridge". Domestic refrigerators are not designed or suitable for most commercial operations.

**Defrosting and cleaning**

Each unit must have an adequate number of defrost cycles to prevent ice build-up on the evaporator coil. This would reduce air flow across, and the surface area of, the coil and result in decreased efficiency and increased temperatures and costs. Assisted defrost systems prevent ice build-up and product warming.

Both exterior, especially door handles, and interiors should be cleaned regularly and internal surfaces of fans disinfected. Base plates and baffle plates should be removed to check for debris such as price tickets and packaging which can obstruct air flow and block drains in multi-deck units. Drip trays, if present, should be emptied and cleaned. Dust on evaporator coils and air ducts must be removed to maintain performance.

After cleaning, units should be completely dried and allowed to attain the correct operating temperature, usually 1°C to 4°C, before being reloaded. Stock should be kept in back-up chill stores during cleaning operations.

Food which experiences a significant increase in temperature, above 10°C, due to breakdown or power cut should be destroyed. Regular cleaning and maintenance will improve efficiency and reduce breakdowns.

**Operating temperature**

To prevent the growth of most pathogens and reduce spoilage the majority of high-risk foods, including cans of pasteurized ham, should be stored below 5°C. The optimum temperature for multi-use refrigerators is therefore between 1°C and 4°C. Higher temperatures allow greater bacterial activity and also prolong the time taken to reduce the temperature of food placed in the refrigerator, i.e. prolonging the time the food remains in the **danger zone**.

The storage of some foods just below freezing results in the formation of large ice crystals and consequential loss of food quality and texture. Fan assisted cooling is recommended as the circulated cold air maintains uniform temperatures, and quickly establishes correct temperatures after the door has been opened.

Cook-chill foods with a maximum shelf-life of five days must be kept between 0°C and 3°C to ensure safety and reduce the risk from *Listeria monocytogenes*. It is recommended that raw meat, poultry, fish and raw meat products such as sausages should be stored at −1°C to 1°C to maximize shelf-life. Furthermore, regulations originating from EC legislation specify that carcases and cut meat in slaughterhouses and cutting premises should not exceed 7°C, offal 3°C and poultry meat 4°C.

**Hot food**

Hot food should be cooled rapidly and not placed directly into a refrigerator as this will raise the temperature of food already stored, as well as increasing the ice build-up on the cooling unit. Condensation may also occur on some foods, resulting in an unacceptable drip on to foods stored below. However, depending on the amount of food and the capacity of the refrigerator, it may be preferable to place a small amount of food which has cooled to around 60°C into a large capacity unit instead of leaving it in a warm kitchen for prolonged periods.

**Contamination**

It is essential that precautions are taken to avoid contamination. Raw food must always be kept separate from cooked food. Ideally two refrigerators should be used, one for raw meat and the storage of food prior to cooking and the other refrigerator to store high-risk food. Each refrigerator should be clearly labelled to indicate its intended use. If only one refrigerator is available, high-risk food must be stored on shelves above raw food. Shelves previously used for raw foods must not be used for high-risk foods without disinfection. Again it is preferable to label shelves according to their intended use. All foods should be adequately covered to prevent drying out, cross-contamination and the absorption of odour.

**Packing and rotation of food**

Refrigerators should not be overloaded and they need packing in a manner which allows good air circulation. Food should not be placed directly in front of the cooling unit as this reduces efficiency. Non-perishables should not be stored in a refrigerator as this takes up valuable space. Good stock rotation is essential to avoid the spoilage of foods and daily checks should be made for out-of-date stock.

**Staff responsibilities**

Staff should be given clear instructions on how to use the refrigerator and in addition, should ensure that the door is opened as little, and for as short a time, as possible. Acid foods should not be stored in opened cans within the refrigerator because of the acid attack on the internal surface of the can. The temperature of the refrigerator should be checked at least three times per day and a record of all readings should be kept. Spillages should be cleared up immediately.

**The storage life of perishable food under refrigeration**

The storage life varies considerably depending on the operating temperature of the refrigerator and the specific perishable food. For example, at 1°C most vegetables will keep for at least two weeks, butter for two months and fresh beef up to a week. A reduction in the initial numbers of bacteria on food can, provided it is stored correctly, increase its shelf-life significantly.

**Chilled display cabinets**

Display cabinets should comply with BS 3053. Cabinets should be loaded correctly so that cold air inlets are not obstructed and load-lines are not exceeded. Only chilled products should be loaded.

Radiant heat can have a significant effect on food stored in chilled cabinets, particularly on the upper shelves. Air temperatures may vary from 1.5°C at the back to

6.5°C at the front, and the isotherms of such product as cartons of yogurt stored at the front of such units may vary from between 7°C and 11°C. Cabinets should be sited away from heating units, high-intensity lights and out of direct sunlight.

**Monitoring temperatures**

Cabinet thermometers rarely reflect product temperature accurately. Refrigerator temperatures should be checked using an accurate digital or infrared thermometer. Bare wire thermocouples provide a quick response and can also be used for testing between packs. Indicating or recording thermometers are essential and premises with a large number of units will need automatic monitoring equipment and alarms to warn of unacceptable temperatures.

Code of Practice No. 12 suggests a three stage approach to determining compliance with statutory food temperatures:

(1) an examination of daily records of air temperature monitoring at the premises;
(2) if records are unsatisfactory then non-destructive testing, between packs, should be carried out; and
(3) if concern remains then probing of the food should be undertaken.

The correlation between air and product temperature can be obtained by pre-chilling a probe thermometer (leave it in a refrigerator for five minutes), taking the product temperature, after at least 24 hours storage, then checking the unit's air temperature.

Each section in a long, refrigerated cabinet should be checked for defective fans and it should be noted that multi-deck cabinets vary by up to 2°C with the cold air being at the top. Variations of 2°C can also occur due to the compressor cutting in and out. Temperatures may be raised slightly during defrost and this can be checked as any highly polished surfaces are usually misted up. "Air on" temperatures are the most reliable indicator of performance as this is the warmer air at the return air vent. ("Air off" refers to the cold air leaving the evaporator coil where it enters the cabinet.)

All temperature monitoring should be logged, preferably first thing in the morning, after a busy period, for example, midday and at the end of the day. Records of in-house checks must be retained and available for enforcement officers and will be essential to establish a due-diligence defence in the event of complaint.

*Infrared thermometers*

Infrared thermometers, which work by measuring the amount of radiant energy, are assuming increasing importance for monitoring food temperatures. Products can be scanned very rapidly and any identified problems can be checked immediately with a digital thermometer. Additional advantages include the fact that it is non-destructive testing and there is no risk of cross-contamination. It is particularly useful for scanning retail cabinets, frozen food, deliveries and despatch as large consignments can be checked for hot spots.

Although simple to use, staff require training to ensure accuracy of measurement. The object to be measured needs to fill the field of view, or the reading will be an average of the object and its surroundings. Infrared is unsuitable for measuring temperatures of foods packaged in reflective foil unless a matt black spot is painted on the surface. It is also inappropriate to use for checking centre temperatures during cooking, thawing or cooling as only the surface temperature is measured.

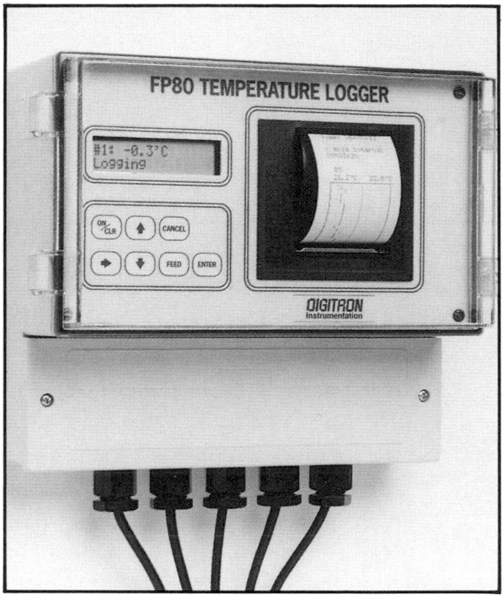


**Fig. 17.** Infrared Thermometer. **Fig. 18.** Temperature logger.

( Courtesy of Digitron Instrumentation Ltd. )

*Temperature/data loggers*

Data loggers and printers will provide a variety of useful information about refrigerated storage including current temperature, maximum, minimum and trends of temperature over a specified period. Should temperatures rise above a predetermined level they can also trigger an alarm.

**The selection of effective refrigeration units**

When purchasing refrigeration units for commercial use, it is important to consider a whole range of factors apart from the obvious one of capacity. Choice must not be based solely on price, and units built for domestic use are unlikely to have the life or qualities that could be expected from a refrigerator purpose-built for commercial organizations. When selecting a unit regard must be had to the following:

(1) *Storage temperatures* - units must be capable of maintaining satisfactory storage temperatures in the high ambient temperatures of commercial kitchens. Some busy kitchens, with inadequate ventilation, have been recorded as high as 43°C. Some units may need to operate at 10°C, for example, if used for wine storage, or others at temperatures of –1°C to 1°C, for example, for the storage of fresh meat or fish. Fan assisted cooling is essential to circulate cold air throughout the storage compartment and maintain uniform temperatures. After opening and closing the door the correct temperature will be quickly re-established.

(2) *Construction* - door(s) and floor should be stainless steel to provide the greatest resistance to impact damage. Heat-reflecting aluminium sides and interior surfaces are often used to save energy. White painted finishes are prone to chipping, cracking and rusting. Plastic liners are easily damaged.
(3) *Automatic defrost* - ensures that the coil remains free of insulating ice and keeps down running cost. Staff do not have to remember to defrost the unit on a regular basis. Air temperatures of units should not rise above 10°C when defrosting.
(4) *Thermometers* - all units should be fitted with an indicating or recording thermometer positioned to show the temperature of the warmest part of the unit. Thermometers should be located externally and should be easily readable with the door(s) closed. It is also useful if there is a light which indicates when the unit is on automatic defrost.
(5) *Fittings* - a comprehensive choice of fittings is available including: adjustable, nylon-coated, wire shelves; gastronome pans; locks; meat rails and fish drawers.
(6) *Labour saving options* - an increasing number of modifications are being provided to save staff time and at the same time increase safety, for example:
   (i) pass-through cabinets which reduce staff fatigue and prevent congestion between the kitchen and the servery;
   (ii) roll-in cabinets which enable fully-loaded trolleys to be wheeled directly into storage so reducing handling;
   (iii) heavy-duty drawers which are used to minimize stooping and reaching;
   (iv) door opening foot pedals which leave hands free for carrying;
   (v) glass doors which enable stock checks without opening doors; and
   (vi) counter models which can be sited under workbenches so reducing walking and minimizing the time high-risk food is kept at ambient temperatures.

**Cooling of hot food**

Rapid cooling of cooked foods to be chilled or frozen is extremely important. Bacteria may survive cooking as spores or even in the vegetative state and there is always a risk of contamination after cooking. By whatever route bacteria enter the food it is essential that their multiplication during cooling is minimized. It is recommended that food is cooled below 10°C in less than 1.5 hours and blast chillers are available that can achieve this specification, but only for relatively thin portions of food. Furthermore, cooling units are often damp and must be cleaned regularly to avoid problems with mould growth.

**Fig. 19.** Monitoring food temperature in a blast chiller (Foster Refrigerator UK).

Unfortunately, it is very difficult to cool even relatively small joints of meat (or poultry) within the recommended times. A study undertaken by the AFRC Institute of Food Research, Langford, Bristol found that:

| **Rolled Joints** | **Approximate wt (kg)** | **Cooling time (min) 70°C to 10°C (50°C to 10°C)** Convection | Immersion | Pressure vacuum |
|---|---|---|---|---|
| Beef silverside | 2.7 | 291(237) | 186(153) | 39(36) |
| Beef forequarter | 2.7 | 304(261) | 216(185) | 24(21) |
| Boneless turkey | 5.9-6.5 | 396(325) | 335(275) | 16(13) |

Convection cooling was in air at 0°C and 1.2ms$^{-1}$
Immersion cooling was in water at 0°C

Most catering/retail premises will not have the necessary equipment to achieve even this rate of cooling, unless they have a blast chiller. Without such equipment or the knowledge regarding possible pathogenic contamination, especially spore-forming bacteria, cooling of joints is likely to be a potential health risk. If spores are present and activated during cooking, then cooling over several hours may provide ideal conditions for subsequent multiplication. Furthermore, if the joint is sliced and/or hot liquids drained off into shallow containers to assist cooling, extreme caution is necessary to avoid the risk of introducing pathogenic bacteria such as salmonella.

*Blast chillers*

To avoid the formation of large ice crystals and consequential loss of quality, it is important that chilled foods do not freeze during the chilling process. Usually, chilled air at 2°C to −7°C is circulated around the product but some blast chillers use the vapour from liquid nitrogen and solid carbon dioxide.

Chillers are intended for the rapid removal of heat and not for the storage of food which is already chilled. Consequently, they operate at air velocities well in excess of those used in refrigerators, for example, 5ms$^{-1}$.

**Distribution of high-risk food**

Vehicles used for the distribution of high-risk food must always be insulated and preferably refrigerated, even for short journeys. Insulation of the roof and floor is just as important as the insulation of the walls. Properly located thermometers should be fitted to all vehicles. The maximum temperature will be recorded by a sensor fitted in the returned air system and the minimum temperature can be measured near the outlet of the evaporators.

Refrigerated vehicles are designed to maintain temperatures of chilled or frozen food and must not be loaded with warm food. Vehicles should be pre-cooled prior to loading. The refrigeration unit should be switched off whilst the doors are open to avoid icing-up of the cooling units. During loading or unloading breaks, the doors must be closed and the unit switched on. Loading must be carried out quickly to avoid unacceptable temperature rises.

Vehicles must be maintained in a clean and tidy condition. Raw food should never be transported with high-risk food unless they are completely segregated to avoid any risk of contamination. Stacking of vehicles should facilitate sufficient air circulation around the food.

*Deliveries of high-risk food*

The temperature of food should be checked on arrival. Food requiring refrigerated storage should be rejected if above 10°C and frozen food rejected above −12°C. Deliveries must be placed in refrigerated storage as quickly as possible to avoid temperatures exceeding the above rejection temperatures.

## THE STORAGE OF FROZEN FOOD

At temperatures of around −40°C, most frozen food should keep for several years without noticeable deterioration. However, most domestic and retail freezers operate at −18°C and at this temperature a gradual loss of flavour and a toughening of texture occurs. Above −10°C spoilage organisms, especially osmophilic yeasts, moulds and halophilic bacteria, commence growth and together with biochemical reactions cause serious problems including souring, putrefaction and rancidity.

Spores and significant numbers of pathogenic bacteria are usually able to withstand freezing and prolonged frozen storage. After a suitable lag phase, survivors will commence multiplication on thawing. Strict precautions must therefore be taken in the manufacture of frozen foods to ensure the absence of pathogens. The storage life of frozen food depends on the initial number of microorganisms, the final storage temperature and the temperatures, and times, of distribution and manufacture. Short periods at a temperature of approximately −15°C will have little effect on quality or shelf-life.

The manufacturing temperature of frozen food is usually −23°C or below. Commercial cold stores are usually operated at an air temperature of between −25°C and −30°C. The quality of frozen food will be affected if:

(1) food is frozen too slowly or not to a low enough temperature;
(2) there is a breakdown in the cold store which results in a significant temperature rise. Cold stores should always be fitted with temperature recording charts so that fluctuations in temperature, and times, are accurately recorded;
(3) distribution vehicles are incapable of maintaining temperatures of −18°C. Problems may occur if there are many small delivery points necessitating the opening of doors a large number of times;
(4) there are excessive delays in loading or unloading which result in frozen food being left at ambient temperatures for considerable periods of time; and
(5) storage facilities at retail or catering outlets are inadequate.

All frozen food should be coded to enable the recall of suspect batches which have escaped manufacturing controls.

**The storage of frozen food at retail premises**

All cabinets used for the storage and display of frozen foods should comply with BS 3053: 1983. To ensure that customers receive the highest quality of frozen food, managers must:

(1) only use reputable suppliers;

(2) reject deliveries above −12°C or which show signs of thawing or having been refrozen, for example, packs of peas which have welded solid;

(3) not allow frozen food to remain at ambient temperatures for longer than 15 minutes. Food will, of necessity, be at ambient temperatures during unloading of deliveries and stocking display units from back-up stores;

(4) not use display freezers for freezing fresh food, as they are only capable of maintaining the temperature of food which is already frozen;

(5) ensure that display units are not filled above the load-line;

(6) carry out regular inspections of freezers and check temperatures at least daily but preferably more frequently. Electronic probe thermometers should be used to ensure the accuracy of the indicating thermometers which should be fitted to all units in an easily readable position;

(7) ensure that back-up stores are fitted with strip-curtains or air blowers and the doors are opened as little as possible to avoid unacceptable fluctuations of temperature. Ice build-up on the walls or floor of units must not be allowed;

(8) implement effective systems of stock control and stock rotation. It is advisable to code food on delivery to assist rotation; and

(9) ensure that food is not mishandled. Damage to packaging may result in loss of product, contamination and freezer burn. For similar reasons packaging, designed to protect frozen food, must not be removed. Stable air temperatures are important as warm air will result in a fall in vapour pressure and the sublimation of water vapour from the food to restore the balance. Dehydration of the product (freezer burn) results in a pale discoloured food surface, rather like balsa wood, that cannot be restored.

**Storage times**

All food should be used within the time recommended by the manufacturer. However, a general guide for food kept at −18°C is:

| | Months |
|---|---|
| vegetables, fruit, most meat | up to 12 |
| pork, sausages, offal, fatty fish, butter and soft cheeses | up to 6 |

Salad vegetables, non-homogenized milk, single cream, eggs and bananas should not be frozen. Cream can be whipped and stabilized to overcome the separation in desserts.

The star marking system is used to indicate the temperature and storage times of food in a frozen storage compartment:

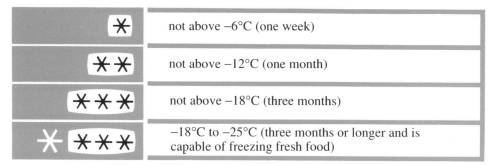

| | |
|---|---|
| * | not above −6°C (one week) |
| ** | not above −12°C (one month) |
| *** | not above −18°C (three months) |
| * *** | −18°C to −25°C (three months or longer and is capable of freezing fresh food) |

**Fig. 20.** The star marking system for frozen food compartments.

### Freezing and refreezing

Freezing of food will not improve its quality. The slow freezing of food in domestic freezers results in the formation of large ice crystals which rupture cells, leading to a slight deterioration in quality, due to changes in the composition of proteins in the presence of enzymes. This deterioration is much more noticeable if food is thawed and refrozen, apart from the obvious dangers if the thawed food is maintained above 10°C for a considerable time. Large ice crystals are particularly noticeable in ice-cream which has been refrozen. However, food which has been frozen, thawed and thoroughly cooked may be refrozen quite safely, although flavour and texture will be altered and nutritional value lowered.

### Effect of fluctuating temperatures

Clear plastic packaging of food may act as a greenhouse and the radiant heat from fluorescent tubes and air conditioning may increase the temperature of frozen food significantly. Fluctuations from −3°C to −18°C have been observed with the lower temperatures only being achieved during the night when heat sources have been switched off.

The presence of ice in packets of frozen food usually indicates fluctuating temperatures have allowed water to evaporate from the product and subsequently freeze. Individually quick frozen products such as peas weld together in a solid mass if exposed to fluctuating temperatures.

### Freezer breakdown

If the freezer breaks down or food becomes thawed, for example, due to a power failure, the food may occasionally be treated as fresh. In certain circumstances the food may be cooked and refrozen. If the food has a solid core of ice it may be safe to refreeze without cooking. If in doubt advice should be obtained from the local Environmental Health Department.

In the event of breakdown, the lid of the freezer should be left closed and the unit covered in newspapers and blankets until repaired. Food may remain frozen for at least two days in a well-stocked, well-insulated freezer.

**Thawing of frozen food**

Most food taken from the freezer can be cooked immediately but poultry, joints of meat and other large items must be completely thawed before cooking. The manufacturer's instructions should always be followed. If food is not completely thawed, ice is likely to be present at the centre and the heat from subsequent cooking will be used to melt the ice and not to raise the internal temperature above that required to destroy pathogens.

However, thawing of food poses several problems and inadequate thawing of poultry frequently results in undercooking and subsequent food poisoning. Thawing at room temperatures (25°C to 30°C) results in the multiplication of bacteria on the warm surface of food, whilst the centre remains frozen. Thawing in a small refrigerator can be even more hazardous. A 20lb turkey will take several days to thaw and the surfaces of the refrigerator, and high-risk food, may become contaminated with thawed liquid containing pathogenic bacteria. Furthermore, the temperature at which the refrigerator is operating has a significant effect on thawing times. Work carried out by Mr T.C. Grey at the Bristol AFRC Institute of Food Research showed that a 1.1kg broiler took around 8 hours at 20°C, 11 hours at 15°C, 13 hours at 10°C, 40 hours at 5°C and 70 hours at 1°C for the temperature to go above 0°C in the deep thigh. Birds left in polythene bags took longer especially at the colder temperatures. It is therefore essential for advice regarding thawing times under refrigeration to state actual temperatures. Thawing of frozen poultry is best carried out at 10° to 15°C in an area entirely separate from other foods, in cold running water or in a thawing cabinet.

**TABLE XXI** THAWING AND COOKING TIMES OF FROZEN POULTRY

| Oven ready weight Kg (lbs) | Approx. thawing time at room temp (hours) | Min. cooking time at 180C/350F Gas 4* (in foil) (hours) |
|---|---|---|
| 2.25 (5) | 15 | 2.5 |
| 4.5 (10) | 18 | 3.5 |
| 6.75 (15) | 24 | 4.75 |
| 9.0 (20) | 30 | 5.75 |

*These are minimum times. The bird is cooked when the juices run clear, and should be checked with a disinfected probe thermometer.

Food thaws slowly because of the low thermal diffusivity of food at 0°C. As soon as the surface thaws it acts as an insulating layer and this reduces the rate of heat flow into the product. Thawing in refrigerators is even slower because of the small temperature difference between the refrigerator operating at 1°C to 4°C and frozen food. Consequently, it takes a considerable time to provide the latent heat of thawing, i.e. the heat necessary to change ice to water.

Several techniques have been suggested for thawing food and some of these have been used commercially. Electrical methods of thawing, namely dielectric, microwave and resistive are not affected by the low thermal diffusivity of food but unfortunately may give rise to an effect known as runaway heating: thawing does not occur evenly throughout the frozen food and areas that thaw absorb energy preferentially to areas which remain frozen. This results in some parts of the food cooking before the whole mass of food is thawed.

*Rules for handling frozen poultry*

(1) segregate from high-risk food;
(2) thaw completely in a cool room at less than 15°C or in a thawing cabinet. Clean, cold running water is preferable to thawing in warm kitchen temperatures or in refrigerators with limited space. Poultry will be ready for cooking when the body is pliable, the legs are flexible and the body cavity is free from ice crystals;
(3) remove giblets;
(4) once thawed keep in the refrigerator and cook within 24 hours;
(5) cook thoroughly and cook the stuffing separately;
(6) all utensils and surfaces used for the preparation of raw meat and poultry should be thoroughly cleaned and disinfected before being used for high-risk food. It is preferable to use separate work surfaces;
(7) eat straight after cooking or, if the bird is carved cold, cool it quickly and store in the refrigerator. As with all meats **refrigerated storage is essential within 1.5 hours;** and
(8) avoid handling the cooked bird unnecessarily.

## COOK-CHILL

Cook-chill is the name given to a catering system in which food is thoroughly cooked and then chilled rapidly in a blast chiller to a temperature of 3°C or below within 1.5 hours. The food is stored between 0°C and 3°C until required for reheating. In mass catering, some form of cooking and chilling is essential. There is no other way of bringing together all the components of a meal simultaneously without a disproportionately large labour force and an excessive cooking equipment provision. As such the chilling of cooked food is not a completely new concept. The rudiments are practised by virtually every large catering establishment. Sometimes, the regime is as basic as "chilling" the food to ambient in a cool part of the kitchen but in most operations, there tends to be an initial pre-chilling at ambient followed by retention in a cold store or refrigerated cabinet. Such practices have significantly contributed to a number of food poisoning cases in the UK.

The formalization of cook-chill as a specific form of catering has, in this context, done nothing more than introduce specialist equipment for chilling and reheating, enabling that which was already practised to be undertaken safely and more efficiently. Large scale schemes are, however, more than just cook-chill. To meet the costs of re-equipping with expensive equipment, a number of operations have centralized production in a single kitchen, known as a Central Production Unit (or CPU). The most cost-effective results are achieved using large scale equipment such as bratt pans, tilting kettles, large steamers, computer controlled fast fryers and convection ovens. A major distribution system is then organized to get the food to the former producing kitchens, now known as end kitchens, where it is reheated.

There are usually eight stages in a cook-chill system:

(1) bulk storage;
(2) preparation;
(3) cooking;
(4) portioning, packaging and labelling;
(5) blast chilling;
(6) storage at or below 3°C;
(7) distribution at or below 3°C and;
(8) reheating (regeneration) and serving.

With the introduction of cook-chill schemes there have been coincidentally, and necessarily in respect of centralization, developments in production aimed at systemizing and standardizing the catering process. The fundamental nature of these operations is that they have more in common with food processing than catering. However, there are significant differences. Batch size tends to be smaller than would be handled in food processing and the menu is considerably more varied. An absolutely key difference, however, is that the CPU can rarely, if ever, cook all the food used in a scheme. Anything up to 60% of total consumption may simply pass through after being portioned and packed. The CPU, therefore, as well as being a manufacturing plant is also a distribution centre, often handling a high proportion of pre-cooked foods. These high-risk foods must be integrated into the mainstream production line. Composite foods like salads and sandwiches may also require integration. In effect, the CPU is two separate operations under one roof, combining to form a single operation at the end. This mixing of functions has a far-reaching effect on the layout. The simple "dirty in one end - clean out the other" flow, favoured in operations as diverse as food factories and sterile supply units, cannot usually be achieved. A far more sophisticated flow and layout is required.

The responsibility of the designer is even greater than for conventional kitchens. The operations heavily influence the design requirements, but the design controls the operation to an even greater degree. The designer should seek to impose a specific regime and set methods of working to ensure a systemized operation. The aims are to ensure that the operation works in the most efficient and safe way and to prevent it working in any other way.

The following benefits are claimed for the cook-chill system:

(1) cost-effectiveness savings are possible because:
  (i) of centralization and better utilization of equipment;
  (ii) centralized purchasing and accurate portion control results in less wastage;
  (iii) careful design and planning can reduce energy consumption;
  (iv) less floor space is required;
  (v) fewer staff are required in both the central production unit and satellite kitchens;

(vi) of a reduction in overtime. Careful planning results in a steady workload instead of troughs and peaks throughout the day;

(2) better staff conditions and less work in unsociable hours. Staff turnover is usually reduced;

(3) flexible - orders for meals can be accepted at much shorter notice; and

(4) improved quality and palatability compared with meals kept hot, above 63°C, for long periods. Complaints of dried-up and overcooked food should not occur. Meals are also more consistent.

**The safety of cook-chill**

Because of the emphasis on strict temperature control throughout the system and the provision of recording thermometers on all units, a properly controlled cook-chill system is safer than most conventional systems of mass catering. Furthermore, as staff are not working under immense pressure for short periods of time, there is less rushing about and mistakes are less likely. However, the reduction in risk tends to be offset, at least on a statistical basis, by the larger scale of production. Where more meals are produced, a unit has to be safer than a smaller operation, just to maintain the same statistical risk of food poisoning. There is also the essential matter of extended shelf-life: foods to be consumed some days after cooking have obviously to be at a higher standard than food produced for immediate consumption. The general approximation that cooking kills germs, which governs conventional catering, does not apply. The cooking process is seen as a reducing factor only. Where initial bacterial loading of the raw product is too high, the cook-chill process cannot produce food at an acceptable standard, no matter how well it operates or how hygienic it is. Raw produce standard assumes a much greater importance.

The potential of the low temperature pathogens such as *Yersinia entercolitica* and *Listeria monocytogenes* to cause problems must not be overlooked, notwithstanding that it appears that multiplication and toxin production over a five day period is insignificant at temperatures below 3°C. Furthermore, most low temperature pathogens should be destroyed during the reheating process.

In order to ensure the safety of cook-chill the following rules should be observed:

(1) All raw materials should be of good microbiological quality. Purchasing contracts should include product specifications and suppliers should be monitored to ensure compliance. Raw products should be stored at appropriate temperature and humidities which are monitored.

(2) Cross-contamination must be avoided; the preparation of raw materials must be in areas physically separated from cooking and post-cooking areas. Personnel handling raw foods should be confined to the raw material area. Separately identifiable equipment should be used for raw products.

(3) Controlled thawing equipment is required if frozen raw materials are used.

(4) The highest standards of hygiene, especially personal hygiene must be observed throughout all stages of preparation, cooking, storage and reheating. Staff will require additional training.

(5) Immediately prior to cooking, excess prepared food must be held below 10°C.

(6) To ensure the destruction of *Listeria monocytogenes,* food should be cooked to a temperature above 70°C for not less than two minutes, at the slowest heating point (checks should be made with a probe thermometer). Recording thermometers should also be used.

(7) Food should be portioned and chilled to below 3°C within two hours of cooking. Chillers must be capable of reducing the temperature of a 50mm layer of food from 70°C to 3°C in not more than 90 minutes when fully loaded. Automatic controls are required including an accurate (±0.5°C) indicating thermometer and temperature recorder. Product depth during chilling should not exceed 50mm and may need to be reduced to achieve chilling specification. Joints of meat should not exceed 2kg and 100mm in thickness. Uniform shapes of joint should be used. Handling of food should be minimized and the use of disposable gloves does not remove the need for frequent hand washing.

(8) Reusable lidded containers, capable of being cleaned and disinfected, or disposable containers may be used for cooked food portions. (Use of lids during chilling reduces dehydration but slows down chilling.) Containers should be date marked to ensure strict stock rotation. The label can also indicate type of food and reheating time (with or without the lid).

(9) The refrigerated store, fitted with indicating and recording thermometers and alarms, should maintain food between 0°C and 3°C and should only be used for cook-chill products. The maximum life of cooked products is five days, including the days of cooking and consumption.

(10) Should the temperature of the food exceed 10°C during storage or distribution and before reheating, it should be destroyed. If the temperature exceeds 5°C the food should be eaten within 12 hours.

(11) Insulated containers, chilled before use, may be used for short distribution runs but refrigerated vehicles are preferred and are essential for long journeys, especially during warmer months.

(12) Food should be reheated as soon as possible after removing from chill and never longer than 30 minutes. The centre temperature of the food should reach at least 70 °C and be maintained for at least two minutes. Service of food should commence as soon as possible and within 15 minutes of reheating. Temperatures must not be allowed to fall below 63°C. Unconsumed, reheated food must be destroyed.

(13) Reheating is preferable using infrared units, forced air and steamer convection ovens (traditional ovens may cause dehydration).

(14) Foods intended to be eaten cold should be consumed as soon as possible and within 30 minutes of removal from chill.

(15) To avoid health hazards a strict system of Quality Assurance, involving the use of hazard analysis and monitoring and control at those points critical to food safety, must be implemented. Action plans should be formulated to deal with deviations from what is acceptable.

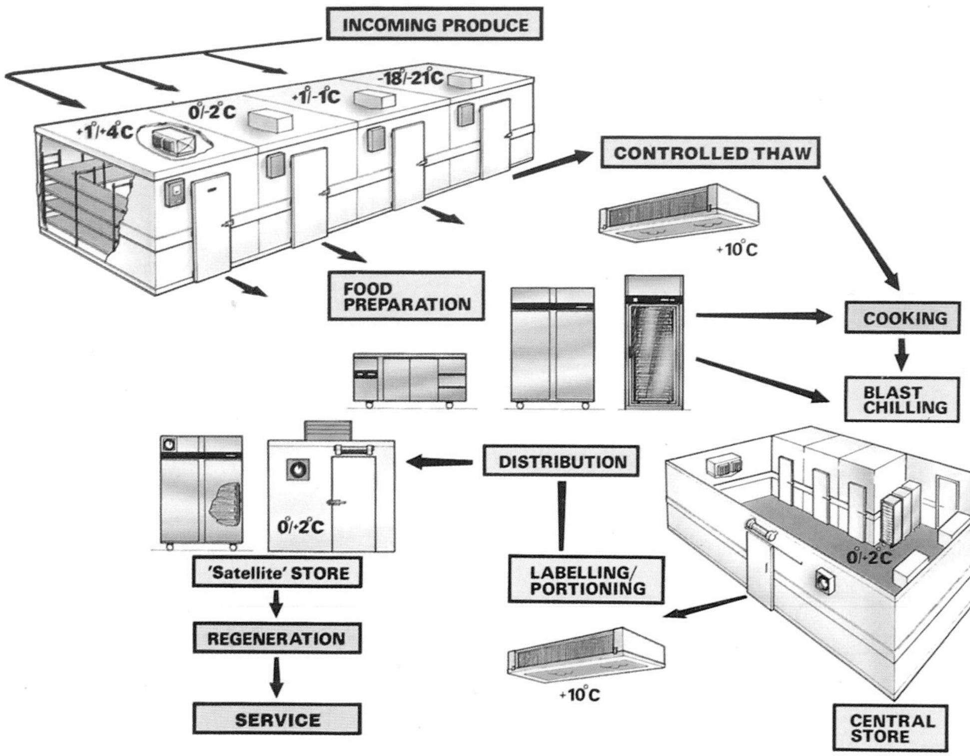


**Fig. 21.** Refrigeration for cook-chill.
( Courtesy of Foster Refrigerator (UK) Ltd.)

## Management

Cook-chill demands considerable management and supervisory skills. Menu planning must take account of the keeping quality of different types of food. Foods with a high unsaturated fat content may oxidize more quickly and may not be suitable for the full five day storage. Work scheduling so that chilling times are rigidly observed, taking into account the differing rates of chilling of food for different types and densities, is also challenging for managers.

Equipment failure and abnormal temperature readings can lead to difficult decisions and high losses. Increased complexity of equipment demands increased expertise from both managers and maintenance staff.

PERSONAL HYGIENE, CLEANLINESS AND CROSS-CONTAMINATION

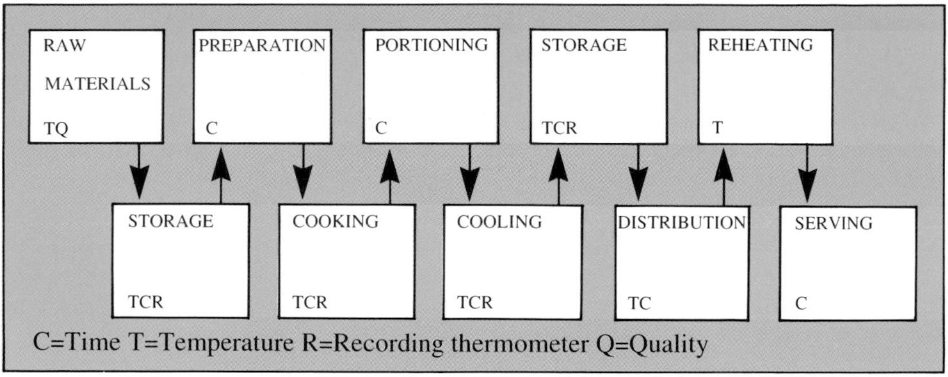


**Fig. 22.** Critical control checks for a cook-chill system.

**Microbiological guidelines to be used for setting up the system (Chilled and Frozen Guidelines on Cook-Chill and Cook-Freeze Catering Systems: DH 1989)**
Total aerobic colony count (48 hours @ 37°C) < 100,000 per gram
Salmonella and *Listeria monocytogenes* not detected in 25 grams
*Staphylococcus aureus* (coagulase+ve) and *Clostridium perfringens* < 100 per gram
*Escherichia coli* < 10 per gram
(100g samples to be taken immediately prior to reheating).

## SOUS VIDE COOK-CHILL

Sous vide cook-chill, also known as cuisine sous vide, is an interrupted catering system in which raw or par-cooked food is sealed in a vacuumized plastic pouch or container, heat treated by controlled cooking, rapidly chilled and then reheated for service after a period of chilled storage. The advantages include:
(1) extended shelf-life;
(2) enhanced sensory quality; and
(3) improved nutritional quality.

Disadvantages include:
(1) significant capital and operating costs;
(2) limited number of products are suitable for this operation; and
(3) poorly designed systems and badly controlled systems may result in serious consequences such as the growth of *Clostridium botulinum* in the product.

**The process**
*Ingredient purchasing, delivery* and *storage*
All raw materials should be of the highest quality and stored at correct temperatures and humidities for the minimum time.

*Preparing and portioning*

High standards of hygiene must be maintained at all times. Prepared food must be held, or if pre-heated chilled to, below 10°C prior to vacuum packaging. Single portion pouches are preferred but if multi-portion pouches are used product thickness should not exceed 50mm, to ensure acceptable heat transfer. Adequately sized pouches are essential. It should be possible to pinch 12.5mm of plastic together on all four sides of the product and the opening of the pouch should be folded back to prevent soiling during filling.

*Vacuum packaging*

After the removal of air and heat sealing of the pouch, it should mould tightly to the contours of the food. All pouches should be checked and any with defects such as air or product movement should be repackaged.

*Prime cooking/pasteurization*

Controlled heating may be undertaken using atmospheric steamers, combination ovens (set on "steaming" mode) or water baths. Food should be heated as soon as possible after preparation and always within two hours. Pouches of differing thickness should be processed separately and pouches must not be stacked on top of each other.

One of the following time/temperature treatments should be used:

| Core temperature (°C) | Minimum holding time (Minutes) |
|---|---|
| 80 | 26 |
| 85 | 11 |
| 90 | 4.5 |
| 95 | 2 |

*Chilling*

Chilling may be achieved by blast, immersion or cryogenic chillers and should commence immediately after pasteurization and always within 30 minutes. Food must be chilled to at least 3°C within two hours of cooking.

*Chilled storage and distribution*

Products must be labelled with their name, date of production (or batch number), use-by-date and reheat instructions. In the UK the maximum shelf-life is usually considered to be eight days including days of production and consumption. Storage and distribution must be between 0°C and 3°C. If the food temperature rises to between 5°C and 10°C the food must be consumed within 12 hours, if it exceeds 10°C the food should be destroyed.

*Reheating and service*

Prior to reheating (regeneration), any defective pouches should be destroyed. Reheating should take place immediately after removing from chilled storage and always within 30 minutes and never more than 15 minutes prior to service. A minimum centre temperature of 75°C should be achieved and the temperature of the food must not fall below 65°C before being served. Unconsumed reheated products must be destroyed.

## THE SAFETY OF CHILLED FOODS

In 1992 The Advisory Committee on the Microbiological Safety of Food recommended that in addition to maintaining the temperature of prepared, chilled foods with a shelf-life of more than 10 days below 10°C, at least one of the following controlling factors should be used, to prevent the growth and toxin production of psychrotrophic *Cl. botulinum*:

(1) a heat treatment of 90°C for 10 minutes or equivalent lethality;
(2) a pH of 5 or less throughout the food;
(3) a minimum salt level of 3.5% in the aqueous phase throughout the food;
(4) an $a_w$ of 0.97 or less throughout the food; or
(5) a combination of heat and preservative factors which can be shown consistently to prevent growth and toxin production of pyschrotrophic *Cl. botulinum.*

The Advisory Committee also recommended that a Code of Practice for the manufacture of vacuum and modified atmosphere packaged chilled foods should be drawn up containing detailed guidance on:

(1) raw material specification;
(2) awareness and use of HACCP;
(3) process establishment and validation (including thermal process);
(4) packaging requirements;
(5) temperature control through production, distribution and retail;
(6) factory auditing and quality management systems;
(7) the requirements to establish a safe shelf-life;
(8) the control factors necessary to prevent the growth of bacteria and toxin production;
(9) the application of challenge testing;
(10) equipment specifications, particularly with regard to heating and refrigeration; and
(11) training.

## COOK-FREEZE

Traditional catering involves considerable fluctuations in workload with a peak of around two hours, based on the time of meals. Cook-freeze is a system of catering devised to ensure a planned daily workload which utilizes division of labour techniques and reduces wastage. The system takes advantage of economies of scale and operates on the same principle as a factory production line. Requirements can be forecast months in advance but fluctuations in demand can be dealt with as they occur. Furthermore, skilled staff are fully utilized throughout the day and a greater proportion of unskilled staff can be employed, for example, in serving kitchens.

The first four stages of cook-freeze are the same as cook-chill, namely bulk storage, preparation, cooking and portioning, packaging and labelling. The fifth stage is blast-freezing. Pre-cooked, lidded packs are loaded on to trolleys which are wheeled into tunnel-type blast-freezers which reduce the temperature to –20°C in less than 90 minutes. Rapid freezing is essential to avoid the formation of large ice crystals which result in poor texture and loss of nutritional value on regeneration. The frozen containers are kept at –20°C and may be stored for up to 12 months.

The exact number of meals required can be removed from storage on demand and regenerated to a temperature of at least 75°C in serving kitchens using, for example, forced-air convection ovens.

Cook-freeze systems may be installed as purpose-built, self-contained production units which ensure a positive flow line or alternatively, existing equipment can be used with the addition of portioning, wrapping, blast-freezing and low-temperature storage. Cook-freeze is most suitable for operations requiring at least 1,000 meals per day, although some units have proved viable serving 200 meals per day.

### Hot storage of food

Temperatures used for keeping food hot, prior to service, must be high enough to prevent bacterial multiplication, especially pathogenic bacteria. However, appliances such as hot cupboards and bains-marie are designed for storing hot food which has been thoroughly cooked; they must not be used for warming up cold food. Storage temperatures must not be relied on to destroy pathogens.

Very few bacteria are able to multiply above 55°C, including those that commonly cause problems of food poisoning. Consequently, the law requires all food businesses to keep hot food at or above 63°C.

It is important to remember that temperatures of cooking may cause the germination of *Clostridium perfringens* spores and the vegetative bacteria will commence rapid multiplication at approximately 50°C. Consequently, a slight reduction in storage temperatures can have disastrous consequences.

## VENDING MACHINES

The use of automatic vending machines is constantly increasing. The complexity and types of machine and range of food dispensed are considerable. Beverage machines include:

(1) *simple drink dispensers* - separate ingredients deposited in a cup followed by hot water;

(2) *in-cup dispensers* - pre-mixed ingredients already in cups, to which hot water is added; and

(3) *post-mix machines* - ready-mixed hot or cold drinks are dispensed.

Post-mix machines are the most popular but require careful cleaning and maintenance.

Food vending machines include:

(1) *column and drawer machines* - the earliest type of machine, used for dispensing items such as bars of chocolate; and

(2) *rotating drum machines* - single items of food or complete meals, kept under refrigeration, stored in separate compartments on rotating shelves. Pre-cooked meals may be reheated using microwave ovens and this system is particularly convenient for factory shift workers requiring substantial meals late in the evening or in the early morning.

Vending machines must be sited, designed, constructed and maintained to ensure the safety and wholesomeness of all dispensed food. They must be durable and capable of being kept clean, both internally and externally. Pests must be denied access. Food contact surfaces should be smooth, impervious, non-toxic, corrosion resistant and be able to withstand the repeated cleaning and disinfection to which they will be subjected.

Machines must not be sited in direct sunlight or adjacent to sources of heat, for example, boilers, which could affect the temperature of food. Lights and other heat generating mechanisms within machines must be fitted so that the temperature of food is not significantly affected. Location of machines should facilitate the thorough cleaning of adjacent wall and floor surfaces. External, or internal, sites which expose food to risk of contamination, including dust, condensation or odour, should not be used for vending machines. The name and address of the machine operator should be clearly visible on the machines. Adequate litter containers, which are emptied as frequently as necessary, should be provided next to machines.

Stock rotation of food is essential. All items should be given a use-by-date, or a suitable code, to ensure that unsatisfactory food is removed. It is extremely desirable for vending machines dispensing high-risk foods, which are stored under refrigeration or above 63°C, to be fitted with chart recording thermometers, to ensure that food which has been subjected to unacceptable temperatures, for example, during a power cut, is not sold. At the very least, an indicating thermometer, visible externally, should be provided.

Vending machines must not be used for heating up cold food or for cooling down high-risk food from ambient temperatures. Hot food placed in vending machines must be thoroughly cooked and placed in the unit above 63°C.

Regular and thorough cleaning and, if necessary, disinfection of vending machines is essential to ensure food safety and quality. Machines should display precise cleaning instructions on the inside of the front service door, and operators must always follow these instructions. The date and time of each cleaning should be noted in the machine.

Further information on vending machines may be obtained from the Automatic Vending Association of Britain, Basset House, High Street, Banstead, Surrey SM7 2LZ (Tel: 01737 357211).

CHAPTER 8

# *Food spoilage and preservation*

## FOOD SPOILAGE

Immediately vegetables and fruit are harvested or animals slaughtered, they usually commence to decompose due to the action of bacteria, moulds, yeasts and enzymes. The rate of decomposition will vary depending on the type of food and the manner in which it is handled. The food may be considered spoiled when it is undesirable to eat. As off-flavours and odours develop and a breakdown in texture occurs, the food will eventually become unfit for consumption.

Spoilage may also be caused by insects or vermin, parasites, chemical contamination, physical damage such as freezer burn, and oxidation. However, spoilage by microorganisms is the most significant and is brought about by the normal function of organisms attempting to degrade complex organic matter into their constituent molecules. Multiplication of spoilage organisms depends on the type of organism, competition, initial numbers, the composition of food, $a_w$, pH, temperature, oxygen tension and the presence of inhibitory substances. Perishable foods such as meat, poultry, fish, dairy products*, fruit and vegetables, unless preserved in some way, are the most susceptible to microbial spoilage and must be handled carefully. Some foods such as sugar, flour and dried fruit are often described as stable or non-perishable and are unlikely to be affected by spoilage unless they are handled badly, for example, by storing under damp conditions.

As spoilage bacteria multiply more rapidly than moulds and use up the available surface oxygen, meat at ambient temperatures or stored in refrigerators of high humidity will usually be spoiled by aerobic bacteria, such as *Pseudomonas,* growing on the surface. Off-odours and slime will be produced. However, in low humidities the surface of meat may be too dry for rapid bacterial growth and consequently moulds such as *Cladosporium herbarum* (Blackspot) and *Thamnidium elegans* (Whiskers) will develop. The presence of mould usually results in food having a musty odour and flavour and, although usually considered to be harmless, increasing concern is being expressed because of the possible presence of mycotoxins.

---

* The spoilage of canned foods and dairy products is dealt with in Appendix I.

The acidity of fruit ensures that most primary spoilage is caused by moulds and yeasts which are able to multiply at a lower pH than bacteria. Although several species of bacteria do cause spoilage of vegetables, moulds are much more commonly involved, for example, those belonging to the genera *Botrytis, Rhizopus* and *Penicillium.*

Vegetables stored in vinegar such as beetroot may be attacked by yeasts which gain access to jars after processing, for example, if the lid on the jar is defective, damaged in transit or removed and replaced by inquisitive customers. The beetroot turns a rusty-brown colour and a pinky-white precipitate may be observed on the base of the jar which is attributable to fermentation by the yeast. Yeast spoilage of food can often be detected by the alcoholic taste and smell and the presence of bubbles in liquid.

Moulds are responsible for most of the spoilage of baked products, especially bread and pies. As mould spores are destroyed by normal cooking temperatures, post-process contamination from airborne spores and contact with contaminated surfaces must be prevented. Particular care must be taken to remove debris and waste food which would support mould growth. Cleansable surfaces and effective ventilation to stop condensation are also important to prevent growth.

Products should be cooled quickly and not wrapped whilst warm as the resultant condensation will encourage rapid mould growth, especially if the food is stored at ambient temperatures. Moulds commonly involved include *Rhizopus* and *Mucor spp.* (white growth with black spots), *Penicillium spp.* (green) and *Monilia sitophilia* (red/pink).

**Rope**

Rope in bread is caused by *Bacillus subtilis* and spores of this bacterium may be present in flour. They are able to withstand baking temperatures, and slow cooling and warm, humid storage ensure rapid germination and multiplication. Affected bread develops a fruity, sickly smell and a soft, sticky texture. Internally the loaf discolours, becoming yellow or brown. Rope is prevented by the use of proprionates. Other products such as cakes and doughnuts may occasionally be affected by rope.

Staleness of bread usually develops with prolonged holding due to physical changes in the carbohydrates. Refrigeration increases the rate of staling, however, staling does not occur during frozen storage at −18°C.

**Rancidity**

Fat in dairy products may be broken down into free fatty acids by microorganisms or by naturally occurring enzymes, lipases, with the production of off-odours and flavours. This process is described as hydrolytic rancidity. Heating may destroy lipase-producing bacteria but not any lipase already formed and rancidity may still occur.

Oxidative rancidity may also occur in dairy products, often due to the presence of copper or iron contamination. Off-odours and flavours are due to the formation and decomposition of peroxides. The prolonged cold storage of fatty fish, bacon and pork results in rancidity unless vacuum packed.

**TABLE XXII** COMMON FOOD SPOILAGE BACTERIA

| Food | Spoilage bacteria commonly isolated | Typical signs of spoilage |
|---|---|---|
| Fresh meat and poultry | *Clostridium*<br>*Pseudomonas*<br>*Achromobacter*<br>*Acinetobacter*<br>*Micrococcus*<br>*Flavobacterium* | slime, greenish discolouration, white spots (bacterial colonies), souring, putrefaction, off-odours and flavours |
| Processed meats | *Achromobacter*<br>*Pseudomonas*<br>*Lactobacillus*<br>*Streptococcus**<br>*Clostridium*<br>*Micrococcus* | souring, gas production, discolouration, surface slime |
| Bacon** | *Streptococcus**<br>*Micrococcus*<br>*Lactobacillus* | slime formation, white spots, discolouration, off-odours. Souring of vacuum packs (which may blow) |
| Fish | *Pseudomonas*<br>*Acinetobacter* | off-odours, discolouration |
| Vegetables*** | *Pseudomonas*<br>*Erwinia/Leuconostoc*<br>*Corynebacteria*<br>*Bacillus/Clostridium* | soft rot, foul odour, discolouration, black spots |
| Raw milk | *Streptococcus*<br>*Micrococcus*<br>*Lactobacillus*<br>*Bacillus*<br>*Pseudomonas* | tainting, off-flavours and odours, souring (above 15°C), rancidity |
| Pasteurized milk | *B. cereus*<br>*Streptococcus*****<br>*Lactobacillus***** | bitty cream (sweet curdling), off-odours and flavours |

**Streptococcus faecalis* is quite salt tolerant.
**Packs of bacon with faulty seams are vulnerable to mould spoilage.
***Frozen green vegetables which defrost become yellowish and eventually khaki, odours a slime may develop. The organism commonly responsible is *Leuconostoc mesenteroides*.
****Thermoduric strains which resist temperatures of pasteurization, for examp *Streptococcus faecalis*.

## Spoilage of poultry

The spoilage rate is dependent on the storage temperature and the number and type of spoilage organisms present. Spoilage is evident at around $10^8$ organisms per $cm^2$.

The smell of spoilt chicken is due to the production of hydrogen sulphide by spoilage bacteria. The hydrogen sulphide diffuses into the muscle tissue and combines with the haem pigments of blood and muscle in the presence of air to form the green pigment sulphaemoglobin just under the skin.

**TABLE XXIII** SPOILAGE RATE OF POULTRY*

| Temperature | 100 organisms/cm$^2$ | 10,000 organisms/cm$^2$ |
|---|---|---|
| 0°C | 11.5 days | 7.6 days |
| 5°C | 6.2 days | 4.1 days |
| 10°C | 3.9 days | 2.6 days |
| 15°C | 1.8 days | 1.2 days |

*Mead G. C. (personal communication).

## FOOD PRESERVATION

Preservation is the treatment of food to prevent or delay spoilage and inhibit growth of pathogenic organisms which would render the food unfit. Preservation may involve:

(1) the use of low temperatures or high temperatures;
(2) the use of dehydration, i.e. moisture control;
(3) the use of chemicals;
(4) controlled atmospheres and the restriction of oxygen; and
(5) physical methods including smoking and irradiation.

## FOOD PRESERVATION BY THE USE OF LOW TEMPERATURES

This form of preservation is based on the fact that all metabolic reactions of microorganisms are enzyme catalyzed. The speed of enzyme reaction depends on temperature and the colder it is, the slower the reaction. Temperatures used in preservation may be:

(1) above freezing (refrigerator);
(2) at freezing (commercially used with chilled beef); or
(3) below freezing (freezer).

### Temperatures above freezing

Refrigerators are used both commercially and domestically and should usually operate at between 1°C and 4°C. They are suitable for the storage of most perishable foods over a relatively short period of time. Most common pathogenic organisms cease multiplication below 6°C, although increasing concern is being expressed about *Yersinia enterocolitica, Aeromonas hydrophila* and *Listeria monocytogenes,* all of which are capable of growth under refrigeration. Psychrophilic spoilage bacteria which cause problems include those belonging to the genera *Pseudomonas, Acinetobacter, Flavobacterium* and *Alcaligenes.* Mould genera capable of growth at low temperatures include *Penicillium, Mucor, Cladosporium* and *Botrytis.*

### Temperatures below freezing

As well as the inhibition of enzyme reactions, freezing also relies on reducing available moisture to ensure effective preservation. The $a_W$ of water at 0°C is 1.0

whereas at –15°C the $a_W$ of ice is approximately 0.85. The freezing of food destroys some bacteria, including pathogens, and a gradual reduction of survivors occurs during storage. Generally, the lower the storage temperature of frozen food the greater is the survival rate of microorganisms. Spores and toxins are practically unaffected by freezing or frozen storage. The greatest number of bacteria are killed between –2°C and –5°C; unfortunately, many enzymes are extremely active at around –2°C and food stored at this temperature would soon deteriorate.

Some parasites can be destroyed by freezing, for example, Trichinella cysts in pork stored at –18°C for 21 days, *Cysticercus bovis* in beef carcases stored at –10°C for 14 days and the fish nematode Anisakis which is destroyed at –20°C in 24 hours.

The lowest recorded temperature for the growth of a bacterium is –20°C, and –34°C for a yeast.* In fact moulds and yeasts are more likely to grow on frozen food than bacteria as they are better able to withstand lower $a_w$ and temperatures. In practice very few organisms grow below –8°C. Even at temperatures of around 0°C it takes the most rapidly growing psychrophiles a day to achieve a tenfold increase in numbers.

On thawing, after a short lag time, a rapid growth of those bacteria which survive freezing will soon compensate for those destroyed, especially if food is allowed to reach temperatures of 20°C to 30°C.

Before vegetables are frozen they must be blanched. Blanching is carried out by immersion in hot water for a short period, approximately one minute. Its function is to destroy enzymes, such as peroxidases which produce off-odours and flavours, reduce bacterial load, fix colour, remove trapped air and induce wilting in some vegetables to aid packing. Overblanching will result in excessive loss of vitamin C by leaching and must be avoided. Care must be taken when operatives handle frozen food to avoid contamination, especially by staphylococci.

As the temperature is reduced, pure water will commence freezing at 0°C. (The freezing point is depressed by the presence of solutes such as salts and sugars.) However, the rate of cooling slows due to the loss of the latent heat of fusion prior to ice formation. As most of the water is converted to ice, the rate of cooling once again increases. Quick freezing involves passing through this zone of maximum crystallization of ice as quickly as possible. The faster the process the smaller the ice crystals, the better the food quality and the smaller the amount of liquid (drip) produced on thawing.

The actual rate of freezing depends on:

(1) the shape and weight of the product;
(2) the initial and final temperature;
(3) the surface heat transfer coefficient and thermal conductivity;
(4) the amount of heat to be removed (enthalpy);
(5) the temperature of the refrigerant; and
(6) the type of packaging.

---

* Michener H. and Elliot R. 1964. Minimum growth temperatures for food poisoning, faecal-indicator and psychrophilic organisms. Advances in Food Research 349-396.

Most foods will keep for prolonged periods in a freezer, although a recommended shelf-life is given because of loss of texture, flavour, tenderness, colour and overall nutritional quality.

Foods must be properly wrapped to avoid loss of moisture from the surface, i.e. freezer burn. The oxidation of food is slower at −18°C and this also assists in preservation. However, vacuum packing is essential to extend the shelf-life of frozen food susceptible to oxidative rancidity, for example, bacon, and the shelf-life of kippers can be extended from three to nine months. Very sophisticated laminate packaging is used for some ready-to-eat meals and boil-in-the-bag products. Films of low-density polyethylene, polyesters, aluminium foils and polypropylene are all used to improve packaging characteristics. Some products such as fish fillets are given a thin coat of ice to avoid dehydration during storage.

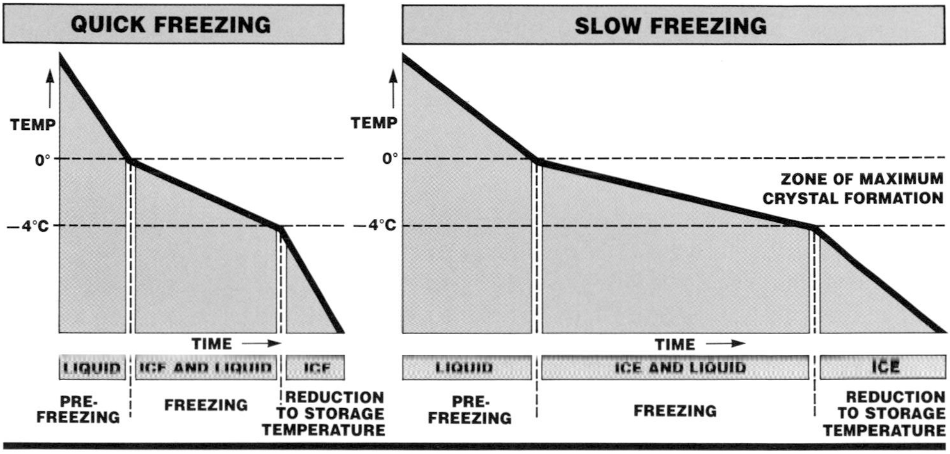


**Fig. 23.** Rates of freezing: the latent heat zone and zone of maximum crystal formation overlap and, if food is frozen slowly, considerable damage and loss of quality occurs.

## Freezing systems

### *Fluidized-bed freezing*

Particulate vegetables such as peas are moved along a tunnel on a perforated tray, through a blast of very cold air. They are normally borne along by a cushion of freezing air forced up from below. This ensures that each item is individually quick frozen, so ensuring that the product does not weld together. The process takes about three to eight minutes.

### *Air-blast freezing*

Air-blast freezers are the commonest method of freezing and include: static tunnels where trolleys of boxed product such as beef and cakes are pushed through; solid continuous belt freezes which are used for fish fillets, patties and pizzas; and spiral belt freezers which are relatively small and allow the refrigerated air to pass through the open link belt. They are used for pizzas, fish fillets, meals and cakes. Air circulates around the food at temperatures of –30°C to –40°C and as with all freezing systems, the freezing time depends on the dimensions of the food. The process usually takes two to three hours.

*Plate freezing*

This method is used for food packed in flat cartons, for example, fish blocks and meals. The cartons are placed between narrow metal shelves in which a very cold refrigerant circulates, so ensuring freezing. Revolving plate freezers are used, for example, for boil-in-the-bag products. Plate freezing usually takes two to three hours.

*Cryogenic freezing*

The food is sprayed by, or dipped into, a refrigerant such as liquid nitrogen. It is a very quick technique and, although capital costs are relatively low, high refrigerant costs restrict its use to high-cost, small products such as raspberries and prawns. Studies have shown that after a few months of frozen storage there is no significant difference between liquid nitrogen frozen and air-blast frozen foods.

*Pellofreeze system*

The "pellofreeze" system is an interesting development in freezing technology which involves freezing liquids and semi-solids in pellet form. Spinach, cream, orange juice, egg and soup have all been frozen commercially by this method.

## FOOD PRESERVATION BY THE USE OF HIGH TEMPERATURES

High temperatures are used to destroy both spoilage and pathogenic organisms and so preserve food. However, heat resistant bacteria, some toxins and spores may survive heat treatment. The number of organisms that survive heating is related to the initial numbers and strain of organism, the time and temperature used, the pH and the presence of protective substances such as proteins and fats. Experimental data* has shown that boiling chicken to an internal temperature of approximately 95°C reduced the number of viable cells of *Salmonella typhimurium* by around 99%.

Most raw poultry is only contaminated by a few salmonellae and consequently, the poultry can be rendered safe by proper heating. An exceptional situation may arise if high numbers of salmonellae are present, for example, $1.0 \times 10^7$ organisms per gram would, if reduced by 99%, leave $1.0 \times 10^5$ viable organisms. Although it is most unlikely that this number of salmonellae would be present, it clearly illustrates the importance of minimizing the number of pathogenic organisms on raw food.

---

* Haussemann D. L. and Wallace M. A. (1951). Studies on the possibility of the transmission of Salmonella by cooked fowl. Food Res., 16: 89-96.

Care must always be taken to avoid the recontamination of food after processing, or the multiplication of bacteria not destroyed during heating will occur. This involves the use of suitable packaging, for example, bottles or cans, or storage under conditions which inhibit bacterial growth, usually refrigeration.

The use of heat can be considered under the following headings:

**Pasteurization**

Pasteurization normally involves heating food at a relatively low temperature for a short time. For example, milk may be heated at 72°C for 15 seconds. The time and temperature combination chosen depends on the particular type of food and must be sufficient to destroy vegetative pathogens and a considerable proportion of spoilage organisms. Toxins and spores generally survive pasteurization and, to avoid the growth of heat-resistant organisms and vegetative bacteria which may be present because of spore germination during heating, refrigerated storage is often essential.

Organisms preferring to multiply at temperatures above 45°C are known as thermophiles and those capable of withstanding heat treatment, but not necessarily multiplying at the higher temperatures, are known as thermoduric.

The main advantage of pasteurization is that food is rendered safe with the minimum effect on flavour and nutritional value. Foods which are pasteurized include: milk, ice-cream, liquid egg, wines, canned fruit and large cans of ham. Guidelines to the types of food products stabilized by pasteurization treatments, and recommendations for the design of pasteurization processes are provided in "Food Pasteurization Treatments: Technical Manual No. 27. Campden Food and Drink Research Association, 1992".

**Sterilization**

Sterilization involves the destruction of all microorganisms and as this is sometimes difficult to achieve, heat treatment adequate to destroy all viable organisms may be utilized. In this case food may be considered commercially sterile. This means that any organisms remaining after treatment will be of no significance under normal methods of storage. Low-acid canned food is given such a treatment. Temperatures required for sterilization normally exceed 100°C and are usually achieved by means of steam under pressure.

There are several factors affecting the heat resistance of organisms including:

(1) *Humidity* - the lower the moisture the more resistant the organism, i.e. dry heat is not as lethal as steam at the same temperature.
(2) *Fat, sugar and proteins* - the presence of these substances usually increases heat resistance.
(3) *pH* - neutral pH is preferred, acid and alkaline conditions increase heat sensitivity. For this reason acid foods such as fruit require a much lower temperature to render them commercially sterile.
(4) *Chemicals* - the presence of certain chemicals such as nitrites may decrease heat resistance.

(5) $A_w$ - the heat resistance of salmonellae and other bacteria increases significantly by reducing the $a_w$.

The main advantage of sterilization is the prolonged shelf-life. The main objections are a lowering of nutritional value, including loss of vitamins, and a marked difference in texture and flavour.

**Ultra heat treatment (UHT)**

The ultra heat treatment of milk is a result of research carried out to find a product with an extended shelf-life without the noticeable organoleptic changes caused by sterilization. Milk is heated to a temperature of 132°C for one second before filling aseptically into sterile containers. This reduces the amount of caramelization and also enhances keeping quality. UHT milk will keep for several months without refrigeration.

**Cooking**

Cooking is a form of preservation but is essentially used to make food more palatable and safe for immediate consumption. Temperatures achieved during cooking are usually sufficient to ensure an effective reduction, or the elimination, of vegetative pathogens, although some preformed toxins and spores may be unaffected. In some cases, cooking activates spores and a significant multiplication of vegetative bacteria may occur during subsequent cooling. Internal temperatures of around 75°C should be achieved to ensure bacteriological safety, although heating food to a lower temperature for longer periods of time may be equally as effective. Faecal streptococci may survive these temperatures, especially in cooked ham.

The centre temperature of cooked meat should be checked regularly with an accurate thermometer which is always disinfected before use. The external surface of, for example, a joint may give the appearance of being thoroughly cooked but closer examination often reveals unacceptable centre temperatures. Rare beef will always have received a terminal centre cooking temperature of less than 63°C (above 63°C the myoglobin changes from red to grey) and this may cause problems if pathogenic contamination is introduced to the centre of rolled joints during boning. Some products such as cakes and pork pies may be cooked satisfactorily but are exposed to risk because of the subsequent addition of contaminated cream or gelatin. Storage of these products must always be under refrigeration.

The United States Department of Agriculture requires that cooked and roast beef receives a minimum internal temperature of 63°C, pork 66°C and poultry 71°C, although in practice higher temperatures are more likely to be used.

**Ohmic heating**

Ohmic heating involves heating food by passing a high-voltage electric current through a liquid and solid type food such as chilli con carne. The commercially sterile food is then cooled and packed under aseptic conditions to provide a product which has a prolonged shelf-life at ambient temperatures. Products must be capable of being pumped and can have a solids content of up to 60% with particulates having a diameter of around 25mm.

## DEHYDRATION AS A MEANS OF PRESERVATION

This method of preservation relies on the fact that all microorganisms require moisture to facilitate their metabolic reactions. Dehydration reduces the amount of available water, and dried foods normally contain less than 25% moisture with an $a_w$ of less than 0.6. Most bacteria require an $a_w$ of at least 0.95 and very few microorganisms can exist at levels around 0.6. However, some bacteria form spores which will germinate on reconstitution of the dried product, for example, *Bacillus cereus*. Gram –ve rods are the most sensitive bacteria to drying and Gram +ve cocci are usually the most resistant, with some able to grow down to an $a_w$ of 0.85. Yeasts and moulds usually grow at lower levels of $a_w$ than do bacteria. Organisms growing under dry conditions are usually referred to as xerophilic (dry loving).

The role of dehydration in food preservation became more important in the food industry with the development of packet convenience foods. Mould and enzyme spoilage is also prevented and, provided that food is stored in suitable air-tight packs, it will keep for a considerable period of time.

Sun drying was the earliest method of dehydration and is still practised in hot climates, for example, for drying currants, raisins and figs. Artificial drying is quicker and normally more effective than natural means. Unfortunately, food undergoes irreversible changes to the tissue structure during drying which affects both texture and flavour.

Methods of drying may be divided into those using hot air, for example, tunnel drying, fluidized-bed drying, roller drying and spray drying and those using warm air such as accelerated freeze drying. Hot air denatures protein; foods are more difficult to reconstitute and it induces greater changes in flavour. However, the choice often depends on the type of foodstuff and the degree of dehydration required. Blanching of vegetables must be carried out before drying to obviate enzyme activity during storage.

In spray drying a solution, paste or slurry is dispersed as small droplets into a stream of hot air. The small droplets result in a rapid loss of moisture and a large proportion of the colour, flavour and nutritive value of the food is maintained. However, because the evaporative cooling effect keeps the temperature of the droplets low, a pasteurization process is usually required prior to spray drying.

In roller drying, a paste of the food is made and feeds on to a heated drum from which the moisture is driven off and the dried cake is scraped from the drum. Generally, the quality of the product is not as good as the spray dried product.

For fruits and vegetables a tunnel drier is used. This consists of a tunnel 10 to 15 metres long in which trays of product are passed along. Hot air is blown across the trays and a continuous process leads to a gradual loss of moisture.

Total removal of moisture may not be necessary. Water that does remain forms a strong solution of salts and soluble proteins. This water remaining is not available to microorganisms and thus the food has a low water activity.

*Accelerated freeze drying*

Food is frozen quickly and then subjected to a mild heat treatment under vacuum. The ice in the food changes directly to water vapour which is then removed, a process known as sublimation. The cells of the food are substantially less affected than by other methods of drying and the product reconstitutes with very little change.

**The advantages and disadvantages of dehydration**

The advantages of dehydration over other methods of preservation include:

(1) the food is lighter and takes up less space; this results in cheaper transport and storage;
(2) costly insulated or refrigerated distribution vehicles and storage facilities are not required; and
(3) the relatively long shelf-life of the food.

The disadvantages include:

(1) considerable care is necessary in packaging to eliminate oxygen; if the packaging is damaged or permeable then spoilage will occur and oxidative rancidity may be a problem in foods containing fats;
(2) non-enzymic browning may occur in foods;
(3) there may be a significant alteration in flavour and a lowering of nutritional value, especially vitamin C;
(4) spore-forming bacteria survive and on reconstitution will germinate;
(5) many foods do not rehydrate very well and may become tough; and
(6) rehydration damages cell walls which increases the rate of decomposition.

To minimize chemical changes, particularly browning, in dried foods it is important to:

(1) keep the moisture content as low as possible;
(2) minimize the level of reducing sugars;
(3) use clean blanching water with low levels of leached soluble solids; and
(4) use sulphur dioxide as a preservative.

All dried food should be stored at low levels of relative humidity and kept dry in order to prevent spoilage, especially mould growth.

## CHEMICAL METHODS OF PRESERVATION

A wide range of chemical additives is available for food preservation and may be used to prevent microbial spoilage, chemical deterioration and mould growth. The use of additives is strictly controlled by legislation and maximum permitted levels are usually specified. Ministers are advised by the Food Standards Committee and the Food Additives and Contaminants Committee and are empowered, under the Food Safety Act, 1990, to make regulations and orders to control their use. However, a preference for milder flavours, and in some instances increasing public resistance, has resulted in a reduction in the amount of some preservatives such as nitrite used in food manufacture. Although this is desirable, extreme caution must be exercised if preservatives are being used not only to increase shelf-life but also to prevent pathogen multiplication. As the amount of preservative is reduced, satisfactory handling and refrigerated storage are becoming even more important. Initially, therefore, the safety of an altered or new recipe containing reduced preservative must be microbiological challenge tested. (The "new" product is inoculated with appropriate pathogens and then subjected to various temperatures to ascertain the effect on, for example, previous recommendation for cooking and storage.)

Any chemical used in food processing must be used in the best interests of the consumer and not as a device to deceive the consumer or to hide faulty processing and handling techniques. All food additives used must be shown to be safe for the consumer. In the UK a **positive list** principle is applied, that is only those compounds specifically listed can be used for food and, in most cases, the maximum amount of material allowed in specific types of food is also specified.

### (1) Salt

Salt has been used as a preservative since ancient times. In part, preservation is due to osmosis. When salt is added to food, water passes out of the cells by diffusion to create an equilibrium concentration. This moisture becomes unavailable for microorganisms. When added to 100g of water, 1.7g of sodium chloride will depress the $a_w$ by 0.01, 3.4g by 0.02, 5.1g by 0.03, etc. The effectiveness depends on the concentration and this is related to many factors including water content, contamination levels, pH, temperature, protein content and the presence of other inhibitory substances. The salt tolerance of microorganisms is usually decreased by lowering the temperature or the pH. Moulds are less exacting in their water requirements than bacteria and consequently, for effective preservation the available moisture must be less than will permit mould development. Curing of protein foods such as meat and fish is carried out by mixing the raw food with dry salts or by immersing the foods in a brine solution.

Organisms which can grow in high concentrations of salt are known as halophiles (salt loving). Those that can withstand high levels but do not grow are termed haloduric. Staphylococci will grow in relatively high salt concentrations and are often associated with food poisoning from semi-preserved salted meats.

In preservation the use of salt, with the addition of other chemicals, is termed curing whilst its use for flavour or colouring is termed brining.

### (2) Nitrates and nitrites

Sodium nitrate ($NaNO_3$) and sodium nitrite ($NaNO_2$) are used in curing meat to stabilize red pigmentation and reduce spoilage. They are also essential for use in such products as pasteurized ham to stop the production of botulinum toxin by preventing the germination of spores. Traditionally, salt and nitrate solutions were injected into the meat which was then immersed in the brine solution to enable salt tolerant bacteria to convert nitrate to nitrite. However, the current trend is to use nitrites direct as they are much more effective than nitrates. Unfortunately, nitrites react with amines to form nitrosamines, many of which are said to be carcinogenic. For this reason the levels allowed are strictly controlled. Both nitrates and nitrites gradually disappear during storage and heating.

The effectiveness of curing salts depends on various factors, including the pH of the meat, the number and types of microorganisms present and the curing temperature.

**(3) Sugar**

Sucrose acts in a similar manner to salt but concentrations need to be much higher (approximately six times). Moulds and yeasts are less susceptible than bacteria and can withstand up to 60% of sucrose. Organisms that are able to grow in high concentrations of sugar are designated osmophiles (loving high osmotic pressures) and those that withstand high levels without multiplying are osmoduric. The substitution of sucrose by artificial sweetening agents must be carefully evaluated because of the implications for reduced product stability and increased potential for growth of food pathogens.

This method of preservation is commonly used for jam and other preserves, candied fruit and condensed milk. Certain types of cake have increased shelf-life due to the effect of sugar.

The sugar or salt used for food preservation must be pure and free from contaminants and extraneous matter, for example, sea-salt can often contain a range of mineral substances in addition to sodium chloride.

**(4) Benzoic acid/sodium benzoate**

This chemical occurs naturally in some foods, for example, cranberries. It is used to inhibit the growth of moulds and yeasts in high-acid foods such as fruit juice, pickles and dressings, but is not generally effective in neutral foods. It acts by inhibiting the cellular uptake of amino acids. Excess benzoate can cause an unpleasant burning taste.

**(5) Sulphur dioxide/sulphite**

Sulphur dioxide may be used in gaseous or liquid form or as a salt. It is an antioxidant and also inhibits growth of bacteria and moulds. It is utilized in the dehydration of some foods to prevent enzymatic browning. Sulphur dioxide is used in wine, beers, fruit juice and comminuted meat products including sausages, where it is allowed up to 450 μg/g. Apart from reducing the growth of spoilage organisms, sulphur dioxide also limits the growth of salmonellae.

**(6) Sorbic acid/potassium sorbate**

Like benzoate, sorbate is only effective in acid food. It is particularly effective against moulds and yeasts and it is also reported to inhibit the growth of salmonellae, faecal streptococci and staphylococci but not clostridia. It may be used in hard cheese, as lactic acid bacteria are unaffected. It is also used in bread, jam, syrups and cakes.

**(7) Acetic and lactic acid**

These acids are produced within food by lactic acid bacteria. They preserve by lowering the pH below the normal growth range of most microorganisms, although some yeasts and moulds may be unaffected. Vegetables such as sauerkraut and cucumbers may be placed in brine, to suppress the growth of Gram –ve bacteria, and allowed to undergo fermentation. The natural sugars are converted, by microorganisms, to lactic acid and a prolonged storage of the food is possible.

The pH limit for bacterial growth is around 4.5 for *Cl. perfringens, Cl. botulinum* and *Staphylococcus aureus*; 4.2 for most *Bacillus, Salmonella* and *E. coli,* and below 4.0 for *Lactobacillus*. However, many yeasts and moulds will grow below a pH of 3.0.

*Pickling and acidification*

This process involves introducing the food into an environment with low pH. Thus, pickling of foods is the acidification of the food. The most common acid used for this is a solution of acetic acid, i.e. vinegar. It is essential that the acidification process is controlled so that the pH of each part of the product is as specified and reliably below 4.5, for example, within four hours of a heat process being completed.

**(8) Sodium and calcium propionate**

Propionates are active in low-acid foods and very useful to prohibit mould growth. They are used in bread, cakes, cheese, grain and jellies.

**(9) Antibiotics**

These chemicals have a preservative role in addition to their normal function. Their use is strictly controlled by regulations to avoid the build-up of resistance by pathogenic organisms. An example of an antibiotic is nisin, sometimes used in cheese and canned foods. Nisin is heat resistant but is destroyed in the stomach by trypsin and should not cause problems of pathogen drug resistance.

## PHYSICAL METHODS OF PRESERVATION

### Controlled atmospheres

*Modified atmosphere packaging*

One of the simplest food processing/preservation methods using a physical method is to change the atmosphere around the food. This is termed modified atmosphere packaging (MAP). The air around a product is modified to contain a different proportion of the gases normally present, for example, lower levels of oxygen and higher levels of nitrogen and carbon dioxide and will slow down the growth of many spoilage organisms thus giving an extended shelf-life to the product. MAP should also be combined with correct chilled temperature control in order to further guarantee the control of microbial proliferation. Concentrations of 10% carbon dioxide may be used to keep chilled beef free from spoilage for up to 70 days. Comprehensive guidelines for the good manufacturing and handling of modified atmosphere packed food products have been produced.*

---

*Source: Technical Manual No. 34, 1992. Campden Food and Drink Research Association.

*The restriction of oxygen*

The development of oxidative rancidity and the growth of strict aerobes such as moulds can be prevented by vacuum packing. However, removal of oxygen allows the growth of anaerobes such as *Clostridium perfringens,* and sufficient oxygen normally remains in so-called vacuum packs of meat to facilitate the growth of some aerobes.

Regular sampling shows that vacuum packs of ham are generally no better bacteriologically, and may even be worse, than ham sliced off the bone. Vacuum packs of cooked meat must be stored under refrigeration to achieve a reasonable shelf-life. A vacuum pack of cooked ham with an initial count of $10^2$ organisms per gram will have a count of $10^6$ after 39 days if stored at 2°C; 20 days at 5°C; and seven days at 15°C.

## Smoking

Smoking is used primarily with meat and fish, after brining or pickling, by suspending the food over smouldering hardwoods such as oak and ash which should be free from chemical preservatives. The principle purpose nowadays is to enhance the flavour. The smoking process also has some dehydrating effect and, when properly controlled, there may be some preserving action due to the presence of bactericidal chemicals such as phenols, alcohols and aldehydes which are absorbed by the food. Most non-sporing bacteria will be destroyed but moulds and *Cl. botulinum* type E may survive, especially if there is a low salt concentration. Smoked products should, therefore, always be stored under refrigeration, preferably below 3°C to prevent toxin formation if *Cl. botulinum* is present. Poor control of the process may allow incubation and hence an increase in numbers of spoilage organisms.

Another way of adding a smoke flavour to the food is to use a liquid, produced by trapping smoke in water and spraying this onto the food. The preserving effect of this process is limited and no dehydration of the food takes place.

## Food irradiation

There has been a considerable debate regarding the use of irradiation as a method of food preservation. It involves subjecting the food to a dose of ionizing radiation, for example, gamma rays emitted from an isotope such as cobalt 60. (X-rays with energies up to 5 MeV (million electron volts) or electrons with energies up to 10 MeV could also be used). Several countries irradiate food, and from the scientific studies carried out it seems to present an effective and safe method of extending the shelf-life of food. It destroys parasites, insects and most forms of microbial life thus reducing the risk of food spoilage and food-borne illness. However, microbial spores and toxins remain unaffected. Foods most commonly irradiated include chicken, fish, onions, potatoes, spices and strawberries.

One particular advantage of food irradiation as a food preservation method is that it introduces virtually no temperature rise in the treated product and is often referred to as a "cold pasteurization process". Fish, fruits and vegetables remain "fresh" and unchanged. Irradiation of packaged food is possible and may be particularly important in areas where hygiene is difficult to maintain or control. Frozen food can be treated but higher doses are required. However, irradiation must never be considered as a substitute for good hygiene practices.

The dose of irradiation used (which is measured in Grays or kiloGrays) is a measure of absorbed energy by the food. One Gray (Gy) is equivalent to one joule per kilogram. (1 Gray =100 rads.) It should be noted that doses of around 5 Gy can be lethal to man.

Spores are least sensitive to radiation, then viruses, Gram +ve bacteria and moulds with Gram –ve bacteria being the most sensitive. Type E botulinum spores have survived the irradiation of fish and produced toxin more rapidly than those in non-irradiated fish.

Food irradiation as a method of preservation has the same limitations as many other food preservation technologies. Vitamins may be destroyed and enzymes are not deactivated. Other disadvantages include the encouragement of oxidative rancidity in fatty foods, the possible production of free radicals in food that stimulate a range of chemical reactions and the softening of some fruit.

The dose of irradiation received varies throughout the product depending on thickness, orientation and packaging. It is important to ensure that the minimum dose necessary to achieve the end result is delivered to all parts of the food but that the maximum average dose of 10 kGy is not exceeded in order to limit the adverse effects.

**TABLE XXIV** DOSE RANGES NEEDED FOR EFFECTIVE TREATMENT

| | kGy |
|---|---|
| Inhibition of sprouting in onions and potatoes | 0.03-0.1 |
| Sterilization of insects and parasites | 0.03-0.2 |
| Killing insects and parasites | 0.05-5.0 |
| Reduction by $10^6$ of vegetative bacteria | 1-10 |
| Complete sterilization of food (would result in unacceptable off-odours and flavours together with a cooked texture) | 20-40 |

As regards the acceptability of the food irradiation process, the following matters need to be considered:

*Production of toxic agents*

Irradiation of food will result in some chemical reactions in the food but it seems no toxigenic compounds have been demonstrated in treated foods.

*Possible carcinogenicity*

There is no real proof that food that has been irradiated shows any carcinogenic activity.

*Induced radioactivity*

Only at very high doses could the food become radioactive. At the levels used for food processing there is no danger of the food developing radioactivity.

*Nutritional quality*

The changes produced in the nutrient content of food will depend on many factors including the type of food, the radiation dose and the processing temperature. Generally, vitamins A and E are the most susceptible to irradiation damage.

*Microbiological interactions*

A high dose of irradiation sufficient to achieve commercial sterility should cause no health problems, however, at lower dose levels when some microorganisms survive, problems may arise. An increase in radiation-resistant organisms will occur but normally only on repeated exposure to irradiation.

A second problem in the use of sub-lethal treatments is that they might result in shifts in microbial flora and the possibility of spoilage being unrecognized through odour before toxin levels reach dangerous levels. In practice this does not seem to occur and irradiated foods appear to follow the normal spoilage pattern.

At the dose level proposed, irradiation could be used to:

(1) destroy a percentage of spoilage and pathogenic bacteria on food;
(2) control mould growth particularly on soft fruits such as strawberries;
(3) disinfest fruit and grain;
(4) inhibit the sprouting of potatoes, onions or garlic;
(5) inactivate parasites such as *Trichinella spiralis*; and
(6) delay the ripening of fruit.

Although the shelf-life of food is prolonged, some bacteria survive and irradiated food must be handled hygienically and stored at correct temperatures. Irradiation cannot replace refrigeration.

The main disadvantages claimed by opponents of irradiation include:

(1) inadequate information exists to assess the long-term effects of consuming irradiated food;
(2) some reduction in the nutritional value of food, particularly vitamin loss;
(3) the absence of a test to ascertain whether food has been subjected to irradiation;
(4) the production of undesirable flavour changes in some foods, for example, eggs and some dairy products;
(5) food of poor bacteriological quality and shelf-life may be irradiated to disguise this fact;
(6) hygiene standards will be reduced as some manufacturers will rely on irradiation to produce an acceptable final product;
(7) spoilage bacteria are more easily destroyed than pathogens and reducing competition may allow more prolific growth of pathogens in certain circumstances; and
(8) more dangerous mutants of pathogens may be formed.

The Food (Control of Irradiation) Regulations, 1990 authorized the irradiation of food in the UK, subject to licensing controls on treatment facilities administered by

Central Government. The Food Labelling (Amendment) (Irradiated Food) Regulations, 1990 require food which has been irradiated to be so labelled.

In 1992 MAFF renewed the licence to Isotron PLC which allows the irradiation of a seasoning blend to a maximum overall average dose of 10 kGy.

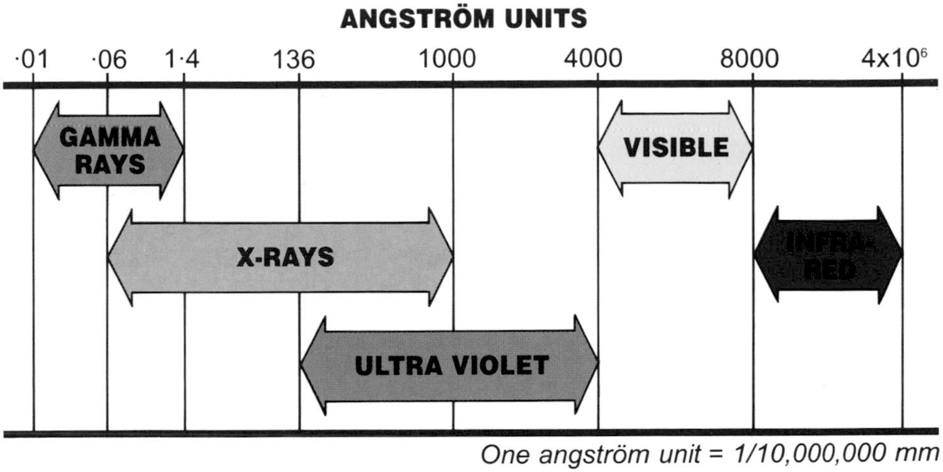


**Fig. 24.** Part of the electromagnetic spectrum of interest to the food industry.

CHAPTER 9

# *Personal hygiene*

Food handlers have a moral and legal responsibility to ensure that food poisoning organisms and other contaminants are not introduced into food, by a failure to observe basic principles of good personal hygiene. Food handlers should be in good health and have clean habits to prevent the direct contamination of food. They should show a willingness to learn to prevent the indirect contamination of, and the multiplication of bacteria within, food. Good eyesight and the ability to read are essential attributes of food handlers who must check thermometers, instructions on chemicals, date coding and the spoilage of food (colour changes). Dirty staff exhibiting unhygienic practices will increase the risk of food poisoning and hasten a decline in business and reputation.

All visitors to food premises should observe the same hygiene rules and wear the same protective clothing as employees engaged in the handling of food. Potential customers will be impressed by strict adherence to Company rules.

## STAFF SELECTION

The foundations of high standards of hygiene are built by the employment of the right calibre of staff and the provision of satisfactory training. The first stage in successful recruitment is the formulation of job specifications and descriptions which clearly define the level of responsibility and skill required. A reasonable salary commensurate with these requirements must then be offered. The following points should be considered when interviewing and appointing staff.

### Personal appearance and attitude

Food handlers must have:

(1) a clean, neat and tidy appearance;
(2) an absence of skin infections;
(3) good dental hygiene;
(4) clean hands with short finger nails and no evidence of nailbiting;
(5) an absence of excessive personal jewellery or make up;
(6) clean shoes, suitable for the work area; and
(7) a belief in the need for hygiene.

Persons who cannot take the trouble to present a good appearance at interviews will not respond to hygiene disciplines imposed in the food environment.They should show enthusiasm and have a suitable attitude relevant to the position for which they are applying. Hygiene awareness and/or a recognized qualification is also advantageous.

**Medical screening**

It is advisable to ascertain some details of an applicant's medical history, particularly relating to food-borne illnesses, food poisoning or persistent diarrhoea. Applicants should have to complete a medical questionnaire (see Appendix II) and preferably be interviewed by a doctor or nurse. When necessary, persons should be asked to submit a faecal or blood specimen, although this is not normally recommended for routine screening of all applicants. Chest X-rays may also be required.

## POST APPOINTMENT

**The role of management**

Before any staff are allowed to commence work they should be advised, in writing, of their personal obligations in respect of hygiene. They should be informed of the training they will be expected to undertake, including attendance on courses. It should be made clear that a breach of hygiene rules could result in disciplinary action. It is particularly important to stress that they have a legal obligation to notify their supervisor if they are suffering from any condition which exposes food to risk. Food handlers should be aware that if they are suspected of having, or have been in, close contact with a person who has had food poisoning, they will be expected to co-operate by providing faecal specimens. Interference with the personal freedom of the individual is likely to arouse resistance and possibly resentment, unless staff appreciate the reasons for particular restrictions.

After attending hygiene courses, food handlers must be encouraged and allowed to practise what they have been taught. Effective instruction, supervision and competency based testing will be essential to maintain high standards of hygiene. Refresher courses are important to keep staff up to date and to reinforce the need for high standards.

Management must lead by example and provide a hygienic working environment together with adequate resources to facilitate the achievement of high standards, for example, suitable and sufficient protective clothing, constant replenishment of liquid soap, paper towels and cleaning materials with adequate cleaning time. For example, a wash-hand basin at the entrance of food rooms, together with close supervision, is the best way of ensuring staff always wash their hands before handling food.

**Clean hands**

Hands are one of the principal agents in transferring pathogens to food, and handling should be reduced to the minimum. Fingernails should be kept short and clean. Nail varnish should not be used.

Bacteriological examination of the hands of food operatives often demonstrates the presence of a large number of potentially harmful organisms generally originating from contaminated foodstuffs. Consequently when there is no satisfactory alternative and food must be handled, regular and thorough hand washing is essential. It is particularly important that hands are washed on entering a food room before handling food or equipment, after visiting the W.C., in between handling raw and cooked food, after handling waste food and as frequently as necessary during the day.

Hands should be washed in hot water (45°C to 49°C) with a suitable non-perfumed liquid/gel/foam soap stored in a wall-mounted dispenser. Recent models have a cartridge replacement reservoir which avoids contamination that can arise from topping-up. Liquid soap is preferable to the communal tablet but whichever product is chosen, it must not cause skin irritation and should not have any residual odour which may discourage its use or taint food.

Effective means of hand drying must be provided and the choice is considerable. Disposable paper towels, warm air and linen cabinet towels are all used successfully but each has its drawbacks. Paper towels and properly separated and maintained cabinet towels have the greater drying efficiency but paper towels require a disposal bin for collection of soiled wipes. Some warm air units are too slow, hands may remain bacteriologically contaminated and operatives may resort to drying their hands on their overalls. It is recommended that one warm air drier be provided for every two wash-hand basins. The cabinet towel is frequently seen trailing on the floor midway through the day because of the difficulty in deciding exactly when it should be replaced by a new towel. If used, two separate compartments must be present in the cabinet to avoid the contamination of unused towels. Charges made by servicing companies vary considerably. A cabinet towel usually allows up to 200 pulls, although many users prefer two pulls.

When selecting a hand-drying system the following points should be considered:

(1) hygiene and safety factors including ease of cleaning;
(2) the cost of purchase (or rental) and installation;
(3) the cost of servicing and maintenance;
(4) the efficiency and speed of the system;
(5) the ease, reliability and standard of service;
(6) the cost of electricity and paper towels (including disposal costs of waste paper);
(7) the control that can be exercised to prevent abuse, vandalism and pilferage; and
(8) the risk of product contamination from paper.

Notices requesting persons to wash their hands on entering the food rooms should be displayed adjacent to the entrance and notices requesting hand washing should be prominently displayed in the sanitary accommodation.

*Nailbrushes*

Nailbrushes are a vehicle of contamination and they should be cleaned and disinfected frequently and at the end of each day. After soaking in a suitable disinfectant, for the correct contact time, they should be removed and allowed to dry. Alternatively, they should be boiled. Disposable or plastic nailbrushes with nylon bristles are recommended.

### Cuts, boils, septic spots and skin infections

Employees with boils and septic cuts should be excluded from food handling areas, as such lesions contain *Staphylococcus aureus*. Uninfected wounds should be completely protected by a conspicuously coloured waterproof dressing. Cuts on hands may need the extra protection of waterproof fingerstalls. Waterproof dressings are necessary to prevent blood and bacteria from the cut contaminating the food and also to prevent bacteria from food, especially raw meat or fish, making the cut septic. Furthermore, waterproof dressings do not collect grease and dirt. It is preferable that green or blue-coloured detectable plasters be used, to improve their visibility in food should they become detached. Metal strips incorporated in dressings assist detection where metal detectors are in use. Loss of dressings must be reported immediately. Perforated plasters are not recommended. Staff who report for work wearing unacceptable dressings must have them changed before they enter a food room or commence food handling duties.

### The hair

Hair is constantly falling out and, along with dandruff, can result in contamination of food. As the scalp often contains pathogenic organisms such as *Staphylococcus aureus,* steps must be taken to prevent contamination from this source. The hair should be shampooed regularly and completely enclosed by suitable head covering. Hairnets (blue) worn under turbans, helmets and hats are recommended. Combing of hair and adjustment of head covering should only take place in cloakrooms and should not be carried out whilst wearing protective clothing, as hairs may end up on the shoulders and then in the product. Hairgrips and clips must not be worn. After having a haircut staff should wash their hair before handling food or working in food rooms.

### The nose, mouth and ears

Up to 40% of adults carry *Staphylococcus aureus* in the nose and 15% on their hands. Coughs and sneezes can carry droplet infection for a considerable distance and persons with bad colds should not handle open food. The hands should be washed after blowing the nose and soiled handkerchiefs should not be used; single-use paper handkerchiefs are preferable. The mouth is also likely to harbour staphylococci and food handlers should not eat sweets whilst working.

Apart from being aesthetically unacceptable, spitting can result in food contamination from staphylococci or streptococci and is illegal.

### Smoking

Smoking must be prohibited in rooms containing open food or whilst handling open food. This is not only because ash or cigarette ends may find their way into open food but also because:

(1) it encourages coughing;
(2) it may result in an unsatisfactory working atmosphere for non-smokers;
(3) of the risk of contaminating food from fingers touching the lips while smoking;

(4) cigarette ends, contaminated with saliva, are placed on work benches.

Legible notices must be clearly displayed, emphasizing the requirement not to smoke in food rooms.

## Protective clothing

All food handlers should wear clean, washable (withstand up to 85°C), light-coloured, durable protective clothing, without external pockets. Protective garments should be appropriate for the work being carried out, should completely cover ordinary clothing and should not be removed whilst food handling. Jumper and shirt sleeves must not protrude and if short-sleeved overalls are worn, only clean forearms must be visible. Press studs are preferred to buttons as they are less likely to become detached. Clean overalls must be available as needed and stored away from contaminants. New products and practices require a reappraisal of protective clothing provided.

Staff must be aware that protective clothing is worn primarily to protect the food from risk of contamination and not to keep their own clothes clean. Dust, pet hairs and woollen fibres are just a few of the contaminants carried on ordinary clothing. Protective clothing must not be worn outside food premises or for travelling to and from work. When selecting protective clothing the manager must consider:

(1) the duties of the wearer and which parts of the body should be covered;
(2) how the garments are fastened;
(3) the colour and type of material;
(4) the smartness and fit (to improve customer image and generate pride in the wearer); and
(5) whether to purchase or use a laundry rental service.

**Fig. 25.** All food handlers must wear the appropriate protective clothing. (Courtesy of Foster Refrigerator (U.K.) Ltd.)

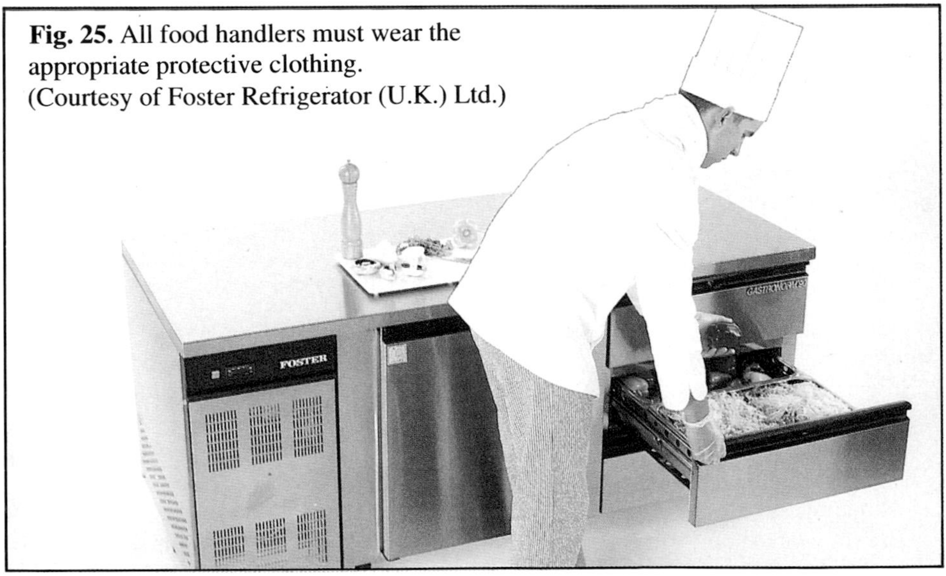

Outdoor clothing and personal effects must not be brought into food rooms, unless stored in suitable lockers. Lockers should be adequately ventilated to keep them dry, eliminate odours and prevent mould growth. Cloakrooms, which are well-ventilated and cleaned regularly, are preferred.

Aprons, if worn, should be suitable for the particular operation, blue (to aid detection if damaged) and capable of being thoroughly cleansed. Disposable aprons (blue) may be obtained and should be disposed of after each use. When used in factories, aprons are normally impervious. Aprons which are torn or have badly worn surfaces, which render them incapable of being cleaned, should be discarded. Facilities should be provided for cleaning aprons at various times during production and at the end of each working day. Cleansable hooks should also be provided for hanging up clean aprons.

Boots may be provided for wearing in wet areas. They should be anti-slip, unlined and easy to clean. Suitable facilities should be provided for cleaning, and storing cleaned boots.

Rubber gloves may be worn for various jobs, for example, on inspection belts in factories or for cleaning operations. Gloves should be maintained in a clean condition and torn gloves should be discarded. If in contact with food, gloves should be of a different colour so that any detached pieces can be easily detected. After use, gloves should be thoroughly cleaned and dried. Only plain, unperfumed talc should be provided for use with gloves. The inside of gloves provides a warm, moist environment ideal for the multiplication of bacteria and, gloves should not be left on food contact surfaces during, for example, breaks.

Thin, disposable gloves are being used more frequently by food handlers in both catering and retailing, to prevent the hands coming into direct contact with high-risk foods, particularly cooked meat, for example, when using a gravity feed slicing machine. The use of these gloves, disposed of at breaks, is probably more effective in reducing the contamination of high-risk food than the use of a hand disinfectant. The hands should be thoroughly washed before putting on the gloves.

**Jewellery and perfume**

Food handlers should not wear earrings, watches, jewelled rings or brooches which harbour dirt and bacteria. Furthermore, stones and small pieces of metal may end up in the food and result in a customer complaint. Strong-smelling perfume or aftershave should not be worn by food handlers as they may taint foods, especially food with a high fat content.

**Practices**

Bad habits are not easily broken and if they are exhibited by a food handler, and present a risk of contaminating food, careful and conscientious control is required. Common bad habits include:

(1) wetting fingers to open bags or to pick up sheets of wrapping paper;
(2) picking the nose;
(3) scratching the head or spots;

(4) tasting food with an unwashed spoon;
(5) coughing and sneezing on to hands and handling food without first washing;
(6) using a food sink for hand washing;
(7) using a wash-hand basin to rinse utensils;
(8) handling the inner parts of crockery or glasses; and
(9) chewing gum, eating food or sweets in food rooms other than dining areas.

Managers must ensure that staff are not only familiar with the do's and don'ts of food hygiene but that they are always observed.

**Exclusion of food handlers**

Management should be aware that even with the strictest application of health standards, a healthy, symptom-free employee may be excreting pathogenic bacteria or viruses. Furthermore, laboratory tests cannot be relied on to detect small numbers of pathogens even though they are being excreted. Consequently, it must be emphasized that high standards of hygiene are essential to prevent the contamination of food rather than a laboratory report, indicating the absence of pathogens from a faecal specimen. Because absenteeism is undesirable and continuous attendance is appreciated by management, staff must be well-motivated to report ailments which they believe may result in a salary reduction or even a loss of their job. All such reports should be noted on medical records.

Warm, wet cans, post retorting are extremely susceptible to contamination if handled and consequently, the following guidelines should be applied to post processing staff in canneries and similar factories. Furthermore, they should be applied to engineers, maintenance workers and cleaners if they could expose food to risk of contamination.

Food handlers with food poisoning symptoms, i.e. diarrhoea/vomiting, or suspected of carrying food poisoning organisms, for example, because of close contact with a confirmed case or consuming a meal known to have caused illness, should be excluded from any job which would expose food to risk of contamination. Persons who are subsequently confirmed as excreting food poisoning organisms must not be allowed to engage in food handling, until they have been symptom free for 48 hours, once any treatment has ceased, and they present no risk to food safety.

Persons returning from holidays abroad, particularly from countries with warm climates and suspect sanitation, should complete a short medical questionnaire. Even if they have recovered from symptoms of diarrhoea or vomiting experienced on holiday, they should be excluded from food handling until they have provided at least one negative faecal specimen.

Persons suspected of suffering from food poisoning, typhoid, paratyphoid or dysentery can be excluded from food handling by the Local Authority and compensation paid to cover loss of wages. Several other conditions such as eczema and psoriasis which are often associated with secondary infection; boils and septic cuts; respiratory tract infections from heavy colds to chronic bronchitis; infection of the eyes; recurrent discharge from the ears and dental sepsis or purulent gingivitis may also require the suspension of food handlers until successfully treated.

**TABLE XXV** EXCLUSION OF FOOD HANDLERS FROM NORMAL DUTIES
(Recommendations of the PHLS Salmonella Sub-committee 1995)

| | **Criteria for clearance to return to work** | |
|---|---|---|
| | **Case when symptom-free** | **Symptomless contact** |
| *Aeromonas spp.*<br>*Bacillus spp.*<br>*Campylobacter spp.*<br>*Clostridium perfringens*<br>*Cryptosporidium spp.*<br>*Escherichia coli* (not VTEC)<br>*Salmonella spp.* (excluding typhoid & paratyphoid<br>*Vibrio parahaemolyticus*<br>Viral gastroenteritis<br>*Yersinia spp.* | 48 hours after first normal stool providing adequate hygiene is practised | None |
| *Staphylococcus aureus* | Septic lesion treated & healed | None |
| *Shigella spp.* | Passing formed stools | None |
| *Clostridium botulinum* | None | Treatment of those at risk |
| *Escherichia coli* (VTEC) | 2 negative specimens | Screen microbiologically |
| Hepatitis A | 7 days after onset of jaundice anNone or symptoms | |
| *Entamoeba histolytica* | 3 negative specimens | Screen microbiologically |
| *Giardia lamblia* | None | Screen microbiologically |
| Typhoid and paratyphoid | 6 consecutive negative stool specimens at 2 weekly intervals starting 2 weeks after the completion of antibiotic therapy | 3 negative consecutive stools at weekly intervals starting 3 weeks after last contact with the case |
| *Taenia solium* and thread worm | Until treated | Until treated |

Faecal specimens should be taken at intervals of not less than 24 hours.

In 1995 guidance from the DH, "Food handlers: Fitness to work", stressed that the greatest risk of pathogenic contamination of food is from persons with diarrhoea and vomiting and that good hygienic practices of food handlers are essential to prevent such contamination. The guidance confirmed the same criteria as above for determining when food handlers should be considered fit to return to work following most gastrointestinal infections, i.e. no diarrhoea or vomiting for 48 hours, once any treatment has ceased and good hygiene, particularly handwashing, is observed.

However, the author believes that managers should also take into account the likely reaction of customers finding out that, for example, salmonella carriers are involved in food preparation. Furthermore, in the event of a food poisoning outbreak, the due-diligence defence may be more difficult to argue, if carriers are employed.

# CHAPTER 10 Training and education of food handlers

Most food poisoning outbreaks are caused by the negligence or ignorance of persons involved in the preparation, storage, distribution or processing of food which results in the introduction of contamination and/or allows the multiplication of large numbers of food poisoning bacteria. The disturbing number of food poisoning incidents and food complaints graphically illustrates the need for a national hygiene education programme aimed at staff and managers employed throughout the food industry, as well as food producers and consumers.

The first essential is for managers to accept their responsibilities with regard to food hygiene and to ensure that food handlers are provided with sufficient knowledge and training to avoid making mistakes that may result in food poisoning or customer complaints. Subsequently, food workers must be motivated and effectively supervised and instructed to ensure this knowledge is put into practice.

## The importance of training

Training should be considered as an investment and evidence is available to show that companies providing high levels of training usually have better growth and profits. Training is necessary to:

(1) enable staff to fulfil their potential by understanding their responsibilities and improving their skills;
(2) promote confidence, increase job satisfaction, improve performance/morale and develop team spirit; and
(3) reduce the amount of supervision required.

## The benefits of hygiene training

Hygiene training of staff should stress the importance of hygiene to the commercial viability of the organization and how a food poisoning incident or serious food complaint is likely to affect them. Such training will contribute significantly to the profitability of a food business by:

(1) assisting in the production of safe food;
(2) safeguarding the quality of the product and reducing food wastage;
(3) reducing complaints;

(4) generating a pride in appearance and practices, increasing job satisfaction and probably reducing staff turnover;
(5) contributing to increased productivity;
(6) ensuring that all the correct procedures, including cleaning, are followed;
(7) complying with any legal provisions or the requirements of Industry Guides or codes of practice;
(8) promoting a good company image which should result in increased business; and
(9) improving the supervisory skills of managers.

The food industry will also benefit by having available a pool of trained food handlers.

## Requirements for effective hygiene training

If training is to be successful, there are five important prerequisites:

(1) the owners of the business must have a genuine commitment to achieving and maintaining high standards of hygiene and this policy must be clearly communicated to staff to engender a positive attitude towards hygiene. Staff must know what is expected of them;
(2) the provision of good working conditions, including lighting, temperature, ventilation and adequate facilities for securing personal hygiene;
(3) the active commitment, support and interest of senior management;
(4) the availability of the necessary finance and organization; and
(5) the availability of suitable expertise in the subject area and the necessary training skills to impart this knowledge.

## Management responsibility

In practice, hygiene standards are controlled by management who must usually accept full responsibility for any problems caused by poor hygiene. In particular, managers should:

(1) communicate the company policy on hygiene to staff and demonstrate full management support for the policy;
(2) lead by example. Managers must wear the appropriate protective clothing, wash their hands on entering a food room and always follow correct procedures; and
(3) appreciate the relationship between hygiene and profit.

## Management knowledge and skills

Managers of high-risk operations must themselves be trained to a level appropriate to their position and should:

(1) be able to prepare and implement a satisfactory food hygiene policy for their company;
(2) know the requirements of legislation relating to their operation;
(3) have a basic understanding of food microbiology and hazard analysis and know how to minimize the risks of food spoilage, food contamination and the multiplication of food poisoning organisms;

(4) have the skill to select staff who have the necessary attributes to become competent food handlers; and

(5) have the knowledge and ability to implement effective control and monitoring procedures at all points in the food business operation which are critical to food safety.

**The legal requirement for training**

Section 16(1) and para 5(3) of schedule 1 of the Food Safety Act, 1990 empower Ministers to make regulations requiring the hygiene training of persons engaged in food businesses. Section 23 of the Act empowers Food Authorities to provide food hygiene training courses for such persons. Chapter 10 of the Food Safety (General Food Hygiene) Regulations, 1995 states "The proprietor of a food business shall ensure that food handlers engaged in the food business are supervised **and** instructed **and/or** trained in food hygiene matters commensurate with their work activity".

The Code of Practice on Food Hygiene Inspections (Code of Practice No. 9) states that the level of training, instruction or supervision of food handlers is a responsibility placed on the food business to determine, having regard to the nature of the business and the role played by food handlers within it, and should be assessed as part of a hazard analysis system. Authorized officers should take into account any relevant UK or EC Industry Guides to Good Hygiene Practice when assessing training levels but it is expected that persons handling high-risk open food will require the level of training equivalent to that contained in the basic or certificate courses accredited by the CIEH, REHIS, RSH, RIPHH, SOFHT or other similar training organizations.

It has also been suggested that food businesses may not successfully utilize the defence of due diligence, provided under section 21 of the Food Safety Act, unless staff are properly trained and adequate records of training are kept.

**The objective of hygiene training**

The main objective of hygiene training is to change the behaviour and attitude of food handlers at work and so minimize the risk of food poisoning and food complaints. To achieve this objective, staff will need to be provided with the knowledge and skills to operate hygienically and then motivated and supervised to ensure that they implement what they have learned. Training should not be undertaken haphazardly but must be carefully planned. The most effective way of undertaking hygiene training is to develop and implement a training programme, the principles of which are applicable to all businesses, although the programme will be less formal for smaller businesses.

## PLANNING AND IMPLEMENTING A TRAINING PROGRAMME

A structured approach to training will enable organizations to obtain the maximum benefits. Managers should consider future skill requirements, identify training objectives and set targets to achieve by specific dates. An appropriate budget allocation will be required. The first step is to determine whether sufficient expertise is available to plan and implement a training programme in-house, although most organizations will probably benefit from the use of experienced hygiene training consultants. Successful training programmes will usually involve the following stages:

**(1) Management of the training programme**

One person should be responsible for the programme and continually monitor its progress and effectiveness. Management support will be essential and regular reports should be made to directors or the proprietor. A hygiene policy statement should be signed by the chairman or proprietor to demonstrate his/her support for, and the commitment of the company to, training and high standards of hygiene. He/she must ensure, as far as practicable, that appropriate managers are appointed and systems established to ensure this policy is implemented.

**(2) Workforce assessment**

The range of tasks and the risk to food safety of each task will need to be established together with the existing level of skill and knowledge of all operatives, including managers, supervisors, cleaners and maintenance staff. (The definition of a food handler suggested by the Catering Industry Guide is "any person in a food business who by his actions, or management, or decision, or advice, can *directly* influence the hygiene of any food handled by that business at any stage".) The academic ability (the ability to assimilate knowledge, study, sit examinations and read and write) and qualifications of each person will need to be determined from personal records or interviews. This will need to be carried out sensitively in the case of staff with literacy problems to avoid possible ridicule.

Assessment must also be made of the hygiene awareness, skill and knowledge of new employees who should not be allowed to work in high-risk situations without appropriate induction training and close supervision. A recognized hygiene qualification is a good indication of hygiene awareness but not a guarantee by itself.

**(3) Establishing a training committee**

A training programme will probably be more successful if the views of the workforce are taken into account and it is not considered to be imposed.

In large organizations it may be beneficial to establish a training committee with representatives from appropriate departments and/or disciplines. Members may include the hygiene training/personnel manager, the production/catering/retail manager, an engineer, a supervisor and a first tier worker. All groups of staff should be given the opportunity to contribute, for example, by questionnaire or through discussion.

The committee will be responsible for considering the information collected and comparing the actual standards of hygiene with the required standards to determine the training needs. Objectives should be determined and targets set for the development and implementation of various parts of the programme. As far as practicable the committee should ensure that the training undertaken is of benefit to individuals and the company as a whole.

**(4) The content of training programmes**

The content of the programme will depend on the shortfall in standards/levels of skill, the time to be allocated and the finance available. These factors will also influence how, when, where and by whom the training will be undertaken. Competence assessment of operatives must be built into the programme at the beginning to ensure it is effective and provides value for money. The following questions will have to be answered:

*(i) Is the training to be provided in-house or are Environmental Health Officers/external consultants to be used?*

To be effective, hygiene training should include:

(a) induction training;
(b) on-the-job training;
(c) attending an appropriate food hygiene session/course; and
(d) refresher training. (Training must be kept up-to-date.)

Trainers must have the ability to educate and motivate and the necessary skill and knowledge to effect a change in behaviour of those persons being trained. In large organizations, managers with training skills who have attended an appropriate advanced hygiene course may be able to provide basic hygiene training specifically designed for the company. However, an external consultant or Environmental Health Officer could also be asked to provide a modified basic hygiene course to suit the requirements of the particular food business. One major advantage of in-house training is that it can be linked with training for hazard analysis and the monitoring of critical points.

*(ii) Who will be trained and to what level?*

Training should start with managers/supervisors who will be responsible for:

(a) formulating hygiene policies;
(b) providing appropriate facilities;
(c) supervising and motivating food handlers;
(d) induction, on-the-job training and assessment;
(e) reinforcing hygiene requirements; and
(f) enforcing hygiene rules.

Most food handlers will require core training which may include:

(a) the company's hygiene policy, confirmation of the company's commitment to hygiene and the consequences of a breakdown in hygiene;
(b) the potential of bacteria to cause illness;
(c) personal health and hygiene, including the legal responsibilities of food handlers;
(d) preventing contamination, including foreign body contamination;
(e) cleaning procedures (when undertaken by food handlers);
(f) food storage(protection and temperature control);

(g) recognition of pests and signs of pests; and
(h) waste disposal.

The actual content of, and requirement for additional, training will depend on the type of food being handled and the risk to food safety posed by the tasks undertaken together with the level of supervision. Organizations with a high turnover of staff will require more emphasis on instruction and supervision, although training should still be provided. The syllabuses of available hygiene courses are outlined in Appendix III.

Training identified as essential, whilst undertaking risk assessment and determining control measures for hazards at points critical to food safety, must be provided.

*(iii) What provision has been made for induction training?*

It is essential that all new starters receive induction training prior to carrying out any high-risk food handling duties. All companies should provide new employees with a basic induction book which confirms the company hygiene policy and details the hygiene rules which they will be expected to follow. Operatives should sign to confirm they have received the book and will follow the hygiene rules contained therein. The booklet could be used as a basis for short induction training sessions which will be necessary to emphasize the dangers of bad hygiene, what is expected of him/her and the consequences for the employee failing to adhere to essential hygiene rules. On-the-job training is critical in developing the correct attitude of new food handlers. Staff must be shown the most hygienic way of performing their job as bad habits, once cultivated, are difficult to break. As well as explaining how to carry out a task, staff must be told the reason for carrying it out in a particular way.

*(iv) What training and examination techniques will be used?*

Most food handlers involved with the preparation of high-risk food will need to attend a formal course of lectures provided by an outside body, consultants or in-house. However, certified courses presented in a classroom style with written examinations may be inappropriate for some operatives and other methods of training designed to improve hygiene standards may be necessary. NVQs and other competence based routes to attaining national food hygiene qualifications are now appropriate for all food operatives. Open learning programmes with workbooks may also be of use in certain circumstances. Testing by the use of projects and assignments relevant to the specific food business is receiving increased support in preference to the theoretical examination of intermediate and advanced courses.

*(v) Have arrangements been made to continually assess the competence of the trained food handlers?*

Increased knowledge, obtained by food handlers attending hygiene courses, may soon disappear. Prior to sending staff on courses a record should be made of their understanding and implementation of hygiene procedures. A further assessment should be made on completion of the course to ensure it provided value for money. In addition competence assessment should be incorporated within the day-to-day role of supervisors to ensure hygiene practices are continually observed and to determine the need for refresher training. Comprehensive systems should be established to record accurately task assessment, standards achieved, courses attended and progress through training of each employee. Staff appraisals can be linked to staff development to determine future training needs.

The following checklist will not be appropriate for every food handler in every situation. It is provided as an example of the level of knowledge that it would be reasonable to expect of some food handlers involved in high-risk operations. It should be used as a framework which can be modified to suit the specific requirements of food handlers depending on the particular food operation.

**TABLE XXVI** CHECKLIST FOR THE ASSESSMENT OF KNOWLEDGE OF FOOD HANDLERS BEFORE AND AFTER ATTENDING APPROPRIATE FOOD HYGIENE TRAINING

Does the food handler know:

- Where to get information on company rules affecting them.
- What conditions prohibit them from working with food.
- What to do in the event of suffering from diarrhoea and/or vomiting.
- What practices are prohibited in a food room.
- What protective clothing should be worn, how it should be put on, when it should be removed, when it should be changed and where to obtain replacements.
- When and how they should wash their hands.
- What first aid dressings must be worn and where they can be obtained.
- How they can contaminate food both microbiologically and physically.
- How they can prevent such contamination.
- Why temperature control is important with regard to the food product they handle/prepare.
- How to handle and deal with waste.
- How to clean to avoid risk to the product.
- Their legal obligations.
- The consequences of food complaints/food poisoning.
- The hazards which they may influence.
- Their responsibilities with regard to hazard control and monitoring of critical control points.
- The procedures for reporting problems and taking corrective action.
- How to complete records satisfactorily.

### (5) Training sessions

When planning a training session it is important to consider the background of the trainees including their age, previous experience, ability, language difficulties and interests. Objectives for the session must be established and, more importantly, achieved. Finally the content must be decided and visual aids selected. Trainees must be encouraged to participate and this may be accomplished by asking questions beginning with the words, how, why, what, when, who, where and which.

There are many ways in which information can be presented and the technique used will, to a large extent, depend on the particular group and number of trainees involved, the objectives of the trainer, the type of information to be presented and the cost-effectiveness of the various techniques. The more common techniques include lectures, talks, job instruction, discussion groups, case studies and counselling on a one-to-one basis. Hygiene committees, similar to safety committees, could be established to discuss ways in which hygiene can be improved and customer complaints reduced.

Whichever type of session is adopted, it should be designed to ensure that the particular group of trainees retain as many important facts as possible. The length of training sessions depends to a large extent on the complexity of the material being presented relative to the ability of the trainees to concentrate and comprehend. However, for the majority of trainees, sessions should be held frequently and kept short and simple.

It is often advantageous to invite visiting lecturers, such as Environmental Health Officers, to reinforce hygiene training, as they usually present a slightly different approach which may stimulate renewed interest, even if it is only to highlight the legal obligations placed upon food handlers. The use of guest lecturers also demonstrates the importance the company places on hygiene training.

*Learning methods*

Hygiene education revolves around some simple but important principles:

if all **I** do is *hear* - **I** will *forget*;
if **I** *hear* and *see* - **I** will *remember*;
if **I** *hear, see* and *do* - **I** will understand.

Understanding helps *remembering* which leads to *learning*.

The first step in training is to motivate the employees to learn. They must appreciate that they could be a vital link in a chain of events leading to food poisoning and that suitable training and education will give them the knowledge to provide safe food.

The second stage in training involves explanation and demonstration to provide knowledge and skill respectively.

The third stage involves the trainee practising the task and the fourth stage should be to test that the task can be performed satisfactorily.

*Communication skills*

To get the message across, the hygiene trainer must take account of factors which interfere with effective communication and these may be considered as factors affecting either the trainer or the trainee.

*Factors affecting the trainer:*

(i) *Voice* - should not be monotonous, too quiet or too loud.
(ii) *Appearance* - should be smart and the trainer suitably dressed.
(iii) *Habits* - should not be distracting, for example, rattling loose change, walking up and down, frequent repetition of words or phrases such as "ok", frequent touching of the hair or face.
(iv) *Eye contact* - should be maintained with as many of the group as is possible. Each trainee should feel that he or she is being addressed.
(v) *Enthusiasm* - should be conveyed to the trainees who must be given the impression that the trainer believes in the importance of what is being said. Questions should be encouraged.
(vi) *Knowledge of the subject* - should be thorough as reasoned arguments are more likely to succeed than dogma.
(vii) *Presentation* - must be at the appropriate level. Trainers must not talk down to people or over their heads. Sessions must be well-planned as disjointed, unrehearsed sessions are not effective.
(viii) *Vocabulary* - must be appropriate. Long difficult speeches, words and jargon will not be appreciated.

*Factors affecting the trainee:*

(i) *Motivation* - are the trainees aware of the importance of the subject and how it affects them either directly or indirectly.
(ii) *Comprehension* - if trainees do not understand what is said they will soon lose interest.
(iii) *Time of day* - large lunches, too much drink or training sessions after a hard day's work may result in student indifference.
(iv) *Design of training room/area* - can everyone see and hear the trainer/visual aids.

**(6) The location and timing of training sessions**

Provided adequate training facilities are available it is usually more cost-effective for training sessions to be organized on the food premises. Most Environmental Health Officers/consultants will undertake on-site basic training. Although six hour basic courses can be completed in a day, improved results may be obtained by organizing sessions of 30 minutes or an hour over several days or weeks. A frequent compromize is 3 x 2 hour or 2 x 3 hour sessions. Advanced courses will usually be organized at training centres, hotels or colleges where appropriate facilities are available to allow use of videos and other hygiene aids as well as any necessary demonstrations.

Training should be undertaken at a time which is convenient to the business operation but also acceptable to the food handlers.

**(7) Visual aids equipment**

Videos, slide and tape packs, hygiene games, films and exhibits such as pests and food complaints are useful to break up training sessions and maintain interest. They are also useful for highlighting actual situations which would be difficult to recreate in a training room. Care must be taken to ensure the information presented does not become dated. Slides and transparencies should be carefully prepared and used to emphasize, clarify or supplement talks. They should be clear and legible to everyone in the audience and not be crammed with too much information. It is better to use two or more transparencies rather than cramming information. Graphs and illustrations are preferable to tables, and dark-coloured backgrounds are more effective. Handwritten scrawl is unacceptable. The number of words should be limited to a maximum of around 40 with adequate spaces between lines.

Slide presentation should be rehearsed to ensure familiarization with sequences. If possible, slides should be loaded into magazines and checked prior to lectures. Remote control operated from a lectern will result in a more professional presentation.

*Overhead projectors*

The main advantage of the overhead projector is that it enables trainers to maintain eye contact with trainees and lectures must not be presented to the screen. The projector should be switched off when positioning or removing transparencies or when not in use - blank screens or the presence of information which is no longer being discussed is distracting. Information on transparencies should be revealed a little at a time, as and when it is relevant.

Trainers should be familiar with equipment and be able to carry out minor repairs such as changing bulbs or fuses. Focusing and volume control should be attended to before trainees assemble. If a room cannot be blacked out, projection should be towards the window rather than away from it.

**(8) Piloting of the programme**

Prior to the introduction of the programme it should be piloted to a cross-section of employees. Close supervision and monitoring is essential to obtain accurate feedback from those trained to enable the programme to be evaluated. Competence assessments following training should be compared with assessments prior to training.

**(9) Implementation of the training programme**

Provided the evaluation of the pilot exercise is satisfactory and any necessary corrective action is approved, the programme may be introduced to all parts of the organization. Consultation with the local Environmental Health Department during the planning and implementation of training may be beneficial.

The programme must be flexible and monitored and evaluated continually to ensure the objectives are being achieved and, if necessary, modifications can be made.

**(10) Evaluation of the programme**

Evaluation of the whole programme and each training session/course is essential. Evaluation of staff, supervisors and managers should be undertaken to determine:

(i) whether objectives have been achieved;

(ii) improvements in practices/skills/standards;
(iii) knowledge retention; and
(iv) further training needs.

Various techniques of evaluation have been used following attendance at training sessions and courses, including:

(i) pre and post course inspections;
(ii) pre and post session interviews to assess knowledge gained;
(iii) pre and post course testing, including practical assessment of competence and written assignments;
(iv) the use of pre and post course questionnaires;
(v) bacteriological swabs taken of hand and food contact surfaces;
(vi) bacteriological food sampling (especially for the presence of indicators); and
(vii) trends in food complaints.

If possible a control group of food handlers who have not attended the course should be compared to ensure that improvements in hygiene resulted from attendance on the course and not, for example, improved supervision or on-the-job training. Managers who have attended advanced hygiene courses could be asked to report on hygiene improvements or achievements implemented three and six months after completing the course.

**(11) Reinforcement of training and staff motivation to ensure that hygiene standards are maintained**

Effective supervision, reinforcement, enforcement and refresher training will be essential to ensure behavioural changes are maintained after attending training sessions. Incentives should be used to encourage high standards. In some countries deterrents have been used to maintain standards, for example, frequent hand swabbing, closed circuit television and fines.

Posters and notices may be used to encourage good practices and to reinforce the legal obligation of the individual. Posters may shock, amuse or instruct and should be prominently positioned and changed as often as necessary to maintain attention. Hygiene displays may be useful and free literature may be available from the local Environmental Health Department.

Small groups of staff participating in hygiene sessions, for example, discussing case studies can stimulate significant interest. External speakers may be brought in to chair such discussions.

Recognition should be given to employees who obtain hygiene qualifications and who operate hygienically. This may take the form of increased remuneration, awards, or perhaps, more importantly, a suitable qualification could become a prerequisite to employment as a food handler.

Many companies use some form of appraisal to determine whether or not supervisors and managers justify receiving larger increases in salary. Hygiene should be included as one of the categories on which this decision is made. Once managers realize that poor hygiene affects their salary, improved standards should be assured.

CHAPTER 11

# The design and construction of food premises

A considerable amount of thought must always be given to the design and construction of food premises, to ensure a cost-effective and hygienic operation. Newly-built premises should comply fully with the requirements of the appropriate hygiene and safety legislation and the elimination of potential hazards and risks should be a key objective. Plans should be discussed with enforcement officers as it is much easier and cheaper to provide satisfactory finishes and facilities such as sanitary accommodation during construction than it is to be told to provide alternative finishes or additional sanitary accommodation when the building is completed.

The use of satisfactory building materials and a well-planned layout is essential to achieve high standards of hygiene. The size of the premises must be adequate to allow efficient operation and the site must be large enough to accommodate possible future expansion.

## Selection of a suitable site

Choosing a suitable site for new food premises is of paramount importance. During the selection procedure, consideration must be given to the provision and availability of services, i.e. electricity and gas, water supply and effluent disposal and the accessibility for delivery and refuse collection. The site should not be liable to flooding or unacceptable contamination from chemicals, dust, odour or pests.

Close proximity of residential properties may cause problems for many food premises, especially factories. Most food businesses generate noise, to a greater or lesser extent, and complaints from nearby properties can be expected, especially if noise is generated before 8am or after 6pm. Shift working, unloading or loading vehicles, extractor fans and refrigerated vehicles parked overnight are just a few examples of commonly occurring complaints. When the site has been selected, and outline planning permission obtained, time and effort must be devoted to the design of the premises.

## General principles of design

Achieving a satisfactory design, which provides a linear workflow and so eliminates cross-contamination, facilitates effective cleaning and can be operated profitably, is far from simple. Full consultation between all involved parties, including architects,

Environmental Health Officers and users is recommended. It should always be borne in mind that an increase in capital expenditure may well result in both increased life of the premises and a reduction in operating and cleaning costs. When designing food premises the following principles should be considered:

(1) cross-contamination should be physically impossible under the proposed working conditions; clean and dirty processes must be separated. Where possible the work areas in large-scale manufacture should be segregated into pre-cook and post-cook, and staff should not be allowed to move from one area to the other. If practicable, a separate area should be provided for de-boxing and unwrapping raw materials, especially when there is a risk of contaminating food with staples, paper, cardboard and string. Accumulations of refuse should not be permitted;

(2) workflow should be continuous and progress in a uniform direction from raw material to finished product. Food should not be kept at ambient temperatures for longer than is absolutely necessary. Distances travelled by raw materials, utensils, food containers, waste food, packaging materials and staff should be minimized;

(3) facilities for personal hygiene and disinfection of small items of equipment should relate to working areas and process risks;

(4) adequate temperature control must be facilitated;

(5) the premises must be capable of being thoroughly cleaned and, if necessary, disinfected at the end of production;

(6) insects, rodents and birds must be denied access;

(7) yard surfaces and roads within the boundary of the premises must have a suitable impervious surface with adequate drainage, and provision made for refuse storage. Facilities for cleaning yards must be provided, for example, a stand-pipe;

(8) suitable provision must be made for staff welfare, including cloakroom and, if necessary, canteen and first aid facilities.

## THE CONSTRUCTION OF FOOD PREMISES

If the design of a food premises establishes the method of operation, the construction and structure determine how easily it can be cleaned. It is essential that the correct materials are chosen for all ceiling, wall and floor finishes and even more important that they are properly fixed or applied. Insufficient attention to fixing generally results in a potentially satisfactory material becoming totally unsuitable and advice should be sought from specialists. Many companies provide a complete package of consultancy, supply and installation. Before a material is selected, the supplier should be requested to provide details of similar premises using the particular product and existing applications should be visited. Whichever surface is chosen it should be kept in good repair and be capable of withstanding the frequent cleaning to which it will be subjected.

### Ceilings

Ceilings may be either solid or suspended. The latter are advantageous as horizontal pipework and services are concealed. Access for inspection, pest control and maintenance must be built in. Structural walkways are often necessary and should always be provided in large premises. Suspended ceilings are normally made of metal lattice incorporating cleansable panels. Aluminium backed and faced fibre-board has proved successful in many food factories. Flush-fitting ventilation grilles should normally be provided.

Solid ceilings give less scope for a hygienic finish, as pipework and ventilation trunking normally protrude. They should be well insulated to avoid condensation and mould growth. Generally, ceilings should be smooth, fire resistant, light-coloured, coved at wall joints and easy to clean. Plasterboard with taped joints, skimmed with plaster and finished with a washable emulsion is common in smaller premises, although in factory areas with little steam, corrugated sheeting treated with suitable anti-fungal paint has proved satisfactory. Special attention must be paid to ceiling finishes above heat and/or steam-producing appliances such as ovens, sinks and retorts.

Ceiling height will vary depending on the type of operations being carried out but should only be high enough to provide satisfactory working conditions and allow the installation of equipment. Maintenance and cleaning is much easier if the ceiling is around 3.5m from the floor.

**Fig. 26.** Examples of unsatisfactory food premises.

## Walls

Smooth, impervious, non-flaking, light-coloured wall surfaces are required. Whichever finish is chosen it must be capable of being thoroughly cleaned and, if necessary, disinfected by the methods employed in the premises. Internal solid walls are preferable to those with cavities which may harbour pests. Crevices and ledges which cause cleaning problems should be eliminated. False panelling must not be used.

Regard must be had to the operations carried out adjacent to the wall, as the surface may need to be resistant to spillages, chemicals, grease, heat and impact. Wall surfaces in use include resin-bonded fibre glass, ceramic-faced blocks, glazed tiles with water-resistant grouting and rubberized paint on hard plaster or sealed brickwork, which is used in some food factories. Some paints incorporate a fungicidal additive but absorbent emulsion paint should not be used on walls.

Galvanized steel, aluminium and stainless steel are used, although they may warp and strain their fixings. In addition, these metals are prone to corrosion and attack by some cleaning chemicals. Plastic sheeting is becoming more popular, although standards and suitability vary considerably. Some sheets can be heat formed to fit corners and angles. Fire resistance of materials must always be considered. Stainless steel splash backs are recommended behind sinks and working surfaces which may be exposed to impact damage.

Wall or floor stops are needed to prevent doors damaging wall surfaces, and wall corners should be protected by non-corrosive metal or PVC angles. Stainless steel angles bedded in mastic with countersunk screw fixings are recommended. Galvanized or stainless steel crash rails should be used if trolleys are likely to damage wall surfaces.

Pipework and ducting should be bracketed at least 150mm from walls to facilitate cleaning. All lagging to pipes must be smooth and impervious. Pipes passing through external walls must be effectively sealed to prevent the ingress of pests.

## Precautions for painting within food premises

(1) Select the correct paint. The paint chosen should:
- (i) adhere firmly so that flaking is minimized;
- (ii) be of low toxicity; the minimum standard should be in compliance with BS 4310: 1968 for low-lead paints;
- (iii) be cleansable; the higher the gloss the better the washability. If vigorous cleaning is used, for example, using hoses, specialist paints will be required;
- (iv) dry rapidly. It may be possible to use a rapid-drying, emulsion-based primer and undercoat system followed by an eggshell. This would allow a two-coat system to be applied within a working day and so minimize production losses.

(2) Cease production during redecoration. This requires careful planning. It may be possible to decorate out of normal production times, for example, at weekends.

(3) Ensure tainting of food does not occur. Solvent vapour may spread to other sections not being decorated and is especially likely to contaminate food rich in fat or oil such as butter.

(4) All fixed equipment must be well-covered.
(5) All paint must be kept in properly marked containers which are not made of glass.
(6) Ensure the contractor is aware of hygiene and safety rules.
(7) On completion of painting ensure that the area is clean, free from odour and painting materials before processing starts.

Further information may be obtained on specialist paints for the food industry and precautions to be taken, by contacting paint manufacturing firms.

### Doors, windows, stairs and platforms

The use of windows in factories is often dispensed with as they take up valuable wall space, and if used for ventilation purposes will allow the entry of insects and dust. If windows are provided they should be fixed on north-facing walls to reduce glare and solar heat gains. Where this is unavoidable solar film will assist in counteracting heat gain. Cleansable, well-fitting fly-screens must, where necessary, be fitted to opening windows.

Windows should be constructed to facilitate cleaning. If present, internal window sills should be sloped to prevent their use as shelves. The design of frames, of both windows and doors, should avoid acute angles. Right-angled joints between frames and walls should be beaded or filled to form continuous surfaces. Architraves should be avoided and reveals tile-surfaced rather than wood carcased. All woodwork should be well-seasoned, properly knotted, stopped, primed and given three coats of polyurethane paint.

Doors should have smooth, non-absorbent surfaces capable of being thoroughly cleaned. They should be tight-fitting and self-closing. Finger-plates are useful where hand contact is expected. Many food factories use polypropylene or toughened rubber doors as they require little maintenance and are easy to keep clean. Clear plastic strips are also used. External doorways should, where necessary, be proofed against the entry of insects, and metal kick-plates should be provided to prevent gnawing by rodents.

Doorways must be large enough to allow for the movement of mobile equipment and possible replacement of fixed equipment. Swing doors which open both ways should be fitted with sight panels. Stairs, ladders and platforms must be capable of being thoroughly cleaned and should not expose food to risk of contamination.

### Floors

When selecting a floor covering, the following criteria should be considered:
(1) the volume and nature of traffic, for example, fork-lifts;
(2) whether the area is wet or dry;
(3) how the area will be cleaned, particularly if steam is used;
(4) what chemical resistance will be necessary;
(5) whether production will need to be curtailed to effect repairs to the floor; and
(6) the type of sub-floor.

To assess the cost-effectiveness of a finish, regard must be had to initial cost, durability, performance and safety. In food premises, floors should be durable, non-absorbent, anti-slip, without crevices and capable of being effectively cleaned. Where appropriate they must be resistant to acids, grease and salts and should slope sufficiently for liquids to drain to trapped gullies; a slope of 1 in 60 is the minimum recommended. The angle between walls and floors should be coved. Regard must be had to the possible odour taint of food during installation or repair. The base of H section vertical girders should be filled with concrete to avoid difficulties in cleaning.

Several types of floor covering may be used. For example, epoxy resin, granolithic (concrete incorporating granite chippings), welded anti-slip, vinyl sheet and slip-resistant ceramic or quarry tiles. Wooden floors are unacceptable. Whichever type of floor covering is chosen, it must be laid in accordance with the manufacturer's recommendations. Special attention must be paid to the jointing of quarry tiles and the sub-floor must be very smooth if anti-slip, vinyl sheeting is laid. If concrete is used, it must be steel-float finished and sealed with, for example, an epoxy sealant, to ensure that it is dust free.

**Fig. 27.** Altro Whiterock walls and ceilings and Altro Designer 25 safety flooring (Courtesy of Altro Floors.)

**Services**

These include gas, electricity, water supplies, drainage, lighting and ventilation. Proper provision of services is essential to the hygienic and effective functioning of all food businesses.

**Gas supplies**

Specific hygiene implications are covered by more general safety and equipment fixing requirements. Supply pipes should always be mounted clear of the floor and never so close to other pipes as to restrict access for cleaning. Flexible connections are recommended.

**Electrical supplies**

Adequate numbers of power points should be available for all electrical equipment, without the use of adaptors or the need for lengthy flexes. Provision should be made for maintenance, repair and cleaning operations. Cut-out switches for power circuits should be accessible and separate from lighting and ventilation supplies, so that cleaning can take place in safety. Separate cut-out switches should be provided for refrigeration equipment.

Controls should be fixed clear of equipment to avoid becoming dirty or wet during cleaning. Removable electrical components are advantageous. Electrical wiring should be protected by waterproof conduits. All switches should be flush-fitting and waterproof (especially in production areas).

**Water supplies**

All cold water supplies used for washing, or addition to food, should be mains supplied and not fed via an intermediate tank unless chlorinated. Hot water should be supplied to every sink, regardless of the intended use, with a target water discharge temperature of 60°C. In hard-water areas, hot water supplies should be softened, otherwise scale build-up will cause cleaning and operational problems and add significantly to detergent usage. An external water supply for flushing refuse areas and loading bays should always be available.

**Drainage**

Premises should have an efficient, smooth-bore drainage system which must be kept clean and in good order and repair. Drains and sewers should be adequate to remove peak loads quickly without flooding. Sufficient drains should be installed to facilitate effective cleaning of rooms by pressure jet cleaners or other means.

Shallow, glazed, half-round floor channels within food rooms are best left uncovered, provided that they are not a safety hazard. If covers are necessary, these should be non-corrosive, continuous, of suitable strength and easily removed for cleaning. In certain circumstances trapped gullies are preferable.

To avoid fat solidifying and causing blockages, drainage systems must be well designed and constructed, with the minimum number of bends and have an efficient self-cleaning velocity. Cleaning and flushing, at least six monthly, is essential. Grease traps, if fitted, should be large enough to allow adequate time for fat to separate. They should be emptied as frequently as necessary and, as the contents are foul-smelling and obnoxious, traps should be positioned outside food rooms.

Inspection chambers should be placed outside food rooms but if interior location is unavoidable they must be airtight. Manhole covers should be double sealed, bedded in silicon grease and screwed down with brass screws. All drainage systems must be provided with sufficient access points to allow rodding in the event of blockages. Petrol interceptors may be required for yard drains.

Items of machinery such as potato peelers and dishwashers connected directly into the drainage system, should be trapped to avoid waste pipes acting as vents for sewers. Waste pipes to fittings should be plastic, screw or push-fit connections to enable easy dismantling in case of blockage.

Drains should be constructed to inhibit the harbourage and movement of vermin. Defective drains may result in effluent, foul odours and rodents entering food rooms. They must be repaired as quickly as possible. All external rainwater fall-pipes should be fitted with balloon guards to prevent rodent access. Circumference guards should be fitted around all vertical pipes fastened to walls, to prevent rodents climbing up them. Waste pipes exposed to constant high temperatures should be constructed of Alkathene. Foul drains passing through kitchens should be British Standard cast iron. Systems conforming to building regulation standards will normally be hygienic.

**Ventilation**

Suitable and sufficient ventilation must be provided to produce satisfactory working conditions and to reduce humidities and temperatures which would assist the rapid multiplication of bacteria. The ventilation system, which should always flow from a clean to a dirty area, must prevent excessive heat, condensation, dust, steam and remove odours and contaminated air. The air from kitchens should not be drawn into storage or dining areas. Good ventilation will assist in reducing grease and staining of ceilings, so reducing the need for frequent decoration.

When planning a ventilation system, expert advice should be sought to ensure that food rooms will all have the recommended number of air changes, for example, in kitchens, 10 to 20 changes per hour. Plenum and extract systems may be necessary to obtain the recommended air change and deal with high temperatures. Inlets must be suitably filtered to prevent dust, dirt and insects being brought into the food room. The input capacity should be approximately 85% of the rated extract capacity to ensure a slight positive pressure and eliminate draughts. Natural ventilation through screened windows normally needs supplementing by mechanical ventilation to ensure effective air circulation. If windows are positioned without regard to the shape of the room, they may cause short-circuiting and so leave certain areas of the room effectively unventilated.

Ducting should be as short as possible with man-sized access points at three metre intervals to facilitate cleaning. Fan motors should be located outside the kitchen otherwise the noise produced may result in staff switching them off. Fans should be of a low-noise type but silencing may result in cleaning difficulty and fire risk.

Steam-producing equipment such as cookers, boilers and blanchers should be provided with adequately-sized canopies constructed of anodized aluminium or other suitable material. A satisfactory fan ducted to the atmosphere in a manner which does not cause a nuisance to neighbouring properties should be provided. Filters, if fitted, should be cleaned frequently to eliminate fire hazards and maintain efficiency. Drainage gutters at the base of canopies should be provided to collect condensate. Self-cleaning ducting arrangements can be provided as an alternative to filters.

Much of the equipment used in food rooms, especially for heat processing and cooking, emits radiant heat which is not directly affected by air flow. Provision of lower heat-emitting equipment such as pressure vessels and microwave ovens, and upgrading insulation on ovens should be considered to reduce heat production.

*Workroom temperature where food is handled*

Generally, food hygiene law regulates food temperatures, and health and safety law regulates air temperature. However, health and safety requirements can usually be met by:

(1) maintaining a "reasonable" temperature of 16°C (13°C if work involves serious physical effort); or if this is not practical
(2) providing a warm work station; or if this is not practical
(3) providing suitable protective clothing, suitable heated rest facilities and minimizing the time in uncomfortable temperatures.

*Hygiene of ventilation and water systems*

Clean air and safe water are vital for a pleasant working environment and hygienic food production, and failure to carry out routine maintenance and cleaning of ductwork, pipes and cooling towers can result in increased risk of infection. The Sick Building Syndrome, involving a dry throat, sore eyes, dry nose and drowsiness, and Humidifier Fever, involving raised temperature, respiratory problems, headaches and lethargy, may be partly caused by poor temperature and poor humidity control from a badly-maintained and dirty air conditioning system.

Water in cooling towers for industrial processes and air conditioning systems is often contaminated with legionella bacteria. This organism develops in neglected water and air conditioning systems and is spread by aerosols, for example, from showers and cooling towers. Poorly-maintained water systems result in a build-up of slime and dirt which support many bacteria and algae and can result in product contamination. Furthermore, biocides and corrosion inhibitors work more effectively in clean systems.

Those organizations without the necessary equipment or in-house experience should consider employing a reputable contractor to carry out regular surveys and maintenance. Filters, header tanks, cooling tower sumps, packing and drift eliminators, overflows and plant rooms should be cleaned and, where necessary, disinfected. Ventilation ducts should be cleaned to remove accumulated dust and debris, birds, mites and insects. Such servicing enables water treatment programmes to operate efficiently, reduces the risk of infection, prolongs the life of pipes and reduces the risk of fire in ducting.

**Fig. 28.** Rentokil's Watersafe Service. Sampling a header tank for harmful bacteria.

**Fig. 29.** Monitoring the level of chlorination in a water supply system.

**Lighting**

Suitable and sufficient lighting must be provided throughout food premises, including store rooms, passageways and stairways. High standards of lighting will produce an environment conducive to clean and safe working without eye strain. Other advantages include the enhanced appearance of food in service and retail areas together with the fact that insects and rodents generally shun well-lit areas.

Artificial lighting is often preferred to natural lighting because of problems of solar heat gain, glare, shadows, and insects entering open windows. Fluorescent tubes, fitted with diffusers to prevent glare and product contamination in the event of breakage, are recommended. Suspended ceilings can incorporate flush light fittings which are also satisfactory but in certain premises, particularly bakehouses, panel lights incorporated into the ceiling may buckle due to excessive heat.

Standards of lighting for specific interiors and activities are provided in the Chartered Institution of Building Services Code, 1984 and these should be the minimum standards maintained. As a general guide, in areas where decoration is bright and ceiling heights do not exceed three metres, 20 watts from a fluorescent fitting per square metre of floor space will give 400 lux.

**Washing facilities**

Adequate facilities for hand washing and drying should be provided wherever the process demands. In particular, a suitable number of basins or troughs should be sited at the entrance of food rooms to ensure all persons entering wash their hands. Wash-hand basins must be easily accessible and should not be obstructed. They must be kept clean and maintained in good condition. Non-hand operated, spray taps providing warm water at 49°C are essential to minimize the risk of cross-contamination. A minimum of two wash-hand basins should usually be fitted in premises where both raw and high-risk foods are handled. Washing facilities provided in food rooms should be additional to those used in conjunction with sanitary accommodation. All basins and troughs, preferably made of stainless steel, should be connected to drains by properly trapped waste pipes.

**Cleaning and disinfection facilities**

Where appropriate, adequate facilities for the cleaning and disinfection of utensils and equipment should be provided. These facilities should be constructed of corrosion-resistant materials, normally stainless steel, capable of being easily cleaned. If sinks are used these should be provided with adequate supplies of hot and cold water. Taps should be wall-mounted with no direct connection to the sinks. Waste pipes should be plastic push-fit ware. The sink itself should be freestanding so that it can be removed easily after unscrewing the lower trap joint and easing free the waste pipe. "Sterilizing" sinks and units should be capable of operating at 82°C, as should the rinse cycle of dishwashing and tray-cleaning machines. It is recommended that if any of the above are positioned against the wall, a suitable stainless steel upstand of 450mm, or a splashback, be provided. If glasswashers are used they should clean and disinfect.

**Sanitary conveniences, washing facilities and cloakrooms**

All new premises should be provided with adequate staff sanitary accommodation in accordance with the Workplace (Health, Safety and Welfare) Regulations, 1992 and the approved Code of Practice and Guidance L24. Suitable and sufficient sanitary conveniences must be provided at readily accessible places, in adequately ventilated and lit rooms which are kept clean and tidy. Rooms containing sanitary conveniences must not communicate directly with a room where food is processed, prepared or eaten. Internal wall and floor surfaces should permit wet cleaning.

Foot-operated flushing devices are recommended. Doors to intervening spaces and sanitary accommodation should be self-closing and clearly illustrate the sex of the user. A notice requesting users of the W.C. to wash their hands before leaving should be conspicuously displayed in the sanitary accommodation. Suitable and sufficient washing facilities must be provided at readily accessible places. In particular, facilities must be provided in the immediate vicinity of every sanitary convenience and supplied with clean hot and cold or warm water, liquid soap and appropriate drying facilities. Rooms must be sufficiently ventilated and lit, and kept clean and tidy.

**Cloakrooms**

Adequate accommodation for outdoor clothing and footwear, not worn by the staff during normal working hours, must be available. Such articles must not be stored in a food room unless in suitable cupboards or lockers provided only for this purpose.

Adequate facilities for drying wet clothing should also be provided. Cloakrooms must be kept clean and tidy and food scraps should not be allowed to accumulate under benches and behind lockers as this may result in cockroach or rodent infestations.

**TABLE XXVII** STAFF SANITARY CONVENIENCES AND WASH STATIONS

| Males or females at work | | | Alternative, males only | | |
|---|---|---|---|---|---|
| Males/Females | W.C.s | Washstations | Males | W.C.s | Urinals |
| 1 - 5 | 1 | 1 | 1 - 15 | 1 | 1 |
| | | | 16 - 30 | 2 | 1 |
| 6 - 25 | 2 | 2 | 31 - 45 | 2 | 2 |
| 26 - 50 | 3 | 3 | 46 - 60 | 3 | 2 |
| 51 - 75 | 4 | 4 | 61 - 75 | 3 | 3 |
| | | | 76 - 90 | 4 | 3 |
| 76 - 100 | 5 | 5 | 91 - 100 | 4 | 4 |
| Each additional 25 or fraction of 25 | 1 | 1 | Each additional 50 or fraction of 50 | 1 | 1 |

**Public sanitary accommodation**

Section 20 of The Local Government (Miscellaneous Provisions) Act, 1976 enables a local authority to require the provision of sanitary appliances at places of entertainment and places selling food or drink to the public for consumption on the premises. The number of sanitary appliances is not stipulated in the Act, although hot water can be required. The guidelines normally used by authorities when deciding on the number of appliances for a given number of persons at a particular place may be those adopted by the Greater London Council or those suggested in the British Standard 6465:Part 1:1984.

**TABLE XXVIII** PUBLIC SANITARY ACCOMMODATION FOR RESTAURANTS, PUBLIC HOUSES AND CANTEENS

| | Males | Females |
|---|---|---|
| W.C.s | 1 per 100 | 1 per 50 |
| Urinals | 1 per 25 | |
| Wash-hand basins | 1 per W.C. + 1 per 5 urinals | 1 per 2 W.C.s |

Wash-hand basins to be provided with hot and cold water supplies.
Provision should also be made for at least one cleaner's sink.

**Sanitary disposal**

Wherever women are employed or catered for, the law requires that suitable and hygienic provision is made for the disposal of sanitary dressings. Customer welfare should also be considered when selecting a disposal method.

Problems may arise from soiled dressings if the disposal of sanitary towels and tampons is inefficient or inadequate, and there is also a risk of blocked drains if attempts are made to flush such items down the W.C. Pedal bins are inevitably unhygienic and present cleaners with the unpleasant task of emptying and cleaning them. Mechanical macerators and incinerators may produce unpleasant smells and may not completely destroy used sanitary dressings - especially where dressings contain synthetic cellulose rather than natural fibres.

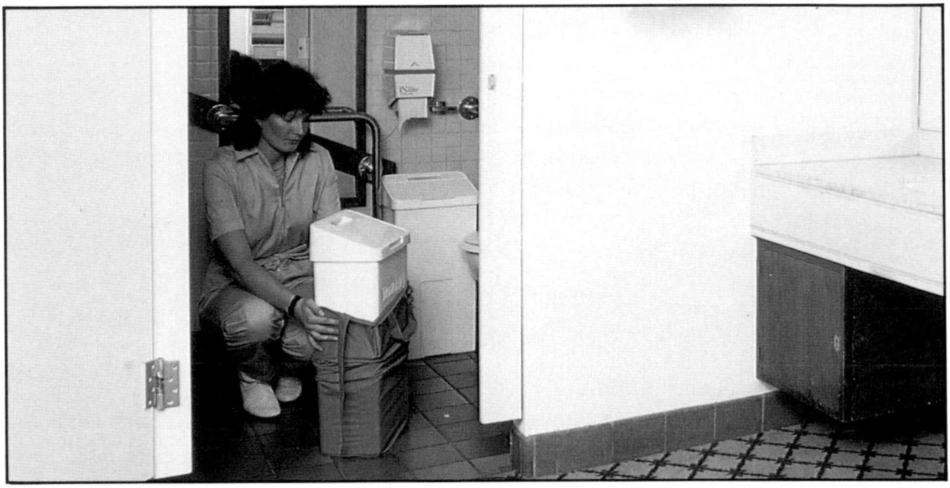

**Fig. 30.** Rentokil Healthcare.

An alternative method of disposal is a regular contract service using specially designed containers placed within W.C. cubicles to afford privacy and which are regularly collected and replaced by fresh, sterilized ones. The contractor is responsible for the safe disposal of the contents away from the customer's premises.

Some containers use a bactericide that works as a vapour as well as a liquid to ensure adequate protection and elimination of unpleasant smells. The bactericide should be capable of keeping the contents sterile for periods well in excess of the normal frequency of exchange.

Contractors should be asked to undertake a survey to establish the optimum number of sanitary towel dispensers, rate of replenishment and the number, and siting, of disposal units required. Some contractors may also provide other hygiene services or amenities such as air fresheners, coin-operated dispensers of sanitary dressings and a disposal service for such things as hypodermic needles.

**The storage and disposal of waste**

Waste disposal systems must be planned, along with other services, when food premises are designed. Refuse must not be allowed to accumulate in food rooms and should not be left overnight. Waste generated within the premises may be stored in polythene bags which are removed when full and at the end of each working day. Stands for such bags must be maintained in a clean condition. Employees must be educated to "clean as they go", to replace lids and wash their hands after receptacles are used. Sacks should not be overfilled and should be tied to prevent problems from insects. Refuse collectors should not have to enter food rooms or dining areas.

Waste food should be kept separate from paper and cardboard packaging. In some instances, waste may be stored under refrigeration pending collection, for example, bones in butchers' shops. It is preferable for all waste food to be removed from food premises at least daily and general refuse to be removed at least twice a week.

Suitable facilities must be provided for the storage of waste externally, prior to removal from the establishment. The number and type of receptacles used will depend on the type and quantity of waste, the frequency of collection and the access available for the refuse vehicle. Dustbins or bulk containers are commonly used, although skips and compactors are more appropriate for food factories.

**Fig. 31.** Examples of satisfactory and unsatisfactory refuse storage.

Dustbins should be stored clear of the ground, for example, on tubular steel racks, to facilitate cleaning and removal of spillages. They should be constructed in accordance with the British Standard Specification for dustbins. All receptacles should be capable of being cleaned and provided with suitable tight-fitting lids or covers to prevent insects, birds and rodents gaining access.

The refuse area must have a well-drained, impervious surface which is capable of being kept clean. Stand-pipes, hoses and, possibly, high-pressure sprayers should be provided for cleaning purposes. The receptacles, and the refuse area, should be thoroughly cleaned after each emptying. Covered areas to protect refuse from the sun and rain are recommended.

Refuse areas should not be too far from food rooms to discourage their use but they should not be too close to encourage flies to enter the food rooms. Covered ways between refuse areas and food rooms are useful to protect staff against inclement weather. Receptacles used for the storage or collection of food must not be used for refuse.

**Refuse compaction**

Charges for refuse collection are continually rising and, since levies are usually based on volume of waste produced, often a price per bin, it is advantageous to use a refuse compaction system. Compactors vary from units similar to a large dustbin to refuse-sack compactors and skip rams. A well-run compaction system improves hygiene, as flies and other pests are less likely to be attracted. Cleaning of refuse areas is also easier as spillages are considerably reduced. Capital costs for purchasing compactors should be compared against collection charges, cleaning and pest control. However, before ordering a compactor the local authority cleansing department should be consulted, as special arrangements may have to be made for emptying.

**Perimeter areas**

A concrete path, at least 675mm wide, abutting the external walls should be provided around all food buildings. This removes cover for rodents and enables early signs of pests to be discovered, for example, rodent droppings. Paths should be kept clean, free of vegetation and inspected regularly. A smooth band of rendering, around 450mm, at the base of external walls will discourage rodents from climbing.

Whenever possible, a perimeter fence should be constructed around food premises to deter unauthorized entry. Areas within perimeter fences must be kept clean and tidy. Rubbish, old equipment and weeds must not be allowed to accumulate or provide harbourage for insects or rodents.

**Kitchen design**

The layout of a well-designed, commercial kitchen will have three main characteristics:

(1) clearly identified and separated flows;
(2) defined accommodation, specific to the purposes allocated; and
(3) economy of space provision (commensurate with good hygiene practice).

The unit will also be so arranged that it can be easily managed. The layout will afford management personnel easy access to the areas under their control and good visibility in the areas which have to be supervised. Space will be allocated for the management function and for equipment such as telephones and computers.

*Flows*

Four separate flows need to be considered: product; personnel; containers, utensils and equipment; and refuse.

Product flows should be subdivided into high-risk and contaminated (raw food) sections. Clear segregation should be maintained between the two. As far as practicable, flows should be unidirectional, without backtracking or crossover.

*Accommodation*

Accommodation should be sized according to operational need. Essentially, the working areas, stores, the equipment and its relative spacing should all be determined and laid out to suit the operation.

Areas should be allocated according to environmental compatibility; hot functions with hot, dirty with dirty, wet with wet, dry with dry, defined overall by segregation between high-risk and contaminated food handling.

*Size*

There should be a minimum of circulation and dead space, commensurate with the efficient functioning of the unit. Size should be neither too small nor too large; there are penalties in the over-provision of space as much as there are problems with too small a provision.

The size of the kitchen can only be determined when its exact purpose and function have been defined. A unit designed for the fast food operation will not work effectively for à la carte service. When a catering operation is planned, the kitchen should be designed first and the rest designed around it. Haute cuisine, for example, will require ample storage space for fresh vegetables, a larder and pastry area. Fast food will require none of these but will need ample space for freezer storage. Other items to take into consideration include:

(1) the state of raw materials, for example, ready prepared or not;
(2) the extent of the menu and number of sittings;
(3) the equipment used, for example, microwave ovens; and
(4) the amount of dishwashing. Disposable plates, etc. may be used.

*Siting of equipment*

Great care is needed to ensure that the operation works as a single system, with equipment required for specific functions grouped and accessible, to avoid excessive walking and the temptation to take shortcuts. For instance, mis-en-place refrigeration should be close to the working areas it serves, otherwise excessive amounts of food may be brought out to save the trips to and from the unit. Wash-hand basins should be strategically located to ensure that operatives entering clean areas wash their hands. Personnel should also be encouraged to wash their hands when leaving the dirty area. Depending on the size of operations, additional wash-hand basins should be provided close to work stations. Non-hand-operable warm water sprays are recommended.

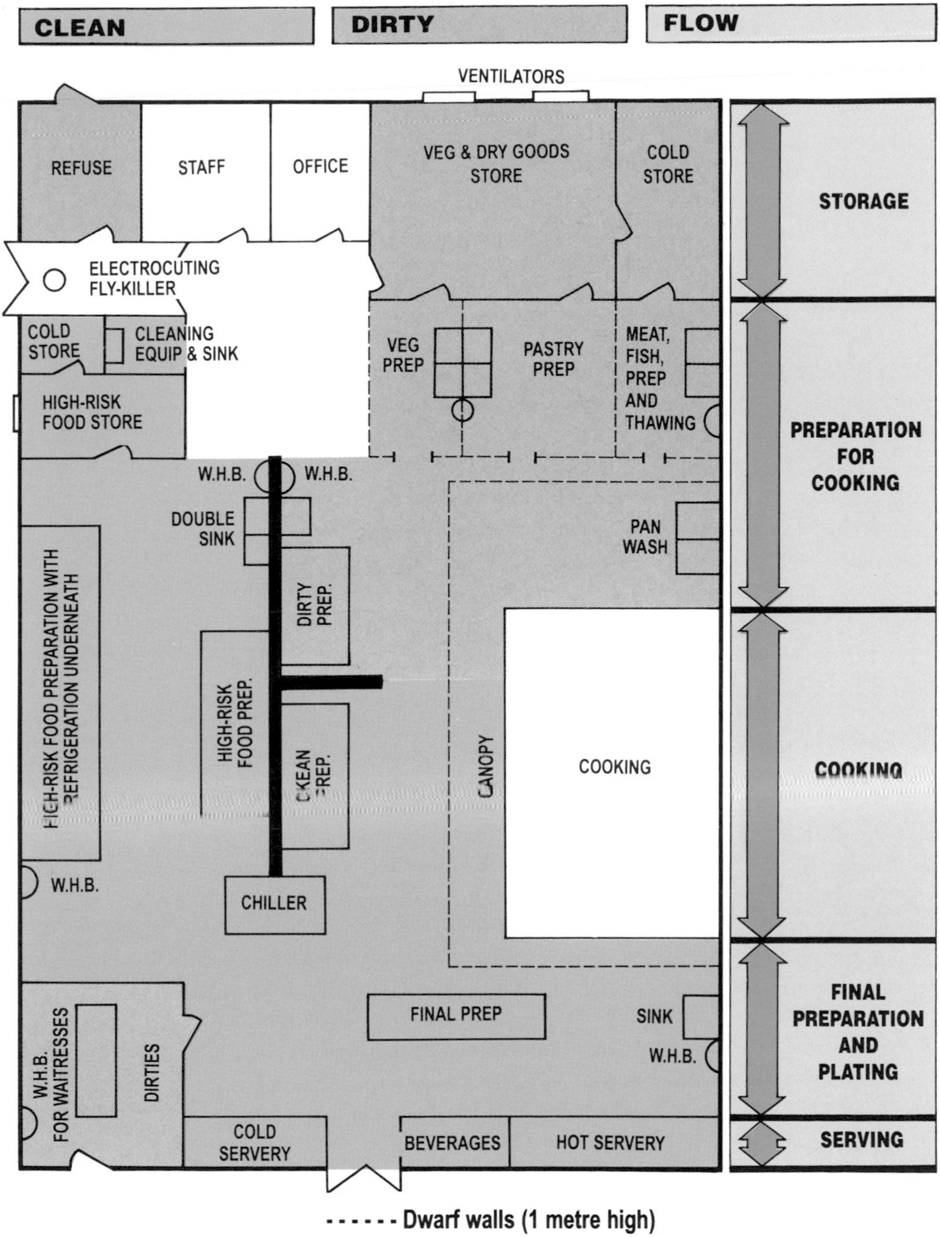


**Fig. 32.** Plan of large kitchen incorporating principles of continuous workflow and segregation of clean and dirty processes (not to scale).

CHAPTER 12

# The design of equipment

Hygienic design of equipment is necessary to comply with legislative requirements, avoid product contamination and facilitate cost-effective cleaning and, if necessary, disinfection (downtime for cleaning will be minimized). Good design necessitates the consideration of the complete process, the environment and methods of cleaning and maintenance and not just the equipment in isolation.

Poorly-designed equipment, which cannot be dismantled, may be uncleanable, incapable of being chemically disinfected and may result in product contamination by pathogenic bacteria which will be disastrous in the case of high-risk food. Even if equipment can be dismantled, unhygienic design may make cleaning and disinfection prohibitively expensive. The ultimate test of whether or not a machine is hygienic is the standard of the product.

## The Legal Requirements

The Food Safety (General Food Hygiene) Regulations, 1995 require all articles, fittings and equipment with which food comes into contact, to be kept clean and be so constructed, of such materials and maintained in such condition and repair as to minimize risk of contamination and enable thorough cleaning and, where necessary, disinfection. Furthermore, equipment must be installed in a way which allows the surrounding area to be cleaned. Proprietors of businesses governed by specific regulations will need to comply with similar requirements and all businesses should be aware of the advice contained within any relevant UK or EC Industry Guide.

The cleanliness of, and risk of contamination from, equipment will need to be considered as part of the identification of steps in the activities of the businesses which are critical to ensuring food safety.

In June 1989 the Council Directive relating to machinery (89/392/EEC) as amended by Directive 91/368/EEC, was published. Although mainly concerned with safety an important section deals with the hygienic design of agri-foodstuffs machinery.

In the UK the requirements of the Directive are enforced using the Supply of Machinery (Safety) Regulations, 1992 (as amended in 1994). The responsibility for compliance rests primarily with the manufacturers and suppliers (including importers), although the user must ensure that the machine is properly installed and maintained and used for the purpose for which it is intended. The Directive requires that new machinery used for preparing and processing foodstuffs carries a CE marking and must be designed and constructed to avoid health risks and in particular:

(1) contact materials of foodstuffs must satisfy the conditions set down in the relevant Directives. Machinery must be designed and constructed to facilitate cleaning;
(2) all surfaces and joints must be smooth, without ridges or crevices which could harbour organic materials;
(3) projections, edges and recesses should be minimal. Continuous welding is preferable. Screws and rivets should not be used unless technically unavoidable;
(4) contact surfaces must be easily cleaned and disinfected. The design of internal surfaces, angles, etc. must allow thorough cleaning;
(5) cleaning residues must drain from equipment surfaces, pipework, etc., there must be no retention in voids;
(6) the design should prevent organic accumulations or insect infestation in uncleanable areas, e.g. by the use of castors or alternatively, sealed bases; and
(7) lubricants must not come into contact with product.

In addition, equipment manufacturers must provide information on recommended products and methods of cleaning, disinfecting and rinsing. This requirement is particularly relevant as, no matter how well designed, equipment will lose the potential to be hygienic if clear instructions for installation, operating, cleaning and maintenance are not provided. The simpler the instructions the better, as workers often attempt to short cut complicated and time consuming systems, sometimes with disastrous consequences.

**The European Committee for Standardization (CEN)**

The European Committee for Standardization has been charged with the task of preparing new European Standards and harmonizing documents and promoting the implementation of international standards in relation to machinery safety and hygiene.

A series of technical committees have been established. CEN/TC 153 is concerned with food processing machinery, safety and hygiene specifications. Another working group is considering the principles of hygiene design which apply to all equipment. In addition, there are nine groups working on standards for specific machines: bakery; meat; catering; slicers; edible oils; pasta; bulk milk coolers; cereals; and dairy.

**Construction materials**

Materials in contact with food must be non-toxic, non-tainting and constituents from their surfaces must not migrate into the food or be absorbed by the food in quantities which could endanger health. Materials must have adequate strength over a wide temperature range, a reasonable life, be corrosion and abrasion resistant and be easily cleaned/disinfected.

The Machinery Regulations state that materials in contact with foodstuffs must satisfy conditions set down in the relevant Directive. Council Directives 92/5/EEC (Meat Products) and 91/497/EEC (64/433/EEC as amended) (Fresh Meat) require contact equipment to be made of corrosion-resistant, non-tainting material which is easy to clean and disinfect. The use of wood is forbidden except in rooms used for the storage of hygienically packed fresh meat. Directive 93/43/EEC (Hygiene of Foodstuffs) requires equipment to be constructed of such materials and kept in such good order repair and condition as to minimize the risk of contamination of the food.

The most widely used material is food grade stainless steel, either type 304 containing 18% chromium and 8% nickel or the more corrosion resistant, and expensive, type 316 with a 10% nickel content and 2% molybdenum. Handles of knives, brushes and other equipment should all be made from cleansable materials such as stainless steel or high-density polypropylene.

Aluminium is attacked by sodium hydroxide, which forms the basis of some detergents, and sodium hypochlorite. Even hard anodizing fails to protect against severe pitting corrosion. Copper and alloys of copper hasten oxidation if in contact with oil or fat. Several metals, for example, copper, zinc and cadmium are unsuitable as they are absorbed by acid food and may cause illness.

Some plastics may be suitable, but must be approved for food use. A useful indication can be obtained if materials comply with safety standards of the American Food and Drug Administration or the German Bundsgesundheitsamt. In the case of uncertainty, advice should be sought from the manufacturers, particularly with regard to high temperatures achieved during cleaning and disinfection.

**Surface finish**

Directive 93/43/EEC requires surfaces to be in a sound condition and easy to clean and, where necessary, disinfect. This requires the use of smooth, washable, non-toxic materials unless food business operators can satisfy the competent authority that other materials used are appropriate.

Surfaces should be continuous, non-porous, non-flaking and free from cracks, crevices and pits. Surfaces will need to retain a satisfactory finish throughout their life including anticipated abuse and normal wear and tear. Instruments are available for measuring surface texture and a profile graph can be made of the shape, height and spacing of surface irregularities. The American National Standard for Food, Drug and Beverage Equipment suggests a value of no greater than the equivalent of 0.8μmRa for surface roughness of food contact surfaces. Unpolished cold rolled sheet from steel mills is well below this. (Roughness average Ra is the arithmetic average value of the department of the profile above and below the mean line throughout the specified sampling length.)

A rough surface provides a better mechanical "key" for soil. Furthermore, soiling is more apparent on bright surfaces which is why it is cost effective to electropolish stainless steel. (Care is needed with siting to avoid problems with sunlight reflecting.)

**Joints**

Joints should be made by welding or continuous bonding to reduce projections, edges and recesses to a minimum. Butt welding is preferred to lap joints provided the welds are ground and polished to the same standard as the rest of the surface, unless it can be demonstrated that the untreated weld is cleanable. Solders used in the construction of food-contact surfaces must also be non-toxic and should not contain cadmium or antimony. Silver soldering may be used to seal joints but must not contain cadmium.

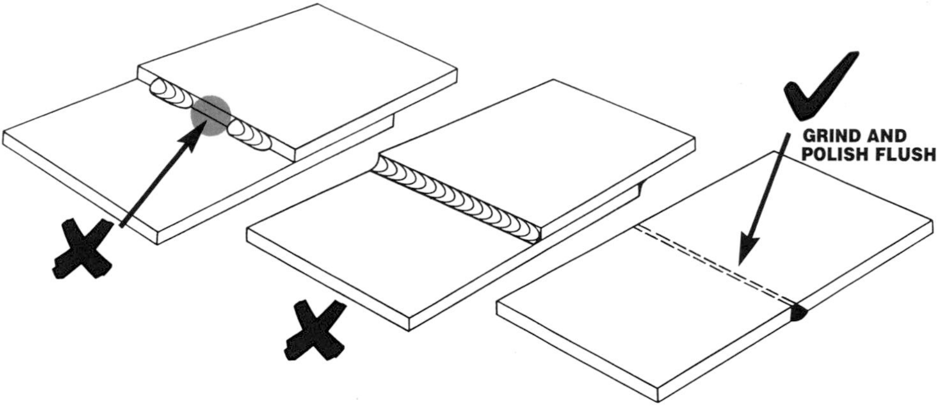


**Fig. 33.** Examples of good and bad welded joints.

Dismountable joints, for example, those relying on bolts, may contain product residue and high bacterial counts when disassembled. If such joints are not cleaned daily they should be sealed against the ingress of product and microorganisms by means of a gasket. (Controlled compression of gaskets is essential.) Metal to metal joints, even if leak tight, may still permit the ingress and egress of microorganisms. Flanged joints must present a smooth, continuous internal surface and be sealed with an appropriate gasket. (Some gaskets are made of materials such as rubber which harden and crack over time.)

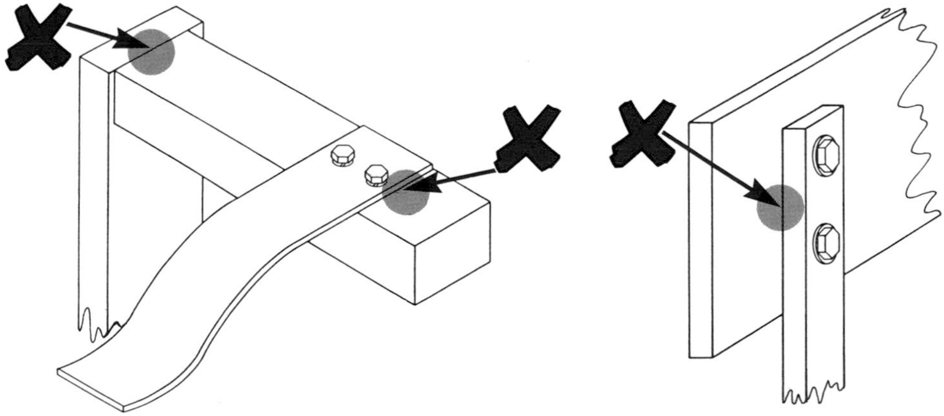

**Fig. 34.** Unhygienic dismountable joints.

**Fasteners**

Exposed screw threads, nuts, bolts and rivets should be absent from food contact surfaces, although if removed daily for cleaning purposes are less likely to cause a problem. Annular recesses and screwdriver slots retain product residues. Nuts and bolts, etc. should be located on the non-product side where this can be achieved.

The hygienic design of equipment also includes avoiding physical contamination of the product. The accidental ingress of foreign matter such as bolts, nuts, washers and gasket materials must be prevented.

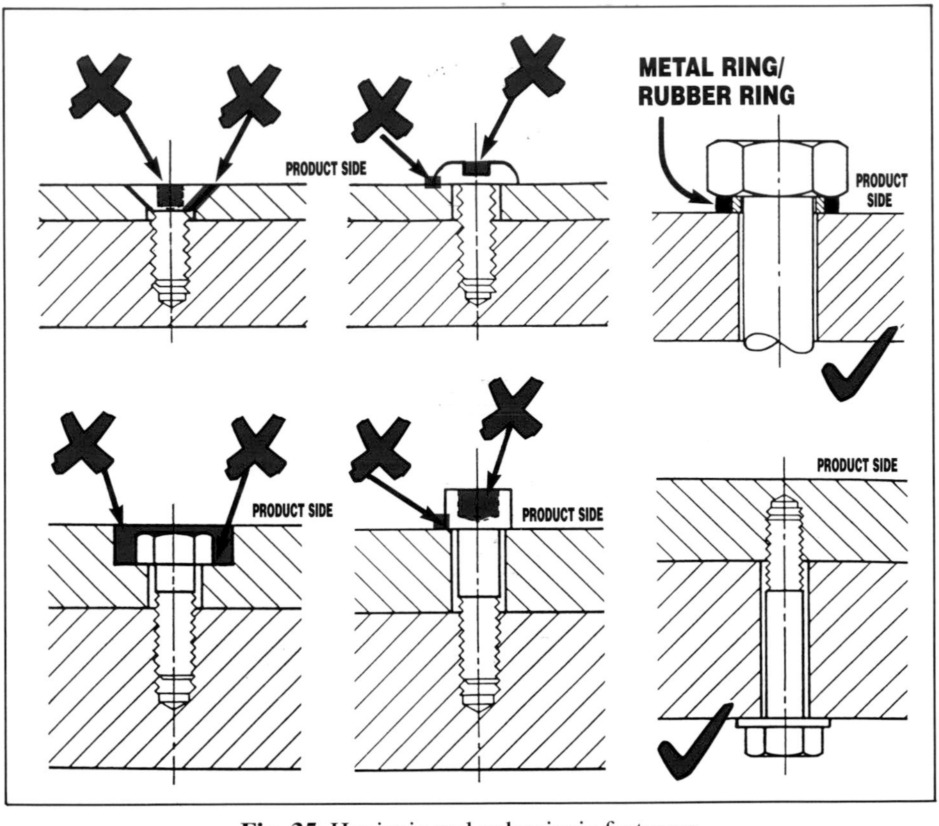


**Fig. 35.** Hygienic and unhygienic fasteners.

**Internal angles and corners**

The Machinery Regulations require inside surfaces to have curves of sufficient radius to allow thorough cleaning. When components are bolted or screwed together, sharp corners are usually unavoidable and metal which is bent or machined is preferred. Routine dismantling and cleaning is the only way to deal with unsatisfactory internal angles.

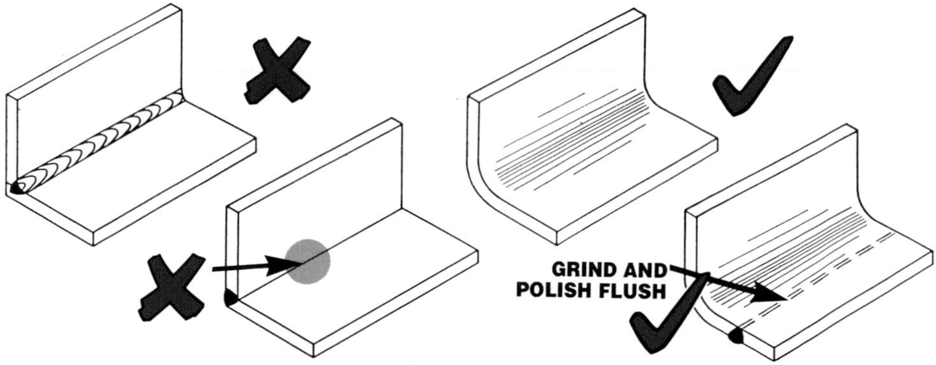


**Fig. 36.** Examples of good and bad internal angles.

### Dead spaces

Dead spaces allow product retention, bacterial growth and product contamination. They must be avoided in the design of equipment and not introduced during installation or as a result of modifications. The Machinery Regulations require the design and construction of equipment to prevent organic matter accumulating in, or liquids or insects entering, areas that cannot be cleaned. In effect, this means that gaskets of material approved for food use or contact must be used, or the design must enable regular dismantling for the space to be cleaned and disinfected.

### Bearings

Bearings should, wherever practicable, be mounted outside product areas to avoid contamination by lubricants. Where this is not possible edible lubricants, or if liquid the product itself ( as in the case of foot bearings ), should be used.

### Equipment exterior

The external surfaces of equipment must avoid ledges and dust traps, for example, round stretchers are preferred to rectangular. It is important to avoid recessed corners, sharp edges, unfilled seams, uneven surfaces and hollows and projecting bolt heads, threads, screws or rivets that cannot be cleaned. Inaccessible spaces, pockets and crevices where product may accumulate must be absent.

### Instrumentation

Instrumentation must be constructed from appropriate materials and any transmitting fluids should be approved for food contact. Hygienic installation of instruments is essential. Controls such as push buttons must also be of hygienic design so they can be maintained in a clean condition and be capable of being cleaned by whatever system is in use. Dials which are fitted to machines must have adequate clearance to allow cleaning.

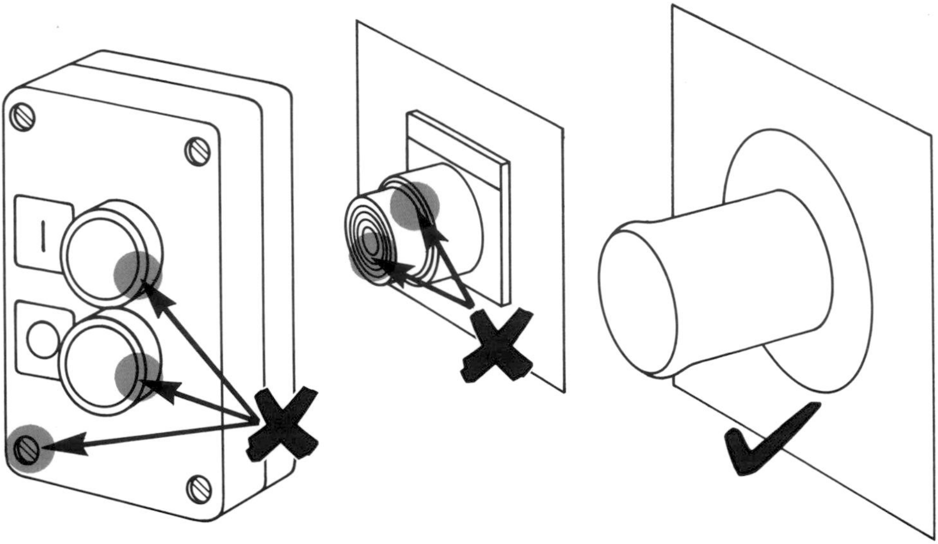

**Fig. 37.** Examples of good and bad controls.

## Fixing and siting of equipment

Equipment must be sited so that there is sufficient space to facilitate access to all external and internal surfaces and, where required, to allow for rapid dismantling and reassembly. Stationary equipment should be at least 500mm from walls and have a clearance of at least 250mm between the floor and underside of the equipment, to allow thorough cleaning of wall and floor surfaces. Alternatively, machines should be fixed firmly to the floor and sealed. Narrow areas or angled contact with the floor should be avoided. Machinery may be mounted on coved, raised platforms of concrete to facilitate cleaning. Where necessary, additional space may need to be provided. The bases and lower parts of machines, including motors and gears, may be difficult to clean and consequently collect dust and spillages which make ideal breeding sites for insects. Skirting or cover plates tend to trap dust.

Where practicable, and with due regard for safety, equipment can be mobile to facilitate its removal for cleaning. This is particularly important if sited close to walls. Tubular metal storage racks, refrigerators and ovens should be castor-mounted with brakes on all wheels. Tables and benches should not be fitted with castors as even when braked, slight movement can still occur posing a hazard to knife users.

When pipework is installed, future cleaning must be considered and sufficient space left between the pipes and floors or walls to allow easy access for cleaning. Alternatively, pipes may be built into the walls. Lagging of pipes must have an impervious cleansable finish. Pipework and equipment directly above open food must not expose food to risk of contamination from condensation, rust or flaking paintwork.

Conveyors can be designed to enable automatic cleaning. Manufacturers must be pressured to ensure that if dismantling is necessary it is as simple as possible.

Guards, required under health and safety legislation, should be capable of being cleaned and, where necessary, removed quickly and easily, even if special tools are required. Sheet-metal and wired-perspex guards are preferable to painted mesh.

## Gas and electrical connections

The presence of electrical equipment such as motors and switches poses problems for cleaners, as even routine cleaning may expose users to some danger of electrocution. Such equipment must always be waterproof and/or capable of removal without tools, prior to cleaning the main equipment. If practicable, electrics should be sited outside food rooms, to reduce cleaning problems. It also enables servicing and maintenance to be carried out by electricians who do not need to enter food rooms.

Gas and electricity supply pipes to ovens should be flexible and capable of being disconnected. In the case of gas, the coupling to the mains must incorporate a self-sealing valve and a shut-off cock immediately upstream of the fitting. The flexible tube must conform to gas board requirements and the appliance must be secured to a fixed point by a strong, detachable wire or chain, shorter in length than the tube, to avoid accidental stretching. Trailing wires and cables must be avoided.

## Drainage

All pipelines, vessels and equipment should be self-draining, not only to enable liquid deriving from foodstuffs to be discharged but also for cleaning and rinsing fluids. It is particularly important that pipelines and vessels cleaned by CIP systems are designed to facilitate complete drainage.

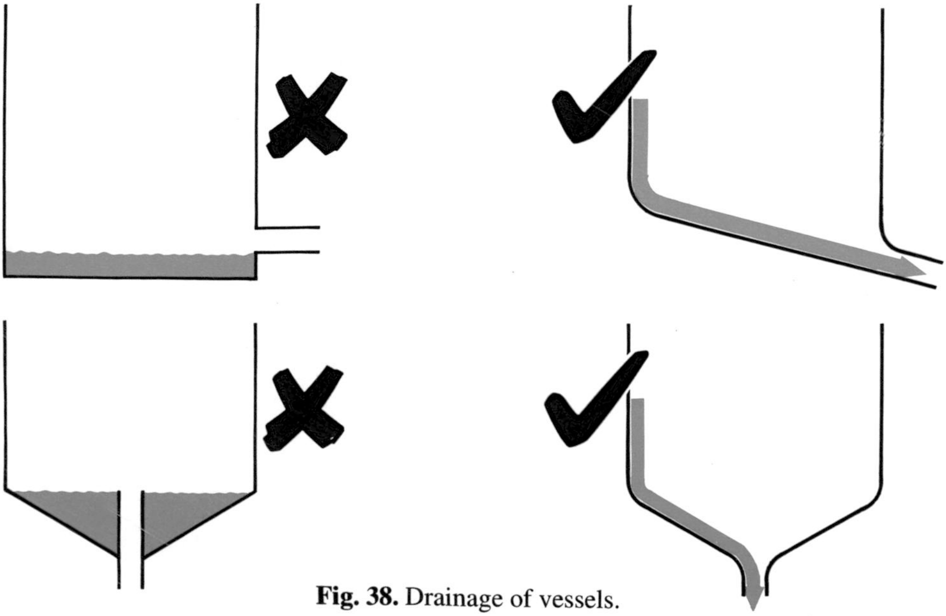

**Fig. 38.** Drainage of vessels.

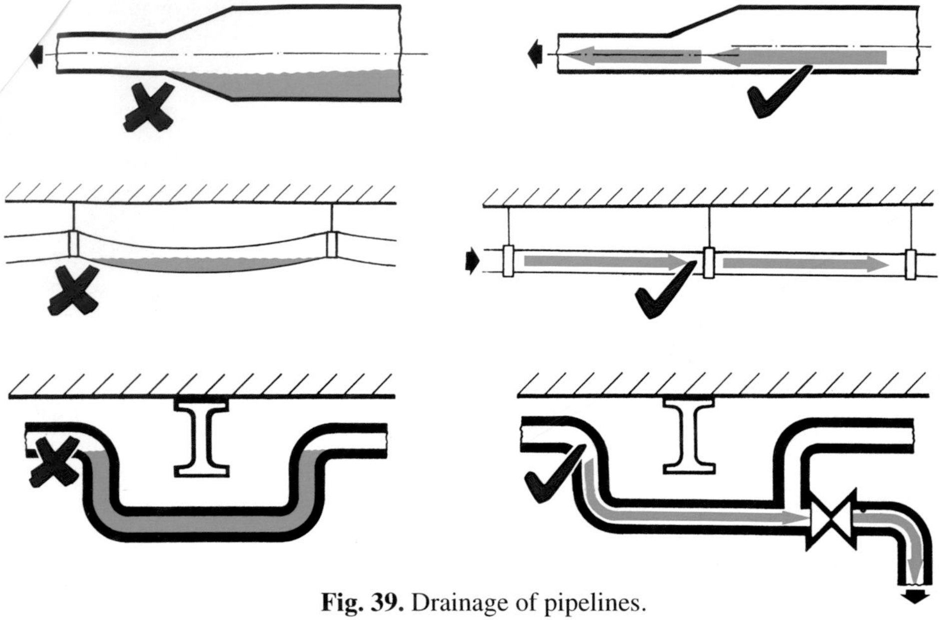

**Fig. 39.** Drainage of pipelines.

**Preparation surfaces**

Preparation surfaces should be jointless, durable, impervious, the correct height and provide a firm base on which to work. If materials other than stainless steel are used, for example, plastic laminate, care should be taken to seal the edges and gaps which may harbour food scraps. They must be able to withstand repeated cleaning at the required temperature without premature deterioration, pitting or corrosion. Flanged-lip designs for tables and shelves which harbour food residues, and are difficult to clean, should be avoided.

**Cutting boards**

A variety of non-absorbent hygienic cutting boards is now being produced. However, some are unsatisfactory. When selecting a cutting board regard should be had to its:

(1) water absorbency;
(2) resistance to stains, cleaning chemicals, heat and food acids;
(3) toxicity and odour; and
(4) durability.

Furthermore, a good board should not split or warp and it is advantageous if it can be passed through a dishwasher. Good quality polypropylene is being increasingly used. As yet no ideal replacement has been found for hard wood chopping boards. However, these should be maintained in good condition and used solely for chopping or sawing meat.

**Contamination**

To avoid cross-contamination, it is important that the same equipment is not used for handling raw and high-risk products without being disinfected. To prevent the inadvertent use of equipment for high-risk and raw food it is recommended that, where possible, different colours and/or shapes are used. Colour coding may be extended to include washing facilities, trolleys, protective clothing, cloths and packaging material.

**Deterioration**

Equipment deteriorates with age and eventually becomes incapable of being thoroughly cleaned. Routine maintenance is essential. Chipped, broken and badly pitted equipment allows the harbourage of dirt and bacteria and should be replaced. String or tape must not be used to repair defective equipment, including knife handles.

**The cleaning of equipment**

All operating instructions and procedures must be clearly communicated to equipment users and cleaners. The equipment should be capable of being cleaned and, if necessary, disinfected safely, thoroughly and rapidly without the need for skilled fitters and specialized tools. If dismantling is necessary this must be achieved relatively easily, as should reassembley.

Sharp edges are a serious hazard for cleaners. A reluctance to clean equipment because of poor design will result in a lowering of hygienic standards. Hinges should be capable of being taken apart for cleaning. Angle iron is difficult to clean and tubular construction is preferred, open ends to tubular legs must be sealed.

**Storage of clean equipment**

Having spent a considerable amount of time cleaning and disinfecting equipment and utensils, it makes sense to ensure that subsequent storage does not result in contamination. The USA Food and Drug Administration Food Service Sanitation Manual states that clean equipment and utensils should be stored at least 450mm above the floor in a clean, dry location, in a way that protects them from contamination by splash, dust and other means.

The illustrations used in this chapter
were provided by courtesy of Campden & Chorleywood Food Research Association.

CHAPTER 13

# Cleaning and disinfection

Even in the most highly automated food business, operating under the most controlled conditions, soiling of both surfaces and equipment is unavoidable. The type and extent of soiling will vary considerably but, whatever the operation, it is essential that such residues are not allowed to accumulate to levels which expose food to the risk of contamination. Removal of these residues is the process of cleaning.

The objective of the clean varies depending on the standard required. A physical clean may be used to prevent physical contamination of the product. However, operations involving high-risk foods will require a microbiological clean which involves cleaning and disinfection, usually as a two stage process.

## The benefits of cleaning

Cleaning is an essential and integral part of a profitable food business. In addition to satisfying legal requirements, cleanliness will:

(1) ensure a pleasant, safe and attractive working environment which will encourage effective working and reduce the risk of accidents to both staff and customers;
(2) promote a favourable image to the customer and assist in marketing the business;
(3) remove matter conducive to the growth of microorganisms so facilitating effective disinfection and reducing the risk of food poisoning and spoilage;
(4) remove materials that would provide food or harbourage for pests and prevent early discovery of infestations;
(5) reduce the risk of foreign matter contamination and thereby obviate customer complaints; and
(6) prevent damage to, or a reduction in, the efficiency of equipment and services, and reduce maintenance costs.

## Problems caused by ineffective or negligent cleaning

Negligent cleaning may achieve a satisfactory physical appearance but can result in hazardous bacterial contamination, for example, cleaning from raw to high-risk areas. Selection of the appropriate cleaning chemicals often requires expert technical advice as the use of the wrong chemicals, or the right chemicals at the incorrect strength, temperature or contact time, may have serious financial consequences. This not only applies to direct costs relating to product, equipment and premises but also, the cost of effluent treatment. Ineffective or negligent cleaning may result in:

(1) a poor quality product which may lead to a reduction in shelf-life, customer complaints, loss of reputation, court proceedings, food poisoning, redress from suppliers and loss of sales;
(2) wastage of food and production re-runs;
(3) taint and other forms of food contamination;
(4) corrosion and premature replacement of equipment;
(5) production breakdowns, for example, following the incorrect use of caustic soda which has removed grease from bearings; and
(6) unacceptable deterioration of floor surfaces and drainage systems.

## MANAGEMENT FUNCTIONS OF CLEANING

Cleaning is essentially a management function and the physical process of removing dirt is only the final stage. The prime responsibility is to ensure that premises and their contents are capable of being effectively cleaned. Not only does this make economic sense but it is also a legal requirement.

### Securing the commitment

Paying lip service to standards is not enough. Everyone involved in a food business must be personally committed to ensuring that satisfactory standards are achieved. Requisite standards must be clearly defined, effectively communicated and reinforced by management. Staff must be motivated, instructed, supervized and controlled.

### Providing the means

Sufficient numbers of adequately trained cleaning staff, properly supervised and supplied with appropriate materials and equipment, must be employed. Adequate supplies of hot water are essential. To avoid confusion the number of different cleaning chemicals used should be minimized.

### Cleaning schedules

Cleaning schedules are a communication link between management and staff and are necessary to ensure that equipment and premises are effectively cleaned and, if necessary, disinfected as frequently and as economically as possible. When planning a cleaning schedule, the following items should be considered:

(1) the size, type and temperature of area to be cleaned, the structure of the building and the wall, floor and ceiling finishes;
(2) the type of equipment and the material from which it is made. The manufacturer's recommendations should always be followed;
(3) whether or not the equipment can be dismantled;
(4) the type of soiling and the water hardness;
(5) the presence of electrics;
(6) the available water pressure and drainage system;

(7) the time constraints, manpower and training needs;
(8) if cleaning is necessary during food preparation, or if food should be removed;
(9) whether or not disinfection is required;
(10) the requirements of the Health and Safety at Work etc. Act, 1974, and all relevant health and safety legislation;
(11) the controls available to monitor the effectiveness of cleaning; and
(12) the overall cost, including labour, equipment, chemicals, water and heat. In large premises the cost of effluent treatment must also be considered.

The cleaning schedule itself must be clearly and concisely written, without ambiguity, to ensure that instructions to staff are easy to follow and result in the objective of the schedule being achieved.

Written schedules should specify:
(1) what is to be cleaned;
(2) who is to clean it;
(3) when it is to be cleaned;
(4) how it is to be cleaned;
(5) the time necessary to clean it;
(6) the chemicals, materials and equipment to be used;
(7) the cleaning standard required;
(8) the precautions to be taken;
(9) the protective clothing to be worn; and
(10) who is responsible for checking and recording that it has been cleaned.

### Monitoring and control of cleaning

A system for identifying problems must be established. Faults may be caused by poor management, administrative deficiencies, unsatisfactory staff, inadequate training or unreasonable expectations of individual performance.

Standards should be routinely monitored by inspections carried out by management personnel not directly involved in cleaning operations. All findings should be recorded and utilized to rectify faults and improve the effectiveness of cleaning.

## ADMINISTRATION

To implement management policy, certain administrative functions must be carried out and these include:

### Selecting a chemical supplier

Price is obviously important but cheap chemicals can result in expensive cleaning. Suppliers should have a knowledge of the type of operation, a satisfactory range of products, a knowledge of all appropriate health and safety legislation, the expertise to undertake a comprehensive audit to determine cleaning needs, the time to spend to demonstrate how to use the product to best effect and easy to understand literature that does not mislead. They must be reliable and have the ability to respond to emergencies and preferably be quality assured.

**Stock control**

Provisions similar to those applicable to food stocks should apply, with proper stock rotation, delivery checking and inventory control. Comprehensive records should be kept of all transactions and minimum and maximum stock levels should also be established. Authorization to order should be restricted to named personnel.

**Distribution**

Transfer of materials from the store to the point of use should be properly organized to ensure that the right materials in the right quantities reach the right people at the right time. Over supply, or storage of bulk stocks in working areas, should be avoided.

**Financial control**

Records of expenditure on each item, identifiable with the area of use, should be kept. Expenditure norms should be established and any deviations investigated, as this is often the first indication to management that procedures are amiss. Underspending is as significant as overspending.

## TECHNOLOGY OF CLEANING

Management and administration apart, the remainder of the cleaning function is the application of technology. In this sense cleaning is defined as "the systematic application of energy to a surface or substance, with the intention of removing dirt". Central to the definition is the concept of energy.

**Energy in cleaning**

Energy is available for cleaning in three distinct forms:

*kinetic energy:* physical - manual labour;
mechanical - machines;
turbulence - liquids (CIP);
*thermal energy:* hot water; and
*chemical energy:* detergents.

Normally, a combination of two or more energy forms is used. Manual labour is the most expensive and chemical energy the most economic, although adequate contact time is also important. The correct energy balance is essential for cost-effective cleaning.

**Cleaning costs**

Cleaning costs may be apportioned as follows:

| | |
|---|---|
| labour 70% | chemicals 6% |
| equipment 12% | heating 4% |
| water/effluent 6% | corrosion 2% |

The above figures should only be considered as a rough guide, for example, if only buckets and mops are used, equipment costs will be lower and labour costs increased. If the wrong chemicals are used corrosion costs may be significantly greater than 2%. Water and effluent costs have increased significantly over the last 10 years and water use should be minimized.

## Chemical cleaning

The usual cleaning medium is water which dissolves certain residues and forms a solution that can be rinsed away. Water, however, is not efficient in dissolving many of the soils that occur in the food industry. To improve the efficiency of water as a cleaning chemical, and to counteract the effect of the impurities in water (hardness salts), other chemicals, for example, detergents are added.

## Detergents

Detergents are chemicals, or mixtures of chemicals, made of soap or synthetic substitutes, with or without additives, which are used to remove grease or other soiling and promote cleanliness. They are available as powders, liquids, foams or gels. Detergents usually exhibit the following specific characteristics:

### *Surfactancy*

This is the property of a detergent which enables it to increase the "wetting power" of water by reducing the surface tension. This increases the contact between the soil and the detergent solution which is able to penetrate the minute irregularities of the dirt more effectively.

### *Dispersion*

This is the ability of a detergent to break up large accumulations of matter into smaller particles.

### *Suspension*

When dirt is broken up into particles, they become coated with a thin film of detergent which keeps the particles apart and buoyant, i.e. in suspension, allowing them to be rinsed away. This characteristic is commonly referred to as the emulsifying action of detergents.

Manual detergents used in the food industry should be non-toxic, non-tainting, non-corrosive, free-rinsing, soluble in water and not form scum in hard water.

### *Alkaline detergents*

The most commonly used alkaline detergent is caustic soda (sodium hydroxide). It is corrosive to skin, aluminium and zinc, has poor wetting properties, but is effective for fat and protein solubility and is relatively cheap. Sequestering agents (chelates), such as the amino carboxylic acids, EDTA and NTA, are added to prevent scale formation in hard water. Inorganic phosphates are effective sequestrants used in the UK, mainly in powder products, but are banned in some European countries because of the eutrophication of rivers.

*Acid detergents*

These are mainly used to remove mineral, protein and vegetable deposits and commonly contain phosphoric acid which is one of the least corrosive acids. It must never be allowed to come into contact with chlorinated compounds because of the consequential release of toxic chlorine gas.

**Detergent action**

The reduction of surface tension enables detergent solutions to penetrate dirt and grease and lift them from the surface to form a suspension.

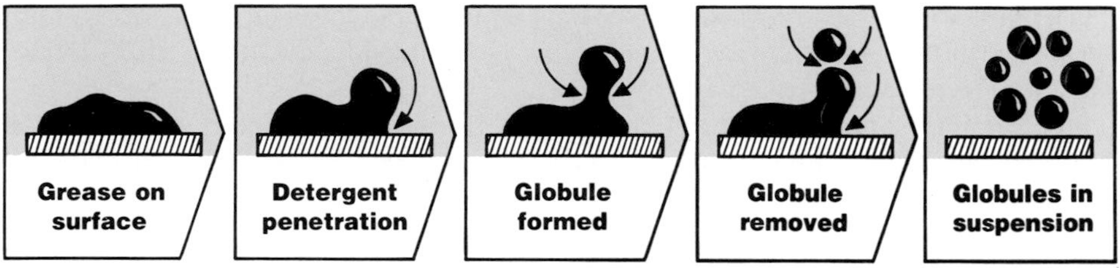


**Fig. 40.** Detergent action.

**Types of soil**

In very general terms there are two types of soil: organic and inorganic.

*Organic soils*

These are derived from living matter and include animal fat, vegetable oils, starch, sugars and proteins from milk, egg, meat or blood. Normally they may be removed by using neutral or alkaline detergents. However, if heated, dried or allowed to remain for a prolonged period, then alkalis must be used to remove them.

Grease or oil will, if heated, form a tenacious, dark, sticky deposit known as polymerized grease. This may be removed by a mild alkali such as sodium carbonate (washing soda) or sodium metasilicate. Further heating of polymerized grease results in the formation of carbon which must be removed by the more aggressive, caustic alkalis such as sodium hydroxide or potassium hydroxide (caustic potash).

Another type of organic soil is tannin which is derived from tea, coffee or wine. It is normally removed by an oxidizing agent such as sodium hypochlorite (bleach) or sodium perborate. However, if the tannin is present with water hardness salts it may be better to use an acid detergent.

*Inorganic soils*

These include water hardness salts (scale), oxidized metals (rust), uric acid salts (urinal stains), beerstone and calcium salts deposited from milk (milkstone). Inorganic soils are normally removed by acids such as hydrochloric and phosphoric, although these should not be used on aluminium due to potential corrosion problems.

Soils are very rarely made up of one component, for example, a hard scale in a meat processing area may be a complex of a mineral scale and protein.

## COST-EFFECTIVE CLEANING

Cost-effectiveness of the whole cleaning operation depends on:
(1) choosing the correct chemical;
(2) applying it at the optimum temperature and concentration;
(3) allowing it time to function; and
(4) using it with the correct equipment.

The correct mix of the above will reduce the work required.

### Choosing cleaning chemicals

The primary choice of a chemical depends on the soil. However, other factors must be considered. Selection may be aided by the following checklist: soil; surface; situation; and safety.

For example, soil may be identified as carbon. Normally caustic soda would be used, however, the surface may be aluminium and this would corrode. Consequently, an alternative chemical must be selected, such as a sodium metasilicate based detergent. The situation must then be considered. Is the room occupied? How much time is available? What equipment is required to apply the chemical? The final criterion is safety, as no chemical should create an unacceptable hazard to users or food product.

Some surfactants react with some plastics which turn black and may cause off-flavours in the product.

### The optimum temperature

Temperature can be critical to chemical performance, generally the higher the better. However, heat may denature the chemical or fix proteins such as egg, in which case warm or cold applications must be used initially.

### Dosing aids and applicators

This classification applies to devices used to deliver or control chemicals. They may be manually operated or automatic. Dispensers may be of the plunger or proportioning or metering type. Applicators include aerosol, trigger spray, pump-up sprayer, backpack sprayer, air or electrically driven sprayer and foam or gel applicators.

*Hand sprayers*

Sprayers may be trigger-pump or pressure-operated and vary in size from 500ml to 25 litres. They can be adjusted to deliver an atomized mist or a fine, long-reaching jet.

*Tap proportioners*

These draw detergent by water suction from a drum.

*Swan-neck or mushroom dispensers*

These are spring-loaded, push-operated pumps, screwed vertically into concentrate containers.

**Time to function**

Chemicals must be given sufficient time to act. This period is normally referred to as the contact time. Vertical surfaces may not allow sufficient contact time due to run-off. Alternative cleaning methods, such as repeated applications, or the use of foams, gels, highly viscous liquids, or even soaking, can be used to extend contact times. Attempts to remove dirt before the chemical reaction is complete, results in a considerable amount of extra work.

**Equipment**

A growing range of specialist equipment is available for cleaning operations and the correct choice will ensure that the most cost-effective cleaning is carried out. Common types and systems include:

**Manual cleaning aids**

Consistent, high standards of cleanliness will only be achieved if the cleaning tools have been specifically manufactured for the stringent demands of the food industry. Correct choice is essential if operatives are to avoid recontamination of a cleaned surface with dirt or bacteria or, in the case of brushes, the contamination of product with bristles. The quality and cleanliness of tools which touch surfaces in direct contact with food is particularly important.

A comprehensive range of tools is now available and when selecting cleaning tools effectiveness depends on choice of materials, quality of construction, design and suitability for a particular task.

*Design*

The design must ensure that tools can be effectively cleaned and there are no hiding places for residues or bacteria to accumulate. If handles are hollow they must be properly sealed. The use of ergonomics in design minimizes operator fatigue, improves safety and consistently results in higher standards. Correct length and diameter of handles reduce the risk of muscle tension and provide the most comfortable grip. Handles should reach the chin of the user, when measured from the floor.

*Materials*

Modern materials such as high-density polypropylene, polyester and rilsan are resistant to acid and alkaline cleaning agents and will withstand repeated heat sterilization up to 130°C.

*Colour coding*

The use of colour coding for cleaning equipment, for example, handles of brushes, bristles and cloths used in high-risk situations, with different colours being used in potentially contaminated raw food areas, assists in reducing the risk of cross-contamination and reinforces hygiene training relating to the need to separate raw and high-risk food.

*Cloths*

Cloths vary from the durable, high-strength textile to the semi-disposable, non-woven with high absorbency and relatively low mechanical strength. Disposable paper is commonly used in preference to cloths.

*Brushes*

Brushes constructed from modern materials such as high-density polypropylene for stocks with bristles of polyester or rilsan give improved performance and resistance to wear. They are capable of withstanding boiling water and the normal cleaning chemicals used throughout the food industry. Wood and natural bristles must be avoided and worn out brushes must be replaced. As brushes become worn they become less effective, they discolour and bristles are more likely to drop out. Blue coloured bristles are often preferred as they are more easily detected if they become loose. Nylon filaments are porous and quickly lose their stiffness in wet conditions, and inferior materials may even distort in hot water.

Care is necessary to ensure damage to surfaces does not occur because the bristles are harder than the surface being cleaned.

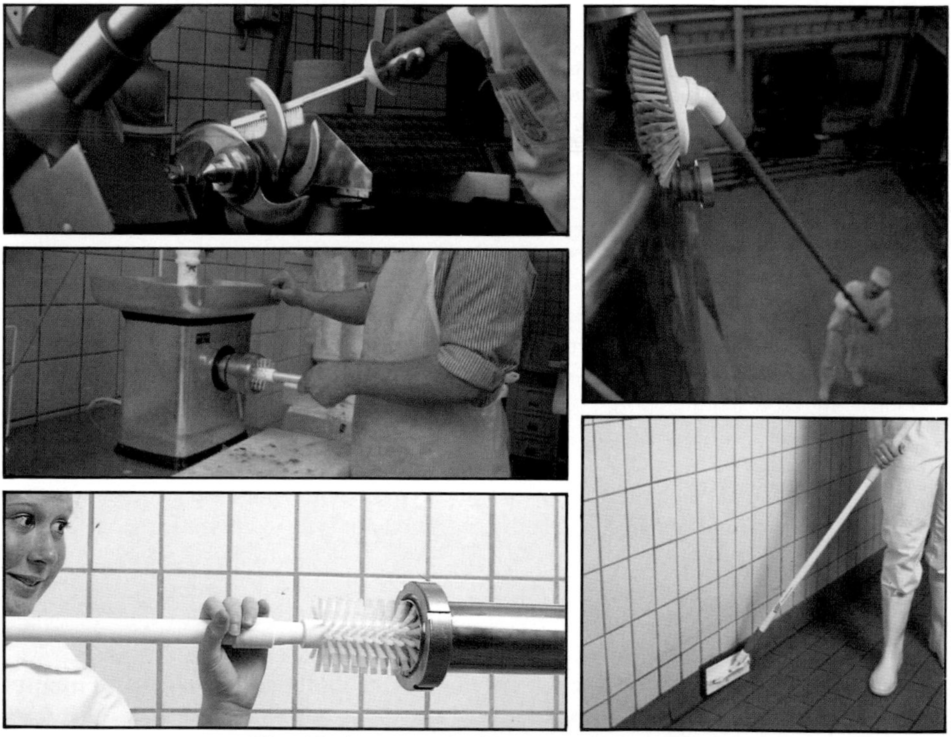

**Fig. 41.** A range of Vikan hygienic brushes.
( Courtesy of Hygienius Ltd. )

*Mops*

The common or socket mop should not be used in the food environment. The twist mops and the Kentucky mop, with its detachable head which can be washed and boiled, are much more appropriate. Mops must be thoroughly cleaned after use and then left to dry. The storage of mops in buckets, with or without disinfectants, should not take place as this may allow the multiplication of, or the development of resistant, bacteria.

*Buckets*

Buckets may be high-density nylon or polypropylene with steel handles. Domestic-grade buckets should be avoided.

**Selecting the right equipment**

The quality of cleaning equipment varies considerably and is usually price related. Effectiveness and durability depend on the choice of materials used in manufacture and the quality of construction. When selecting, for example, brushes, the following points should be considered:

(1) high density polypropylene stock is preferable (not foamed). Generally the heavier the brush the more durable;
(2) bristles made of polyester are preferable;
(3) whether the brush will withstand boiling or even higher temperatures;
(4) the range of brushes available. Those designed specifically for a particular task are likely to be more effective; and
(5) if the supplier is quality assured, for example, BS 5750/ISO 9000 accredited.

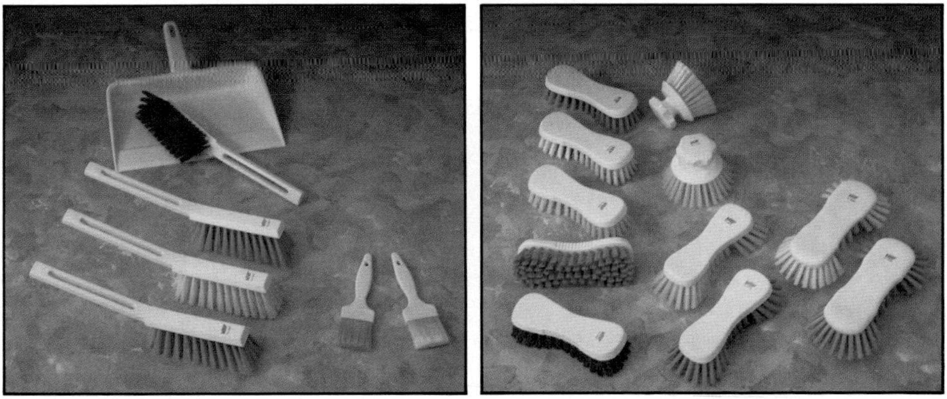

**Fig. 42.** Colour coded brushes can reduce the risk of cross-contamination. ( Courtesy of Hygienius Ltd. )

**Sinks and tanks**

Sinks are the basis of any manual utensil and small equipment cleaning and are essentially fixed vessels for the containment of a cleaning solution. Sizes may vary from 20 to 450 litres. Construction material should be food grade stainless steel.

Tanks are similar to sinks but are used for soaking. They tend to be under-exploited. A stainless steel tank containing an aggressive cleaning solution can be used to soak a variety of equipment, removing encrusted carbon with a minimal labour input.

**Mechanical aids**

These include floor scrubbers, rotating washers, power washers, air lines, steam cleaners, vacuum pick-ups, dish washing and tray-cleaning machinery. Judicious use of mechanical equipment can significantly reduce labour requirements, but considerable care should be taken in selection to ensure that it is suitable for the use intended.

*Vacuum cleaners*

Suitable industrial vacuum cleaners, which suck up dirt and dust in a stream of air and then filter the air to trap the dirt, should be used to clean such areas as dry stores and carpeted public rooms. The suction must be powerful enough to ensure efficient operation and some models may be used to remove liquid spillages. Extension pipes are available to clean ceilings. The use of suction vacuum cleaners is preferable to sweeping as dust clouds are avoided.

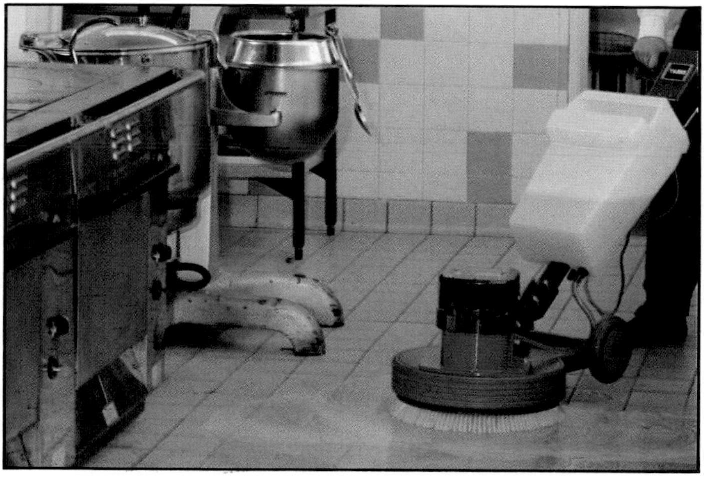

**Fig. 43.** A single disc scrubbing machine. *(Courtesy of Lever Industrial.)*

*Power washers*

An increasing number of food premises are being designed to facilitate cleaning by the use of power washers. Satisfactory fall and drainage of floors is essential and wall and floor finishes, and joints, must be capable of withstanding high-pressure sprays.

Pressures range from 20 to 196 bar (300 to 2,800 psi), although extreme care must be exercised at the higher pressures. Increasingly, lower pressures of around 20 bar are being used for many applications and particularly when combined with foam or gel detergents. The correct machine must be selected for a particular job. Inadequate pressure may result in poor cleaning, whereas excessive pressure will cause unnecessary splashing and misting and increase the risk of damage to surfaces and equipment. A volume of water of at least nine litres per minute is required to wash away dislodged soils.

Power washers may be electric, diesel or petrol driven and may be mobile or fixed. The large electric washers require a three-phase supply. Safety must be considered in relation to mobile electric units which should be protected by an approved earth-leakage, circuit breaker. All electrical installations should satisfy the requirements of the Electrical Engineers Regulations and should be checked regularly. Care must be taken to protect electrical components against the ingress of water. Fumes from petrol and diesel driven washers may make them unsuitable for use in food premises unless fixed outside food rooms.

Various fan nozzle designs are available giving a spreading angle of between 15° and 40°. Some washers are capable of heating cold water feeds but units that are not provided with heating elements may be fed with hot water up to 75°C. Cold water may be quite effective, provided the correct detergents are used, although hot water will usually be required to remove grease. There are many situations when satisfactory results will only be achieved by pre-spraying stubborn deposits and grease with an appropriate degreaser and allowing adequate contact time before using the power washer to rinse away the residues. Steam washers are not usually necessary or desirable for cleaning food premises.

A considerable number of specialized detergents have been developed to ensure the efficiency of power washers, including foam. The greater contact time of foam, which clings to vertical and overhead surfaces, is claimed to improve performance and make it easier to detect any areas which have not been cleaned.

**Fig. 44.** Foam or gel cleaning can improve performance. (Courtesy of Lever Industrial.)

**Clean-in-place (CIP) equipment**

Cleaning-in-place has replaced hand cleaning in dairies, breweries and potable liquid installations. It involves circulating non-foaming detergents and disinfectants through process equipment in the assembled state. The combined effects of solution turbulence, chemical energy and heat remove soil debris and microorganisms from pipework and ancillary plant without time-consuming dismantling and manual cleaning. Efficiency of cleaning depends on type of soil, temperature, concentration of detergent, velocity, turbulence and the design of the CIP system.

The use of heat changes the physical state of the soil, for example, it alters turbulence, accelerates chemical reaction and melts fat. As a rough guide an increase of 10°C may be considered to double the speed of chemical reaction. The most cost-effective results are usually obtained by using detergents at as high a temperature as possible, taking into account equipment, venting, stressing and detergent manufacturers' recommendations. Allowances must also be made for the expansion of pipe lengths during CIP when hot solutions are used. It may not be possible to use hot solutions for cleaning refrigerated systems or tanks because of the risk of damaging heat-sensitive thermometers and thermostats. For light soiling, a concentration of detergent between 0.1 and 1.0% causticity is preferred.

Careful design of CIP systems is essential to avoid unsatisfactory results. Inaccessible crevices and pockets, which can become foci for bacterial multiplication, must be eliminated. Valves and other components must be installed in the correct orientation and configuration to avoid uncleanable dead legs and tees which retain air or debris. The maximum length of dead legs and height of tees should be three times the pipe diameter to ensure satisfactory cleaning. Direction of flow into a pocket is superior to flow away from the same pocket.

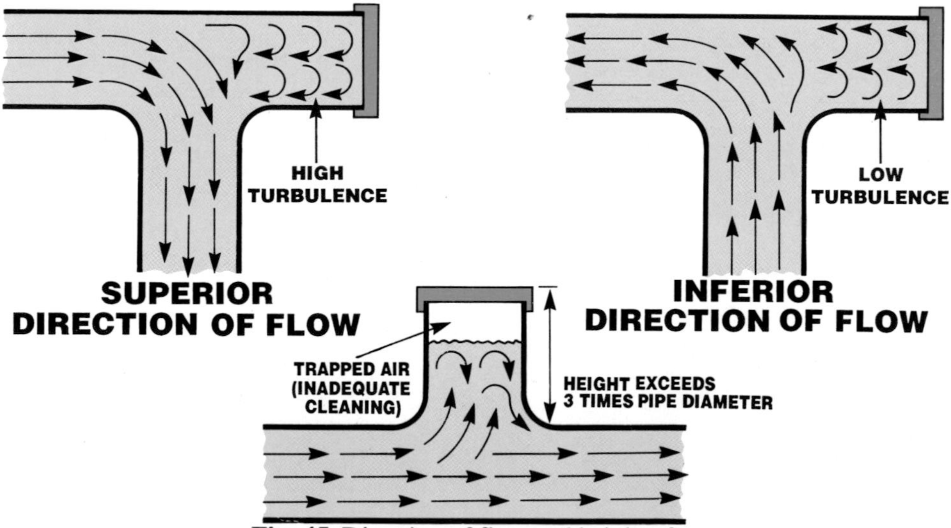


**Fig. 45.** Direction of flow and height of tees.

All sections of the pipe line, including valves and fittings, must be filled with solution without leaving any pockets of air. A fluid velocity of around 1.5m per second is satisfactory for most applications, although 2m per second may be required to remove stubborn soil with low temperature solutions. Suitable fall must be built in to horizontal pipes as all parts of the system must drain completely.

Tanks, exceptionally large diameter pipes and large containers may be thoroughly cleaned using spray balls or rotating jet devices and this avoids the unnecessary and uneconomical filling of vessels with solution. It also obviates the need for men to climb into vessels to carry out manual scrubbing.

Mains services required by CIP units may include: electricity, which may be single or three phase; a suitable clean, softened water supply of 7.5 litres per second; a clean, filtered, oil-free air supply; a saturated, filtered steam supply; and a suitable splash-proof drain or gully, resistant to temperatures of up to 90°C, capable of transporting CIP acids and alkalis and removing effluent discharge of 7.5 litres per second. All systems include cleaning solutions, reservoirs, pumps, feeds and control equipment, which may vary from simple timers and manually operated switches and clocks to complex, fully integrated computer operations.

**Fig. 46.** A twin pump CIP system.
(Courtesy of APV Co. Ltd.)

A typical basic CIP sequence consists of five stages:

(1) pre-rinse with cold water to remove gross soil;
(2) detergent circulation to remove residual adhering debris and scale;
(3) intermediate rinse with cold water to remove all traces of detergent;
(4) disinfectant circulation to destroy remaining microorganisms; and
(5) final rinse with cold water to remove all traces of disinfectant.

The time allowed for each operation can be determined for each particular plant or circuit being cleaned.

**Reducing unnecessary labour**

Careful planning and assembly of materials and adopting the most suitable method will save considerable time and effort. Systematic wiping or spraying will avoid duplication of coverage and the risk of areas being missed. If "clean as you go" is in operation, cleaning will be easier as residues will not have hardened. Organizing work in teams is often highly efficient.

**The use of contractors**

It is often worth considering the use of specialist cleaning contractors to supplement in-house cleaning by intensive deep cleaning of the structure, ventilation trunking, drains and difficult-to-reach surfaces. Contractors may use steam, special solvents, degreasers and sophisticated equipment to establish and maintain standards of hygiene not otherwise readily obtainable in inaccessible areas. However, contractors must be selected carefully and suitable references should always be obtained before allowing the use of potentially dangerous chemicals which could, in inexperienced hands, cause thousands of pounds worth of damage and extensive contamination of food.

## CLEANING TERMS

Technical terms commonly used in cleaning science include:

*Abrasives*

Abrasives include hard abrasives such as pumice and fine sand which may be compounded with soaps to form pastes, and mild abrasives such as lime and chalk which are used in cream cleaners.

*Amphoteric surfactants*

The active ions of amphoterics can be either positively or negatively charged, depending on the pH (acidity or alkalinity) of the solution. They are anionic in alkaline conditions and have both penetrating and wetting properties which enable them to remove grease and give them cleaning properties. In acid solutions they exhibit cationic behaviour and act as bactericides. They have low human toxicity but high unit cost.

*Anionic surfactants*

Anionic surfactants separate in solution to form ions. The active ion is negatively charged. They are the most commonly used surfactants and are often mixed with non-ionic surfactants to form basic commercial detergents such as washing-up liquid. They are biodegradable, non-toxic and have good wetting properties.

*Biodegradability*

Biodegradability refers to the property of a surfactant which allows it to be broken up by bacteria in sewage works, so reducing pollution and toxic hazard to fish. All modern surfactants tend to be biodegradable, although some form intermediate toxic compounds and have been banned in some countries.

*Cationic surfactants*

Cationic surfactants ionize in solution, the active ion being positively charged. Mixed with non-ionics, they are usually sold as sanitizers, sometimes called germicidal detergents. They are high foaming and have relatively poor wetting characteristics.

*Compatibility*

Detergents with different ionic charges should not be mixed as they are not compatible and become inactivated. Even mixing similar types of detergent may impair performance, as blends are carefully balanced to optimize synergistic effects.

*Emulsion*

An emulsion is a suspension of one liquid in another. Detergents have the ability to surround microdroplets of oil or fat and hold them in suspension as an "oil-in-water" emulsion which can be easily rinsed away.

*Foaming activity*

Foam is not an essential part of a detergent and can interfere with mechanical cleaning. In manual cleaning, however, foam increases the surface area of a solution, increasing the speed of activity and enables more dirt to be suspended. Too much foam can cause rinsing difficulties.

**Fig. 47.** Emulsifying action (diagrammatic).

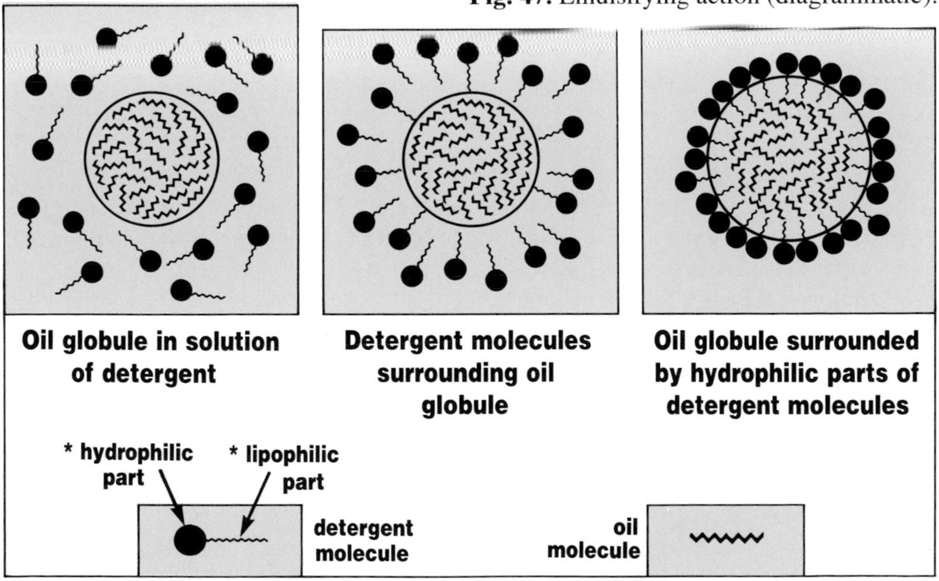


* hydrophilic means water loving and lipophilic means fat loving.

*Non-ionic surfactants*

Non-ionic surfactants do not ionize in solution and therefore do not carry a charge. They are compatible with anionic, cationic and amphoteric surfactants, commonly being used as components of blends to improve overall cleaning performance. They can also be mixed with acids to form acid cleaners. They are biodegradable, non-toxic, have good wetting properties and may be high or low foaming.

*Saponification*

Saponification is the process of making soap, usually by boiling vegetable and mineral fats and oils with an alkaline material such as caustic soda. This also occurs in cleaning when alkalis react with fatty or oily organic soils. The soap thus formed assists in the further cleaning action. Soap is anionic in character and forms a scum in hard water when it reacts with the calcium and magnesium ions.

*Scouring powder*

Scouring powders are cleaning powders combining abrasive and often minute amounts of bleaching agent. They will seriously damage enamel or stainless steel surfaces and should not be used for cleaning these materials.

*Sequestrants*

Sequestrants are chemicals which counteract the effect of water hardness salts, preventing the formation of scum which would interfere with the cleaning action of chemicals.

*Solvents*

Solvents are chemicals which have the effect of dissolving specific types of soil. Solvents, such as glycol ether, are often used in small amounts as a part of a detergent formulation to improve its performance for dealing with oils and fats.

*Synergism*

Synergism is an enhanced performance achieved by the mixture of two or more chemicals, the sum of the activity being greater than the total effect of the components acting separately. This effect occurs with ionic and non-ionic detergent blends and can also be important in disinfectant formulations.

## DISINFECTION

Although cleaning may remove large numbers of microorganisms it does not kill them. In fact there is evidence to demonstrate that an unsatisfactory cleaning operation can itself be a major vehicle of contamination within food premises. The process of destroying microorganisms is known as disinfection. Normally, disinfection is carried out after cleaning, although sometimes the two processes are combined.

Disinfection is defined by British Standard 5283 as, "the destruction of microorganisms, but not usually bacterial spores; it may not kill all microorganisms but reduces them to a level which is neither harmful to health nor the quality of perishable foods". Disinfection may be achieved by using heat, chemicals, irradiation or UV radiation. UV is usually effective for atmospheres and clear water but not for surfaces.

The term sterilization relates to the destruction of all microorganisms and spores and is normally unnecessary and impracticable to achieve within the food industry.

### Heat disinfection

The application of heat is the most reliable and effective means of destroying microorganisms, although it may not be the most practicable, especially for surfaces. It is used in machines, such as dish washing machines, with a water temperature of 88°C and a contact time varying from one to 15 seconds. It is also used in sterilizing units where articles may be fully immersed for a period of 30 seconds at 82°C.

### Steam disinfection

Lances producing steam jets may be used in large food factories to disinfect machinery or surfaces which are difficult to reach. Steam cleaned equipment is self-drying, although disadvantages may include:

(1) an adverse effect on some materials, for example, some plastics and certain wall and ceiling finishes, such as paint, may be stripped off;
(2) the removal of grease and lubricants from machinery;
(3) a safety hazard if steam lances are used by untrained personnel; and
(4) the formation of condensate on other equipment, especially overhead pipes and metal girders.

### Chemical disinfection

Disinfectants suitable for use in the food industry are limited to those which, when used correctly, will not have a deleterious effect on food, equipment or personnel. Types of chemical disinfectants available include:

*Chlorine release agents*

Properly used, these substances are amongst the most suitable for the food industry. The commonest are hypochlorites which are salts of hypochlorous acid (HOCl). The most useful is sodium hypochlorite which disinfects by oxidation of protein, an essential part of the structure of bacteria, viruses, yeasts and fungi.

They are normally supplied in solutions containing 6 to 10% available chlorine and should be diluted to between 100 and 2,000 ppm of available chlorine, depending on the particular situation. A freshly made-up solution of hypochlorite containing 100 ppm of available chlorine will satisfactorily disinfect a completely clean surface, provided a contact time of approximately three minutes is allowed. However, depending on the amount and type of soil, pH, contact time, temperature and organisms or spores present, a concentration of up to 2,000 ppm of available chlorine may be necessary to ensure disinfection. In the event of doubt the manufacturer's advice should be obtained. For general use, to minimize corrosion, it is recommended that hypochlorites are used below 40°C, at a maximum of 200 ppm with a contact time of up to 20 minutes. Upon completion of disinfection they should be rinsed off with clean, cold water. They must never be used in conjunction with acid cleaners due to the production of chlorine gas. Hypochlorites may react with phenols, present in some resins used in glass fibre vessels, to form chlorophenols which result in taint problems.

Hypochlorites are relatively cheap and are active against most microorganisms. They are unaffected by hard water. However, they exhibit staining/bleaching characteristics, have a pungent odour, are corrosive to man and many metals and are readily inactivated by organic soil. They have no wetting power and therefore a detergent may be added to aid surfactancy. Liquid hypochlorite should be stored in a cool, dark place. The use of chlorinated powders containing, for example, sodium dichloro-isocyanurate, eliminates most of the above disadvantages.

Provided they are used on clean surfaces, allowed adequate contact time, residues are rinsed off and suitable safety precautions are taken during handling, the advantages of hypochlorites far outweigh their disadvantages.

*Quaternary ammonium compounds (QACs)*

Cationic in characteristic, QACs are safe, odour-free, non-corrosive, stable and taint-free bactericides with some inherent detergent properties. In isolation they have a narrow range of activity and are not as effective as hypochlorites against Gram −ve bacteria, viruses and fungi. Effectiveness can be significantly improved by the incorporation of a sequestrant as part of a well-built formulation with non-ionic detergent and alkali ingredients. Because of their inherent residual properties (which can be advantageous in certain situations), QAC's should be used with care by the brewing and fermenting industries when this characteristic is undesirable.

*Iodophors*

Iodophors are expensive but effective bactericides consisting of iodine and non-ionic surfactant in an acid medium. They have both detergent and disinfecting properties and their acid characteristics make them suitable for the dairy industry, breweries and soft drink manufacturers. Advantages include the ability to kill a wide range of organisms, effectiveness at low temperatures (iodine may sublime above 40°C), tolerance of soiling and hard water and brief contact time. Iodophors are stable, of low toxicity and virtually odourless if properly used, although they may combine with food to cause taint. Furthermore, if used negligently they may be corrosive.

Iodophors stain soiling matter such as milkstone and so indicate poor physical cleanliness. Plastics may be stained but metals are not. In use, the yellow-brown colour of the iodophor is absorbed by organic matter and the colour disappears, a useful indicator of potency. They should not be used on aluminium or copper.

*Biguanides*

Cationic bactericides, similar in function to QACs but with better all round performance. They have no wetting properties and are therefore compounded with non-ionic detergents. They are sometimes used in the licensed trade for glass washing and are non-foaming. They are unsuitable for use in highly alkaline conditions and should not be used after caustics.

*Amphoteric surfactants*

Amphoterics exhibit bactericidal properties in acid solutions. They are of low toxicity, relatively non-corrosive, tasteless and odourless. They are good detergents but are expensive and exhibit limited antibacterial activity. Furthermore, they are inactivated by many materials and being high foaming are unsuitable for use with machines and high-velocity sprays.

*Peroxy compounds*

These fairly specialized products are increasingly used for terminal disinfection in large dairies (per-acetic acid, replacing hydrogen peroxide) and as peroxy compounds within a detergent blend for agricultural and other applications.

*Per-acetic acid*

This acid, which destroys microorganisms by an oxidative action, remains effective at temperatures as low as 0°C. Once diluted it has a limited life and is only suitable on glass or stainless steel surfaces.

*Alcohols*

Where there is a requirement for light cleaning and disinfection in essentially a "dry" area, for example, delicatessen point of sale or packing belts on a production line, the use of an alcohol based spray/wipe product is particularly useful. This is typically a blend of alcohol, QAC, and possibly mild detergent additives, formulated to provide good disinfection in lightly soiled conditions without the use of water. The product flashes dry after application thus removing the need for an undesirable wipe-dry operation. Care must be exercised because of the flammability of alcohols.

Ethanol and iso-propanol are two of the alcohols commonly used for surface and hand disinfection.

*Aldehydes*

Formaldehyde and glutaraldehyde have a wide spectrum of activity but are not used because of their high toxicity and irritancy characteristics.

**Choosing a disinfectant**

The choice of disinfectant depends on many factors including:

(1) amount of soiling;
(2) water hardness;
(3) contact-time available;
(4) type of microorganisms that need to be destroyed;
(5) type, imperviousness and smoothness of surface to be disinfected;

(6) possibility of taint;
(7) temperature of application;
(8) toxicity of the disinfectant and the effect on personnel;
(9) ionic nature of the detergent used before disinfection; and
(10) way the disinfectant is to be used/method of application.

There is no official standard for disinfectants in the food industry and users should satisfy themselves that a product is suitable for the use intended.

**Where to disinfect**

Disinfection is not a universal process applicable to all surfaces. It should only apply to those surfaces where the presence of microorganisms, at the levels found, will have an adverse effect on the safety or quality of the food handled. If disinfection is considered necessary, it should normally be restricted to:
(1) direct food-contact surfaces;
(2) hand-contact surfaces;
(3) food workers' hands; and
(4) cleaning materials and equipment.

**Disinfection of food and hand-contact surfaces**

As microorganisms are rarely mobile and need to be physically carried onto food, the disinfection of non-food contact surfaces, such as floors and walls, is rarely necessary. Surfaces not directly coming into contact with food, but frequently touched by food handlers, need disinfection to avoid build-up of microorganisms on hands.

**Hand disinfection**

Hand disinfection is only necessary in critical situations, for example, when the handling of high-risk food is unavoidable or to protect food handlers such as fish filleters from developing septic cuts. In the majority of food handling situations washing the hands properly in hot water, using a liquid soap, is quite satisfactory. If hand disinfection is considered necessary it should be carried out after normal hand washing. Hand disinfectants should be fast-acting, rapid-drying and contain ingredients to protect the skin.

**Disinfection of cleaning materials and equipment**

Cleaning equipment is often an important vehicle of contamination and should be disinfected frequently. Normal machine laundering at 65°C or above, in the case of cloths and towels, will achieve this.

**Disinfection frequency**

In most operations, contamination by microorganisms takes time to build up to a significant level unless extraneous contamination is introduced by poor operational practice. Under normal circumstances, therefore, disinfection can correspond with cleaning intervals dictated by visual soiling or with work cycles. However, intermediate disinfection may be needed to counter the effects of inherent bad practice, such as the use of the same surface or equipment for cooked and raw meats.

**Resistance**

Some bacteria, under certain circumstances, develop resistance to disinfectants at concentrations that would normally be lethal. This problem can be avoided by:

(1) ensuring that a fresh solution of disinfectant is used, at the correct concentration;
(2) ensuring that the components of a system are compatible with the disinfectants used;
(3) using disinfectants of adequate performance against the bacteria requiring control;
(4) using only disinfected equipment and/or disposable or freshly laundered cloths;
(5) applying disinfectants to clean surfaces.

Only in extreme cases, where the above conditions have not been observed, is it necessary to change the type of disinfectant used.

**Inactivation**

This phenomenon occurs when a disinfectant mixes, or comes into contact, with a substance that interferes, partially or completely, with its ability to kill microorganisms. Such substances are called inactivators, the primary one being dirt which affects all disinfectants to a greater or lesser extent. Hard water will inactivate uncompounded QACs, and plastics, cork, cellulose and certain organic materials will inactivate cationic disinfectants in free solution.

**Control procedures**

It is unfortunate that there is no visible difference between a physically clean, but bacteriologically contaminated surface and one that has been effectively disinfected. Furthermore, even minor deviations from manufacturers' instructions may render the disinfection process ineffective. Where appropriate, a product with a visual indicator, such as an iodophor, may assist in control.

If necessary, the effectiveness of disinfection should be monitored by bacteriological swabbing of surfaces and also examination of the food product. It is important to establish trends over a period of time and not to react to isolated unsatisfactory results.

## PROCEDURES AND METHODS OF CLEANING

Whatever the location, industry, soiling type or circumstances, cleaning and disinfection comprises six basic stages:

(1) pre-clean: sweeping, wiping or scraping-off loose debris, pre-rinsing and/or pre-soaking;
(2) main clean: applying detergent and loosening of the main body of dirt;
(3) intermediate rinse: removal of loosened dirt, chemical neutralization of cleaning agent residues;
(4) disinfection: destruction of residual microorganisms;
(5) final rinse: removal of disinfectant residues; and

(6) drying: removal of final rinse water.

In light-soil conditions, the pre-clean may be combined with the main clean. Disinfection can be omitted on non-critical surfaces. Drying can either be natural, as in air drying, or physical, using disposable paper towels, hot air or a clean dry cloth.

Disinfection can take place in combination with the main clean using specific chemicals known as sanitizers, although this is not as effective.

## Cleaning methods

Various methods exist including: small item cleaning; soaking; manual cleaning; pressure washing; the use of foams, gels or mist; cleaning-in-place; and machine dish-washing.

## Preliminary and post-cleaning actions

In the case of dangerous or electrical equipment, preliminary safety procedures and final safety checks will be required. Several types of equipment will need partial or complete dismantling to ensure effective cleaning.

## Dish washing

Unfortunately, many catering premises only use a single sink for dish washing. Wherever possible this should be supplemented by a dishwasher. Where a single sink is used it is essential to use water as hot as possible, just below 60°C, and to replace the water frequently as it becomes cool or greasy. Air drying will not usually occur and disposable paper towels should be used in these circumstances.

Although the use of a single sink is not as effective or hygienic as either the double sink or the dishwasher, provided the crockery and cutlery are clean, free from grease and dry, then there will be minimal risk of causing illness to customers.

Detergents must be compatible with the local water supply and correct amounts, in accordance with manufacturers' instructions, must be used. Measuring equipment must be cleaned frequently.

## Double-sink washing

This procedure is recommended for washing-up in catering premises, public houses and retail outlets selling high-risk foods, when suitable dish washing machines are not available. It also applies to food-processing, packing and distribution plants where small items are hand washed. Thermal disinfection is preferable if double sinks are used but if this cannot be achieved, a suitable chemical disinfectant such as hypochlorite in a tablet form may be used. However, the rinse water should still be hot enough to allow air drying. The requisite temperature will depend on the particular piece of equipment/utensil and the material from which it is made, the temperature of the item prior to immersion and the time the item is left in the second sink. Melamine plates were found to air dry rapidly after immersion for 30 seconds at 65°C. The full, six-stage procedure should always be followed:

(1) remove any heavy or loose soil by scraping and rinsing in cold water;

(2) place articles in the first sink in detergent solution at 53°C to 55°C, scrub with a nylon brush and/or wipe with a clean cloth to loosen dirt residues;
(3) re-immerse in the first sink to wash off loosened dirt;
(4) place articles in the second sink to rinse off chemical residues;
(5) leave for sufficient time at a high enough temperature to ensure rapid air drying. Baskets for disinfecting purposes should be maintained in good condition and inspected regularly. They should be loaded so that all surfaces of crockery and equipment are fully exposed to the rinse water. Hollow items such as cups should be placed on their side; and
(6) remove articles, allow to drain and evaporate dry on a clean, disinfected surface.

A rinse aid may be added to the rinse water to promote smear-free drying. Items should then be removed and stacked in a clean, protected area ready for re-use.

The order of washing-up should be planned so that glasses and lightly-soiled articles are cleaned first. For safety reasons, glasses should be washed one at a time. Some articles may need pre-soaking and treatment with abrasive pads. The temperature of the wash water should be so high as to be uncomfortable, necessitating the wearing of rubber gloves, but should never exceed 60°C to avoid fixing proteins. Gloves must be washed and dried after use, as must the sinks, drainers and any other surfaces involved in the process. Disposable paper towelling placed on the draining surface helps absorb water and reduces noise.

Dishcloths should be semi-disposable, discarded daily or, if woven fabric, should be withdrawn daily and laundered; normal laundry procedures being sufficient to secure disinfection. Cloths should never be left wet or soaked in disinfectant overnight as this can result in a build-up of resistant bacteria. Bleaching, if desirable, may take place prior to laundering but should not be considered as a substitute. High-density polypropylene brushes are preferable to cloths as they withstand autoclaving temperatures and can be cleaned and disinfected frequently.

**Mechanical dish washing**

Mechanical dish washing is preferable to, and often more economic than, manual washing provided the machine is used according to the manufacturer's instructions. Machines, in addition to cleaning, are also a highly efficient means of disinfecting small items of equipment and should be used for articles such as the removable parts of slicing machines, polypropylene cutting boards and other items which come into contact with high-risk foods, provided that no damage to the item will result. The sequence is as follows:

(1) remove excess food into suitable waste bins; if necessary pre-soak or spray, unless the machine is fitted with a pre-wash cycle;
(2) pack articles in a neat, orderly fashion so that items do not overlap, place in the machine and operate the wash cycle of hot detergent solution (49°C to 60°C), unless automatic;
(3) operate the rinse cycle (82°C to 88°C), with injection of rinse aid; and
(4) remove racks, allow cleaned items to drain and evaporate dry.

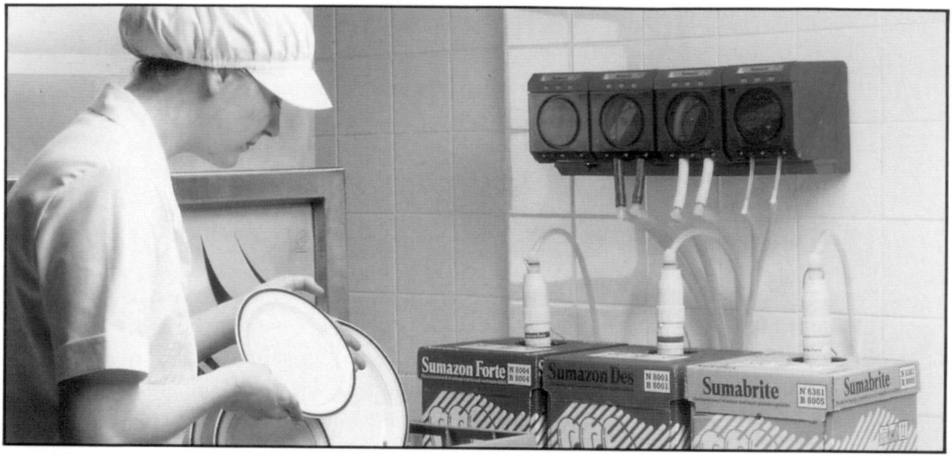


**Fig. 48.** A mechanical dishwasher incorporating detergent/rinse aid dosing system using the "safebox" safety system. ( Courtesy of Lever Industrial.)

To ensure that the best results are obtained, it is important that machines are serviced regularly and operated in accordance with manufacturers' instructions and that:

(1) utensils are washed as soon as possible after becoming soiled;
(2) the correct detergent for the level of water hardness is used. It is often more economic and efficient to install a water softener;
(3) the detergent dosing equipment is working properly and detergent rinse levels are properly adjusted;
(4) sprayer arm jets are clear from obstruction and strainers are in place. Both should be cleaned daily; and
(5) track speed, where appropriate, is properly adjusted to give the contact time required for the detergents used.

As a rule of thumb guide to the efficiency of a machine, if items coming out are too hot to handle and dry rapidly to a clean, smear-free finish, then the machine is operating correctly.

**Cleaning a work surface**

The procedure for work surfaces will vary according to the finish and the types of cleaning chemicals used. For stainless steel and similar surfaces the routine is as follows:

(1) remove loose debris with a clean, loosely-folded cloth (pre-clean);
(2) wash with hot detergent solution and a clean cloth or brush (main clean);
(3) rinse with hot water and a clean cloth (intermediate rinse);
(4) apply a suitable disinfectant and allow sufficient contact time;
(5) rinse off with fresh water and a disposable paper towel (final rinse); and
(6) allow to evaporate dry (drying).

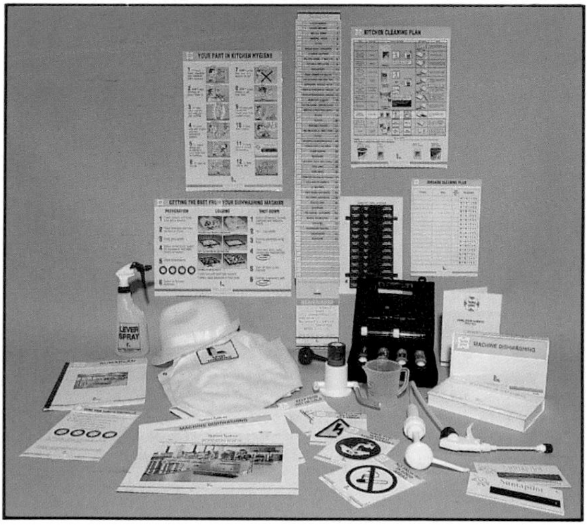

**Fig. 49.** A selection of cleaning instruction wallcharts and dosing devices.
( Courtesy of Lever Industrial.)

## Cleaning a slicing machine

*Pre-clean*

(1) switch off power socket and remove the plug;
(2) set the slice thickness control to zero; and
(3) dismantle the machine and pass removed parts through the dish washing machine.

Where the machine is of a type that has a removable blade, a blade guard must be fitted before the blade is removed. Cleaning may then commence, with the proviso that no person may clean a slicer or other dangerous machine unless they have reached their eighteenth birthday and have been properly trained.

*Post-clean*

(1) reassemble the machine;
(2) redisinfect parts handled;
(3) check the guards are properly fitted, reconnect the power and switch on the machine. Test run to check safe working. This procedure is vital because accidents have been caused by guards having been improperly fitted after cleaning. If any adjustments have to be made, the machine should be switched off and disconnected and the test run repeated; and
(4) switch off the machine, disconnect the plug and cover with a freshly laundered tea towel or other suitable covering.

## Cleaning a soft ice-cream machine

(1) remove all ice-cream from the machine;
(2) rinse thoroughly with cold water;
(3) switch off, disconnect the plug and dismantle the machine;
(4) wash the parts and machine interior with a suitable detergent, reassemble the machine;
(5) clean the outside of the machine and reconnect;

(6) fill the machine with a suitable disinfectant solution, circulate for two minutes and drain. Leave the machine empty; and
(7) prior to use the next day, fill with fresh clean water, circulate and drain before filling with ice-cream mix.

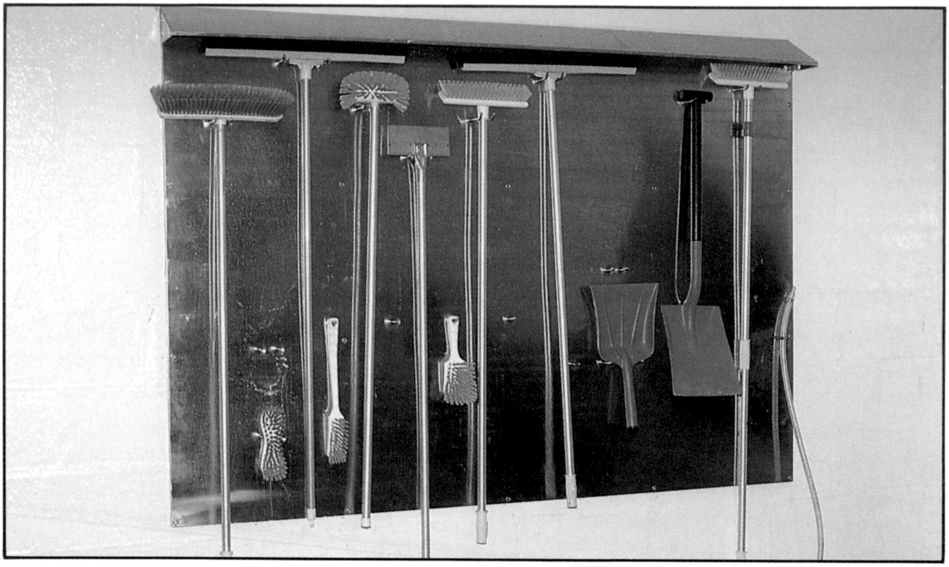

**Fig. 50.** Cleaning tools must be kept clean and tidy.

**Beverage vending machines**

These machines may present difficult cleaning problems. The complexity of some of the working parts, the time allocated for cleaning and the tenacious nature of the soil deposits has often resulted in machines being imperfectly cleaned as well as accelerated surface damage from the use of abrasives.

While the prevalent and most troublesome soiling is often identified as tannin, it has been shown that the stubborn nature of the soil is caused by an intermediate layer of water hardness scale bonding to machine parts. The scale and tannin deposits can be removed by soaking in a suitably formulated acid detergent for a few minutes. Specific tannin removers merely remove the tannin without affecting the scale.

Problems have also been identified with feed tubes. Conventional procedures do not remove all soil and when a brush is pushed down a tube and pulled out from the same end an amount of the soil is redeposited. Brushes have therefore been adapted by crimping the end loops so that a whole brush can be passed through a tube in one direction. Complete soil recovery and disinfection are effected by inserting a small piece of disinfectant-soaked cloth in the crimped end-loop, which is pulled through in much the same way that a rifle barrel is cleaned.

**Cleaning procedure**

(1) remove all contact parts from the machine, dismantle where necessary and soak in acid detergent solution. (The waste bucket, after emptying and cleaning, can be used.);
(2) remove ingredient containers, clean auger discharges with a nylon scraper, refill as necessary, wipe down the exteriors and set aside;
(3) wipe down the interior of the machine and dry thoroughly with a disposable paper towel;
(4) remove soaked parts, wipe, brush and "pull through" as appropriate, disinfect and dry. Reassemble and replace;
(5) replace ingredient containers;
(6) empty, clean, disinfect and dry the waste bucket to prevent fungal growth. Replace bucket; and
(7) flush all lines with clean, hot water from the machine system, test-vend all drinks, close the cabinet and wipe down the exterior.

Provided that high-risk beverages such as soups are closely monitored, the above procedure may be carried out every three days.

## THE HEALTH AND SAFETY OF CLEANING

The main Act applying to the safety of cleaning is the Health and Safety at Work etc. Act, 1974. This Act requires employers to ensure the health and safety of all persons on site, including employees, visitors, members of the public and sub-contractors.

Specific legislation made under this Act includes:

**The Control of Substances Hazardous to Health Regulations, 1994 (SI. 1994 No. 3246) (COSHH)**

These Regulations require employers to assess the hazards and provide suitable controls. Implementation is by means of risk assessment.

COSHH is concerned with substances that are classified as toxic, harmful, corrosive, irritant or very toxic but excludes properties such as flammable or explosive.

**Risk assessment**

An assessment of risk involves a careful examination of the workplace to identify **hazards** (anything that has the potential to cause harm), **exposure** (the likely contact with the hazard) and **risk** (the likelihood and seriousness of someone being harmed).

**Stages in risk assessment**

(1) Look for the hazards which may result in significant harm, for example, slipping on wet floors, toxic chemicals, moving parts of machinery, work at height (steps), pressure systems (steam, water or air), electricity (contact with water), manual handling, noise, poor lighting and low or high temperatures.
(2) Consider who might be harmed and how.

(3) Evaluate the risks arising from the hazards. Establish the chance of exposure occurring, level, time and frequency of exposure. Conclude whether or not a significant risk exists.

(4) Is the risk adequately controlled? Control measures will involve providing information, training, instruction and setting up safe systems and procedures. Precautions must comply with legal requirements, reduce the risk as far as practicable and a list must be made of the risks not adequately controlled. Protective and preventive measures may involve:

(i) removing the risk completely;
(ii) using a lower risk option;
(iii) preventing access;
(iv) organising the work or area to reduce exposure;
(v) issuing personal protective equipment; and
(vi) welfare and health surveillance.

(5) Assessments should be suitable and sufficient and recorded.

(6) Periodic reviews should be undertaken to establish any significant change.

**Chemicals (Hazards, Information & Packaging) Regulations, 1993 (CHIP)**

*Information required*

If a dangerous chemical is supplied in a package it must be labelled with:

(1) the name, address and telephone number of the supplier;
(2) the name of the substance or preparation; and
(3) an indication of the danger and the associated symbol risk and safety phrases.

**Fig. 51.** Hazchem symbols.

A material safety data sheet must be provided for the purchaser, which includes detailed information about the product, its hazard classification under the CHIP Regulations and the information needed by the user to carry out a COSHH assessment.

**Rules for the storage, handling and dispensing of hazardous products**

*Receipt*

All containers should be checked for damage, labelling and actual delivery against delivery note.

*Chemical stores*

Lockable, clearly identified storage, separate from foodstuffs, should be made available for cleaning materials. Access to the store should be restricted. Stores should be dry, cool, well-lit and ventilated and out of direct sunlight. There must be adequate space for safe and tidy storage, with sufficient racking to allow systematic placement of stocks. Information on storage and safety should be displayed.

Stores should be kept clean and spillages should be cleared away promptly. Stores should not freely drain and chemicals should not be allowed to enter the drainage system in quantities that could cause problems. Chemicals should be stored in original containers and used before the expiry date which is usually written on the label or the container. Acidic and alkaline (or chlorinated) products should be kept apart.

Stores must be specially designed if bulk containers of potentially harmful chemicals are broken down, and a sink, water supply and adequate working surfaces should be provided. Care must be taken when making up cleaning solutions, and manufacturer's instructions must always be followed. For example, caustic soda flakes must always be added to water. If water is added to flakes, problems are likely because of heat and effervescence.

*Handling*

(1) Chemicals should never be transferred into unmarked containers.
(2) Lids must be firmly screwed on containers, especially when being carried.
(3) There must always be adequate washing facilities for both routine and emergency situations.
(4) There should be no contact with concentrated products.
(5) When transporting, decanting or dispensing concentrated products, appropriate protective clothing must be worn including waterproof overalls, waterproof gloves, and eye protection to the appropriate British Standard.
(6) Protective clothing must be kept in good condition, dry and not contaminated with chemicals.

*Dispense*

Where available, automatic equipment is preferable for dispensing. Products should not be mixed because they may neutralize each other, form a very corrosive chemical, produce poisonous gases, or heat up rapidly causing boiling or an explosion.

**Personal Protective Equipment (PPE) at Work Regulations, 1992**

These Regulations require the employer to provide suitable personal protective equipment for employees exposed to health and safety risks, when such risks cannot be adequately controlled by other means. Personal protective equipment may include eye protection, respiratory protection, protective overalls and hand protection.

Employees must be fully trained in the use of such equipment, must be aware of the risks which the equipment will prevent or limit, must be aware of purpose and the manner in which the PPE is to be used and the maintenance required. Furthermore, employees must wear the PPE provided, take care of it and report any faults or damage.

**First aid**

The aims of first aid are to preserve life, to limit the effects of the condition and promote recovery. The first aid for cleaning chemicals generally involves the dilution of the product in or on the body.

(1) *Eye and skin contact:* dilute and remove the chemical by flooding with water. If necessary, arrange for the removal of the casualty to hospital. (Always take material safety data sheets.)

(2) *Ingestion:* maintain airways, breathing and circulation, obtain medical assistance and identify the substance swallowed. Do not induce vomiting.

(3) *Inhalation:* remove the casualty from the affected area, restore adequate breathing and obtain medical aid if necessary.

**Accidental spillage**

In the event of spillage there is an immediate risk to site personnel, to surfaces, and if chemicals mix in the drains there will be a subsequent risk to persons working in sewers.

Procedure in the event of spillage:

(1) contain the spillage to stop it reaching the drain;

(2) pump/decant the spillage into suitable containers for disposal/reuse, or absorb the spillage using sand or an absorbent material such as attapulgite; and

(3) if disposed of use a registered waste disposal company.

*Spillages entering the drain*

The sewers may become dangerous for personnel working in them and the effluent treatment plant may be damaged/overloaded so that the chemicals end up in a river. The Water Authority/National Rivers Authority must be contacted for advice and prosecution may follow. (Make sure the emergency numbers for the Water Authority and the National Rivers Authority are readily available.)

CHAPTER 14

# Pest control

Pests are the direct cause of most of the statutory closures of food businesses, they are a major factor in the thousands of food complaints reported to Environmental Health Departments each year and they feature prominently in many of the prosecutions taken under food hygiene regulations. Furthermore, pest attack is responsible for a significant proportion of the unfit food surrendered each year. If one also takes into account the amount spent on pesticides, the damage to buildings and fittings, the distress to customers and the spread of disease, it is obvious that pest control is an inseparable part of profitable and hygienic food production.

It should be the responsibility of a senior person to ensure effective pest control. Persons involved in pest control should be fully trained, and it is essential to ensure that the treatment itself does not expose food to risk of contamination.

The common pests found in the food industry include:

(1) rodents: rats and mice;

(2) insects: flies, wasps, cockroaches, psocids, silverfish, stored product insects and ants;

(3) birds: mainly feral pigeons and sparrows; and

(4) mites.

Effective pest control necessitates rapid identification of the species causing concern, a knowledge of its life cycle and the most economical, rapid and safe way of eliminating it. Pests require food, shelter, warmth and security. Denial of these environmental factors (access (proofing), food and harbourage) will prevent their survival. This form of control may be termed environmental control and is the first line of defence against possible infestations.

Environmental controls may not be entirely successful and other steps must be taken to destroy any pests which gain access to food premises. Eradication methods may be considered under two main headings:

(1) physical;

(2) chemical.

Usually, physical control methods are preferable as the pest is caught, either dead or alive, and consequently is not able to continue contaminating food. Examples of physical control include electronic fly killers and rodent traps. Unfortunately, physical control methods are not always completely effective and pesticides have to be used.

When chemicals are used the pest is not killed immediately and may, therefore, drop or crawl into food if adequate precautions are not taken. Furthermore, the safety implications of using pesticides must not be overlooked.

**Reasons for pest control**

(1) *To prevent the spread of disease*

Rodents, insects and birds can all spread diseases which affect man and other animals. Rodents, sparrows, flies and cockroaches are all capable of transmitting food poisoning organisms, either by direct contact with food with their contaminated bodies or legs, by faecal deposits, or in the case of rodents, by urine. Furthermore, disease may be spread by:

(i) consuming food contaminated by rodent urine or droppings;
(ii) contact with rat urine which may result in Weil's disease (leptospiral jaundice). In the food industry, fish filleters and slaughterhouse operatives are most at risk;
(iii) eating undercooked pork affected by Trichinella cysts which may infect pigs which have eaten dead rats;
(iv) parasites which live on rats; and
(v) rat bites.

(2) *To prevent wastage of food*

Considerable financial loss is incurred by pest infestations in food and packaging materials. The presence of insects, either dead or alive, rodents, droppings or hair, bird feathers or droppings in food results in loss of production, recall of contaminated foods and the destruction of large quantities of food. Bagged foodstuffs under long-term storage can collapse due to heavy rodent attack and the cost of rebagging and cleaning can be considerable. Furthermore, birds and insects, but particularly rodents, eat food in fields, warehouses, commercial and domestic premises.

(3) *To prevent damage*

To wear down the incisor teeth, which grow throughout their life, rodents gnaw continuously; woodwork, soft metal pipes and electric cables are common targets. The damage caused by rodents from fire, flooding due to burst pipes, and subsidence caused by burrowing results in considerable financial loss each year. Furthermore, at least one death has been recorded as a result of rodents gnawing gas pipes.

(4) *To comply with the law*

The Food Safety (General Food Hygiene) Regulations, 1995 require that food must be so placed and/or protected as to minimize any risk of contamination and that food premises must be maintained in good repair and condition and designed and constructed to prevent contamination by pests. The Food Safety Act, 1990 makes it an offence to sell food which is unfit or contains foreign bodies. Food contaminated with pests, parts of pests or droppings, etc. could be dealt with under this Act. Furthermore, food premises with serious infestations of rodents, insects, particularly cockroaches, or birds that are a danger to the health of customers could be the subject of closure procedure under the Food Safety Act. The loss of business resulting from the prosecution of a food premises for offences involving pests can be considerable and may even result in bankruptcy.

The Prevention of Damage by Pests Act, 1949 requires the occupier of any land or buildings to notify the local authority of any rodent infestation (not applicable to agricultural land). The authority can insist that the occupier carries out any necessary treatment including the removal of harbourage and repair of buildings. This Act also requires local authorities to take steps to ensure that their district is kept free from rats and mice.

Under the Health and Safety at Work, etc. Act, 1974 employers have a legal obligation to ensure, as far as reasonably practicable, the health, safety and welfare of employees. The presence of an infestation of certain pests could result in unsafe working conditions.

**The design, maintenance and proofing of buildings**

Harbourage in food premises is not only provided in dark, undisturbed areas but also within the very structure of some buildings. For this reason false ceilings must always have access points to enable inspection and treatment to be carried out. Boxing or ducting of pipes creates ideal conditions for harbourage and should normally be avoided. Where ducting is installed, it should be fitted with access plates at two metre intervals and should never finish in an open end. Surface panels and finishes which are not properly fixed and sealed to walls often provide ideal harbourage. Cavities within internal walls should also be avoided. All parts of the structure should be capable of being easily cleaned. High ledges, pits for elevators and ovens must be fully accessible. Elevators and conveyor intakes must have tight-fitting doors at the delivery end. Shutter boxes for roller doors must be checked to ensure they are not used as nesting sites for rodents or birds. The use of cupboards should be minimized and no gaps should exist around pipework passing into cupboards.

The design and installation of cables, electrical trunking and motors should eliminate harbourage. Motor housings for refrigerators make ideal nesting sites for mice. All structural damage such as holes in walls, broken windows, loose tiles and damaged insulation should be repaired immediately to obviate its potential for insect harbourage. Silicon mastics are particularly useful for sealing small gaps.

All buildings should be adequately proofed; doors should be close-fitting and provided with metal kick-plates. Gaps where pipes and girders pass through walls should be adequately proofed. Defective drains, both above and below ground, must be made good. Tight-fitting inspection chamber covers must always be provided and replaced immediately if they become broken. Chamber walls should be kept in good condition with the mortar joints intact, otherwise rats may break through the walls. Disused drains should be properly sealed, especially foul drain inlets from W.C.s which should be stopped with concrete mixed with broken glass. Water seals in gullies, sinks and W.C. pans must be maintained. All external ventilation stacks must be provided with wire balloons fixed in the top of each pipe. Insects and rodents thrive in warm conditions and effective ventilation is required to keep food rooms as cool as possible. All ventilation openings, including opening windows, must be adequately proofed to avoid pests gaining access, for example, air bricks should be fitted with metal gauze. It should be noted that if a pencil can pass through a gap, so can a young mouse.

Rats drink about three times the amount they eat and denying sources of water will therefore assist control. Dripping taps, defective gutters, leaking roofs and puddles are all examples of common sources which must be removed.

**Good housekeeping**

Despite all proofing precautions, pests will inevitably get into a building at some time. There is a difference, however, between the occasional invader and the establishment of a stable population. To reduce the risk of an infestation it is important to deny the lone invader the conditions it likes and in particular to ensure that:

(1) premises are kept in a clean and tidy condition to reduce sources of food and harbourage. Attention must be paid to staff locker rooms, changing, dining and washroom areas. The consumption of food should be restricted to dining areas. Lift shafts must be regularly inspected to remove debris and food deposits. Adequate cleaning and dust extraction equipment is essential to avoid dust build-up, especially when handling dry powders such as flour. Fixtures and fittings should be at least 250mm above the floor to facilitate cleaning. Co-operation between cleaners and pest control contractors is essential to ensure baits are not removed, repositioned or washed away;
(2) spillages are cleared away promptly;
(3) food is kept in rodent-proof containers and lids are always replaced; used ice-cream tubs are ideal for use in catering operations;
(4) stock rotation is carried out and all stock is stored correctly;
(5) unused equipment, packaging material and similar articles are rotated and checked frequently as rodents prefer living in undisturbed areas;
(6) special attention is paid to waste disposal. Receptacles should be of adequate capacity to avoid overflowing and should be provided with tight-fitting lids or covers. Waste must be removed promptly and efficiently and refuse areas should be hosed down after waste is collected. Receptacles themselves must be cleaned after emptying to prevent deposits providing breeding sites for flies. Incinerators must not be allowed to cause problems and refuse tips on or adjacent to food premises/sites should not be allowed;
(7) vegetation, old equipment, rubbish and other cover or harbourage must be removed from the immediate vicinity of the site. It may be appropriate to undertake joint action with neighbouring premises to, as far as practicable, keep adjacent areas pest free; and
(8) all raw materials, including food, packaging and equipment must be checked to ensure their freedom from infestation.

## Correct storage

The correct storage of goods is essential to reduce pest incidence. The following principles must be adhered to:

(1) all areas must remain accessible for cleaning and inspection which should be carried out at frequent and regular intervals;
(2) damage to containers must be minimized to reduce spillage;
(3) all goods must be kept clear of the walls, windows and ventilators (at least 500mm);
(4) adequate gangways must be left for inspection between stacks;
(5) all goods must be kept off the floor, for example, on pallets or low stands, taking care enough room is left to clear spillages;
(6) all areas must be well-ventilated and lighted;
(7) storage areas must be in good repair and effectively proofed against pest entry;
(8) storage space should be cleaned and inspected before new stock arrives; and
(9) goods which are infested or susceptible to infestation must be segregated from those which are not; raw materials, packaging and finished products should be stored separately.

## The use of contractors

Most food businesses rely on the expertise of a pest control company, or the local authority, to ensure their freedom from infestations. The final decision on whom to choose normally depends on the type of pest and the methods required for its control. However, the destruction of pests which are observed in the premises is not sufficient; regular inspections should be carried out to ensure the complete absence of pests from the immediate surrounding area.

It should be noted that the use of contractors does not absolve managers from their responsibility of keeping premises pest free. Furthermore, their use, in isolation, is not a defence should legal proceedings be instituted for a complaint regarding food contaminated with insects or parts of rodents or their droppings. However, food authorities should consider the attitude of, and precautions taken by, companies when deciding whether or not to institute proceedings, and the court will also take these factors into account when considering a "due diligence" defence or the level of fine.

## Selecting a contractor

The following matters should be considered when selecting a contractor:

(1) the ability of the contractor to undertake a complete survey and provide a clear report of recommendations and action required. The contract should detail pests covered, frequency of visits and reports, arrangements for additional treatments including emergency response, preventative measures and include an unambiguous quotation;
(2) the experience of the contractor of pest control in the food industry and provision of appropriate references from current clients;

(3) the adequacy of appropriate insurance cover with regard to product, public and employer's liability together with evidence of financial viability;
(4) the contractor must have sufficient resources in terms of trained/qualified staff and the necessary equipment to carry out proper pest control services. It is a legal requirement for all of the contractors' staff to be trained to a competent level ;
(5) clear reporting procedures and accountability must be established;
(6) the methods and materials used for pest control treatment have to be approved under The Control of Pesticides Regulations, 1986 and it is illegal to use as a pesticide any substance not so approved. Contractors should provide the relevant Materials Safety Data Sheets and COSHH risk assessments. Some contractors now provide a pest risk assessment as part of the contract enabling clients to take advantage of the **due diligence** defence in the Food Safety Act, 1990;
(7) the ability of the company to provide a complete service including preventative measures such as proofing and the installation, maintenance and cleaning of electronic flying insect killing equipment. Reports of inspections should include advice on good housekeeping, storage and any preventative work required; and
(8) the company should be a member of the British Pest Control Association and employ staff who hold the Association's certificate of proficiency or its equivalent.

**Liaison with the contractor**

The contractor should provide the client's management with details of all preparations used, supply a written report on each visit and make any necessary recommendations with regard to proofing, waste disposal, stock control, housekeeping, cleaning or access. Action points should then be agreed and follow-up visits made to ensure the remedies are carried out.

Whichever firm is chosen, to ensure successful control it will need the full co-operation of the client and the contractor should be called in immediately evidence of a pest is discovered. Additionally:

(1) the serviceman should be accompanied throughout the visit;
(2) written notes on any unsatisfactory housekeeping should be made and immediate action taken to remedy defects;
(3) the position of bait boxes should be noted;
(4) daily inspections of bait boxes should take place to look for droppings and dead bodies, which should be removed immediately;
(5) if necessary, fresh bait should be laid at the end of a week, by which time weekly inspections may well suffice; and
(6) when no further evidence of infestation appears, intensive baiting can be discontinued and proofing carried out. Permanent baits should be maintained.

## RODENTS AND RODENT CONTROL

The three rodents which may infest food premises in this country are:

*Rattus norvegicus* (common rat, brown rat or Norway rat);

*Rattus rattus* (ship rat or black rat);
*Mus domesticus* (house mouse).

The provision of food stores gives rodents the ideal conditions for rapid multiplication; food, shelter and no predators or competition. Furthermore, the transportation of food in containers has meant that rodents can easily be brought into premises, if suitable precautions are not taken during unloading and emptying.

**Surveys**

Certain members of staff should be specifically trained to identify evidence of rats or mice. These people should carry out regular inspections of the premises, both internally and externally, to look for signs such as:

(1) droppings, if very recent they are shiny and soft;
(2) footprints in dust;
(3) gnawing marks and damage, for example, holes in sacks;
(4) smear marks from the fur of rodents where their bodies are in regular, close contact with surfaces, for example, horizontal pipes adjacent to light-coloured walls;
(5) holes and nesting sites;
(6) rat runs in undergrowth; and
(7) the animals themselves, either dead or alive.

The reporting of signs should not be restricted to specific people, all staff should be aware of the problems of rodents and must observe their responsibility to notify their supervisor if they believe them to be present.

**The house mouse**

The cosmopolitan *Mus domesticus* is normally found inhabiting buildings, where it finds harbourage, warmth, food and nesting materials. Unlike the rat it tends to be attracted to many feeding points while foraging for food - particularly cereals. Intense feeding occurs at only one or two points, although the mouse will nibble at many places. Movement in search of food is limited. The success of the house mouse to co-exist with man can be attributed to its ability to live in a wide range of habitats, to its immense reproductive capacity and its omnivorous feeding habits (a pair of mice can, given ideal conditions, produce up to 2,000 young within a year).

**The brown rat**

*Rattus norvegicus* is the predominant rat in the United Kingdom. It usually lives in burrows in the soil, especially beneath buildings, but may also be found in sewers, railway embankments, foodstores and rubbish dumps. The brown rat is omnivorous but has a preference for cereals. It tends to remain close to its nesting site when searching for food. Theoretically one pair of rats can produce hundreds of offspring within a year, fortunately many fail to achieve maturity. However, once a pair of rats become established, failure to implement immediate eradication measures can soon result in a major infestation.

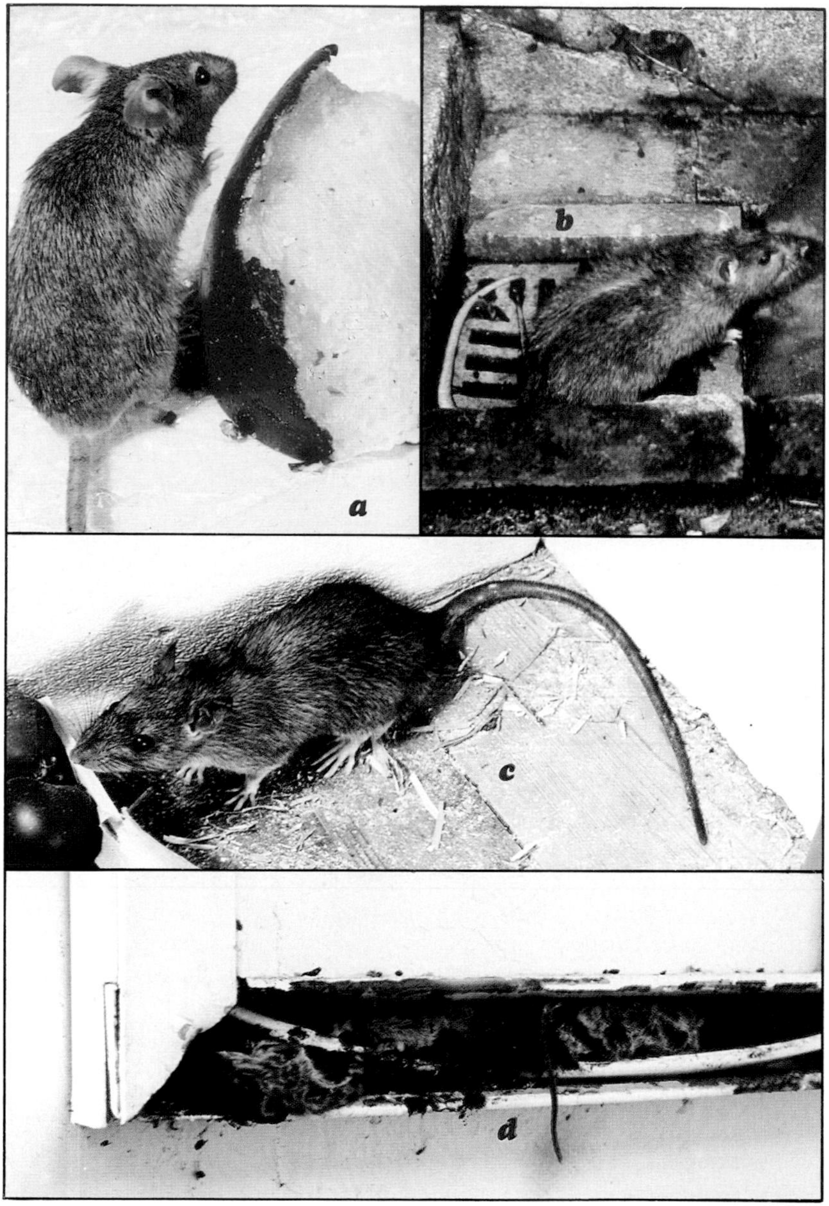


**Fig. 52.** a) House mouse. b) Brown rat. c) Black rat.
d) Barbecued mice - caused by gnawing a live electric cable.

**TABLE XXIX** A COMPARISON OF COMMON RODENTS

| | Brown rat | Black rat | House mouse |
|---|---|---|---|
| Body/weight | Thick set 100-500g | Slender 100-300g | Up to 20g |
| Snout | Blunt | Pointed | Slightly pointed |
| Ears | Small | Large | Large |
| Tail | Shorter than head plus body | Longer than head plus body | Much longer than head plus body |
| Colour | Variable: brown on back, grey belly | Variable: black or brown back, dark grey/white belly | Grey back, light grey belly |
| Feet | Large | Large | Small |

**The black rat**

*Rattus rattus* is also omnivorous but has a preference for fruit and vegetables. It is an excellent climber and is often found in the upper storeys of buildings and roof spaces. The black rat is more difficult to control because of its food preference and its wider foraging activities. In the UK it is unlikely that the black rat breeds on the mainland but it may occasionally be imported to sea-ports, airports and container terminals.

**Treatment**

*Rodenticides*: may be defined as chemicals used for killing rodents.

*Baits*: are rodenticides combined with food, or water, which are palatable to rodents. Bait bases include cereals, fruit, fish, meat and paste.

Successful control requires sufficient numbers of suitably distributed baits to ensure that all rodents have an opportunity of eating enough rodenticide to cause death.

Rodenticides may be divided into two groups:

(1) chronic rodenticides; and

(2) acute rodenticides.

**Chronic rodenticides**

These chemicals need to be ingested by rodents in small doses over a few days to obtain the desired results. Although, it is claimed that a lethal dose of the anticoagulant, brodifacoum, can be ingested during a single feed. Like other anticoagulants death occurs several days after feeding and consequently bait shyness does not occur.

Most chronic rodenticides are anticoagulants. They work by preventing the blood from clotting and as rodents are continually haemorrhaging, those consuming sufficient bait die of internal and external bleeding. Warfarin was the first and most widely used anticoagulant but the increase in resistance has resulted in its decline.

**Resistance**

Rodents may continue to eat bait over several weeks if reinvasion occurs or if they possess a natural tolerance to the rodenticide. This last effect is known as resistance. Where resistance to warfarin occurs, mice may be killed with alphachloralose, calciferol or brodifacoum. Rats may be killed by bromadiolone or brodifacoum. Research is continuing on new rodenticides with a different mode of action.

**Acute rodenticides**

These chemicals kill the rodent in a relatively short time after a single feed. However, they are more toxic to humans and domestic animals. A further disadvantage is the possible development of bait shyness following the consumption of a sub-lethal amount of rodenticide. The rodent refuses to eat any more bait.

After treatment all bodies must be collected and either incinerated or buried. Suitable protective clothing, including gloves, must always be worn when handling bodies or rodenticides.

Alphachloralose is for indoor use only and is commonly used against mice in food premises. It is a sedative which lowers the body temperature and death results from hypothermia. It is not so effective when temperatures exceed 16°C.

**Contact rodenticides**

This is a rodenticidal dust or gel, such as bromadiolone, used to treat dry harbourages and runs. The dust is picked up on the feet and fur and may pass through the skin or be ingested during grooming. It must never be used inside food rooms or if there is a risk of contaminating food or food equipment.

**Traps**

Traps may be used if there is a particular risk of contaminating food, or to catch a sole survivor of a treatment. The advantage of the trap is that it prevents rodents dying in inaccessible places and causing offensive odours or blowfly problems. Traps are normally baited, although they are occasionally laid unbaited. Traps should be placed on runs, at the entrance of harbourage or at right angles to walls, with the bait nearest the wall. They should be examined daily so that if necessary they can be reset or dead rodents removed.

**Sticky boards**

These are most often used to eliminate the occasional survivor of a treatment. A piece of hardboard is coated with 3mm of a very sticky substance which holds any rodent that comes into contact with it. Baiting around the edge of the board increases its effectiveness. It may be advantageous to fasten boards down and they must be checked daily.

## Tracking powder

This is a dry powder, such as flour or talc, which is used to determine the presence and location of rodents, by foot or tail marks. It is non-toxic and does not kill rodents.

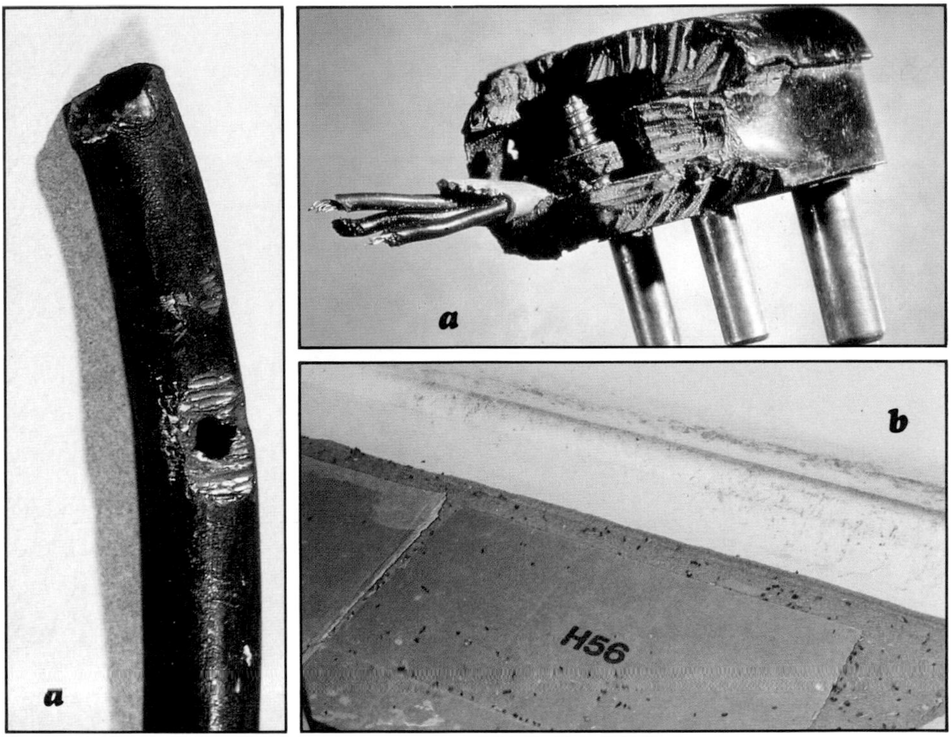


**Fig . 51.** a) Rodent damage caused by gnawing.
b) Mouse smears and droppings.

## Safety precautions

The position of all bait points should be numbered and all bait boxes should be given a corresponding number and be dated to show when the bait was last inspected or replaced. A plan of the premises, showing the location of all bait points, should be kept by the senior person responsible. It is important to keep accurate details of visits by contractors, and a pest control book should be kept on the premises under the control of management. The following information should be recorded:

(1) the results of the initial survey;
(2) the work carried out as a result of the survey;
(3) the degree of infestation found and the type of pests;
(4) details of each treatment carried out and the pesticides used;
(5) the recommendations made by the contractor on each visit and the action taken;
(6) a record of any special or emergency visits made by the contractor; and

(7) all reported sightings by staff, of pests on or around the premises.

Baits must not be positioned where they could expose food to risk of contamination and all boxes must be labelled "poison". A dye is normally added to each bait and the person in charge should be aware of which colour is given to each rodenticide. Suitable protective clothing and waterproof gloves must always be worn when handling rodenticides, rodents or traps. Food contaminated by rodents is usually considered unfit for human consumption. Regard must be had to the Health and Safety at Work, etc. Act, 1974 and the Control of Substances Hazardous to Health Regulations, 1994.

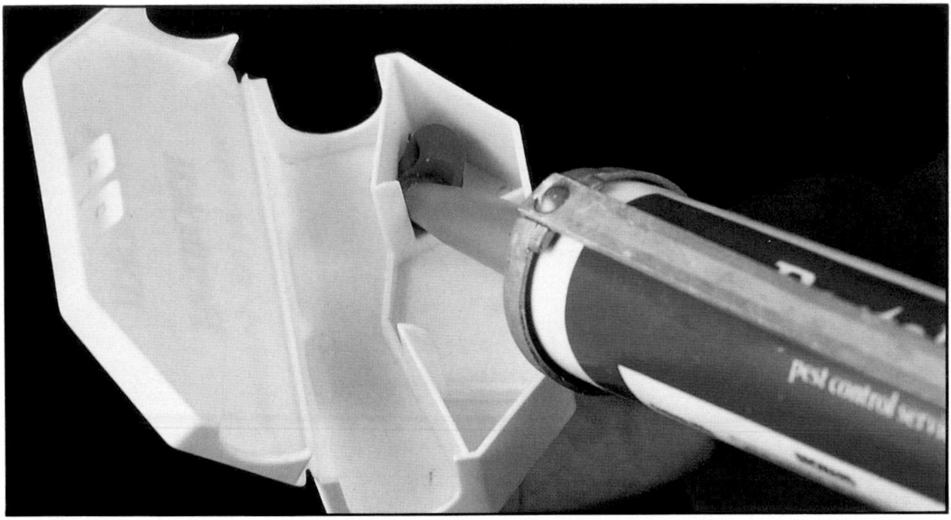

**Fig. 54.** The extrusion of poison into a tamper resistant box reduces spillage. The use of these boxes has been found to increase the weight of bait eaten, as they provide security to a mouse while it consumes bait, and so ensures control is more effective. They also reduce the risk of accidental poisoning of pet animals.

## INSECTS AND INSECT CONTROL

Any insect in food premises is a pest. However, apart from those insects that wander in, there are many that will cause extensive problems if they become established. Insect pests can attack and destroy large quantities of food which become contaminated with their bodies, webbing and excreta. In addition, several insects are capable of transmitting pathogens, including food poisoning organisms. No food is safe from insect attack, although beans, cereals, flour, dried fruits and some dried meats are amongst the most susceptible to infestation.

Common insect pests of food premises include:

(1) flies;
(2) wasps;
(3) stored product insects, including moths;
(4) cockroaches;
(5) psocids and mites;
(6) silverfish; and
(7) ants.

## FLIES

The order Diptera contains approximately 78,000 species. Those of particular importance to the food industry are: *Musca domestica* (common housefly), *Fannia canicularis* (lesser housefly), *Calliphora spp.* (bluebottle), *Lucilia spp.* (greenbottle) and *Drosophila spp.* (fruit fly).

Flies infect food in four ways:
(1) to feed, they regurgitate enzymes and partly-digested food from the previous meal;
(2) they continually defecate;
(3) they carry bacteria on the hairs on their body and legs; and
(4) pupal cases, eggs and dead bodies end up in our food.

The danger to health from flies must not be underestimated. Flies have been allegedly involved in the transmission of many pathogens including *Shigella spp.* and food poisoning organisms.

The life cycle of flies depends on the breeding site temperature and the amount of available food. Typical breeding sites are accumulations of waste organic matter, such as refuse, and refuse tips. The female housefly deposits around 600 eggs during her life span. From egg to adult is normally less than two weeks in warm weather. Maggots grow to around 9mm. Blowflies usually breed on decaying matter of animal origin, especially meat.

Fruit flies generally occur in bakeries, fruit-canning factories and beer cellars. They are often seen hovering around sweet foods. Some species lay their eggs in unwashed milk bottles, when the pupal cases may be found cemented to the inside of the bottles. The presence of these flies should generally be regarded as bad management. They are more of a nuisance than a health hazard and control is usually achieved by removal of the breeding material.

### Wasps

Wasps are basically beneficial to man as they are predators of other insects. However, they tend to be a nuisance during the late summer in such premises as bakeries and fruit factories. If possible, nearby nests should be located and destroyed. Perimeter baiting by pest control operators may be successful.

### Flying insect control

Wherever possible, emphasis should be placed on environmental and physical control methods to reduce the risk of food contamination. The areas around food premises should be kept clean and tidy and all possible breeding sites should be removed. Drainage gullies, effluent treatment plants and waste disposal areas can all cause problems if neglected.

All refuse containers should be kept clean and in good repair. Lids should always be tight-fitting. If skips are used, completely enclosed compacting types are preferable. Waste-food containers, such as syrup tins, which attract insects, should be washed thoroughly before storage outside. All refuse areas should have well-drained hard-standings which are kept clean. Polythene sacks are recommended for internal use.

*Proofing*

Windows and other openings used to provide ventilation must, where necessary, be fitted with cleansable flyscreens. Roof access at apexes and eaves should also be screened. Doors should be kept closed or provided with cleansable screens or clear, heavy-duty plastic strips. Self-closing doors and double door air-locks are useful.

*Electronic flying insect killers*

Those insects gaining entry to food areas should be destroyed using suitably sited electronic fly killers. Flies are attracted by an ultra-violet light and then electrocuted on charged grids. Performance is proportional to total light wattage of each unit.

Units are most effective in subdued light, away from windows and fluorescent lights. They should not be positioned over food or food equipment or in draughts, as dead flies may be blown out. Some units incorporate a system to prevent insect particles falling out, for example, the use of UV light-transmitting polymer film. Catch-trays should be emptied frequently and the units regularly serviced. Tubes should be replaced annually or as recommended by the manufacturers. Due to risk of explosions, they should not be sited where there are high concentrations of flour or sugar dust.

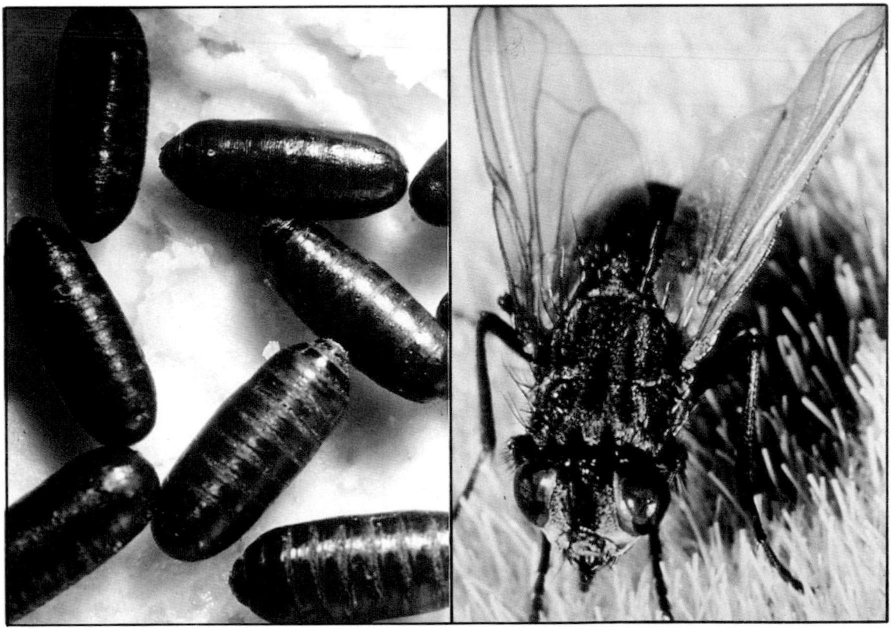

**Fig. 55.** Housefly and pupae.

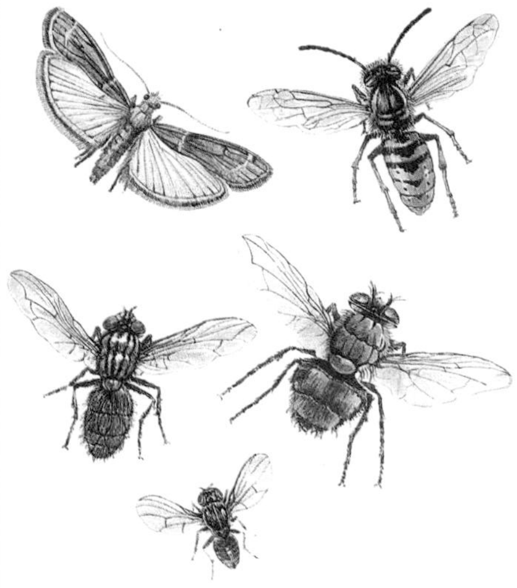

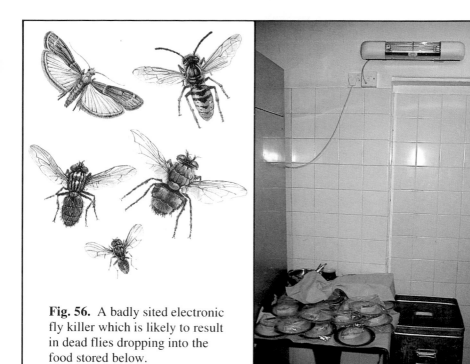

**Fig. 56.** A badly sited electronic fly killer which is likely to result in dead flies dropping into the food stored below.

*Sticky fly-papers*

These are very useful to supplement electronic fly killers in areas to which the public are not admitted. Useful protection can be given to storage areas, refuse areas and bakeries. They should not be positioned near heat sources and should be changed as often as necessary.

*Chemical control of flying insects*

Insecticides are chemical substances which kill insects. They should only be used as a back-up to physical control methods. Only knock-down insecticides with low toxicity, such as pybuthrin, should be used in food rooms. Before treatment, food and equipment should be removed, or protected, to prevent risk of contamination from chemicals or insects. After treatment all surfaces should be thoroughly cleaned and dead bodies removed.

The use of residual insecticides or treatments involving the continuous emission of insecticide during food production, for example, dichlorvos strips, is not recommended because of the danger of dead insects dropping into food. However, treatment of corridors, or vestibules in non-food areas, with residual insecticides may be useful. Synthetic pyrethroids are the most common of the residual insecticides used in these areas.

## STORED PRODUCT INSECTS

This is a large group of insects which attacks foodstuffs in storage, transport and manufacture. It includes beetles, weevils, moths and larvae. Cereals, flour, beans, dried products and nuts may all be attacked.

These insects have no direct health significance, although they do cause considerable economic loss. Infestations are often difficult to detect due to the small size of the insects and because many are only active at night. They remain hidden in the building structure, concealed in the crevices and inaccessible, dark corners. Signs to watch for include tiny moving adult insects, unusual debris or speckling, fine strands of webbing and tunnels in some foods. If evidence of infestation is discovered, a specialist pest control contractor must immediately be asked to carry out treatment.

Infestations may be introduced into the food premises with the raw materials or possibly arise due to breeding in materials which are poorly rotated. Inaccessible, poorly-cleaned structures also provide useful breeding sites. Panelling of walls increases problems significantly. Infested pallets may be a source of infestation. It is essential that all raw materials are thoroughly inspected when unloaded at the premises. Containers or sacks showing evidence of damage or holes should be regarded with suspicion. If adequate inspection is not possible when unloading, the new materials should be segregated from existing stocks. All raw materials which are held for considerable periods should be inspected at least weekly. This includes paper and other stationery stocks. All spillages and residues must be removed as soon as possible.

### Insect control

To successfully control stored product insects it is necessary to know:

(1) the species involved;
(2) the source of the infestation; and
(3) the size of the infestation and its location.

**Fig. 57.** Fumigation may be required to control infestation of stored products.

Should an infestation occur, despite environmental control, insecticides will have to be used. Control should be carried out by trained specialists using approved insecticides. The formulation and insecticide used will depend on the site of infestation and the type of insect. Infestations of raw materials should be dealt with immediately. In some cases treatment may be successfully employed, for example, fumigation. However, quite often the food will need to be destroyed.

Fumigation is the application of a toxic chemical in the form of a gas, vapour or volatile liquid in a closed container or to a food stack under gas-proof sheets. The required concentration of gas must be maintained for a specific period. For some pests, such as insects in cereals, fumigation is the only satisfactory method of treatment. The most common fumigant is methyl bromide.

**Psocids or booklice**

Psocids are small (1-2mm), cream, light brown or dark brown insects which are being reported more frequently in food premises and are resulting in increasing numbers of food complaints. They are omnivorous and commonly infest flour, grain, nuts, chocolate, fish and meat products. They also feed on moulds and yeasts and infestations are often associated with packaging materials and pallets. Their presence usually indicates conditions of high humidity. They are mainly of nuisance value but they may be responsible for disseminating spoilage bacteria.

Control involves high standards of hygiene which prevent mould development. Adequate ventilation and dry conditions are particularly important. Residual insecticides may be applied to pallets, walls or other surfaces, although fumigation of product may also be necessary.

**Mites**

Mites are similar to insects but adults have eight legs. They appear to the naked eye as coarse dust and can only be detected by their movement. A variety of food may be infested including flour, cheese and smoked meats. They are particularly likely to be found in damp, poorly-ventilated stores where they taint food. They may cause dermatitis. Mites are controlled by drying and high temperatures.

**Silverfish and firebrats**

These essentially nocturnal insects are either bright or dull silver, the shape of miniature carrots about 10mm long. Identification is made easier because of the two large antennae on the head and the bristles on the abdomen. They move about very quickly and, although they are frequently found in food premises, they are of little health significance. However, as with all other insects, infestations cannot be tolerated.

Good housekeeping and denial of harbourage are essential for successful control. Crumbs and spillages must be cleared up and particular attention paid to waste disposal. Sources of moisture, including condensation, must be removed. Hundreds of silverfish can live under defective surfaces, especially badly-fixed tiles, and in cracks and crevices. Infestations thrive on tea and coffee waste trapped behind sink units.

**Fig. 58.** Stored product pests
a) *Stegobium paniceum* (Biscuit beetle).
b) *Sitophilus granarius* (Grain weevil).
c) *Liposcelis bostrychophilis* (Booklice).
d) *Ptinus tectus* (Australian spider beetle).

**Fig. 59.** a) Larva, webbing and damage by *Ephestia elutella*.
b) *Plodia interpunctella* (Indian meal moth).
c) *Tineola bisselliella* (Clothes moth).
d) *Hofmannophila pseudospretella* (Brown house moth).
e) *Ephestia elutella* (Warehouse or Mill moth).

Live insects may be killed with an aerosol fly spray provided that the usual precautions are taken. Residual insecticides may need to be applied by a pest control operator where other control measures fail.

## COCKROACHES

Only two species of cockroach are widely distributed in this country:

(1) the Oriental cockroach (*Blatta orientalis*); and

(2) the German cockroach (*Blattella germanica*).

Occasional problems are caused by the larger American cockroach (*Periplaneta americana*), for example, in dock areas, zoos and schools where they have escaped from laboratories.

### Cockroach habits

Cockroaches are gregarious, omnivorous, nocturnal insects and give off an unpleasant characteristic odour. During the day they hide in cracks, pipe ducts, electric motors, behind skirtings and in stores. Their presence is normally detected by faecal pellets or their smell. The periods of maximum activity are just before dawn and just after dusk. Neither species fly, although the German cockroach may glide for short distances.

Cockroaches are capable of carrying various pathogens which may lead to outbreaks of disease, although there is little evidence that they are a common vector for spreading infection. Over 40 pathogenic organisms have been isolated from cockroaches collected from a variety of premises either in the faeces or contaminating their legs or antennae, including:

*Staphylococcus aureus* *Salmonella typhimurium* *Salmonella typhi*

For this reason and the fact that their faecal pellets, moult debris and dead bodies contaminate food, cockroaches in food premises must be destroyed.

**Fig. 60.** Oriental cockroach, with protruding ootheca.

**The Oriental cockroach**

By far the commoner of the two species. The adults grow to about 24mm long and are shiny dark brown to black. They can climb rough vertical surfaces, such as brickwork, and often congregate around water sources. Oriental cockroaches are frequently found in cellars, kitchens, bakeries and drains. Long-term survival and breeding externally, for example, in refuse tips and gardens, is possible.

The eggs are laid in an ootheca and take around two months to hatch at 25°C, but this period is extended in cooler conditions. It takes between six and 12 months to reach adult stage in heated buildings with good food supplies. The female can produce over 150 young in its lifetime.

**The German cockroach (Steam fly)**

The adult is 10 to 15mm long and is yellowish-brown. It is capable of climbing smooth vertical surfaces such as painted walls. German cockroaches prefer warm, moist conditions and are commonly found in kitchens, pantries, restaurants and especially ships' galleys. At 30°C the life span is around 3 to 12 months and the female produces approximately 250 to 300 eggs.

**Fig. 61.** German cockroaches.

**Cockroach control**

Prevention is of prime importance when considering cockroach control in food premises. Cockroaches may be brought into the building with food containers, raw materials or laundry. It is imperative to ensure that commodities entering the food premises are not a constant source of supply of cockroaches.

Sound building structure is important as it precludes the entry of a large number of cockroaches through openings and helps eliminate harbourage. Crevices may be sealed with putty, and service pipes or conduits passing through walls should be cemented in position. Ill-fitting panels that are not removed are often likely to harbour cockroaches. Strict hygiene should discourage infestations. Food should be stored in containers with close-fitting lids and spillage should be removed promptly.

Areas inaccessible for cleaning should be eliminated. Particular attention should be paid to drains and refuse areas. Effective control necessitates the use of specialist operators. The first procedure in any control programme is to make a thorough survey, preferably at night by torch light, to establish the extent of the infestation and the species of cockroach involved. For daylight inspection the application of an insecticide with a flushing action, for example, pyrethrum, may be used. When sprayed into crevices cockroaches will come scurrying out. Small adhesive cockroach traps may be placed in susceptible areas to identify and monitor any cockroach activity.

Internally, the insecticide and formulation employed must be chosen to suit the site and no single application is available for all circumstances. It is advisable to sketch a plan of the rooms, including details of the plant lay-out, to achieve effective control.

To obtain satisfactory results the insecticide should persist on treated surfaces for sufficient time, or be applied an adequate number of times, to break the life cycle. This may involve a period of 12 weeks, which is the time taken for some eggs to develop.

A range of insecticidal contact dusts be puffed into underfloor spaces, ducts and cavities. Other formulations include insecticidal gel or sprays based on fenitrothion, alphacypermethrin, bendiocarb or other residual insecticides. Insect growth regulators such as hydroprene are now commercially available. Bait and gel formulations containing hydramethylnon provide alternatives where sprays are unacceptable. Established infestations are often difficult to eliminate and reinfestation from isolated pockets commonly occurs.

*Cockroach traps*

Several types of cockroach trap have been developed with varying degrees of success. They are particularly useful to monitor the extent of infestations and to determine whether any cockroaches have survived a treatment with insecticide.

## ANTS

### The garden ant (Lasius niger)

The black garden ant nests outside but often becomes a persistent pest of food premises as it forages for food. It is mainly of nuisance value, although contaminated food must be discarded. Successful control depends on the destruction of the nest. This may be achieved using residual sprays, dusting powder or insecticidal baits.

### Pharaoh's ant (Monomorium pharaonis)

Pharaoh's ants are light yellow and approximately 2mm in length. They are often found in seemingly impenetrable food containers. Infestations are usually restricted to permanently heated buildings, especially hospitals, bakeries, hotels, residential properties and kitchens. All kinds of food may be attacked, although there is a preference for sweet and high-protein food. Nests are very difficult to detect and destroy. Physical transmission of pathogens to food is possible as they may visit drains, excreta and soiled dressings.

Control may eventually be achieved using baits containing boric acid or methoprene. Residual sprays, powders and lacquer formulations may all be used depending on the location of the infestation.

## BIRD PESTS AND THEIR CONTROL

Birds which commonly gain access to food premises are sparrows and feral pigeons, although other species, such as starlings, occasionally cause problems. Warehouses and large food factories are prime targets, although bakeries and supermarkets may also be affected.

Reasons for control:

(1) to prevent the contamination of food or equipment by droppings, feathers, regurgitated pellets and nesting materials;
(2) to prevent the transmission of food poisoning organisms;
(3) to remove sources of insect and mite infestation provided by nests, excreta and the birds themselves;
(4) to prevent blockages of gutters which may result in flooding and expensive maintenance;
(5) to prevent defacement of buildings; bird droppings produce an acid which attacks stone;
(6) to prevent roosting on fire escapes and similar structures, which may result in a safety hazard for human occupants; and
(7) to prevent damage to food packaging.

### External control

Control of birds must be considered during the planning stage of new buildings. Food premises should be designed to prevent ingress of birds, as it may be extremely costly to proof against entry once the building is completed. Ledges and perches should be eliminated.

### Good housekeeping

As with other forms of pest control, prevention is better than cure. Good housekeeping is essential. All food spillages which attract birds must be removed as soon as possible. Waste receptacles should be provided with tight-fitting lids and not overfilled. Waste areas must be kept in a clean condition.

### Proofing

All openings, whether large or small, should be proofed to prevent the entry of birds. The roof apex, open eaves, louvres and ventilation openings should be protected with 15mm galvanized chicken wire, expanded aluminium or polythene-coated or tarred nylon netting. Doors should be self-closing and heavy-duty, overlapping plastic strips should be fitted if factory doors are constantly left open or are used for fork-lift trucks.

**Maintenance**

All buildings should be well-maintained and any holes which remain after alterations should be filled as soon as possible. Broken windows must be repaired immediately. Regular checks should be made in roof spaces, as roof linings and girders often provide ideal nesting or roosting sites; nests must be removed and a search made to locate points of entry.

**Repellents**

Thick inert gels have been used, with limited success, to prevent birds perching. Birds feel insecure on contact with the gel and look for alternative sites. A sprung-wire system known as Avistrand has been developed and when installed correctly, it appears to be more successful for some bird species than the earlier repellents.

**Traps**

Traps may be successfully employed against pigeons, provided that they are positioned correctly and birds are using the site to feed, not purely for roosting.

**Internal control**

It is usually more difficult and more expensive to control birds inside buildings than it is to prevent their entry in the first place. Furthermore, unless provisions are made to proof buildings after treatment, reinvasion will occur.

Although the technology to remove birds is available, there is no magic formula for instant success. Control measures are strictly governed by the Wildlife and Countryside Act, 1981 which prevents the use of those measures which may be considered inhumane. The law is strictly adhered to by reputable companies.

**Bird scaring devices**

These are used to frighten birds away from areas where they roost or cause problems and they include loud bangs and flashing lights. They are of limited value and, unless used sparingly and intermittently, will eventually be ignored.

**Shooting**

The use of suitable air rifles may be quite successful, especially if control is carried out at night when birds are roosting. Foods must not be exposed to risk of metal pellet contamination during shooting. Reinvasion is likely unless proofing is carried out.

**Narcotizing**

Alphachloralose is a stupefying substance which may be used successfully in a bait base attractive to birds. Those which succumb may be disposed of by humane methods and protected species can be released. Chances of success are increased if all alternative sources of food, such as spillages, are removed. It is important to ensure that all baits are collected after treatment.

**Mist netting**

The use of mist netting is rather like fishing for birds. The nets are very fine and are not detectable by birds. They are fitted over doorways and other flight paths of birds. It is a humane technique; protected species can be released and pest birds disposed of. Once again only licensed operators are permitted to use mist nets. Nets must be removed when the operator leaves the premises.

**Fig. 62.** Mist netting used internally to control sparrows.

**Wildlife and Countryside Act, 1981**

British law conforms to the EC Birds Directive by the issue of a general licence to authorized persons for the taking of pest species such as feral pigeons, house sparrows and starlings at any time. It is a defence for persons prosecuted for killing some types of protected birds to prove that the control of the birds was necessary to preserve public health or to prevent the spread of disease.

N.B. The photographs used to illustrate this Chapter were provided courtesy of Rentokil Ltd.

CHAPTER 15

# Monitoring and control of food standards and operations

Monitoring and control are an integral part of all hazard analysis systems and essential functions of management which complete the circle of responsibility. Cost-effective operations which produce safe food will only be achieved if managers:

(1) set the requisite standards/objectives;
(2) provide the resources and establish systems and controls, including documentation, to achieve the standards;
(3) communicate the standards required to staff;
(4) train and motivate the staff to undertake monitoring and recording and to achieve the standards;
(5) provide effective supervision; and
(6) monitor, analyze, compare actual standards with those required and, if necessary, take corrective action and improve performance to facilitate achievement of objectives.

Monitoring of all food operations is essential to:

(1) confirm expected standards/controls are achieved;
(2) ensure the production of safe, wholesome food of good quality and shelf-life;
(3) ensure compliance with specific legislation and to facilitate the use of the due diligence defence;
(4) identify problems, for example, sources of contamination;
(5) satisfy customers and enforcement officers and minimize complaints;
(6) facilitate modification of procedures and confirm effectiveness of control systems;
(7) encourage commitment and improve motivation of staff.

## Commitment

Notwithstanding the legal and moral responsibilities of managers, satisfactory standards of hygiene will not be achieved without the commitment of all involved in the food business. Commitment is required from the owners, the board of directors, the managing director, the food handlers and all levels of management. If this commitment is not forthcoming then inadequate resources will be made available to provide the basic framework essential to achieve the necessary standards. Resources are required to: plan, design and construct food premises so that they can operate hygienically;

provide satisfactory facilities and to secure the employment and training of suitable staff. Commitment of owners will only be achieved when it is accepted that, although good hygiene may be expensive, bad hygiene is more expensive.

The commitment of management is essential to motivate and effectively supervise staff. Managers must always lead by example and provide staff with suitable incentives to encourage the maintenance of standards.

| Benefits of high standards of hygiene | Results of low standards of hygiene |
|---|---|
| Satisfied customers, a good reputation and increased business. | Food poisoning/deaths. |
| Compliance with legislation. | Food complaints/loss of production. |
| High staff morale and low staff turnover. | Prosecutions and possible closure. |
| Increased shelf-life of food. | Civil action by customers because of food poisoning or food complaints. |
| | Pest infestation/food wastage. |

**Food safety policies**

A planned approach is a prerequisite of hygienic operations. The standards required, and the way they can be achieved, should be incorporated into a food safety policy in the same way that safety matters are included in the safety policy required by the Health and Safety at Work, etc. Act, 1974. This policy document would be extremely useful to support claims of due diligence. It can be used as an effective way of communicating the requisite standards to staff and for determining their training requirements. To remain effective the document must be reviewed regularly.

A responsibility flow chart showing management structure and individual responsibilities with regard to hygiene should be included. The document should be brought to the attention of all staff and written in a way that demonstrates company commitment to producing safe food. All aspects of hygiene should be covered by the policy, which should include a commitment to:

(1) produce safe food;
(2) observe all relevant legal requirements, industry guides to good hygiene practice and Government codes of practice;
(3) identify hazards and implement effective control and monitoring procedures at those points critical to food safety and to review the hazard analysis and control system periodically and whenever the food business operations change;
(4) staff training and the implementation of a planned food hygiene training programme. (Training records should be maintained);
(5) obtain all food and water from satisfactory/approved suppliers. (Suppliers should be asked for a copy of their food safety policy);
(6) provide the necessary premises, equipment, facilities and maintenance to achieve high standards of hygiene, including personal hygiene;
(7) maintain satisfactory temperature control and monitoring systems for food ingredients and products during storage, preparation/processing, and distribution:

(8) ensure satisfactory cleaning and, where necessary, disinfecting of the premises, equipment and facilities. (Cleaning schedules will be required);

(9) provide adequate pest control measures including proofing and the use of specialist contractors and maintaining records;

(10) provide procedures and systems for health screening and the reporting of staff illness, dealing with visitors, contractors, enforcement officers, food poisoning incidents, customer complaints, delivery of raw materials, product recall and hazard warnings;

(11) implement effective Quality Assurance/Control systems, including stock rotation, foreign body control, organoleptic assessment, sampling, food labelling and in-house audits;

(12) provide the necessary resources and training of managers to ensure the implementation, updating and enforcement of the policy throughout the business.

## THE HAZARD ANALYSIS AND CRITICAL CONTROL POINT (HACCP) CONCEPT

Food product safety is ultimately a management responsibility and is regarded as an absolute requirement by the customer. If a manager is to do more than hope that the hygiene standards he has set are being achieved consistently and that every batch of food sold is safe, it is necessary to establish a food safety control and monitoring system.

It is possible to define a safe food product by setting acceptable limits for relevant pathogenic microorganisms. It is then theoretically possible to control the product safety within these limits, whatever the quality of ingredients or process, by not releasing the food for sale until it has passed microbiological and/or toxicological analysis. Control by such end-product testing, however, is not physically possible if the gap between production and consumption is short, as in conventional catering, and little information is provided as to why a product has failed to meet a standard. Consequently, a preventative approach, involving control of the ingredients, process and processing environment, is always preferable.

The Hazard Analysis and Critical Control Point concept provides a logical and systematic basis for such an approach. The original HACCP concept was proposed in 1973 as a result of a joint effort by the Pillsbury Company, NASA and the US Army Natick Laboratories to apply a nil-defects programme to the production of food.

HACCP involves the systematic assessment of each step in the food production process and the identification of those points which are critical to food safety. Technical and financial resources can then be concentrated at these critical control points. All aspects of food safety, from raw materials to final product user, are included. It is a preventative, Quality Assurance approach which removes the reliance on end-product testing. HACCP requires a multidisciplinary team of specialists with a high level of scientific knowledge of all ingredients, contaminants and processes, and often involves months of hard work. The time and commitment required by team members must not be underestimated.

Hazards associated with the food product (suitability for bacterial growth and preservatives used), the process (handling, lethal effect of heating, drying, cooling, freezing fermentation, curing), personnel, equipment and the environment (premises, atmosphere, water supply) and intended use of the product (storage and conditions, shelf-life, packaging, customer group) are systematically analyzed and points where they occur are identified. Those points which are considered critical to product safety are monitored and remedial action taken if they are outside predetermined safe limits.

The use of a HACCP system and the availability of extensive documentation and records of monitoring of critical control points will contribute significantly to a defence of due diligence.

**Terminology associated with HACCP**

*Control measures* — those actions required to eliminate hazards or reduce them to a safe level.

*Criteria* — specified characteristics of a physical (e.g. time or temperature), chemical (e.g. pH) or biological (e.g. sensory) nature.

*Critical control point (CCP)* — a step in a process which, if controlled, will eliminate or reduce a hazard to an acceptable level.

*Critical limit* — the value of a monitored action which separates acceptable from unacceptable.

*Decision tree* — a sequence of questions applied to each process step with a potential hazard to identify which process steps are critical to food safety.

*Flow diagram/chart* — the detailed sequence of operations involved with a particular product or process, usually from receipt of raw materials to the end-user.

*HACCP* — a structured and documented hazard analysis system based on specialist advice and applied to a standerdized food production process with a view to ensuring cost-effective food safety.

*Hazard* — the potential to cause harm to the consumer and can be microbiological, chemical or physical.

*Hazard analysis and control* — any system which enables a food business to identify points in its activities which are critical to ensuring food safety and to identify and implement effective control and monitoring procedures, and to periodically review these procedures to ensure food safety.

*Monitoring* — the planned observations and measurements of targets and tolerances of control points to confirm that the process is under control.

*Risk* — the estimate of the probability of a hazard occurring.

*Risk assessment* — the process of identifying hazards, assessing risks and severity and evaluating their significance.

*Severity* — the magnitude of the hazard or the seriousness of possible consequence.

*Target level* — the predetermined value for the control measure.

*Tolerance* — the specified degree of latitude for a control measure which, if exceeded, would render the process unsafe.

**Advantages of HACCP**

(1) remedial action can be taken during processing/production, i.e. before serious problems occur;
(2) control parameters are relatively easy to monitor, for example, time, temperature, pH, texture, appearance;
(3) more cost-effective than microbiological or chemical analysis because it is part of the process and avoids the need for expensive statistical sampling plans;
(4) the operation is controlled on the premises;
(5) current and predicted hazards and risks can be identified and removed;
(6) all staff can be involved with product safety;
(7) reduced product loss and avoidance of expensive reprocessing;
(8) complementary to other quality management systems, for example, ISO 9000;
(9) useful in demonstrating due diligence; and
(10) focuses resources on the critical parts of the process.

**Hazard analysis**

To establish a preventative control system for a particular product or group of similar products, the first step is to undertake a detailed analysis of the ingredients, process and processing environment, identifying hazards, risks and severity (microbiological, chemical or physical). In the case of microbiological hazards these will be stages involving one of the following:

(1) the presence of pathogenic microorganisms or toxins;
(2) contamination with pathogenic microorganisms;
(3) multiplication of pathogens or toxin production; or
(4) survival of pathogens.

The hazard analysis must be specific to the food, process, equipment and premises involved but should take into consideration other processes or materials in the same area or using the same equipment which could affect the process under investigation.

A comprehensive hazard analysis for any food product should include a consideration of likely events in distribution, storage and retailing and, also, the potential for consumer abuse. The risks associated with ingredients can be estimated in terms of the following three general characteristics:

(1) the ingredient can usually be assumed to be a potential source of contamination by toxins or pathogenic microorganisms;
(2) the ingredient has not been subject to a controlled process to destroy pathogens;
(3) the pH, water activity and nutritional content of the ingredient make it favourable to the multiplication of pathogens.

Once the detailed hazard analysis has been completed it may be possible to eliminate some of these hazards by making changes to the ingredients, process or processing environment. This is easier to do if a hazard analysis of proposals is undertaken at the planning stage of a new product. Actions such as the creation of physical barriers to prevent cross-contamination are extremely beneficial because alternative attempts to control the hazard will probably involve a complex set of activities which will be expensive in time and resources throughout future production.

**Critical control points**

It may not be cost-effective to exercise tight control over all the identified hazards at every control point. Careful consideration of each one, with special regard to its position in the sequence of operations, will allow the identification of those which are truly critical, i.e. where loss of control would result in an unacceptable food safety risk. The determination of critical control points can be assisted by using the "decision tree".

These significant hazards must then be controlled within acceptable limits which can be easily monitored. Food product safety is thus controlled indirectly by means of a set of critical control points which are specific to a particular product or group of generic products which undergo the same process. Clear and appropriate standards must be defined if the critical control points are to be maintained within acceptable limits and there must be some means of monitoring in order to verify control.

Suitable standards for critical control points can be determined empirically from a basis of experimentation. However, they can also be derived from theory and published information and guidelines. Objective quantitative standards such as those which may be set for time/temperature exposures concerned with limiting the survival of pathogens after a heat treatment or limiting the multiplication of pathogens in the food during cooling, holding and handling operations are generally preferable to more subjective qualitative standards.

Temperature limits may apply to a position within the food but may also, for practical reasons, need to apply to the air or heat transfer medium surrounding the food. In the latter case it is still the temperature of the food which is significant and where such indirect temperature limits are used, it is essential to understand the relationship between these and the actual temperature of the food. Other more indirect standards such as the dimensions of items of food can be particularly relevant to the control of time/temperature exposures in, for instance, roasting or cooling. Standards may also be set for the size of a batch of food which can be withdrawn from chilled storage at one time in order to control the period of exposure to ambient temperature during handling.

Cleaning and disinfection are frequently the means by which contamination of food product from personnel, equipment and environment are limited. When this constitutes a critical control point, standards must be set for either the microbiological load remaining after cleaning or the frequency of, and methods used for, cleaning surfaces and hands. In the latter case it is preferable if the specified methods and frequencies have been proven, by microbiological testing, to maintain contamination within the acceptable limit. With hand washing it is important to remember that the ultimate aim is to limit the contamination of the food from personnel at critical stages in the process. It is thus necessary to establish standards for the type and cleaning of toilet and hand washing facilities which will prevent significant recontamination of the hands after washing.

Where hazards are identified at a step in a process which is not considered to be a critical control point, good hygiene practice must always be applied to minimize hazards and risks.

**Monitoring of control points**

Monitoring of control standards such as time/temperature, staff training, hygiene practices and pest control procedures is essential at all critical control points to ensure product safety. If, however, these standards are not achieved the manager will require all the relevant information about the batch of food to decide whether it is safe to release. Therefore, control systems are most useful and accurate in establishments where it is possible to differentiate discrete batches of food and where the results of monitoring the critical control points are recorded in such a way that they can be related directly to these batches.

Unless production is truly continuous it is usually appropriate to identify a batch of food as that quantity which undergoes the major heat step in one piece of equipment at one time. In a high output cook-freeze production unit, where such a control system is used and where there are limited facilities for microbiological testing on site, batches which have failed to meet the requirements of one or more critical control points should be held and subjected to rigorous microbiological analysis. If the batch is shown to meet the end-product standard it is released, if not, it is discarded. Batches which meet all requirements of the critical control points are released without testing.

Managers are often somewhat distant from production, and the monitoring of critical control points is carried out by operatives who may be the same people responsible for the activities which are designed to limit the hazards. It is therefore essential that understanding and commitment to the system are fostered in all levels of staff within the establishment. Some critical control points are monitored by quantitative measurements whereas others, such as those involving cleaning of equipment and hand washing, can be monitored by self-observation. The staff involved indicate whether the activity has been completed using the method and at the times specified in the production specification document.

It is advisable for each product or group of products to have a detailed written production specification in which the ingredients, formulation and production methods are clearly documented. The document should also include the critical control points, acceptable limits, control methods and instructions for monitoring. If staff training is based on the content of these documents, then operation of the preventive food safety control system becomes an integral part of the job. The responsibility carried by operatives is increased and the scope for improvisation and discretion is reduced.

**Verification**

Verification involves reviewing the entire HACCP system and records to ensure the system is working correctly and that monitoring is effective. Verification includes:

(1) checking records and the accuracy of monitoring;

(2) observing staff and operations at critical control points;

(3) obtaining microbiological samples; and
(4) special studies such as challenge testing.

**Corrective action**

Whenever monitoring of a critical control point indicates that a significant deviation from a defined target level has occurred, corrective actions have to be taken, for example, a refrigerator with an air temperature of 10°C. A specific action plan should be available to restore control and advise on product discard. In these circumstances it is essential that a clear chain of command has been established and that the appropriate manager is informed so that decisions on action can be made and instructions issued.

**Implementing HACCP**

The implementation of a HACCP system involves the following stages:

(1) define the terms of reference. Decide which product or group of products are to be assessed and which hazards, including specific organisms, are to be considered. In addition to food safety, spoilage and unacceptable physical contamination can be included. The starting and finishing point for products must also be decided, for example, harvesting and/or suppliers through to consumption;
(2) assemble the HACCP team. The team will be composed of persons who fully understand the food products, their uses and the hazards and risks involved in their handling and processing, for example, a Quality Assurance specialist, a production specialist, an engineer and other specialists who may be co-opted as appropriate, for example, buyers, operators and cleaning specialists. Most teams will benefit from the occasional input of different food handlers who are directly involved with the products under consideration. Smaller businesses may have to consider the use of consultants. At least one member of the team should be fully trained in the principles of HACCP;
(3) describe the product. Each product or group of products must be considered, including whether the raw ingredients are likely to be contaminated, suitability for bacterial growth, composition, use of preservatives, packaging systems, method of storage and distribution, required shelf-life, instruction for use and intended consumers;
(4) construct a detailed flow chart which clearly identifies every step in the process from selection of raw materials to point of consumption. Times and temperatures of processing/cooking, cooling, chilling and storage should be noted;
(5) verify the flow chart by on-site inspection at various times of production;
(6) identify hazards, risk and severity (physical, chemical or microbiological) at each step in the operation, using the flow chart, and list any preventative measures to eliminate hazards or reduce them to an acceptable level (i.e. control points);
(7) identify which control points are critical to product safety by using the CCP decision tree;
(8) determine target levels and tolerances for each critical control point (CCP) such as time, temperature, pH, $a_w$, available chlorine, etc.;

**TABLE XXX** CCP DECISION TREE

In deciding which control points are critical, the critical control point decision tree may be used. Each question should be answered in sequence at each step for each identified hazard.

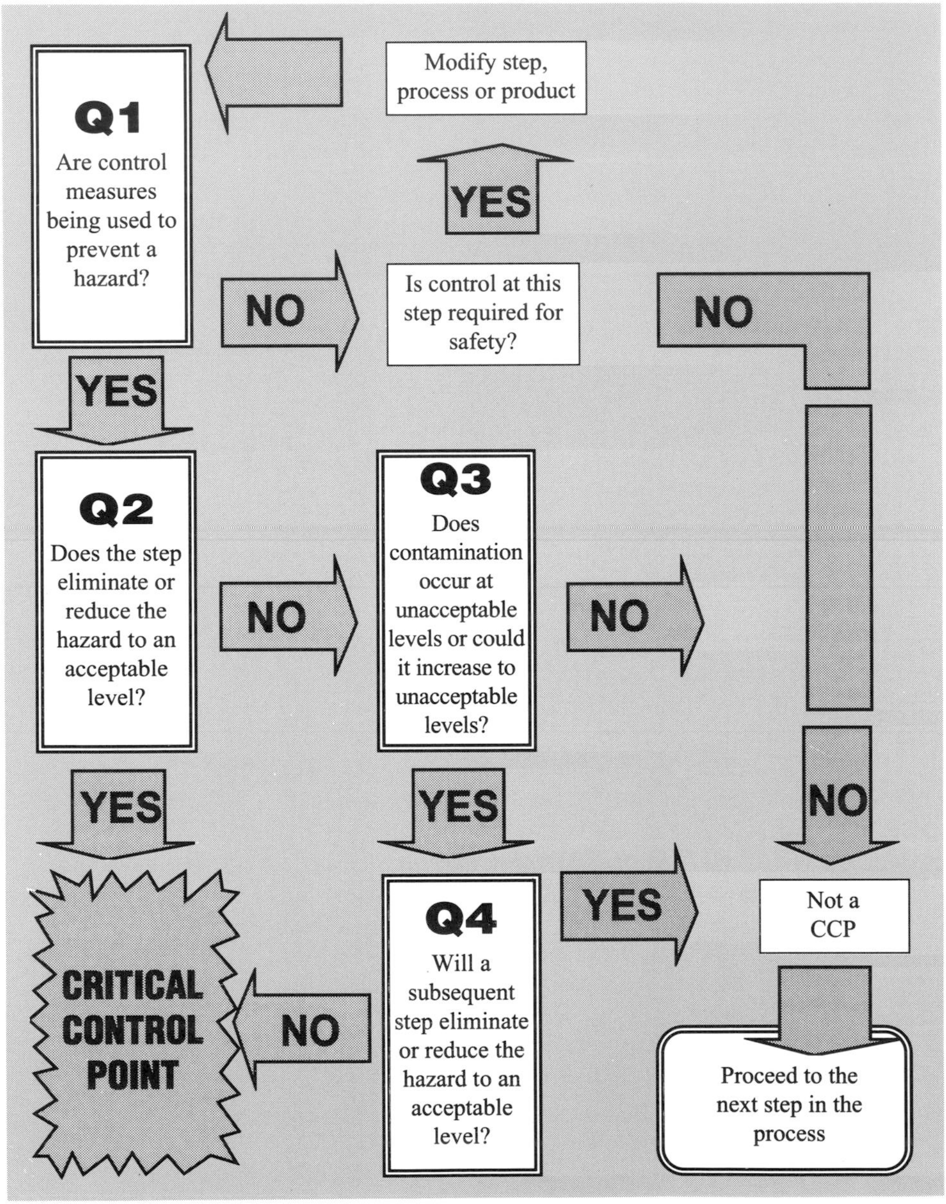

(9) establish monitoring systems for each CCP, including who should act, when and how and what action to take if target levels are exceeded (corrective action);
(10) establish a detailed recording and documentation system;
(11) verification of the HACCP system; and
(12) review the HACCP system at least annually, whenever something goes wrong, for example, food poisoning, and whenever changes to the process or recipe are made, including changes in raw materials, processing equipment, cleaning schedules, packaging, distribution and staffing levels.

Accurate records are essential to the successful application of HACCP. Documentation should relate to raw materials, processing, cleaning and disinfection, pest control, complaints, storage and distribution as well as the basis for decisions relating to product safety, deviations, corrective action and modifications.

## HAZARD ANALYSIS, CONTROL AND MONITORING SYSTEMS

Because of the lack of consistency in production and preparation techniques, the large number of products simultaneously handled and the lack of detailed microbiological and scientific knowledge relating to specific products and processing equipment, most small catering and retail businesses will be unable to apply HACCP to their operation. Consequently, various alternative systems based on HACCP principles have been developed to facilitate hazard analysis and the implementation of control and monitoring procedures, for example, "Assured Safe Catering". Information is also available in the Industry Guides to Good Hygiene Practice. Most of these systems are "generic" in nature and do not require comprehensive ingredient and product knowledge, for example, $a_w$, pH, D values and z values. Furthermore, they can be applied by one trained person with suitable knowledge and they do not require the use of the HACCP decision tree or extensive documentation. However, the more product and processing knowledge that is available and applied, the safer the end product is likely to be. Whichever hazard analysis, control and monitoring system is used, the first stage should always be, as far as practicable, to standardize operations and adherence to documented procedures for all steps in the operation, from receipt of raw materials to consumption. Failure to achieve consistency negates effective control.

To comply with legislation, proprietors will need to examine their operation on the basis of the following five principles:

(1) analysis of the food hazards associated with the food business operation including microorganisms and toxins, chemical contamination and physical contamination;
(2) identification of the **points** in the operation where food hazards may occur. Food hazards should be identified at each step in the operation using a generic flow diagram. The particular hazards to consider at each step are:
   (i) the presence of the contaminant in the raw food or ingredient, for example, salmonella in raw chicken, pesticides on fruit or a foreign body in flour;
   (ii) the likely contamination of the food at a particular step, for example, storage of raw food and high-risk food together or contamination by glass;

(iii) the multiplication of bacteria or toxin production, for example, because food is left at room temperature for too long; and
(iv) the ability of microorganisms to survive a particular process such as cooking or disinfection which should have killed them;

(3) deciding which of the points identified are critical to ensuring food safety (critical points). At each step there is likely to be several hazards and the points at which hazards can be effectively controlled to ensure food safety should be considered as critical control points. Bacterial contamination, of high-risk food, for example, from unhygienic practices, must be controlled as must any steps which would allow multiplication of bacteria. Times and temperatures of cooking and processing and the essential disinfection of equipment are always likely to be critical points;

(4) identification and implementation of effective control and monitoring procedures at critical points. Controls must be implemented to eliminate the hazard or reduce it to a safe level. Measurable target levels should be set and checks introduced to ensure targets are achieved. Temperature and times are two of the most important parameters as they are precise and relatively easy to monitor. For example, high-risk foods should be stored at or below 5°C and during preparation should never be left at ambient temperature for longer than 30 minutes. Personal hygiene controls are not as precise, although effective supervision should ensure instructions are adhered to, for example, staff must wash their hands when entering the food room. Bacteriological cleanliness or equipment will require cleaning and disinfection of equipment at specific times in accordance with cleaning schedules. Records are necessary for managers to ensure that the appropriate monitoring has been undertaken. Written procedures on corrective action in the event of targets not being met are also essential; and

(5) review of the analysis of food hazards, the critical control points and the control and monitoring procedures periodically and whenever the food business's operations change. A review of the system is necessary if:
(i) controls are ineffective or the product is unsatisfactory;
(ii) the type of product, the raw materials, the recipe or ingredients alter, for example, cooked chicken is purchased instead of raw;
(iii) the method of preparation changes, for example, a microwave oven replaces conventional cooking;
(iv) changes are made to the cleaning and disinfection schedules;
(v) staff numbers and/or responsibilities change; and
(vi) new equipment is introduced, for example, a new refrigerator or oven.

Documentation of the system is not a legal requirement but effective documentation and monitoring records may assist a defence of due diligence in the event of prosecution. It is also extremely difficult to apply controls and checks consistently if there is no documentation.

Some form of training in hazard analysis monitoring and control will be necessary for all personnel who can influence the safety of food being produced.

**TABLE XXXI** EXAMPLES OF HAZARDS, CONTROLS AND MONITORING AT STEPS IN THE OPERATION CRITICAL TO FOOD SAFETY

| Step | Hazard | Control | Monitoring |
|---|---|---|---|
| Purchase of raw materials | Presence of contaminants, especially pathogens or toxins. (inherent contamination) | Select least hazardous ingredients. Only use reputable suppliers (approved suppliers list). Specification for product quality and safety including delivery temperatures. | Inspect supplier or request records to show that they follow good manufacturing practice. Historical check of deliveries. Absence of customer complaints. Bacteriological sampling. |
| Receipt of raw materials | Contamination of food, especially by pathogens/toxins. Multiplication of food poisoning bacteria. | Specify delivery requirements, especially time and temperature. Minimize time for unloading/placing in storage. Deboxing area. Staff training. | Check delivery vehicles and drivers, date codes, time for unloading and temperature and condition of food (as per specification). Competency testing of staff. |
| Storage (chilled, frozen and dry) | Multiplication of food poisoning bacteria. Contamination due to poor hygiene practices. | Store at correct temperature (alarmed units). Cover/wrap food. Stock rotation/date codes. Separate raw/high-risk foods. Cleaning/disinfection. Good housekeeping. Pest control/pest proof containers. Staff training. | Check air/food temperatures, date codes, pest control and food complaint records. Audits and visual checks of food. Cleaning schedules. Competency testing of staff. |
| Preparation | Multiplication of food poisoning bacteria. Contamination due to poor hygiene practices. | Prepare minimum amount of food. Minimize time at room temperature. Good personal hygiene/training. Separate raw/high risk foods. Colour coding. Cleaning/disinfection. Good hygiene practices organization/workflow. | Check time/temperature. Audits/visual checks. Competency testing of staff. Cleaning schedules. Bacteriological swabbing. of surfaces. Equipment maintenance. Design. Electronic fly killers. |
| Cooking | Survival of pathogens/toxins. Contamination and multiplication. | Centre temperature at least 75°C. Ensure frozen poultry/joints completely thawed. Staff training. | Check time/temperature. Equipment maintenance. Audits. Competency testing of staff. |
| Cooling | Multiplication of surviving food poisoning bacteria or germination of spores. Toxin production. Contamination. | Weight/thickness of joints. Cool rapidly (blast chiller). Keep covered. No contact with raw food. Good personal hygiene/training. Cleaning/disinfection. | Check time/temperature. Audits/visual checks. Equipment maintenance. Competency testing of staff. Cleaning schedules. |
| Service | Multiplication of food poisoning bacteria. Contamination. | Keep < 5°C or >63°C. Good personal hygiene/training Keep covered Cleaning/disinfection. Sell within shelf-life. Prevent customer contamination. | Check time/temperature. Audits/visual checks. Competency testing of staff. Cleaning schedules. Equipment maintenance. |

**Stages in hazard analysis and control for small businesses**

(1) management commitment. Time, effort and finance will be required;
(2) business operated in accordance with good hygiene practice;
(3) staff trained commensurate with their work activities;
(4) proprietor or manager (person responsible for implementation) to obtain adequate advice/training/knowledge about the implementation of hazard analysis. Attendance at an intermediate or advanced hygiene course would be an appropriate first stage;
(5) planning (information gathering). Relevant details of suppliers, products, hazards, processes and risks will be required;
(6) production of a generic flow chart for each step in the food operation (check by on-site inspection);
(7) generic grouping of food products (as few as possible);
(8) list hazards (and bad hygiene practices that may result in hazards) for each group of food products at each step (microbiological, physical and chemical);
(9) identify controls (good hygiene practices) at each step in the flow chart. Controls should be as precise as possible with measurable targets, for example time and temperature, frequency of hand washing, size of joints, frequency of cleaning and disinfection;
(10) identify monitoring and recording activities. The appropriate equipment will need to be obtained, for example, a probe thermometer;
(11) determine corrective action to be taken at each step if target levels for controls are not achieved;
(12) identify and provide additional training for staff;
(13) implement and verify that the system works; and
(14) review annually whenever changes are made to the operation or justified customer complaints are received.

**The inspection of food premises by managers**

The inspection of food premises is a skilled technique which managers must learn and practise before proficiency can be expected. Certain fundamentals must be observed as follows:

(1) the objectives of the inspection must be established in advance and any equipment, including a clipboard, report form, penknife, torch and white coat, must be obtained before starting. The inspection should include structure and repair, cleanliness, pest control, equipment, practices, lighting, ventilation, staff hygiene and hazards, and the effectiveness of controls and monitoring associated with any of these items. It is advisable to examine each item separately and to employ consultants or contractors for technical items.
(2) the inspection should be formal and exclusive; a manager should not combine an inspection with other functions. A period should, therefore, be allocated within a manager's duties, solely for the purpose of carrying out inspections;

(3) the timing should be appropriate; some points can only be properly examined at certain times; cleanliness for instance, can only be accurately assessed when cleaning has been completed. Timing of pest surveys depends on the type of pest;

(4) the inspection should be methodical. A typical routine will involve starting at a defined point within a room or identifiable area within a building, the progressive examination of all relevant items around the perimeter and then the same ordered examination of central fittings, installations or equipment. The route taken should be such that it can be followed by the recipient of the resultant report;

(5) the inspection should be thorough. Every aspect of the subject under examination should be covered. It may not be enough to look at a piece of equipment; it may need to be dismantled and/or moved from its position. Cupboards and refrigerators may need to be wholly or partially emptied and surfaces may need to be scraped or tapped to assess soundness. In this respect, full use should be made of the senses: sight, smell, hearing and touch; and

(6) notes and subsequent reporting should be precise and comprehensive. It is essential to describe completely and accurately what is seen at the time of the inspection, as notes made later can easily become distorted.

Inspections should be carried out without prior warning and at varying times. Inspection reports should be discussed with supervisors and other appropriate personnel. Defects highlighted for the first time by management inspections usually indicate a failure in existing control systems.

*Spot checks*

Spot checks should be regarded as mini-inspections, limited in area or scope only and not in any of the fundamentals specified earlier. Superficial examinations can be dangerously misleading and convey a distorted picture of standards prevailing.

*The examination of monitoring procedures and processes*

The examination of procedures may be to determine hygienic operation or safe working. As with all other forms of inspection it is imperative that problems are detected and remedied with the minimum of delay. Further checks must be carried out to ensure that the solution is satisfactory. Procedures monitored will include any process which may expose food to risk of contamination; systems provided to prevent contamination such as metal detection and the temperature parameters of storage, processing or cooking, distribution and display.

To determine routes of contamination, visual observation may be augmented by the use of diagrams. A plan of the premises should be drawn and the observed routes of personnel and food traced on the plan using different colours for raw and high-risk foods. The flow diagram produced will indicate efficiency of operation and areas of cross-contamination.

As a general rule, procedures monitoring should follow the route or treatment of a single product or operation from start to finish. Each operation should be timed to establish how long food remains in the temperature danger zone.

**Suppliers and raw materials**

The quality and safety of the final product depends, among other things, on the standard of the raw materials. Consequently, food should be obtained from reputable sources. Hygiene officers are employed by some large food organizations to inspect the premises of main suppliers to ensure that they are capable of providing a satisfactory product which consistently meets the agreed specification. The safety of processes, the condition of the premises and equipment, the hygiene of operatives and the controls exercised by management are essential factors in determining the suitability of suppliers.

When it is impracticable to inspect the suppliers' premises then managers must use other indicators, for example, other customers supplied, the appearance of delivery men and their adherence to basic hygiene rules and the condition of the delivery vehicle may be considered as a likely reflection of the hygiene standards of the supplier. Carriage of cooked and raw meats in the same container, high-risk food delivered at unsafe temperatures or deliveries placed in unsuitable areas can indicate poor standards. Companies which provide formal hygiene training for food handlers and managers are more likely to have a real commitment to high standards of hygiene.

Specifications must be set for all raw materials and these should, where practicable, stipulate bacteriological standards, flavour, colour, temperature and permissible levels of contamination. For example, an occasional pod in a delivery of peas may be acceptable, a rat dropping would not. Certain foodstuffs carry official certificates of inspection, for example, all red meat carcases intended for human consumption must bear an official inspector's stamp. Imported food must be accompanied by documents certifying fitness.

Raw materials should be checked on arrival before unloading and regular samples should be obtained for bacteriological and chemical assessment. Dry herbs and spices are a frequent source of undesirable and pathogenic microorganisms and must not be overlooked. The time of delivery, the weight and condition of the load and the type and condition of packaging should all be noted. The presence of dampness, dirt, insects, mould, unusual odours, blown or leaking containers, incompatible non-food items and severely damaged packaging will usually require the rejection of the delivery, as would unacceptable temperatures of refrigerated food stuffs.

**Organoleptic assessment of food**

The appearance, smell, texture, taste and other physical characteristics of food are valuable for obtaining a rapid assessment of food standards (quality, taint and spoilage). However, food contaminated by pathogenic bacteria may appear in all respects fit to eat and suspect food should not be tasted. Specific indicators include:

(1) *Smell* - good food should smell fresh, pleasant and natural. Unusual, stale, musty or rancid smells should invite suspicions. Chemical smells may indicate chemical contamination. Ammonia smells in some fish are an early sign of decomposition.

(2) *Taste* - unusual bitterness, sweetness, a soapy taste or any untypical flavour may indicate unfitness.

(3) *Appearance* - food should be visibly free from signs of spoilage, fungal growth, slime, darkening or other change in colour, untypical wetness and mechanical damage. Absence of foreign objects and dirt in finished goods, including pests, pest debris and parasites, is important. Meat, poultry and fish should be free from signs of disease or other pathological conditions. In frozen food excessive ice can be an indicator of mishandling, as can large ice crystals within the texture; loose foods such as peas should not weld together. A final judgement of frozen food can only be made after defrosting.

(4) *Sound* - many packed foods, especially canned goods, emit a characteristic sound on being tapped or shaken. Any such food or pack emitting an untypical sound is suspect.

(5) *Texture* - unusual softness, hardness, brittleness or change in texture may be indicative of unfitness. Meat, fish and certain other products such as cheese should display a springy texture. Light pressure from a finger that causes an indentation to remain can be significant.

In all situations, the key to a sound judgement is to use all the relevant senses and to make a decision on the basis of all the available evidence. In cases of doubt, advice should be obtained from local authority Environmental Health Officers or consultants.

**Bacteriological monitoring**

Bacteriological monitoring is concerned with more than end-product testing and can be used to:

(1) build up a profile of product quality;
(2) indicate trends in product quality;
(3) ascertain whether handling techniques are satisfactory;
(4) indicate product safety and the absence of specific organisms (pathogens);
(5) determine effectiveness of cleaning and disinfection;
(6) determine effectiveness of processing; and
(7) confirm that legal standards or customer's specifications are being met.

The number and types of bacteria in a finished food product depend on:

(1) the microbiological quality of the raw materials;
(2) the standards of hygiene implemented during storage, manufacture or preparation;
(3) the type of food, preservatives used and the processes to which it is subjected;
(4) the type and quality of packaging; and
(5) the time/temperatures observed during handling, distribution, storage and service.

All organizations which handle high-risk foods should have access to facilities which enable the bacteriological assessment of food and food equipment. Whether or not in-house laboratory facilities are maintained is mainly an economic judgement. A number of consultant laboratories provide an *ad hoc* or contract service and a certification scheme run by the National Physical Laboratory at Greenwich will direct enquirers to the appropriate laboratory.

Bacteriological monitoring must not rely solely on the examination of the final product. By the time the defect is discovered a large amount of unsatisfactory food may have been produced and sold. This is usually the case with regard to high-risk products with short shelf-life.

To provide information as early as possible, a bacteriological sampling programme based on the type and amount of food produced should be designed and this should include raw materials, efficacy of cleaning and disinfection, water supplies, food containers and samples of the product at all appropriate stages of production, distribution and retail sale. The maximum number of bacteria permissible at each stage of production should be established and departures from this standard normally indicate a breakdown in hygiene or unsatisfactory processing. Unsatisfactory trends may allow remedial action to be taken before a product becomes unsaleable.

Bacteriological monitoring provides targets to achieve and can lead to a gradual improvement in hygiene. It can also be used to demonstrate the safety and quality of a product to customers and demonstrate the effectiveness of controls. However, the following disadvantages are associated with bacteriological sampling:

(1) it is usually retrospective and cannot be used to verify product safety where there is a short time between production and consumption, for example, in conventional catering or for products with short shelf-lives;
(2) it is relatively expensive;
(3) considerable expertise may be needed to interpret results and relate them to product age;
(4) the non-uniform distribution of bacteria in foods and the effect of different laboratory techniques and sampling methods significantly affect the results;
(5) the operation is being controlled by a laboratory technician who may be remote from the food production;
(6) only a limited number of samples can be taken;
(7) not all hazards are identified; and
(8) only a small section of the workforce assumes responsibility for product safety.

The development of rapid assay techniques is reducing the time to obtain results and may overcome some of the above disadvantages. One of the few rapid bacteriological sampling tests available is the resazurin test for milk which enables dairies to accept or reject raw milk supplies from the farm within ten minutes of testing.

When selecting laboratories, preference should be given to those which are NAMAS (National Measurement Accreditation service) accredited, to provide assurances that work undertaken will be accurate and reliable.

## RAPID METHODS FOR MICROBIOLOGICAL TESTING*

The term "rapid method" in microbiology has numerous connotations. To microbiologists, a rapid test is one that has a significant time-saving over more traditional methods. However, a rapid test for one manager (producing a long shelf-life product) may be unacceptable to another. The selection of a particular rapid method therefore depends upon the individual circumstances of a particular company/product.

*Written By Dr Paul Beers (University of Humberside)

## Rapid versus traditional methodology

Assessment of the microbiological quality of food traditionally has been determined by the use of standard plate counts. This has often incorporated the use of specialist media to isolate a particular organism, for example, *Salmonella* or *Listeria,* followed by a confirmatory test. These methods involve a growth stage and hence, usually have a minimum 24 hour gap between analysis of the sample and obtaining the result.

Rapid methods are usually based on metabolic processes within the cells, for example, ATP- photometry or the measurement of some component of the cell such as DNA-probe and immuno methods such as ELISA & DEFT. The results are usually available the same day. This is significantly different from the traditional numbers game where microbiological specifications are designed to reflect the number of permissible viable organisms within a food. This leads to the main problem with rapid methods - drawing inappropriate conclusions from the results obtained.

## Advantages and disadvantages of rapid methods

Rapid methods:

(1) provide real time results, leading to rapid clearance of raw materials and products. This provides savings in warehouse/cold storage space due to shorter release time;
(2) are in some cases very easy to use, for example, ATP-photometry can be carried out by non-specialist staff after a short training session;
(3) will not solve hygiene/spoilage problems, they will only allow them to be detected over a shorter time span - they will **not** make the problem easier to find;
(4) have to be commissioned and this may be relatively slow as protocols will have to be designed and optimized to fit in with the production process. This will ensure that the information obtained is relevant to the process being monitored; and
(5) require the education of line managers and supervisors since a test result will probably not be expressed as CFU/ml or gram and there is often confusion in relating metabolic measurements to the real life situation.

## Rapid methods available

### *Impedance method*

This method refers to the measurement of impedance (the degree of resistance to an electric current) within a culture medium. Microorganisms will metabolize substrates as they grow, decreasing the impedance of the medium. It is possible to directly relate the changes in impedance to cell numbers. The Bactometer™ is a commercial instrument which uses this technique. Numerous specific methods have been developed for the detection of coliforms including the detection in meat samples, and individual organizations can develop their own protocols in consultation with the companies producing the instrumentation.

### *DNA methods*

Different DNA methods include the use of a DNA-probe, designed to detect a single organism or a group of organisms. The future for rapid methods lies in the DNA-based methods, as they can be used to detect and amplify bacteria, for example, the polymerase chain reaction, PCR.

*Adenosine triphosphate (ATP) measurement*

This is the growth area in rapid methods. The technique relies upon the presence of ATP in bacterial cells. All bacteria contain ATP, as it is the primary energy store of all living organisms. Its measurement usually involves the use of the firefly luciferin-luciferase system which emits light that is measured by the use of a luminometer. There are manufacturers of dedicated instrumentation that enable this method to be used on the factory floor. The main disadvantage is that food also contains ATP making it difficult to use this technique to estimate cell numbers. It is used widely in the industry for the monitoring of cleaning efficiency, as microbial cells and/or food contamination will give a high reading.

*Culture media*

The addition of identifiable substrates (i.e. substrate that is used by a particular group of microorganisms leading to an observable change within the media) to existing culture media is another expanding area. These methods may shorten the time to make a positive identification and have the advantage, for food industry personnel, of expressing the results in the same format as traditional methods. One such method is the addition of MUG (4-methylumbelliferyl-β-D-glucuronide) to culture media. Most *Escherichia coli* convert this non-fluorescent substrate into a fluorescent product causing the media to fluoresce under a simple UV lamp.

*Immuno methods*

The most common immunological assay is the ELISA (enzyme linked immunosorbant assay). This method involves the use of antibodies to detect a particular organism or group of organisms and is linked to an enzyme system which changes colour if the organism is present. ELISA systems are currently available to detect *Salmonella, Listeria, Escherichia coli 0157:H7, Staphylococcus aureus* and its enterotoxins, botulinal toxins, moulds and mycotoxins.

**Selection of a rapid method**

Further information can be obtained from food microbiology textbooks, from reviews of current methodology and more importantly from trade literature. If managers intend to introduce rapid microbiological testing the following points should be considered.

Firstly, identify if current methods are adequate for the company's needs. If they are then a change is probably unnecessary. If existing methods are inadequate then:

(1) review the current information available on rapid techniques and identify any that may be of benefit;
(2) collect as much information as possible on the reliability, ease of use and sensitivity (including false positive and negative rate);

(3) contact the manufacturers and ask for a demonstration;
(4) set up a trial of the method to run in parallel to existing tests; and
(5) ascertain if the results of the trials lead to an improvement in the information obtained.

If this is the case the test may be adopted, otherwise continue to use existing methods or select an alternative rapid method.

*Food MicroModel*

This is a computer-based system for predicting the growth, death and survival of food-borne pathogens which can be used to help determine the microbiological safety of food, and reduce the number of challenge tests when developing new products.

**Bacteriological food sampling by enforcement officers**

The Food Safety Act, 1990 formalized the administrative procedures for the taking and examination of food samples. Food liaison groups, involving Environmental Health Officers from adjacent authorities, Public Health Laboratory food examiners, and sometimes, Public Analysts and Trading Standards Officers, have introduced coordinated sampling programmes within their areas. These groups also cooperate with the Department of Health and LACOTS to obtain food samples to comply with the requirements of the EC with regard to national sampling programmes.

EC legislation is increasing the emphasis on bacteriological standards as a way of improving food safety, and standards exist for many foods including egg products, milk and milk products and shellfish. However, EC policy dictates that inspection and sampling is primarily undertaken at the production premises in the country of origin and not at frontiers between member states (EC directives 89/397 and 89/662).

Samples of food may be taken for bacteriological examination to determine the acceptability or safety of a batch of food intended for human consumption, for example, a consignment of imported food or a quantity of food suspected of being contaminated by pathogens. As bacteria are unevenly distributed throughout food, a statistical sampling plan should be used to ensure that an adequate number of random samples are taken on which to base a decision regarding the whole consignment.

However, most routine bacteriological sampling by enforcement officers is carried out at food shops, factories and restaurants, etc., to support observations regarding the standard of hygiene within these premises. When sampling from retail outlets, it is preferable to take samples of several different high-risk foods from one or two premises as opposed to taking samples of the same type of high-risk food from many premises.

Unacceptable numbers of bacteria in the sample usually reflect poor handling techniques, under-processing, post-process contamination or incorrect storage. Due to the uneven distribution of bacteria, unsatisfactory results should not usually be used to support an opinion about any food remaining on the premises. However, the presence of pathogens or a suspicion of under-processing would require the detention and further sampling of any of the original food that had not been used or sold.

If only one or two samples out of many taken from a premises are unacceptable, this may be due to an unsatisfactory delivery of the specific food. If several samples from a single premises are unsatisfactory, for example, because of the presence of *Escherichia coli,* and all of the food originated from different suppliers, this would indicate that it was more likely that there had been a handling or storage problem at the retail outlet or restaurant.

The routine use of statistical sampling plans requiring many samples of the same food to be taken from one premises is not practicable or necessary to determine whether a particular food sample has been handled hygienically. However, a sampling programme should be designed to ensure the appropriate frequency of sampling of specific foods from particular premises. The programme may be based on the risk of food hygiene associated with particular foods, the history of premises with regard to food poisoning and food complaints and the nature of the food industry within a particular area.

When procuring a food sample, the officer obtains as much information as possible concerning its handling, including method of distribution, date of delivery, date of production, temperature of storage, type and condition of packaging, and any significant information regarding hygiene associated with the product, for example, risks of cross-contamination, handling techniques, personal hygiene of operatives and hygiene of premises and equipment.

The food is usually placed in an insulated container, to avoid the multiplication of bacteria prior to testing, and taken to the public health laboratory. The bacteriologist examines the food to establish the total number of bacteria present per gram of food and whether any indicator or pathogenic organisms are present. On completion of incubation, typically 48 hours at 37°C, the number of bacteria are counted and a report forwarded to the Environmental Health Department. As none of the methods used by laboratories can be guaranteed completely accurate, tolerances must be allowed. Furthermore, if comparisons are to be made or standards established it is important that the same methods and procedures are used by all laboratories involved in analysis, as well as by all enforcement officers.

## Interpretation of results

*Bacteriological counts*

The total number of living bacteria in a food sample is usually expressed as the total viable count (TVC) and is used as a microbiological indicator of food quality. The temperature of incubation used varies depending on the type of bacteria which are likely to be present if the food has been mishandled. A temperature of 37°C is usually employed by the Public Health Laboratory Service as they are interested in the presence of mesophilic bacteria and the opportunity for pathogen growth. TVCs, in excess of $10^4$g, in most high-risk foods indicate either gross contamination or old product, together with storage at incorrect temperatures. High counts at 20°C on chilled foods indicate inadequate, or lack of, refrigeration.

*Indicator organisms*

Indicator organisms are organisms which are usually present in very large numbers in environments inhabited by pathogens. The usual indicator organisms used by the food microbiologist belong to the Enterobacteriaceae family, many of which live in the intestine of man and animals, and include coliform organisms, faecal coliforms and *Escherichia coli* ( *E. coli*).

*Faecal streptococci*

Faecal streptococci include *Streptococcus faecalis, Streptococcus faecium, Streptococcus bovis and Streptococcus equinus* - this group is serologically defined as Lancefield group D. They are normally present in mammalian faeces but are more resistant to drying, high temperatures and disinfectants than Enterobacteriaceae. Their presence usually indicates poor plant hygiene or a failure of a specific heat process to destroy them; post-process contamination may or may not have occurred.

**TABLE XXXII** THE ENTEROBACTERIACEAE FAMILY

| Family | Tribes | Genus |
|---|---|---|
| Enterobacteriaceae | Escherichiae | Escherichia* |
| | | Edwardsiella |
| | | Citrobacter* |
| | | Salmonella |
| | | Shigella |
| | Klebsielleae | Klebsiella* |
| | | Enterobacter* |
| | | Hafnia |
| | | Serratia |
| | Proteae | Proteus (spoilage organisms) |
| | Yersinieae | Yersinia |
| | Erwinieae | Erwinia (plant pathogens) |

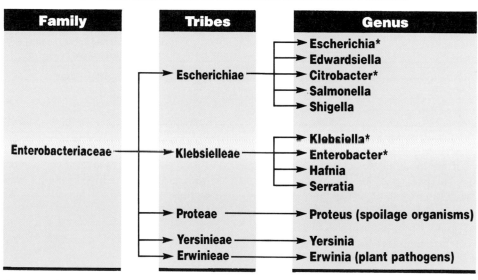

*Lactose fermenting coliforms (also some species of *Salmonella* and *Shigella*).

*Coliforms*

Coliforms are those members of the Enterobacteriaceae which ferment lactose and produce gas. They are sensitive to heat and their presence in food usually indicates post-process contamination or poor hygiene. The presence of coliforms in water, or food, may be a result of recent faecal contamination but as some coliforms exist in soil and on plants this is not always the case. However, the presence of *E. coli* does indicate recent human or animal faecal contamination and also the likelihood of pathogenic contamination. Faecal coliforms are those coliforms which can be successfully incubated at the higher temperature of 44 to 45.5°C and include *E. coli.*

*Pathogenic contamination*

Pathogens should not be present in hygienically handled and effectively processed high-risk food, even though some microbiologists believe that levels of $10^3$ *Staphylococcus aureus, Clostridium perfringens* or *Bacillus cereus* per gram are insignificant. However, notwithstanding the fact that such low numbers are extremely unlikely to cause food poisoning, such food is potentially hazardous and has not been handled hygienically.

The presence of: *Staphylococcus aureus* usually indicates a breakdown in personal hygiene or the handling of food; *Clostridium perfringens* usually indicates prolonged warm storage after cooking and *Salmonella* indicates cross-contamination, under-cooking/inadequate thawing or faecal contamination from a carrier.

The following table of point of sale guidelines is based on practical experience and what is achievable with good manufacturing and retailing practices.

**TABLE XXXIII** POINT OF SALE GUIDELINES*

| **Test** | **Cooked meat pies** | | | **Cooked meats and creams and custard filled confectionery** | | |
|---|---|---|---|---|---|---|
| | Satisfactory | Suspect | Unsatisfactory | Satisfactory | Suspect | Unsatisfactory |
| TVC/*g* (37°C) | $< 2 \times 10^2$ | $2 \times 10^2$-$2 \times 10^3$ | $> 2 \times 10^3$ | $< 2 \times 10^3$ | $2 \times 10^3$ - $2 \times 10^4$ | $> 2 \times 10^4$ |
| *E.coli/g* | < 10 | 10 - 100 | > 100 | < 10 | 10 - 100 | > 100 |
| *S. aureus/g* | < 20 | 20 - $2 \times 10^2$ | $> 2 \times 10^2$ | < 20 | 20 - $2 \times 10^2$ | $> 2 \times 10^2$ |
| *Cl. perfringens/g* | $< 2 \times 10^2$ | $2 \times 10^2$-$2 \times 10^3$ | $> 2 \times 10^3$ | $< 2 \times 10^2$ | $2 \times 10^2$-$2 \times 10^3$ | $> 2 \times 10^3$ |
| *Salmonella/25g* | Absent | Absent | Present | Absent | Absent | Present |

*Arthur Pinnegar, formerly the Principal Microbiologist, PHLS, Regional Laboratory, Leeds.

If the food fails to achieve a reasonable bacteriological quality, then an investigation is usually carried out to ascertain the reasons for this and advice will be given on how to prevent further unsatisfactory results by ensuring that:

(1) the product is acceptable when delivered to the premises;
(2) stock rotation is effective;
(3) handling techniques are hygienic;
(4) cleaning and disinfection is satisfactory;
(5) proper temperature control is exercised at all stages of manufacture, distribution and sale;
(6) packaging is satisfactory; and
(7) staff training is effectively carried out.

Repeat samples should be taken until a sequence of satisfactory results are obtained.

*Microbiological guidelines*

In 1995 the Public Health Laboratory Service published microbiological guidelines for ready-to-eat foods sampled at point of sale. The microbiological quality of the food related to aerobic plate counts and common food-borne pathogens, and ranged from satisfactory to hazardous. Although the guidelines are not a legal requirement they may be referred to in the event of enforcement action.

**Official control of food premises**

In the United Kingdom, Central Government has given the responsibility for protecting public health and ensuring food businesses comply with food hygiene legislation to local authorities. Officers with a wide range of qualifications, experience and expertise are necessary to enable authorities to carry out the significant range of food hygiene and food safety controls that now exist. The most common local authority official involved in food hygiene control is an Environmental Health Officer (EHO). Authorities may also appoint technical officers with specialist food qualifications.

The functions of EHOs and other officers in the field of food hygiene and food safety include:

(1) ensuring product safety and fitness for consumption;
(2) reducing possible sources of contamination entering the food environment;
(3) monitoring conditions and hygienic operations within the food environment;
(4) ensuring compliance with relevant legislation;
(5) establishing the integrity of management and effectiveness of control procedures;
(6) offering professional guidance, including preventative advice, particularly when legislation is changing.

EHOs and other officers undertake the above functions:

(1) during routine visits to and inspections of food premises;
(2) whilst investigating food poisoning outbreaks and incidents;
(3) whilst investigating food complaints;
(4) by lecturing on hygiene courses and seminars and giving related talks;
(5) by using the media, for example, press releases, committee reports and hazard warnings;
(6) whilst dealing with planning and licence applications;
(7) by developing partnerships with businesses' decision-making bases in the local authority's area (often referred to as the "Home Authority Principle"); and
(8) by developing local business forums for the exchange of information and the provision of advice.

**Inspections of food premises by enforcement officers**

Code of Practice No. 9 states that food hygiene inspections have two main purposes:

(1) to identify risks arising from the food businesses' activities and determine the effectiveness of the businesses' own assessment of hazards and control of risks; and
(2) to identify contraventions of food legislation and seek to have them corrected.

In particular, EHOs should encourage food businesses to adopt good food hygiene practices and offer advice where it is appropriate or is requested.

The Local Authorities Coordinating Body on Food and Trading Standards (LACOTS) has issued advice on food hygiene inspections which reflects the main purposes of an inspection as detailed within Code of Practice No. 9. LACOTS guidance emphasizes the need for local authorities to have an appropriate management system to ensure EHOs and other officers undertake inspections in a consistent manner. The various stages of a food hygiene inspection are specifically addressed, including planning for the inspection, preliminary interviews, the inspection of premises, the post inspection interview and post inspection administration.

Before carrying out a food hygiene inspection, EHOs will take account of a number of issues. These will include:

(1) reviewing the premises' previous history - including information on its operations and systems, previous complaints and responses to previous inspection outcomes;
(2) timing of inspection - generally unannounced, although advance notice may occasionally be appropriate to ensure relevant persons are present;
(3) equipment availability, for example, calibrated temperature recording equipment;
(4) appropriate protective clothing; and
(5) assessing the need for additional expertise, for example, food examiners.

Before commencing an inspection, the EHO will explain the purpose of the inspection and what it will entail. Inspections will include:

(1) a preliminary assessment of the food hazards associated with the business; and
(2) determining whether the business has a satisfactory system for assessing food hazards and controlling risks.

The approach to inspection will depend significantly on whether such a system exists. LACOTS guidance on food hygiene inspections therefore emphasizes the central role of a preliminary interview. Discussion at an early stage of the inspection about the hazards associated with the business and any system in place for assessing those hazards and controlling the risks, allows an EHO to properly plan the subsequent detailed inspection of the business operations and premises.

Food businesses are now required to identify any step in their activities which is critical to ensuring food safety. Businesses must ensure that adequate safety procedures are identified, implemented, maintained and reviewed on the basis of the following principles:

(1) analysis of the food hazards in a food business operation;
(2) identification of the points in the operations where food hazards may occur;
(3) deciding which of the points identified are critical to ensuring food safety;
(4) identification and implementation of effective control and monitoring procedures at the critical points; and
(5) review of the analysis of food hazards, the critical control points and the control and monitoring procedures periodically and whenever the food business operations change.

In complying with this requirement, businesses may have various systems in place. Only a minority will have a formal documented HACCP system; most are more likely to have implemented some less formal system. Different approaches to auditing such systems are necessary. LACOTS guidance on risk assessment provides detailed advice on assessing different types of systems. It emphasizes the flexibility EHOs must have in recognizing that food businesses may use a variety of methods to identify and assess relevant food hazards and control risks. It also recognizes that with this new requirement, many businesses will need advice on how to develop systems and EHOs are seen as central to enabling proprietors to develop relevant systems.

In addition to considering any systems in place, an inspection will include a visual and physical examination of the premises and its operations. EHOs will have particular regard to the food hazards and the control and monitoring procedures in place at the critical points. LACOTS guidance on risk assessment includes advice on the broad stages of a risk-based inspection and the judgements EHOs must take. The guidance emphasizes going beyond simply identifying hazards. It recognizes that action taken to control hazards, without any consideration of the risk, can result in unnecessary controls being imposed on food businesses.

Inspections will, therefore, usually include the following areas:

(1) temperature controls during storage, cooking, processing, cooling, reheating, thawing, preparation and distribution. Physical checks will be made and records examined, including action taken in the event of breakdown, for example, the failure of refrigeration;
(2) the absence of cross-contamination and the use of good handling techniques. Work flows will be examined to ensure separation of high-risk food from raw food and waste. The use of staff and equipment will be considered and particular attention paid to thawing and cooling. The protection/covering and packaging of food will be included;
(3) cleansing and disinfection. The physical and bacteriological cleanliness of premises and equipment, evidence of a planned cleaning programme/cleaning schedules;
(4) personal hygiene and training. The hygiene awareness of managers and staff, the standard of supervision, procedures for appointments, medicals and exclusions. Procedures for replenishment of soap, towels and replacement of soiled protective clothing. The use of training records;
(5) the delivery and handling of raw materials, including checking food on arrival and the use of specifications, and dealing with non-food items such as packaging to avoid food contamination;
(6) pest control including absence of pests, proofing and control. Records of visits, treatment and recommendations will be required;
(7) complaints. An examination of records and action taken on receipt of complaints. Recall systems and product traceability will be checked. Foreign body detection equipment such as metal detectors, and systems will be examined;
(8) waste and refuse. Procedures for handling and removal of waste and for dealing with detained or unfit food;
(9) visitors. Procedures for dealing with visitors, including enforcement officers, engineers and contractors;

(10) food storage and stock rotation. Systems and documentation, including staff awareness;
(11) finished product. Handling, wrapping, storage and distribution;
(12) management control systems including the hygiene policy and the application of hazard analysis and control and monitoring procedures at critical points will be examined. Contracts, for example, pest control, cleaning, equipment maintenance, waste disposal and catering. Quality Assurance/Quality Control systems including microbiological monitoring, records and action taken in event of adverse results. Hygiene audit records should be available; and
(13) structure, equipment and facilities including design, lighting, ventilation, drainage, water supply, staffrooms, first aid, storage areas, facilities for washing hands, equipment and food, and external buildings and yards.

It will be clear from the above that comprehensive inspections of food premises by EHOs may take several hours or even days, depending on the size of premises, the type of operation and the standards of hygiene. Furthermore, inspections may take place at any time of the day or night depending on the hours of operation.

Some form of post-inspection interview should occur to enable the EHO to discuss any significant findings including any contraventions of food hygiene laws. At all times EHOs will clearly distinguish those matters that are contraventions from recommendations of good practice. The EHO should discuss possible solutions to problems identified and agree time scales for any proposed action. The EHO will also confirm what enforcement action is proposed, if any.

Code of Practice No. 9 requires EHOs to specifically report back in writing after every relevant inspection. The reports should include the following information:
(1) name and address of premises;
(2) person seen/interviewed;
(3) type of premises;
(4) date and time of inspection;
(5) areas inspected;
(6) records examined;
(7) details of any samples procured; and
(8) summary of action to be taken by the authority.

It is quite common for such reports to be provided at the end of the inspection, in handwritten form. The summary of action should confirm whether any further measures will follow, for example, an advisory letter or service of a notice.

*Action taken as a result of an inspection*

During an inspection, an EHO may identify contraventions of food hygiene legislation and/or poor or unsafe food handling practices. Several options exist to remedy the contravention and detailed guidance is found in a number of the Food Safety Act, 1990, Codes of Practice as to the most appropriate action. In addition, LACOTS has published guidance on food enforcement policies. The guidance stresses the range of options available to local authorities and provides detailed criteria which may be applicable to them. The options available and potential outcomes for all food hygiene inspections include:

(1) verbal advice/warnings or informal written advice/warnings where the EHO is confident the work will be carried out;
(2) an Improvement Notice, where there are contraventions of food hygiene legislation, allowing not less than 14 days to comply;
(3) the detention or seizure of unsafe food where food does not comply with the food safety requirements;
(4) an Emergency Prohibition Notice, where there is an imminent risk of injury to health, requiring closure of the premises or prohibition of processes or use of equipment;
(5) a formal caution where an offence exists but it is not considered in the public interest to prosecute through the courts; and
(6) prosecution, where it is considered in the public interest.

**Frequency of inspections**

Effective inspection programmes recognize that the frequency of inspection will vary according to the type of food business, the nature of the food, the degree of handling and the size of the business. Essentially, those premises posing potentially a higher risk should be inspected more frequently than those premises with a lower risk.

Code of Practice No. 9 details an inspection rating scheme for assessing premises for this purpose. Premises are rated in the following areas:

(1) hazards associated with the premises:
   (i) type of food and method of handling;
   (ii) method of processing; and
   (iii) consumers at risk.
(2) level of current compliance with regard to:
   (i) food hygiene and safety (including practices, procedures and temperature controls); and
   (ii) structure ( including cleanliness).
(3) confidence in management/control systems including:
   (i) previous history;
   (ii) management attitude;
   (iii) level of food hygiene training; technical knowledge; and
   (iv) accredited systems or documented procedures.

The EHO determines the score for each of the categories, in line with the Code's detailed guidance, the total score being used to determine the minimum frequency of inspection and the date of the next inspection. Businesses handling low-risk foods with few customers that comply with food hygiene legislation and are managed effectively may only be inspected every five years. Businesses processing high-risk food, for example, cook-chill operations and supplying vulnerable consumers, are likely to be inspected at least every six months.

Provided premises comply with hygiene legislation, it should be noted that the interval between inspection will be greater if the EHO has confidence in the management and the control systems. This enables local authorities to target their resources at those businesses that fail to make efforts to comply and in which the authorities have little or no confidence. This approach recognizes that it is the primary responsibility of food businesses themselves to ensure legal compliance and safe systems of work and that local authorities should give priority to those businesses unwilling to discharge their responsibilities.

**The investigation of food complaints**

The Food Safety Act, 1990 contains a number of offences which may be relevant to food complaints. There is a general offence regarding selling foods not complying with food safety requirements which includes food that is either injurious to health, unfit for human consumption or so contaminated (whether by extraneous matter or otherwise) that it would not be reasonable to expect it to be used for human consumption in that state. The Act also contains an offence of selling food not of the nature, substance or quality demanded by the purchaser. These offences cover a whole range of types of food complaint including food that would be harmful if it were consumed, food contaminated by foreign bodies, contamination by mould and food in dirty containers (a particular problem with reusable bottles).

Local authorities investigate food complaints as part of the general enforcement service to the public. The purpose of investigating complaints includes:

(1) resolving problems which pose a risk to public health;
(2) the provision of information to the food industry in order to raise and maintain standards;
(3) the prevention of future complaints; and
(4) fulfilling the duty of enforcement contained in the Act.

To ensure a consistent approach to the investigation of food complaints, LACOTS has published specific guidance on dealing with and investigating food complaints made to local authority Environmental Health Departments. A structured and systematic approach is necessary in investigations because what may appear to be a simple isolated problem could have significant, possibly national or international, implications.

The first stage of any investigation will be receipt of the complaint when information will be obtained from the complainant. Various details are necessary to assist the future investigation. At this early stage a decision must be made confirming that it is the responsibility of the authority that has received the complaint to investigate.

The relevant local authority officer, usually an EHO, will then inspect the food in question and arrange, if necessary, to further interview the complainant. The complainant will usually be asked to provide a written statement detailing various matters including information on when, where and by whom the food was purchased, what happened to the food after purchase and when, where and by whom the problem with the food was discovered. Details of the vendor and, if relevant, the manufacturer and importer will be noted. Some form of proof of purchase is desirable to supplement the statement of the complainant, for example, a till receipt or distinctive packaging.

At this early stage, the EHO will consider whether the complaint may relate to national/widespread problems or malicious contamination. If suspected, Food Safety Act, 1990, Code of Practice No. 16 on food hazard warning systems gives guidance on further action to be taken. The EHO will also assess whether the complaint is associated with illness and, therefore, whether it is necessary to initiate a food poisoning investigation.

The retailer, caterer or manufacturer where the food was purchased or produced will then be visited. Where the retailer is within the EHO's local authority area but the manufacturer is outside that authority's area then, after visiting the local retailer, the EHO will make contact with the local authority Environmental Health Department responsible for the manufacturer (often referred to as the home or originating authority) to obtain further information. The Food Safety Act, 1990 empowers authorized officers such as EHOs to enter business premises outside their area to identify evidence of contraventions which may encompass, amongst other things, the investigation of food complaints. However, authorities generally rely on the reports from home or originating authorities for detailed information on such premises as this is seen as a more cost-effective option.

At this stage, further information obtained may suggest that a national or widespread problem exists. In most cases, however, the officer will proceed with a detailed investigation and inspection of all relevant premises. The investigation will seek to confirm if an offence has been committed, the alleged person(s)/enterprise responsible and the precautions taken to prevent such a complaint.

Food complaint investigations will, on occasions, necessitate formal interviews having regard to all the relevant law on criminal evidence and, in particular, the Police and Criminal Evidence Act, 1984 and its associated Codes of Practice. This will occur when the EHO considers that an offence exists and the outcome of the investigation is likely to result in a recommendation to prosecute. In addition to interviews with persons, EHOs may formally request confirmation, in writing, of details from manufacturers and other relevant enterprises relating to the complaint and, in particular, precautions taken to prevent such complaints.

The usual outcome of food complaint investigations is that advisory or warning letters are sent to the business responsible. However, if an EHO believes a prosecution may be appropriate, the Food Safety Act, 1990, Code of Practice No. 2 on legal matters states that the following factors should be considered:

(1) the seriousness of the alleged offence;
(2) the previous history of the business;
(3) the likelihood of the defendant being able to establish a due diligence defence;
(4) the ability of any important witnesses and their willingness to cooperate;
(5) the willingness of the party to prevent a recurrence of the problem;
(6) the probable public benefit of a prosecution and the importance of the case;

(7) whether other action such as issuing a formal caution, service of an Improvement or Prohibition Notice would be more appropriate or effective; and
(8) any explanation offered by the affected company.

The reference in the Food Safety Act, 1990 to the defence of "due diligence" with regard to food related offences is worthy of specific note. The Act creates a number of offences known as "strict liability". In such a case, it does not matter that the person accused did not intend to break the law. The mere fact that there is clear evidence that the statute has been contravened is sufficient for a conviction. This regime of strict liability was perceived as causing injustice if a person was held to have committed an offence for which he had no responsibility at all, or because of an accident or some cause completely beyond his control. In order to create a balance of fairness, a defence was included which has become known as the "due diligence defence".

The Act specifically states that it is a defence to prove that all reasonable precautions were taken and all due diligence exercised to avoid the offence. Through legal precedent, various principles have been confirmed as necessary if a defence is to succeed. Some positive steps will always be required. Taking reasonable precautions involves the setting up of a system of control having regard to the nature of the risks involved. Due diligence involves securing the proper operation of that system. Where there is a reasonable precaution then it should be taken. Nevertheless, what is reasonable will depend on particular circumstances including the size of the business. All relevant aspects of the operations of the business must be included in any control system and the operation of the system must be kept under review and amended as necessary.

Food complaint investigations may, therefore, involve considerable time and effort on the part of the investigating authority. In addition to determining whether there is admissible evidence to provide a realistic prospect of conviction for any food complaint offence, EHOs will also consider whether it is in the public interest to prosecute. It is likely that only those food businesses which have failed to fulfil their legal and moral responsibilities will find themselves in court for food complaint offences.

## The role of the consultant EHO

Some of the largest food manufacturers, retailers and caterers employ Environmental Health Officers or Hygiene Technologists to help them formulate and manage their own hygiene policies.

However, many companies use the services of Hygiene Consultants. There are a number of experienced and self-employed Environmental Health Officers providing consultancy services and some companies offer a national service.

Consultants provide an independent and objective assessment of a food operation and can help companies formulate policies to improve the management of their hygiene standards. Consultants often fulfil a troubleshooting role but increasingly their advice is sought on a pro-active basis as the food industry recognizes the benefits that accrue from a proper investment in hygiene. They may be utilized to assist with the implementation of BS 5750 and HACCP and to approve potential suppliers. The considerable demand for hygiene training created by the Food Safety Act, 1990 has resulted in many consultants specializing in this area of work.

The introduction of compulsory competitive tendering has resulted in some local authorities using consultants in areas not subjected to competition, including food hygiene inspections, and this trend may increase.

**Organizations involved in food control**

The food control service operated by Environmental Health Officers relies from time to time on advice and assistance from other organizations including LACOTS, the Public Health Laboratory Service, the Public Analyst, the Department of Health, the Communicable Disease Surveillance Centre, research establishments, the Ministry of Agriculture, Fisheries and Food and, with regard to animals, Veterinary Investigation Centres. In addition, a considerable amount of work on the microbiology of food is undertaken by the Food Hygiene Laboratory at the Central Public Health Laboratory at Colindale.

**LACOTS and the Coordination of Local Authorities**

LACOTS, the Local Authorities Coordinating Body on Food and Trading Standards, is a local government central body charged with the task of coordinating local authority trading standards and food enforcement activity. Its terms of reference were extended in 1992 to encompass local authority food hygiene and food safety functions. This reflected the need for local authorities to ensure delivery of an effective enforcement service that was both coordinated and consistent.

LACOTS is funded by local government monies and is answerable to a group of local authority elected members, appointed through the local authority associations, that make up LACOTS Management Committee. It has a small administrative and professional secretariat but is reliant on the hard work, experience and expertise of a large group of local authority advisers who volunteer, through the associations, their time and efforts to assist LACOTS in its work. Advisers include directors, chief officers, experienced managers and practitioners who are organized into various technical panels and working groups to address specific enforcement issues requiring coordination. By involving local authority officers who are responsible for the policy and detail of local authority enforcement work, LACOTS ensures its strategies and guidance are relevant and acceptable.

LACOTS has identified three key coordinating strategies which have been applied to food hygiene and food safety. Through LACOTS advisers, it emphasizes the need for common sense and pragmatic interpretations and application of food hygiene laws and a consistent approach to inspections, investigations and outcomes. LACOTS identifies and promotes existing good enforcement practice, encouraging local authorities to ensure enforcement policies are based on protecting the public.

The second strategy involves encouraging the development of local authority food liaison groups. These groupings of local authorities enable EHOs to raise enforcement difficulties and potential inconsistencies and resolve them through peer group discussion. Where difficulties cannot be resolved, or the issues have national implications, the groups can seek the view of LACOTS and its advisers.

The third strategy is known as the Home Authority Principle. This involves local authorities taking particular responsibility for those food business's whose decision making bases are located in their areas (usually the head office). The role of a Home Authority is to assess a food businesses' own system for ensuring food hygiene and food safety issues, including legal compliance, are properly addressed. The Home Authority also provides preventative advice particularly when legislation changes. It acts as a focal point for liaison with other authorities who inspect the business's decentralized branches or units situated in their area. However, the final decision to pursue legal action in the event of a contravention always remains with the authority where the offence occurred.

The strategies of LACOTS have been recognized by Central Government as an essential part of the local authority food control system. All three aspects of LACOTS' strategies are reflected in the relevant Codes of Practice issued under Section 40 of the Food Safety Act, 1990. These Codes contain information which authorities must have regard to (as well as advice for information only). Of particular importance is Code of Practice No. 9 on Food Hygiene Inspection which makes reference to LACOTS advice, the role of local authority food liaison groups and the Home Authority Principle.

*The Public Analyst*

Food Authorities appoint a public analyst to provide, among other things, a service of chemical analysis and advice. Work is also undertaken for private companies. However, public analysts must not engage in any food business that is carried on in the area to which their appointments apply. Food and water is analyzed using extremely sensitive and sophisticated equipment to confirm the presence, or absence, of specific contaminants, pesticides, additives, trace metals or taints. Tests can be carried out to ascertain whether an item has undergone a particular process, for example, the phosphatase test is used to determine whether an insect has been subjected to heat treatment or cooking. The composition of food and the amount of water present can also be ascertained.

CHAPTER 16

# Quality Assurance

### *by Sterling Crew, B.Sc. (Hons.), M.C.I.E.H., M.I.F.S.T.*

Quality Assurance is becoming increasingly important in relation to the management of systems controlling the quality and safety of food. However, many people are unsure of its exact meaning and how it can be applied to the broad areas of work that are encompassed by the food industry.

**What is quality?**

Quality can be defined as the totalling of features and characteristics of a product or service that bear on its ability to satisfy stated, or implied, needs. Within this definition concepts of fitness for a given purpose, customer satisfaction, safety and value for money can be identified. It does not, however, mean the most expensive or the most excellent. A beef fillet steak is perceived as a high quality food and a traditional beef sausage a low quality one. However, if a customer requires a low cost meal which is easy to make and requires minimum preparation, yet is still satisfying and fills that hunger gap, one may consider the sausage a better buy and therefore in certain circumstances a product which merits an equal quality rating. Quality must therefore not be confused with the grade of the product.

**British Standard 5750**

Quality Assurance may be considered as all the planned and systematic actions necessary to provide confidence that a product or service will satisfy the customer's requirements for quality over time. Over the years many people have developed their own Quality Assurance systems. Some of these have been synthesized and formalized into British Standard 5750: 1987. BS 5750 attempts to set out how a group can establish, document and maintain an effective quality system which would demonstrate a commitment to quality and the ability to meet a client's quality needs. It is now an internationally accepted standard. This is reflected in its acceptance in its entirety by the International Standards Organisation in its ISO 9000 series. It is often said that the Standard is common sense set down on paper in an organized fashion. Quality Control is differentiated from Quality Assurance in that it is a series of techniques used to assess compliance with a specification by product sampling, which is usually based on statistical criteria. This often takes place at the end of production and the information is then fed back into the organization. It is in essence a reactive process which identifies things that may be wrong after the event and does not necessarily determine the cause of the problem. Quality Assurance is proactive and attempts to stop things going wrong in the first place, often said to be getting it right first time every time. It usually involves a continuing evaluation of factors affecting the adequacy of specification for intended applications as well as audits of production, installation and inspection operations. This continuous product assessment and fault correction is the responsibility of all staff, especially those involved in preparation and production.

**Fig. 63.**
Lyons Tetley, Greenford, Middlesex.

The first UK food manufacturer to be awarded BS5750 registration.

**The implementation of Quality Assurance**

The three main components in the Quality Assurance process are:

(1) the specification (What is to be done);

(2) documented instruction (How it is to be done); and
(3) the recording system (That it has been done).

Quality must be built into a food product; it cannot be inspected in. To demonstrate how ineffective end testing by people can be, even if it is 100% inspection, simply read the following paragraph and count F's both small and capital. Do not go through the material a second time because this would be 200% inspection:

"The necessity of training farm hands for first class farms in the fatherly handling of farm live stock is foremost in the minds of farm owners. Since the forefathers of the farm owners trained the farm hands for first class farms in the fatherly handling of farm live stock, the farm owners feel they should carry on the family tradition of training farm hands of first class farms in the fatherly handling of farm live stock because they believe it is the basis of good fundamental farm management."

The majority of people identify only two thirds of the 36 F's present. One can imagine the failure rate increasing if this were carried out on a fast production line, for example, spotting defective bottles or jars on a bottling line in a dairy.

The clear message which emanates from BS 5750 is to control all points of the process where not to do so would result in prejudicing the quality and safety of the product. To do this, hazards within the process must be identified through detailed analysis of all operations involved. Indeed Quality Assurance in relation to food must incorporate the principles of HACCP (Hazard Analysis and Critical Control Points) for it to be fully effective. HACCP is an excellent stratagem for identifying and controlling risk, and an effective and integrated Quality Assurance system would contain the necessary elements to ensure that the specified standards are maintained. Both systems should be seen as steps on a journey towards effective hygiene management. They are not a final destination in themselves. The strategic challenge therefore facing the food manager is how to improve the quality and safety of their operations without, in most cases, increasing resources. This may seem an unenviable task, but as the late John F. Kennedy said, "there are risks and costs to a programme of action, but they are far less than the long range risks and costs of comfortable inaction."

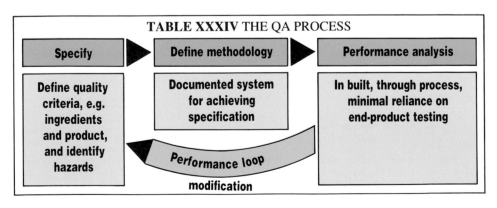

**TABLE XXXIV** THE QA PROCESS

| Specify | Define methodology | Performance analysis |
|---|---|---|
| Define quality criteria, e.g. ingredients and product, and identify hazards | Documented system for achieving specification | In built, through process, minimal reliance on end-product testing |

Performance loop modification

**Quality Assurance and the food industry**

Very few caterers, retailers or food manufacturers have been accredited to BS 5750 or indeed use the Standard as the basis for their Quality Assurance programme. It is anticipated that this situation will rapidly change with the growing appreciation that the system will not only enable companies to comply more effectively with the legal requirements, but that it also has clearly identifiable commercial advantages. Not least of these is the recognition that accreditation is a marketable commodity, as not only can BS 5750 be used as a standard upon which a group can set up a quality system, but it has the facility to be used in recognized third party accreditation. After a satisfactory audit a certificate of registration may be obtained from a body recognized by the National Accreditation Council for Certification Bodies (NACCB). Although this should not be seen in the same way as a driving test, i.e. one examination, as it must be continuously assessed if it is to be retained. Accreditation usually takes around two years to achieve.

To quote a Technical Director of a National Food Retailer: "In the short-term we will be encouraging our suppliers to go for BS 5750, in the medium-term we will be pressing them to have it, in the long-term we will be requiring them to have it". This statement recognizes the fact that one cannot sell a quality item, no matter what elaborate and effective storage conditions are used, if the food being supplied is of a low standard. One cannot build quality into raw materials which are sub-standard. The establishment of checking procedures for a caterer who is buying in cooked ham may include organoleptic and temperature testing (if warranted microbiological tests could be used) and ensuring that the source is a reputable one. The need to build quality into the whole food chain, from the farm to the restaurant plate, is seen as an essential requirement. In the future it is anticipated that the needs for retailers and caterers to have confidence in their suppliers will encourage more companies to adopt Quality Assurance practices. Not only is the ability to meet a client's requirements vital between two separate organizations, it is also essential between different departments within the same company: does the waitress receiving a meal from the kitchen get the correct food in the right quantity?

The benefits of applying Quality Assurance are also real. It should save an organization money because procedures will be more soundly based and efficient. It will ensure customer satisfaction and will reduce waste and time consuming reworking of faults. Making a faulty product costs money as well as creating a dissatisfied and possibly ill customer. By getting it right first time, real economies are created, as the high cost of rejecting unfit food due to inadequate storage procedures demonstrates.

Methods employed in Quality Assurance programmes within the food industry will vary considerably in accuracy and sophistication according to the type of process and the size and nature of the resources available. However, the basic principles can be applied to all areas of the food industry from the smallest caterer to the largest food manufacturer.

It has been recognized that due to the general nature of the Standard, additional interpretation is necessary for certain industries in order to provide for greater consistency. The British Standards Institute has commendably responded to this by publishing, in October 1989, Quality Systems for the Food and Drink Industries, Guidelines for the use of British Standard 5750 Part 2 1987 in the Manufacture of Food and Drink.

The Guidelines highlight aspects specific to the food and drinks industry which are not immediately apparent within BS 5750, but as they only enlarge on the requirements of the Standard, to be used effectively they must be used in conjunction with it. The Guidelines acknowledge extensive reference to the Institute of Food Science and Technology Manual, Food and Drink Manufacture - Good Manufacturing Practice. It is therefore not surprising that the subject headings are familiar to those working within the food industry.

To achieve the objectives of Quality Assurance in relation to food and drink it is necessary to design and plan, as relevant:

(1) raw materials specifications;
(2) ingredients formulations;
(3) processing equipment and environment;
(4) processing methods and conditions;
(5) intermediates in specifications;
(6) appropriate labelling specifications;
(7) specification for quantity per pack;
(8) specifications for management and control procedures; and
(9) a specified distribution system and cycle;
(10) appropriate storage, handling and preparation instructions.

This written documentation provides the means by which the various products comply with their specifications. The enforcement of good manufacturing practice ensures that the capability is translated into reality and that the resulting products do comply with the product's specification.

Quality Assurance must be welcomed by the Industry as a system which will make a substantial contribution to improving food quality and safety. However, it must not be overlooked that assuring the system with a strict product specification is not easily achievable in food manufacture because of the natural variations of raw materials which may be due to climate, cultivation and rearing techniques or non-uniformity within the species concerned. This poses an additional burden on control systems. The concept of "zero defects" should be realistically seen therefore as the desired target to aim for, and which is why the Government have allowed a defence of "due diligence"

**The practical implementation of Quality Assurance**

In order to establish a Quality Assurance system it is necessary to:

(1) prepare a statement of quality;
(2) decide on a system of appraisal and assessment of current company performance;
(3) determine the performance standard that is required;
(4) determine how to measure quality;

(5) ensure that there is a team approach and commitment to understand decision-making;
(6) raise the hygiene awareness and improve the skills of the workforce by training;
(7) improve the relationship with suppliers and clearly state the required quality;
(8) improve the levels of plant and personal hygiene to achieve effective hygiene and comply with good manufacturing practice;
(9) implement hazard analysis and control and monitoring at all points which are critical to food safety; and
(10) eliminate factors which prevent the specification being achieved.

**TABLE XXXV** SETTING UP A QUALITY ASSURANCE SYSTEM IN THE FOOD INDUSTRY

**UNDERSTAND QUALITY**
↓
**COMMITMENT TO QUALITY**
↓
**POLICY ON QUALITY**
↓
**PLAN FOR QUALITY**
↓
**DESIGN FOR QUALITY**
↓
**ORGANIZE FOR QUALITY**
↓
**MEASUREMENT OF THE COST OF QUALITY**
↓
**PROVIDE THE CAPABILITY FOR QUALITY**
↓
**TEAMWORK FOR QUALITY**
↓
**TRAINING FOR QUALITY**
↓
**IMPLEMENT A SYSTEM FOR QUALITY**
↓
**CONTROL OF QUALITY**
↓
**EFFECTIVE QUALITY ASSURANCE SYSTEM**

## Quality Assurance audits

By definition an audit is a documented activity performed to verify, by examination and evaluation of objective evidence, the effectiveness of an organization. It is essentially an information gathering process so structured that improvement or corrective action may be taken. An organization should be able to audit its hygiene in much the same way it would its budget.

To audit a system one must have a standard to which it can be compared and measured against. Effective food hygiene embraces all those matters which are implemented to prevent the incidence of food poisoning, and aims to provide a quality product. BS 5750 addresses this problem by providing an excellent structure for formulating an effective Quality Assurance programme, which can incorporate good manufacturing practices.

Good manufacturing practice is not a new concept in the UK. It has a long history in the pharmaceutical manufacturing industry and is acknowledged as a specific recording method of operation, designed to minimize hazards. It is also capable of being controlled and monitored. The Institute of Food Science and Technology recognized the principles of good manufacturing practice and has synthesized these principles into a guide. This document aims to ensure that products are consistently manufactured to a level of safety and quality appropriate for their intended use. The guide sets out the principles of the effective implementation of well-designed manufacturing operations coupled with the implementation of an effective Quality Assurance system.

Armed with a competent comprehensive standard and an effective inspection framework the manager is prepared for the auditing process. But it should be borne in mind that the mere act of observation changes the conditions being measured. Managers must try to obviate this as far as possible, aiming to create a constructive atmosphere where "normal" conditions may prevail. The presence of the auditor should not affect the practice of food handlers.

The auditor's personal qualities are also very important. Any preconceived ideas, prejudices or subjective attitudes should be expelled. It is essential that the auditor produces complete and accurate findings based on facts and facts alone. The auditor's prime role is simply to observe and draw informed conclusions. It is important that he or she adopts a constructive approach which attempts to disclose facts and make analyses and assessments in a critical manner.

## Audit phases

Audits may be divided into four main phases:

### (1) Preparation

Information is gathered about the system from existing files. If it is an unfamiliar work area it may be beneficial to conduct a reconnaissance exercise to establish a picture of the current situation. The auditor will then be able to evaluate the size, scope and nature of the operations involved. The audit can thus be programmed and appropriate check lists compiled ready for issue.

**(2) The opening meeting**

This involves meeting all the pertinent members of the organization including a wide spectrum of senior management such as the managing director, the production manager and the Quality Assurance/Control manager. The standard to which the premises is to be inspected should be agreed. If reticence is displayed over using a standard higher than that required by legislation the commercial advantages should be stressed. Information should be provided on the areas to be observed and on the co-operation required to facilitate an efficient and effective audit. It is recommended that the audit programme be submitted to the department being assessed. This is also a prudent moment to invite and discuss any queries relating to the audit itself.

Prior notification is given to the management of the date of the audit - usually two weeks. Some may question this practice but it is found that the depth and nature of the matters covered in the audit cannot be ameliorated in a short period of time preceding the inspection. Those that can, for instance, the last minute cleaning and poor practices, are detected in an unannounced visit preceding the main audit. The results of this, married with the auditor's technical expertise give an indication of the "usual" conditions. It is hoped that this prior notification contributes to establishing the atmosphere of co-operation and openness that is essential for a successful, constructive conclusion.

The logistics of the operation also dictate the need for advance warning. A quiet room is necessary to study the paperwork and interview staff. It may also be necessary to arrange for a guide who has a working knowledge of areas to be inspected if it is an unfamiliar operation.

**(3) The investigation**

(i) *The adequacy audit*

This is an office based exercise which attempts to examine to what degree the documented system, represented by the hygiene policy, manual, associated procedures, work instructions, inspection forms and records, adequately sets the standard of good manufacturing practice, and if it provides the objective evidence for which it was designed. (British Standard 5750 provides an excellent format for document formulation and control.) To facilitate this part of auditing procedure it is an advantage for the auditor to have a specifically designed check list not only as an aide memoir but to assist in giving structure to this part of the audit.

The company should be encouraged to formulate a hygiene policy, if it has not already done so. It is unfortunate that this matter is not a statutory requirement and its omission from the Food Safety Act, 1990 is disappointing. The advantages of such a system are clear. The policy should be a general statement of objectives and methods and in practice should consist of three parts:

*General statement of intent*

The statement should outline the company's overall philosophy in relation to the management of hygiene. An example of a general hygiene policy statement could be "to achieve and maintain the highest possible standard of food and environmental hygiene to protect the consumer from food poisoning and associated dangers and to maintain a system to produce a quality food and drink product". This statement must be made by the company board and management, which provides adequate resources to achieve the objectives.

*Organization*

This part should clearly show who is responsible to whom and for what, i.e. the chain of command. A structured diagram is useful for this. It should demonstrate how accountabilities are fixed, how policy implementation is to be monitored and how individual job descriptions set hygiene and quality responsibilities.

*Arrangements*

This part should detail the practical arrangements in force to assist in overall policy implementation. These include hygiene training, hygiene audits/inspections, food poisoning reporting/investigation/control, good manufacturing practices, codes of practice relating to food handling techniques and cleaning procedures and health services. In practice this part of the policy may be very lengthy and is often best presented in the form of a manual with appropriate cross references to the other sections. Each hygiene policy should be signed by the organization's managing director/chief executive, and should be dated to facilitate revision. The policy should be brought to the attention of all employees, through training sessions or other appropriate methods.

To ensure effective policy implementation the organization of hygiene and quality management within a company should:

- (a) clearly and unambiguously show, in written format, an unbroken and logical delegation of duty through the line management operation where risk of food poisoning could occur;
- (b) identify key personnel, by title rather than name, to be held accountable to senior management when ensuring that detailed arrangements such as systems and procedures for safe hygienic working practices are developed, utilized and maintained;
- (c) define the roles of both line staff and management by the use of specific job descriptions;
- (d) provide adequate support for relevant management, for example, hygiene advisers, food scientists, medical advisers and public analysts;
- (e) nominate competent persons to measure and monitor controls;
- (f) provide the means/authority to deal with failures to meet the requirements of the hygiene policy;

(g) specify management accountability for hygiene and quality in a similar manner to other management functions;
(h) ensure that the organization unambiguously tells each individual exactly how to fulfil his or her role;
(i) ensure that the organization makes it known, in terms of both time and money, what resources are available for hygiene and quality; and
(j) be user friendly.

(ii) *The compliance audit*

This audit seeks to establish the extent to which the documented system is implemented and observed by the workforce, i.e. "do they do what they say they do". It should determine objectively the conditions which prevail and make an assessment of them. It is important that the auditor knows exactly what standard is being used and the specified requirements for each instance. The number of people engaged in this exercise would reflect the size, process and complexity of the company being examined and the resources of the organization which is to undertake such a task. If a team is required the participants are designated specific responsibilities. It is important that all of the team are fully conversant with their objectives to avoid any omissions or inefficient duplication of work. A check list may be useful. For example, a member of the team responsible for temperature control may have an inspection sheet relating to chiller units. Questions would relate to:

(a) ambient air temperature;
(b) temperature of food (detailing number of samples required and length of time samples have been in the unit);
(c) method of measurement, for example, by single thermometer or data temperature logger;
(d) whether a thermometer is present on the unit and if it is correctly calibrated;
(e) whether the unit has a data recording system; and
(f) if an effective alarm system is present.

All the auditor can do in a compliance audit is to investigate a limited sample of activities and on the basis of this make an "informed judgement" as to the general status of the hygiene system. Care should be taken that the areas observed are the most germane to the achievement of a safe quality product. It would therefore be prudent to adopt an inspection method based on the lines of Quality Assurance in relation to risk identification. This is a natural component of any Quality Assurance programme where the basic philosophy is prevention of defects by dividing control requirements into product formulations, processing parameters and operating practices.

The results of the adequacy and compliance audits should be analyzed in an objective manner. It may be of advantage to remember the Holmes adage -"when you have eliminated the impossible, whatever remains, however improbable, must be the truth".

At the end of the survey the auditor establishes if the inspection has disclosed any significant non-compliances which require immediate attention. It is the auditor's task to assimilate the surveys into a cohesive report and to present an overall assessment. It is advantageous to prioritize remedial works. However, the members of the organization examined should also be encouraged to do this as it can give a good indication of their capabilities and perceptions.

**TABLE XXXVI** SURVEY AREAS FOR A COMPLIANCE AUDIT

| SURVEY AREAS | MATTERS ADDRESSED |
|---|---|
| Monitoring and control procedures including temperature control/ stock rotation/quality control | Heat treatments to which food is subjected. Storage temperatures. Procedures for dealing with equipment breakdown. Stock control system. Vetting of suppliers. |
| Food Science and Technology | Examination of compositional risks inherent in food and the process to which it will be subjected. |
| Hygiene hazards and contamination | Pest control, waste control practices, personal hygiene |
| Plant and equipment including cleaning and disinfection | Design, structure, facilities, ventilation, lighting, cleaning schedules. |
| Staff training and motivation | Is it systematic and adequate for the task undertaken? |
| Transportation | Vehicle structure, cleanliness, temperature control, inspections. |

**(4) The closing meeting**

The audit findings will normally have been stated verbally in general terms to the relevant representative of the company, especially those findings requiring urgent remedial action. However, they are also formally reported to the company's senior management at the closing meeting. A date for the meeting is set to allow the senior management time to digest and analyze the resulting report. However, if this is not substantial in nature the report may be given verbally at the conclusion of the survey.

The meeting should involve the same people who were present at the opening meeting, and should encourage everyone's participation. At the beginning of the meeting it is important to reiterate the standard to which the premises have been inspected, ideally good manufacturing practice.

The salient conclusions which have been drawn by the auditor are put in a summary statement, then the organization's senior management representatives are invited to discuss specific points of disagreement or matters on which they are unclear. Some organizations may wish the statutory contraventions to be clearly identified. Dates are then agreed on which remedial action will be taken. Following this meeting the implementation of an effective hygiene programme usually takes place. A revisit is organized to verify that corrective action has been taken and that it is suitable.

**Quality Assurance and the law**

The Food Safety Act, 1990 has introduced a new defence into food legislation, that of "due diligence" (section 21). This replaces the old warranty defence, because of the way in which it was enforced, which all too often allowed retailers to evade their responsibilities. The new defence is intended to ensure that the liability for any contravention remains with the appropriate party. It is a defence for the person charged to prove that he took all reasonable precautions and exercised all due diligence to avoid the commission of the offence by himself or by a person under his control. It should be noted that the words "it is a defence to prove" places the onus of proof upon the person charged. The prosecuting authority is not under an obligation to prove that the defence was not fulfilled. The burden of proof is discharged on the balance of probability. This is an important development for all areas of the food industry and clearly it would be advantageous to develop a control system which can reduce or eliminate the risk of prosecution. It is, however, anticipated that each case will depend on its own circumstances. There will be no standard system of due diligence. Although a major contributing factor in any such defence may well be centred on a company's Quality Assurance programme.

A company which has a system that has obtained a Certificate of Registration from an approved certification body (recognized by the NACCB) will obviously have an added security, as it has been assessed to be adequate by an independent, competent third party. It must, however, be emphasized that the "special tick" awarded under the scheme is not a product safety mark, as in the case of the British Standard Kite Mark. It only relates to the systems involved. Such a system may not apply to a company as a whole. It may only concern a particular premises and even a specific operation being carried out on a site.

Many companies will have developed a quality system independent of BS 5750 and may have no intention of seeking a third party approval. Such companies should ensure that whatever system of Quality Assurance is adopted, adequate precautions and checks, dependent on their size and resources, are taken having regard to the inherent risk posed by the product. Such steps must be suitably recorded if a credible defence is to be offered. The Company will not be able to rely on warranties and any reasonable precautions available must be taken: the system must prevent faults, and corrective action must be taken where they occur - all consumer complaints should be recorded and analyzed. The system should be written down with adequate instruction and training being given to staff.

CHAPTER 17

# *Food safety and hygiene legislation*

The law is a complex subject and most acts and regulations affecting the food industry are difficult to interpret. However, ignorance of the law is no defence in the event of a prosecution and all managers must make a special effort to become conversant with legislation which affects their business.

This Chapter is intended only as a general outline of the most important legislation relating to food and food hygiene in England and Wales, and Scotland; Northern Ireland has its own legislation, although any differences are usually minor. It is not intended to provide a concise legal document and as legislation is constantly changing, regard must always be had to any new legislation which may have been introduced since this book was written. Should information or advice be required regarding the interpretation of a particular section, or the current legislation applicable, the local Environmental Health Officer or a solicitor should be consulted.

Legislation consists of:

(1) *Acts of Parliament*

These are statutes passed by Parliament which can only be modified by parliamentary procedure. Acts are normally concerned with principles of legislation and must pass through the House of Commons and the House of Lords before receiving Royal Assent.

(2) *Regulations and orders*

Regulations and orders are delegated legislation made by the appropriate Minister who is empowered to do so under a specific Act. For example, The Food Safety (General Food Hygiene) Regulations, 1995 were made under the Food Safety Act, 1990. Regulations normally deal with specific premises or commodities in much greater detail than Acts.

(3) *Local acts or byelaws*

These are made or adopted by local authorities and are legally binding only within the area of the particular authority. Byelaws must be formally approved by a specified Minister before they can take effect.

Copies of legislation can be purchased from Her Majesty's Stationery Office. Regulations are known as Statutory Instruments (SI) and are numbered to enable rapid identification when ordering.

Acts and regulations applicable to the food industry are concerned with:
(1) preventing the production or sale of injurious, unsafe or unfit food;
(2) preventing the contamination of food and food equipment;
(3) the hygiene of food premises, equipment and personnel (including training);
(4) hygiene practices, including temperature control, hazard analysis, and monitoring and control of hazards at points which are critical to food safety;
(5) the provision of sanitary accommodation, water supplies and washing facilities;
(6) the control of food poisoning;
(7) the importation of food;
(8) the composition and labelling of food; and
(9) the registration and licensing of food premises and vehicles.

*The European Community*

Since the United Kingdom joined the Common Market, several hundred regulations have been introduced to secure compliance with the requirements of EC directives. Occasionally the EC produces binding regulations which are applicable to all member countries without the need for each country to enact its own legislation.

## LEGAL TERMS

*Court of Appeal (Criminal Division)*

This Division deals with appeals from the Crown Court against conviction or sentence. Usually three or five judges sit to hear an appeal.

*Crown Court*

This Court is responsible for serious criminal trials of indictable offences and also hears appeals from magistrates' courts. The County Court is responsible for dealing with civil offences, for example, claims for damages from persons who have suffered food poisoning.

*Indictable offences*

Serious crimes usually tried by a judge and jury in the Crown Court. The accused is given a full written statement setting out each alleged offence. This document is known as an indictment and each offence is called a count.

*Information*

A statement of the alleged contravention(s) which is sent to the justices' clerk by the prosecuting authority. On receipt of the information the clerk issues the summons. This is the usual method of instituting criminal proceedings before a Justice of the Peace.

*Judge*

An Officer of the Crown, appointed on the advice of the Lord Chancellor, who sits in court to administer justice according to the law. Most judges are barristers and will have had several years of experience before appointment, however, some are solicitors.

*Justices of the Peace (JP)*

Persons from all walks of life, appointed by the Crown to preside over magistrates' courts in a particular area. They act judicially in the case of summary offences and initiate proceedings and commit the accused for trial in the case of indictable offences. They receive expenses only and must attend training courses prior to appointment.

*Magistrates' court*

A court that deals with summary offences in a particular geographic area. Usually presided over by three Justices of the Peace or a single stipendiary magistrate. Each bench of magistrates is assisted by a legally qualified justices' clerk.

At the court hearing the accused has to plead guilty or not guilty. If he pleads guilty the magistrates will then sentence him, taking into account previous convictions. If he pleads not guilty the prosecutor will call witnesses to prove his guilt. The solicitor acting for the accused will cross-examine the prosecution witnesses, the accused will give his own evidence and may produce his own witnesses to prove his innocence.

The prosecution has to prove the guilt of the accused beyond all reasonable doubt. After the closing speech by the defence solicitor the magistrates will state whether or not they find the case proved. If the accused is found guilty he will then be sentenced.

*Statutory instrument*

Subordinate legislation, such as regulations and orders, which the appropriate Minister is empowered to lay before Parliament.

*Stipendiary magistrate*

A salaried magistrate who is a legally qualified barrister or solicitor of at least seven years' experience.

*Summons*

A document signed by a magistrate and issued by the justices' clerk on receipt of the information, requiring the attendance of the accused in court on a particular date.

## THE LAW GOVERNING THE SALE OF FOOD

### Food Safety Act, 1990

This is the most important Act relating to the sale of food for human consumption and as such is applicable to all food premises. In addition to strengthening enforcement procedures and increasing penalties, it is an enabling Act to allow Ministers to issue regulations for securing food safety throughout England, Scotland and Wales.

The Act consists of four parts and five schedules.

***Part I Preliminary***

*Section 1.* Extends the definition of "food" to include water which is bottled for sale or used as an ingredient (water supplied to the premises is excluded).

*"Food"* does not include live animals, birds or fish, animal feeding stuffs or drugs.

*"Food business"* means any business in the course of which commercial operations with respect to food or food sources are carried out (whether for profit or not).

*"Commercial operation"* in relation to food (or contact material) includes selling, possessing, preparing, advertising, labelling, storing or transporting for the purposes of sale, importing and exporting.

*"Food source"* means any growing crop or live animal, bird or fish from which food is obtained (whether by harvesting, slaughtering, milking or collecting eggs).

*"Premises"* includes any place, vehicle or stall.

*Section 2.* Extends the meaning of sale to include food which is offered as a prize or reward or given away in connection with any entertainment for the public.

*Section 3.* Food, or ingredients, commonly used for human consumption are presumed, until the contrary is proved, to be intended for sale for human consumption.

*Section 5.* "Food authorities" include the council of London and metropolitan boroughs, districts and counties.

"Authorized officer" means any person authorized in writing by a food authority to act in matters arising under the Food Safety Act, 1990.

*Section 6.* Requires every food authority to enforce within their area those parts of the Act for which they are responsible.*

***Part II Main provisions***

*Section 7.* It is an offence to treat food so as to render it injurious to health with the intent that the food will be sold in that state. Regard shall be had to the cumulative effect of foods consumed over a long period.

*Section 8.* It is an offence to sell, offer for sale or have in possession for sale food intended for human consumption which fails to comply with the **food safety requirements**, i.e. food which has been rendered injurious to health, is unfit for human consumption or is so contaminated (whether by extraneous matter or otherwise) that it would not be reasonable to expect it to be used for human consumption in that state.

---

*The Food Safety (Enforcement Authority) (England and Wales) Order, 1990 (SI. 1990 No. 2462) sets out the division of responsibility for enforcing the Act.

If such food is part of a batch then the whole batch shall, until the contrary is proved, be presumed to fail to meet the **food safety requirements.**

*Section 9.* An authorized officer of a food authority may seize or detain food (for up to 21 days) which fails to comply with **food safety requirements** or which is likely to cause food poisoning or a food-borne disease. Food which is seized has to be dealt with by a Justice of the Peace. Any person liable to be prosecuted in respect of such food is entitled to make representations to the justice of the peace. If the food is not condemned, or detained food is cleared, compensation can be claimed. Any expenses incurred in the destruction of condemned food must be paid by the owner of the food.

*Section 10.* An authorized officer can serve an **improvement notice** on the proprietor of a food business for failing to comply with regulations relating to hygiene or to the processing or treatment of food. The **notice** must state the grounds for non-compliance, specify the contraventions and measures necessary to secure compliance, and the time (not less than 14 days) allowed. Failure to comply is an offence.

*Section 11.* If a proprietor of a food business is convicted of an offence under the above regulations **and** the court is satisfied that the business, any process/treatment, the construction or condition of any premises or the use or condition of any equipment involves a risk of injury to health, they **shall** impose a **prohibition order**.

A **prohibition order** can apply to the use of a process/treatment, the premises (or part thereof) or any equipment. A copy of the **prohibition order** must be conspicuously fixed on the premises and contravention of the **order** is an offence.

The **prohibition order** ceases to have effect when the enforcement authority issues a certificate which states that there is no longer a health risk. On application by the proprietor, the enforcement authority must determine within 14 days whether the health risk has been removed and if so satisfied, issue the certificate within three days.

The court may also impose a prohibition on the proprietor or manager participating in the management of any food business. (Only a court can lift a **prohibition order** on a proprietor.) This prohibition applies for at least six months.

*Section 12.* If an authorized officer of an enforcement authority is satisfied that there is an imminent risk of injury to health he may issue an **emergency prohibition notice.** An application for an **emergency prohibition order** must then be made to the court within three days of serving the notice, and at least one day before the date of application the proprietor must be advised of this intention. (Saturdays, Sundays and Bank Holidays are excluded.)

The **emergency prohibition notice** and **emergency prohibition order** must be served on the proprietor and conspicuously displayed on the premises. Any contravention is an offence. An **emergency prohibition notice** ceases to have effect if no application for an **order** is made to the court. An **emergency prohibition**

**notice/order** ceases to have effect when the enforcement authority issues a certificate which states that there is no longer a health risk.

Compensation is payable by the enforcement authority in respect of loss suffered in complying with the **notice** unless an application is made for an **emergency prohibition order** within three days **and** the court is satisfied that the health risk condition was fulfilled.

*Section 13*. Empowers the Minister to issue an **emergency control order** prohibiting the carrying out of commercial operations with respect to food, food sources or contact materials involving an imminent risk of injury to health. Failure to comply is an offence and expenses for "work in default" can be recovered.

*Section 14*. It is an offence to sell, to the prejudice of the purchaser, any food which is not of the nature (different kind or variety) or substance (not containing proper ingredients) or quality (inferior, for example, stale bread) demanded by the purchaser.

*Section 15*. It is an offence to sell, display or have in possession for the purpose of sale, food which is falsely described or labelled so as to mislead as to the nature or substance or quality.

*Sections 16, 18 & 26*. Empower the Ministers to make regulations including those relating to composition, fitness, processing, hygiene, labelling and for securing food safety and the training of food handlers (Schedule 1).

*Section 17*. Empowers the Ministers to make regulations to secure compliance with Community obligations.

*Section 19*. Empowers the Ministers to make regulations requiring the registration of food premises, and for the licensing of premises to secure compliance with food safety requirements or in the interest of public health or protecting the interests of consumers.

*Section 20*. Enables proceedings to be taken against another person when the offence was due to their act or default.

*Section 21*. It is a defence for a person to prove that he took all reasonable precautions and exercised all due diligence to avoid the commission of the offence, by himself or by a person under his control.

In the case of persons not involved with the preparation or importation, for example, a retailer, charged with an offence under Sections 8, 14 or 15 it is a defence to prove:

(a) the offence was due to another person;
(b) that he carried out all reasonable checks or it was reasonable to rely on checks carried out by his supplier; and
(c) he did not know or suspect his act or omission would amount to an offence.

*Section 23.* Enables a food authority to provide training courses for food hygiene within or outside their area.

*Section 26.* Empowers Ministers to make orders to facilitate the exercise of functions, i.e. to provide for the detailed enforcement of the Act. The section also specifies the circumstances when it will not be an offence for a person to disclose information obtained by means of an order.

***Part III Administration and enforcement***
*Section 27.* Requires food authorities to appoint a public analyst.

*Sections 29 & 30.* Empower an authorized officer to purchase or take samples of food, food sources, contact materials or any article or substance required as evidence. Such samples should, if considered necessary, be submitted for analysis by a public analyst or examination by a food examiner, who shall provide a certificate specifying the result of the analysis or examination.

*Section 31.* Empowers Ministers to make regulations relating to sampling and analysis. (The Food Safety (Sampling and Qualifications) Regulations, 1990 (SI. No. 2463) lay down procedures for enforcement officers when taking samples for analysis or microbiological examination.)

*Section 32.* Empowers an authorized officer, on production of an authenticated document showing his authority, to enter any premises within his area at all reasonable hours to carry out his duties under the Act. In the case of a private dwelling-house entry cannot be demanded unless 24 hours' notice has been given to the occupier. An enforcement officer is also empowered to enter any business premises outside his area for the purpose of ascertaining whether or not there are any contraventions of the Act or regulations/orders made thereunder. Warrants may be issued by a Justice of the Peace authorizing entry, by force if necessary, if entry is refused.

Authorized officers can inspect, seize and detain records, including computer records, required as evidence. Improper disclosure of information so obtained is an offence.

*Section 33.* It is an offence to obstruct persons executing the provisions of the Act, including the failure to assist or provide information (unless it incriminates them) or the furnishing of false information.

*Section 34.* Prosecutions must commence before the expiry of three years from the commission of the offence or one year from its discovery by the prosecutor, whichever is the earlier.

*Section 35*. The penalty for obstruction on summary conviction shall be a fine not exceeding level 5* and/or up to three months' imprisonment.
The penalty for the remaining offences is:
(a) on conviction on indictment to an unlimited fine and/or up to two years' imprisonment; or
(b) on summary conviction to a fine not exceeding the relevant amount and/or imprisonment for up to six months. (In the case of Sections 7, 8 or 14 the relevant amount is £20,000, the amount for the other sections is level 5.)

*Sections 37 & 38*. Enable aggrieved persons to appeal to the magistrates' court (sheriff) or the Crown Court.

*Section 39*. Allows for appeals against improvement notices.

***Part IV Miscellaneous and supplemental***
*Section 40*. Empowers the Ministers to issue codes of recommended practice for the guidance of food authorities as regards the execution and enforcement of the Act and regulations/orders made thereunder.

*Section 41*. Requires food authorities to provide reports, returns and information to the Minister.

*Section 42*. Enables the Minister to empower another food authority, or one of his officers, to discharge the duty of a food authority which has failed to discharge that duty and the failure affects the general interests of consumers of food. The authority in default will be responsible for the payment of reasonable expenses.

*Section 49*. Relates to the form and authentication of documents.

*Section 50*. Relates to the service of documents.

*Section 54*. Deals with the application of the Act to the Crown, i.e. the removal of Crown immunity.

**Statutory Codes of Practice**
Section 40 of the Act empowers Ministers to issue codes of practice to guide food authorities on the execution and enforcement of the Act and secondary legislation made thereunder. One of the main aims of the codes is to assist in producing a uniform

---

*The Criminal Justice Act, 1991 provided for fines for summary offences in magistrates' courts to be placed on a scale of levels 1 to 5 unless otherwise stipulated in a particular Act.
Level 1 - £200 Level 2 - £500 Level 3 - £1,000 Level 4 - £2,500 Level 5 - £5,000

standard of enforcement and food authorities must have regard to any relevant provision in their enforcement activities.

The codes of practice are not legally binding, however, Ministers will be able to **give directions** requiring food authorities to take specific action to comply with a specific code of practice and these directions will be enforceable through the courts.

Examples of Codes of Practice (CP) issued include:

CP No. 1: Responsibility for Enforcement of the Food Safety Act, 1990.
CP No. 2: Legal Matters.
CP No. 3: Inspection Procedures — General.
CP No. 4: Inspection, Detention and Seizure of Suspect Food.
CP No. 5: The Use of Improvement Notices ( Revised 1994).
CP No. 6: Prohibition Procedures.
CP No. 7: Sampling for Analysis or Examination.
CP No. 8: Food Standards Inspections.
CP No. 9: Food Hygiene Inspections (Revised 1995).
CP No. 10: Enforcement of the Temperature Control Requirements of Food Hygiene Regulations. Enforcement of Temperature Monitoring and Temperature Measurement.
CP No. 11: Enforcement of the Food Premises (Registration) Regulations.
CP No. 12: Quick Frozen Foodstuffs. Division of Enforcement Responsibilities; Enforcement of Temperature Monitoring and Measurement.
CP No. 13: Enforcement of the Food Safety Act, 1990 in Relation to Crown Premises.
CP No. 14: Enforcement of the Food Safety (Live Bivalve Molluscs and other Shellfish) Regulations, 1992.
CP No. 15: Enforcement of the Food Safety (Fishery Products) Regulations, 1992 and associated Regulations.
CP No. 16: Enforcement of the Food Safety Act, 1990 in relation to the Food Hazard Warning System.
CP No. 17: Enforcement of the Meat Products (Hygiene) Regulations, 1994.
CP No. 18: Enforcement of the Dairy Products (Hygiene).
CP No. 19: Qualifications and Experience of Authorized Officers and Experts.
CP No. 20: Exchange of Information between Member States of the EU on Routine Food Control Matters.

**The Deregulation (Improvement of Enforcement Procedures) (Food Safety Act, 1990) Order, 1996**

Before serving an **improvement notice** an authorized officer **shall**:

(a) give the proprietor written notice stating that:
  (i) he is considering serving an improvement notice and stating the reasons for the notice; and
  (ii) the proprietor may, within a period specified within the notice*, make written representations to the officer **or** make oral representations to the officer in the presence of a senior officer of the enforcement authority; and

(b) consider any such representations.

*The minimum recommended time for a "minded to" notice is 14 days, and if an oral representation is to be made, a minimum time of seven days is recommended for the proprietor to contact the enforcement authority to arrange the meeting.

There is no requirement to issue a "minded to" notice prior to issuing a prohibition notice, an emergency prohibition notice or commencing legal proceedings.

**The Food Premises (Registration) Regulations, 1991 (SI. No. 2825)**

It is a requirement for most premises used for food businesses, for five or more days within any five consecutive weeks, to be registered with the local, or port health, authority in whose area they are situated. New businesses must apply for registration at least 28 days before they open. There is no charge for registration and it cannot be refused. Failure to register may result in a fine not exceeding level 3, however, any person providing false information may be fined up to level 5 on the standard scale.

Premises exempt from the registration requirement include those used for:

(1) certain agricultural activities (excluding processing);
(2) the retail sale of food from automatic vending machines;
(3) childminding (when registered with the Social Services Department);
(4) the supply of beverages, biscuits or confectionery in the course of a non-food business, for example, drinks supplied to customers by hairdressers; and
(5) the storage for sale of biscuits, crisps, etc., and dry ingredients for the preparation of beverages where the premises are controlled and used by voluntary organizations or charities.

In addition, dairies, dairy farms, milk distributors, slaughterhouses and poultry slaughterhouses or cutting premises are exempt, as are domestic premises where:

(1) the proprietor of the food business does not reside (except for peeling shrimps or prawns);
(2) bed and breakfast is provided in not more than three bedrooms;
(3) fruit and vegetables are produced and sold (farm shops are not exempt).

In the event of uncertainty as to whether or not registration is required, advice should be sought from the local Environmental Health Department.

Every registration authority must keep a register, which is open to public inspection, containing the name and address of the premises/business and the nature of the business.

**The Food Safety (General Food Hygiene) Regulations, 1995 (SI. No. 1763)**

These Regulations, which implement Council Directive 93/43/EEC of 14 June 1993 on the Hygiene of Foodstuffs, apply to most food businesses in England, Scotland and Wales. The Regulations cover all stages of food production, except primary production and businesses carrying on activities covered by regulations implementing product specific directives (for example, manufacturers of animal origin products such as meat, meat products, fishery products, dairy and egg products).

The main objective of the Regulations, as stated in the preamble to the Directive, is to protect human health. The Regulations, therefore, place extensive responsibilities on food businesses. In particular, they introduce three important new requirements into UK food hygiene law: all business must operate hygienically; businesses must identify steps in their activities which are critical to ensuring food safety and ensure that adequate food safety procedures are identified, implemented, maintained and reviewed; and all food handlers must be supervised and instructed and/or trained in food hygiene matters commensurate with their work activities.

The Regulations frequently qualify requirements with the terms "where necessary" or "where appropriate". This means if necessary or appropriate for ensuring food safety or wholesomeness.

***Part I General***

*"Food business"* means any undertaking, whether carried on for profit or not and whether public or private, carrying out any or all of the following operations, namely, preparation, processing, manufacture, packaging, storage, transportation, distribution, handling or offering for sale or supply of food.

*"Hygiene"* means all measures necessary to ensure the safety and wholesomeness of food during preparation, processing, manufacturing, packaging, storing, transportation, distribution, handling, and offering for sale or supply to the consumer, and "hygienic" shall be construed accordingly.

*"Wholesomeness"* means, in relation to food, its fitness for human consumption so far as hygiene is concerned.

In determining whether any matter involves a risk to food safety or wholesomeness, regard shall be had to the nature of the food, the manner in which it is handled and packed and any process to which the food is subjected before supply to the consumer, and the conditions under which it is displayed or stored.

*Reg.4.* A proprietor of a food business shall ensure that the preparation, processing, manufacturing, packaging, storing, transportation, distribution, handling and offering for sale or supply of food are carried out hygienically. (In particular, the proprietor must ensure that the appropriate requirements of Schedule 1 are complied with.) The proprietor shall identify any step in the activities of the food business which is critical to ensuring food safety and ensure that adequate safety procedures are identified, implemented, maintained and reviewed on the basis of the following principles:

(a) analysis of the potential food hazards in a food business operation;
(b) identification of the points in those operations where food hazards may occur;
(c) deciding which of the points identified are critical to ensuring food safety ("critical points");
(d) identification and implementation of effective control and monitoring procedures at those critical points; and

(e) review of the analysis of food hazards, the critical control points and the control and monitoring procedures periodically, and whenever the food business's operations change.

*Reg.5.* A person working in a food handling area who :

(a) knows or suspects they are suffering from or may be a carrier of a food-borne disease or

(b) has an infected wound, a skin infection, sores, diarrhoea or any similar condition which may result in food contamination by pathogens

shall report the condition or their suspicion to the proprietor of the food business.

*Offences and penalties*

*Reg.6.* Any person guilty of an offence against these Regulations shall be liable:

(a) on summary conviction, to a fine not exceeding the statutory maximum; or

(b) on conviction on indictment, to a fine or imprisonment for a term not exceeding two years, or both.

*Reg.7.* Specific sections in the Food Safety Act, 1990 relating to "offences due to the fault of another person", "defence of due diligence", "documentary evidence", "obstruction etc. of officers" and "time limit for prosecutions" apply to the Regulations.

*Enforcement and execution*

*Reg.8.* These Regulations shall be enforced by the food authority which must:

(a) ensure that food premises are inspected with a frequency which has regard to the risk associated with those premises;

(b) ensure that inspectors include a general assessment of the potential food safety hazards associated with the business and pay particular attention to critical control points identified by food businesses to assess whether the necessary monitoring and verification controls are being operated; and

(c) give due consideration to whether the proprietor of a food business has acted in accordance with any relevant guide to good hygiene practice.

(Code of Practice No. 9 places similar requirements on food authorities.)

***Schedule 1 (Rules of Hygiene)***

*Chapter I (General requirements for food premises)*

(1) Food premises must be kept clean and maintained in good repair and condition.

(2) The layout, design, construction and size of food premises shall:

(a) permit adequate cleaning and/or disinfection;

(b) be such as to protect against the accumulation of dirt, contact with toxic materials, the shedding of particles into food and the formation of condensation or undesirable mould on surfaces;

(c) permit good food hygiene practices, including protection against cross-contamination between and during operations, by foodstuffs, equipment, materials, water, air supply or personnel and external sources of contamination such as pests; and

(d) provide, where necessary, suitable temperature conditions for the hygienic processing and storage of products.

(3) An adequate number of washbasins must be available, suitably located and designated for cleaning hands. An adequate number of flush lavatories must be available and connected to an effective drainage system. Lavatories must not lead directly into rooms in which food is handled.

(4) Washbasins for cleaning hands must be provided with hot and cold (or appropriately mixed) running water, materials for cleaning hands and for hygienic drying. Where necessary, the provisions for washing food must be separate from the hand-washing facility.

(5) There must be suitable and sufficient means of natural or mechanical ventilation. Mechanical air flow from a contaminated area to a clean area must be avoided. Ventilation systems must be so constructed as to enable filters and other parts requiring cleaning or replacement to be readily accessible.

(6) All sanitary conveniences within food premises shall be provided with adequate natural and/or mechanical ventilation.

(7) Food premises must have adequate natural and/or artificial lighting.

(8) Drainage facilities must be adequate for the purpose intended; they must be designed and constructed to avoid the risk of contamination of foodstuffs.

(9) Adequate changing facilities for personnel must be provided where necessary.

*Chapter II (Specific requirements in rooms where foodstuffs are prepared, treated or processed – excluding dining areas and those premises specified in Chapter III)*

(1)(a) Floor surfaces must be maintained in a sound condition and they must be easy to clean and, where necessary, disinfect. This will require the use of impervious, washable and non-toxic materials, unless the proprietor of the food business can satisfy the food authority that other materials used are appropriate. Where appropriate, floors must allow adequate surface drainage.

(b) Wall surfaces must be maintained in a sound condition and they must be easy to clean and, where necessary, disinfect. This will require the use of impervious, washable and non-toxic materials and require a smooth surface up to a height appropriate for the operations, unless the proprietor of the food business can satisfy the food authority that other materials used are appropriate.

(c) Ceilings and overhead fixtures must be designed, constructed and finished to prevent the accumulation of dirt and reduce condensation, the growth of undesirable moulds and the shedding of particles.

(d) Windows and other openings must be constructed to prevent the accumulation of dirt. Those which can be opened to the outside environment must, where necessary, be fitted with insect-proof screens which can be easily removed for cleaning. Where open windows would result in contamination of foodstuffs, windows must remain closed and fixed during production.
(e) Doors must be easy to clean and, where necessary, disinfect. This will require the use of smooth and non-absorbent surfaces, unless the proprietor of the food business can satisfy the food authority that other materials used are appropriate.
(f) Surfaces (including surfaces of equipment) in contact with food must be maintained in sound condition and be easy to clean and, where necessary, disinfect. This will require the use of smooth, washable and non-toxic materials, unless the proprietor of the food business can satisfy the food authority that other materials used are appropriate.

(2) Where necessary, adequate facilities must be provided for the cleaning and disinfecting of work tools and equipment. These facilities must be constructed of materials resistant to corrosion, and must be easy to clean and have an adequate supply of hot and cold water.
(3) Where appropriate, adequate provision must be made for any necessary washing of the food. Every sink or other such facility provided for the washing of food must have an adequate supply of hot and/or cold potable water as required, and be kept clean.

*Chapter III (Requirements for movable and/or temporary premises (such as market stalls or mobile sales vehicles), premises used primarily as a private dwelling house, premises used occasionally for catering purposes and vending machines)*

Premises and vending machines must be sited, designed and constructed, kept clean and maintained in good repair and condition to avoid risk of food contamination and pest harbourage, so far as is reasonably practicable. Where necessary, there must be facilities to maintain adequate personal hygiene and for the cleaning of equipment and food to avoid contamination.

*Chapter IV (Transport)*

Conveyances and/or containers used for transporting foodstuffs must be kept clean and maintained in good repair and condition, and must, where necessary, be designed and constructed to permit adequate cleaning and/or disinfection. Foodstuffs must be placed and protected to minimize the risk of contamination.

*Chapter V (Equipment requirements)*

Articles, fittings and equipment with which food comes into contact shall be kept clean, and be so constructed, be of such materials and be kept in such good order, repair and condition, as to minimize any risk of contamination of food and enable them to be kept thoroughly cleaned and, where necessary, disinfected. They must be installed so as to allow adequate cleaning of the surrounding area.

*Chapter VI (Food waste)*

Food waste and refuse must not be allowed to accumulate in food rooms unnecessarily. Waste must be deposited in closeable containers (unless the food authority agree otherwise) which, if necessary, are easy to clean and disinfect. Adequate provision must be made for the removal and storage of waste. Refuse stores must be designed and managed to enable them to be kept clean, to prevent access by pests and prevent contamination of food, drinking water, equipment or premises.

*Chapter VII (Water supply)*

An adequate supply of potable water must be provided and used to ensure foodstuffs are not contaminated. If used, ice must also be from potable water if it could contaminate the food. It must be stored to protect it from contamination.

*Chapter VIII (Personal hygiene)*

Persons working in food handling areas must maintain a high degree of personal cleanliness and wear suitable clean and, where appropriate, protective clothing. Persons suspected or known to be suffering from a food-borne disease or condition which could contaminate food with pathogens must not be permitted to work in food handling areas where there is a likelihood of directly or indirectly contaminating food.

*Chapter IX (Provisions applicable to foodstuffs)*

Contaminated or decomposed raw materials must be rejected unless normal sorting and hygienic preparation will ensure their fitness for human consumption. All food must be protected against contamination during handling, storage, packaging, display and distribution. Effective pest control procedures must be implemented. Hazardous and/or inedible substances, including animal food, must be labelled and stored in separate and secure containers.

*Chapter X (Training)*

The proprietor of a food business shall ensure that food handlers engaged in the food business are supervised and instructed and/or trained in food hygiene matters commensurate with their work activities.

**The Food Safety (Temperature Controls ) Regulations, 1995 (SI. No. 2200)**

***Part I General***

"Ultimate consumer" means any person who buys otherwise than:

(a) for the purpose of resale;
(b) for the purposes of a retail establishment; or
(c) for the purposes of a manufacturing business.

In determining for the purposes of these Regulations whether any matter involves a risk to food safety, regard shall be had to the nature of the food, the manner in which it is handled and packed, any process to which the food is subjected before supply to the consumer, and the conditions under which it is displayed or stored.

***Part II Temperature Control Arrangements in England and Wales***

*Chill holding requirements*

*Reg.4.*(l) No person shall keep any food:

(a) which is likely to support the growth of pathogenic microorganisms or the formation of toxins; and

(b) with respect to which any commercial operation is being carried out

at or in food premises at a temperature above 8°C. (Excludes mail order to an ultimate consumer.)

*General exemptions from the chill holding requirements*

*Reg.5.* Regulation 4 shall not apply to:

(a) food which:

(i) has been cooked or reheated;

(ii) is for service or on display for sale; and

(iii) needs to be kept hot in order to control the growth of pathogenic microorganisms or the formation of toxins;

(b) food which, for the duration of its shelf-life, may be kept at ambient temperatures with no risk to health;

(c) food which is being or has been subjected to a process such as dehydration or canning intended to prevent the growth of pathogenic microorganisms at ambient temperatures, but this paragraph shall not apply in circumstances where:

(i) after or by virtue of that process the food was contained in a hermetically sealed container; and

(ii) that container has been opened;

(d) food which must be ripened or matured at ambient temperatures, but this paragraph shall cease to apply once the process of ripening or maturation is completed; and

(e) raw food intended for further processing (which includes cooking) before human consumption, but only if that processing, if undertaken correctly, will render that food fit for human consumption.

*Reg.6.* If food is kept above 8°C, it is a defence for the person charged to prove that:

(a) a food business responsible for manufacturing, preparing or processing the food has recommended that it is kept:

(i) at or below a specified temperature above 8° C; and

(ii) for a period not exceeding a specified shelf-life;

(b) the specified temperature is on a label on the packaging or is a written instruction;

(c) the food was not kept above the specified temperature; and

(d) the specified shelf-life had not been exceeded.

A food business shall not recommend food is kept above 8°C for a specified shelf-life, unless there has been a well-founded scientific assessment.

*Chill holding tolerance periods*

*Reg.7.* It is a defence for a person charged under regulation 4(l) to prove that the food:

(a) was for service or on display for sale;

(b) had not previously been kept for service or on display for sale at a temperature above 8°C; and

(c) had been kept for service or on display for sale for less than four hours.

It is also a defence to prove that the food:

(a) was being transferred to or from a food business vehicle to premises at which the food was going to be kept at or below 8°C;

(b) was kept above 8°C for an unavoidable reason such as:

(i) to accommodate the practicalities of handling during and after processing or preparation;

(ii) the defrosting of equipment; or

(iii) the temporary breakdown of equipment

and was kept at a temperature above 8°C for a limited period consistent with food safety.

*Hot holding requirements*

*Reg.8.* No person shall in the course of a food business keep any food which:

(a) has been cooked or reheated;

(b) is for service or on display for sale; and

(c) needs to be kept hot in order to control the growth of pathogenic micro-organisms or the formation of toxins

at or in food premises at a temperature below 63°C.

*Hot holding defences*

*Reg.9.* It is a defence for any person charged under regulation 8 to prove that:

(a) a well-founded scientific assessment indicates there is no risk to health if food held for service or on display is kept at a specified temperature below 63°C for a period not exceeding a specified period of time and this time/temperature had been adhered to.

It is also a defence to prove that the food:

(a) had been kept for service or display for less than two hours; and

(b) had not previously been kept for service or on display by that person.

*Reg.10.* No person shall keep raw materials, intermediate and finished products likely to support the growth of pathogenic microorganisms or the formation of toxins at temperatures which would result in a risk to health, although limited periods outside temperature control are permitted for the practicalities of handling during preparation, transport, storage, display and service, consistent with food safety.

*Cooling of food*

*Reg.11.* Food which must be kept at or below ambient temperature shall be cooled, to the temperature at which it must be kept, as quickly as possible following:

(a) the final heat processing stage; or
(b) the final preparation stage.

***Part III Temperature Control Requirements in Scotland***

*Chill and hot holding offences*

*Reg.13.* Food should be kept in a refrigerator or a cool ventilated place or above 63°C unless:

(a) it is undergoing preparation for sale;
(b) it is exposed for sale or has been sold;
(c) it is being cooled under hygienic conditions as quickly as possible to a safe temperature immediately following cooking or the final processing stage;
(d) it is reasonable to store it at a different temperature so as to be conveniently available for sale on the premises to consumer; or
(e) for the duration of its shelf-life it may be kept at ambient temperatures with no risk to health.

*Reheating of food*

*Reg.14.* Food which is to be reheated before being served for immediate consumption or exposed for sale shall be raised to a temperature of not less than 82°C. (It is a defence to prove that reheated food could not be raised to 82°C without a deterioration of its qualities.)

*Reg.15.* (1) Gelatin used for bakers' confectionery filling, meat or fish products shall, immediately before use, be brought to the boil or kept at a temperature of not less than 71°C for 30 minutes.

(2) Any gelatin remaining, other than waste, shall be cooled as quickly as practicable and refrigerated or stored in a cool ventilated place.

*Reg.16.* No person shall keep raw materials, intermediate or finished products likely to support the growth of pathogenic microorganisms or the formation of toxins at temperatures which would result in a risk to health, although limited periods outside temperature control are permitted for the practicalities of handling during preparation, transport, storage, display and service, consistent with food safety.

It shall not be an offence if food is being cooled as quickly as possible to a safe temperature following a final heat processing or a final preparation stage.

*Offences and penalties*

*Reg.17.* Any person guilty of an offence against these Regulations shall be liable:

(a) on summary conviction, to a fine not exceeding the statutory maximum; or
(b) on conviction on indictment, to a fine or imprisonment for a term not exceeding two years, or both.

**Voluntary Industry Guides to Good Hygiene Practice**

Council Directive 93/43/EEC of 14 June 1993 on the Hygiene of Foodstuffs placed a specific requirement on UK and other European Member States to encourage the food industry to prepare and develop voluntary Industry Guides to provide guidance on compliance with legal requirements. Central Government subsequently published a "template" providing advice on the compilation of UK Industry Guides. In particular, it outlines those matters that must be demonstrated for an Industry Guide to be officially recognised in the UK. The industry sector developing a guide must demonstrate that:

(1) it provides guidance on compliance with all parts of the Directive and Regulations relevant to the sector;

(2) it provides an appropriate definition of the sector to which it applies;

(3) it provides guidance appropriate to the range of individual businesses within the identified sector;

(4) wherever appropriate, it has followed the format outlined in the template document, and in particular:

  (i) refers prominently to a system or systems which identify and control food hazards;

  (ii) contains specific guidance relevant to the sector where the Regulations' requirements are qualified by certain terms, for example, where necessary/appropriate;

  (iii) clearly states the reasons why more rigorous standards than found in the Regulations are suggested for the sector; and

  (iv) wherever practicable, uses the Regulations as a model for organizing the contents of the guide;

(5) clearly distinguishes between guidance on complying with the legal food safety requirements and guidance related to good practice; and

(6) it has been drawn up by a representative section of the industry sector affected, including small business representatives, and also in consultation with enforcement and consumer bodies.

The Industry Guides should provide food businesses with a practical guide to complying with the Regulations and must be given due consideration by enforcers. They will also assist in achieving consistency of enforcement. However, food businesses do not have to follow the advice in any Guide as they may wish to comply with the Regulations in some other way.

Several industry guides have been, or are being, produced including guides for:

(1) the catering industry;
(2) the baking industry;
(3) the retail industry;
(4) the markets and fairs sector;
(5) vending and dispensing;
(6) fresh produce;
(7) wholesalers;
(8) flour millers.

**The Police and Criminal Evidence Act, 1984 (PACE)**

Section 67 of this Act requires persons charged with a duty of investigating offences to have regard to codes of practice made under sections 60 and 66. The Act, therefore, applies to Environmental Health Officers investigating contraventions of food legislation. The first code of practice came into force on 1 January 1986 and has superseded the Judges Rules, in relation to questioning.

Persons suspected of an offence must be cautioned prior to asking questions intended to obtain evidence for use in court. The Criminal Justice and Public Order Act, 1994 requires the caution to be in the following terms: "You do not have to say anything. But it may harm your defence if you do not mention when questioned something which you later rely on in court. Anything you do say may be given in evidence." (Minor deviations are allowed.) Persons must also be advised that they are not under arrest and may leave the premises but if they stay may wish to seek legal advice.

In most cases involving food/hygiene offences persons suspected of the offence will be invited to attend an interview at the council's offices and advised to discuss the matter with their solicitor, who may wish to be present at the interview. A signed record of the time and content of the caution, together with relevant information regarding the interview, including all those present, must be retained. Tape recorded interviews are commonly held.

Code B of PACE requires enforcement officers to go through a set procedure for obtaining warrants and conducting searches (and seizures), when there are grounds for suspicion that an offence has been committed. Particular procedures are laid down for dealing with juveniles, the mentally ill or handicapped, persons requiring an interpreter, and written statements.

**The Imported Food Regulations, 1984 (SI. No. 1918)**

These Regulations prohibit the import of food not of animal origin, intended for sale for human consumption, into England and Wales, which is unfit, unsound or unwholesome. Any imported food may be examined by a Port Health Officer (an Environmental Health Officer employed by a port health authority) or deferred inspection may be carried out by an Environmental Health Officer if the food is in an unexamined sealed container which has been allowed to go direct to a specified place of destination in England or Wales. Samples of food may be taken for analysis or bacteriological examination and the consignment can be held for up to six days pending the results of the examination. Unfit food may be seized and destroyed by order of a Justice of the Peace.

**Products of Animal Origin (Import and Export) Regulations, 1992 (SI. No. 3298)**

These Regulations govern the import of food of animal origin, for example, meat, meat products, fish and seafood, from countries outside the EC. They lay down the necessary procedures for the prior notification and checking of such foods, which may only be imported through approved border inspection posts. Consignments of fish and fish products must be accompanied by a health certificate issued by the competent authority in the country of origin.

Since 1 January 1993, food imported from other Member States of the EC has not been liable to inspection at UK ports. Once imported it is subject to the requirements of the Food Safety Act, 1990.

**Office of Fair Trading**

The Director General of Fair Trading is empowered, under Part III of the Fair Trading Act, 1973, to seek written assurances from a person carrying on a business which has persistently operated to the detriment of the interests of consumers. Assurances are usually sought from persons who ignore repeated complaints, warnings and prosecutions.

Where a person refuses to give, or breaks, an assurance, the Director General can apply to a County Court for a Court Order requiring the person to operate within the law, for example, by giving the Court an undertaking to protect food from risk of contamination. If the person fails to observe the Order, the Court can impose very heavy penalties for Contempt of Court.

**The Food Labelling Regulations, 1996 (SI. No. 1499)**

These Regulations principally implement Council Directive 79/112/EEC. They apply directly in England, Scotland and Wales and require most food, sold for human consumption, to be labelled with:

(1) the name of the food;
(2) a list of ingredients;
(3) a "best-before" date which provides an indication of minimum durability (shelf-life) or in the case of food which, microbiologically, is highly perishable and in consequence likely, after a short period, to constitute an immediate danger to human health, a "use-by" date;
(4) any special storage conditions or conditions of use; and
(5) the name and address of the manufacturer or packer or of a seller.

Subject to certain exemptions food must be date marked to indicate its shelf-life. Two types of date marking are allowed:

(1) "best before" or "best before end" followed by the date up to and including which the food should retain its optimum condition and quality, if properly stored (for example, it will not be stale). This type of date marking applies to most foods; and
(2) "use by" followed by the date in terms of either the day and the month or the day, month and year after which time the food is likely to be unfit. This form of date marking applies to highly perishable foods (microbiologically) with a short shelf-life. Correct storage of such food is essential and any storage conditions which need to be observed to ensure the stated shelf-life, for example, store under refrigeration, must be indicated.

The specific requirements of labelling depend on the shelf-life of the food. The following are examples of the various labels allowed.

| Expected shelf-life | Date marking allowable |
|---|---|
| highly perishable and likely to constitute an immediate danger to health | Use by 1st April 1997 (year can be omitted) |
| 3 months or less | Best before 1st April 1997 (year can be omitted) |
| 3 to 18 months | Best before 1st December 1998 or Best before end of December 1998 |
| More than 18 months | Best before December 1999 or Best before end of 1999 |

The following foods are exempt: fresh fruit and vegetables which have not been peeled or cut into pieces; wine, alcoholic drinks (10% or more alcoholic strength); soft drinks (greater than five litres for catering premises); flour confectionery and bread; vinegar; salt; sugar; chewing gum and edible ices.

It is an offence to sell foods bearing an expired "use-by" date and for anyone other than the person originally responsible for applying the date mark to change it.

**The Quick-frozen Foodstuffs Regulations, 1990 (SI. No. 2615) as amended 1994**

These Regulations apply to "quick-frozen foodstuff", i.e. food which has undergone *"quick-freezing"* whereby the zone of maximum crystallization is crossed as rapidly as possible and is labelled for the purpose of sale to indicate it has been subjected to quick-freezing.

Quick-frozen foodstuff intended for supply to the ultimate consumer must be suitably pre-packaged so as to protect it from microbial and other contamination and dehydration and must remain so packaged until sale. Such food shall, if intended for supply without further processing, be labelled with:

(a) an indication of the date of minimum durability;
(b) an indication of maximum advisable storage time;
(c) an indication of the temperature at which, and the equipment in which, it is advisable to store it;
(d) a batch reference; and
(e) a clear message not to refreeze after defrosting.

Quick-frozen food must, subject to permitted exceptions, be maintained at or below −18°C. (Exceptions relate to local distribution and storage in retail display cabinets consistent with good storage practice.) Air temperature monitoring or recording instrumentation must be fitted by businesses involved with the storage, distribution and sale of quick-frozen foodstuffs. Records must be retained for at least one year.

## THE LAW AFFECTING THE MILK TRADE

**The Dairy Products (Hygiene) Regulations, 1995 (SI. No. 1086) as amended 1996**

These Regulations implement various European Directives on milk hygiene and also simplify and consolidate the milk hygiene provisions in previous milk and dairies regulations.

The Regulations cover the production and placing on the market of raw milk, heat-treated milk and milk-based products from cows, sheep, goats and buffaloes. The requirements include:

(1) the hygiene conditions which production holdings (farms producing cow's, sheep, goat's and buffalo milk) must meet in order to be registered by MAFF;
(2) the hygiene conditions which dairy establishments must meet in order to be approved by the food authority and the hygiene conditions relating to all dairy establishments and staff;
(3) standards for raw milk and microbiological standards for raw milk and milk-based products;
(4) requirements regarding health marking;
(5) conditions for packing, labelling, transport and storage; and
(6) conditions for the handling and marketing of dairy products.

The Regulations also include certain provisions from previous UK legislation which have been retained mainly on public health grounds:

(1) retention of raw drinking milk rules for cow's milk, with extension of raw drinking milk standards to raw sheep and goat's milk. Raw cow's milk can be sold at or from a farm, where the milk was produced, to:
(i) the ultimate consumer;
(ii) a visitor to the farm premises, as part of a meal or refreshment; or
(iii) a distributor (who can only sell direct to the final consumer).
(The retail sale of raw sheep and goat milk is still permitted.)
(2) retention of heat treatment rules for milk, cream and ice cream; and
(3) retention of provisions relating to public health protection from infectious diseases on a temporary basis, including the service of heat treatment notices in respect of infected raw cow's milk.

To simplify milk hygiene legislation, requirements for the retail labelling of milk and milk products have been consolidated in the Food Labelling Regulations, 1996.

**The Ungraded Eggs (Hygiene) Regulations, 1990 (SI. No. 1323)**

It is an offence for producers to sell, or offer for sale, ungraded eggs from their own production which have visible cracks.

**The Egg Products Regulations, 1993 (SI. No. 1520)**

The manufacture or heat treatment of egg products must be in an approved establishment. Liquid egg must be pasteurized at 64.4°C for 2.5 minutes (or the equivalent) and cooled to below 4°C immediately. Pasteurized egg must pass the alpha-amylase test.

## THE LAW AFFECTING THE MEAT TRADE

### The Fresh Meat (Hygiene and Inspection) Regulations, 1995 (SI. No. 539)

These Regulations transfer responsibility for meat hygiene inspection from local authorities to the Meat Hygiene service and relate to the licensing, hygiene, packaging and inspection requirements of fresh meat at slaughterhouses, cutting premises and cold stores in England, Wales and Scotland. The transport of fresh meat is also included. All licensed premises must be supervised by veterinarians. Fresh meat passed as fit for human consumption must be given a health mark. Procedures for the ante and post-mortem health inspection requirements are laid down and conditions rendering part or all of the carcase unfit are detailed.

Requirements for the hygiene and construction, layout and equipment of premises, the hygiene of staff and slaughtering and dressing practices are included within comprehensive schedules.

### The Diseases of Animals (Waste Food) Order, 1973 (SI. No. 1936)

All waste food, including meat or animal products, must be processed before being used for feeding to animals. It is an offence for any caterer to allow the removal of waste food unless the person holds a current licence issued by the Ministry of Agriculture, Fisheries and Food (MAFF). Conditions regarding the type and cleaning of vehicles used to convey waste are laid down. The Order also applies to Scotland.

### The Poultry Meat, Farmed Game Bird Meat and Rabbit Meat (Hygiene and Inspection) Regulations, 1995 (SI. No. 540)

These Regulations implement various European Directives and revoke and replace various UK regulations including the Poultry Meat (Hygiene) Regulations, 1976.

The Regulations cover licensing of slaughterhouses, cutting premises, cold stores and re-wrapping centres, supervision and control of premises and conditions for the marketing of fresh meat. Detailed schedules cover construction, layout and equipment in various premises and hygiene requirements relating to handling operations and staff.

### The Meat Products (Hygiene) Regulations, 1994 (SI. No. 3082)

These Regulations implement European Directive 92/5/EEC laying down the conditions for the production and marketing of meat products and certain other products of animal origin. The Regulations cover approvals of premises and certain conditions necessary for the handling and marketing of meat products. These include various information requirements including wrapping, health marking and indications of storage temperature and durability. Detailed requirements cover the hygiene of premises, including practices and personal hygiene. The Regulations do not apply to fresh meat products, retail businesses, caterers and domestic production.

**The Animal By-Products (Identification ) Regulations, 1995 (SI. No. 614)**

These Regulations update and replace the Meat (Sterilization and Staining) Regulations, 1982 and the equivalent Scottish Regulations. The main aim of the Regulations is to continue to provide adequate safeguards against the possibility of animal by-products not intended for human consumption finding their way into the human food chain while reducing the burdens placed on the meat industry and local authorities. Essentially, animal by-products, as described in the Regulations, must generally be sterilized or stained immediately at a slaughterhouse or at any animal by-product premises. Movements to premises are controlled and the Regulations define various specified conditions and records that must be kept in relation to the movement.

## THE LAW AFFECTING THE FISH AND SHELLFISH TRADE

**The Food Safety (Live Bivalve Mollusc and Other Shellfish) Regulations, 1992 (SI. No. 3164) and the Food Safety (Live Bivalve Mollusc (Derogation) Regulations, 1992 (SI. No. 1508) as amended 1994**

These Regulations implement a European Directive laying down health conditions for the production, import and placing on the market of live bivalve molluscs. Areas are designated for the harvesting and production of shellfish and those areas unsuitable for such. The Regulations define the approval of dispatch and purification centres and detailed requirements are specified for hygienic conditions and operation. Requirements for harvesting and transportation of shellfish including relevant documentation and marking are included.

The Regulations empower a food authority to temporarily prohibit the sale of shellfish for human consumption, from a laying within the district if there is likely to be a risk to public health.

**The Food Safety (Fishery Products) Regulations, 1992 (SI. No. 3163) and The Food Safety (Fishery Products) (Derogation) Regulations, 1992 (SI. No. 1507) as amended 1994**

These Regulations implement a European Directive laying down health conditions for the production, importing and placing on the market of fishery products. Establishments, auction and wholesale markets concerned with the processing/handling of fishery products are covered. Detailed requirements relate to factory vessels, landing of products, and establishments on land. Conditions relate to premises and equipment and hygienic handling. Specific requirements apply to fresh, frozen, thawed and processed products including canning, smoking and salting.

## SPECIFIC LEGISLATION RELATING TO FOOD POISONING AND FOOD-BORNE ILLNESS

**Public Health (Control of Disease) Act, 1984**

*Section 11.* Medical practitioners must notify cases, or suspect cases, of food poisoning to the proper officer of the local authority immediately. This requirement also applies to medical practitioners in hospitals.

*Section 18.* The occupier of any premises in which there is, or has been, someone suffering from food poisoning, must provide any information within his knowledge that may be required to enable the proper officer to prevent the spread, or trace the source, of food poisoning.

*Section 20.* The proper officer can require any person to discontinue work to prevent the spread of typhoid and paratyphoid, dysentery, scarlet fever, acute inflammation of the throat, gastro-enteritis and undulant fever. The local authority must compensate persons suffering any loss by discontinuing their work.

**The proper officer**

For the purposes of the Public Health (Control of Disease) Act, 1984 local authorities appoint a proper officer to advise them on medical matters regarding food poisoning and communicable disease. The officer usually appointed is the consultant in communicable disease control who is employed by the health authority.

**The Public Health (Infectious Diseases) Regulations, 1988 (SI. No. 1546)**

*Regulation 9 and schedule 4.* The local authority can, on receipt of a report from the proper officer, require that any person suffering from, or a carrier of, food poisoning, typhoid, paratyphoid and other salmonella infections, dysentery and staphylococcal infections likely to cause food poisoning, discontinues work in connection with food until the risk of causing infection is removed. Managers of food businesses must assist the local authority if it is considered necessary for a medical officer to carry out a medical examination, or bacteriological tests, of a person suspected of carrying one of the above diseases, in order to prevent the spread of infection.

**National Health Service (Amendment) Act, 1986**

This Act, removed Crown immunity from health authorities and health authority premises for the purpose of food and health and safety legislation.

*Section 1* removes Crown immunity from health authorities in England and Wales and health boards in Scotland for the purposes of the Food Safety Act, 1990 and any regulation made thereunder.

*Section 2* removes Crown immunity from health authorities and health boards for the purposes of the Health and Safety at Work, etc. Act, 1974 and regulations, orders and other instruments made thereunder.

The Act also removes any protection afforded to members and officers of health authorities and health boards by Section 125 of the National Health Service Act, 1977 or *Section 101* of the National Health Service (Scotland) Act, 1978. In effect this means that, where appropriate, legal action can be taken against individuals for contraventions of food or health and safety legislation.

**The National Health Service (Food Premises) Regulations, 1987 (SI. No. 18)**

These Regulations provide that health authorities in England and Wales shall be treated as both owners and occupiers for the purposes of food legislation.

**The Public Health Laboratory Service (PHLS)**

The PHLS was established under the National Health Services Acts to provide for the surveillance and control of infectious diseases in England and Wales. There are 52 area and regional laboratories and the Communicable Disease Surveillance Centre at Colindale. The laboratories assist Environmental Health Departments investigating food poisoning incidents by providing epidemiological and microbiological expertise. Suspect food, water and faecal samples and swabs are examined at the laboratories in an attempt to isolate pathogens responsible for illness. Routine food and water samples are also sent to the laboratories for examination.

## THE LAW AFFECTING HEALTH AND SAFETY

**The Health and Safety at Work, etc. Act, 1974**

A major piece of legislation that incorporates a completely new approach to health, safety and welfare. It applies not only to employees but also to members of the general public. The Act creates a unified inspectorate working under the direction of the Health and Safety Commission and also applies to Scotland.

The objectives of the Act include:

(1) to secure the health, safety and welfare of persons at work;
(2) to protect non-employees and members of the public against risks to health and safety arising from the activities of persons at work; and
(3) to control the keeping and use of dangerous substances.

The Act attempts to create an awareness of the need for high standards and encourages management to promote health and safety. Supervision and training must be given to all staff.

A further requirement is the duty placed upon employers to prepare and revise a written safety policy and to bring this document to the attention of their staff. Businesses with less than five employees are exempt. Safety policies should consist of two parts; the first part being a general statement of policy and the second the organization and arrangements for implementing the policy and bringing it to the attention of all employees. Unions may appoint safety representatives and at the request of the representatives an employer must set up a safety committee.

**The Control of Substances Hazardous to Health Regulations, 1994 (SI. No. 3246)**

These Regulations introduce a legal framework for the control of substances hazardous to health in all types of businesses, including factories, farms, retail and catering premises, stalls and delivery vehicles. The Regulations set out essential measures that employers (and sometimes employees) have to take to ensure people are protected from the hazardous substances they may encounter.

Substances **hazardous to health** include substances labelled as dangerous (i.e. toxic, harmful, irritant or corrosive) pathogens and substantial quantities of dust.

Employers must carry out an assessment of all work which is liable to expose any employee to hazardous solids, liquids, dusts, fumes, vapours, gases or micro-organisms. The assessment involves evaluating the risks to health and then deciding on the action necessary to remove or reduce those risks. Equipment must be properly maintained and procedures observed. Employees should be informed, instructed and trained about the risks and the precautions to be taken. Occasionally it may be necessary to monitor the exposure of employees and to carry out an appropriate form of surveillance of their health.

**The Reporting of Injuries, Diseases and Dangerous Occurrences Regulations, 1985 (SI. No. 2023)**

These Regulations require employers to notify the enforcing authority of all injuries resulting from accidents at work which cause incapacity for more than three days. In addition certain diseases associated with specified work activities must be reported and so must major injuries, accidents which result in death, and dangerous occurrences (listed in the Regulations). Some injuries can be reported in writing, others by the quickest practicable means, for example, by telephone. Written confirmation on form F2508 must follow within seven days.

Any acute illness requiring treatment, or loss of consciousness resulting from absorption by inhalation, ingestion or through the skin must be reported (form F2508A). In addition acute illness requiring medical treatment as a result of exposure to a pathogen or infected material must also be reported. A record of all reportable injuries and dangerous occurrences must be kept.

**The Electricity at Work Regulations, 1989 (SI. No. 635)**

Employers must ensure electrical equipment and systems are in good condition and have been correctly installed. Fixed wiring systems and portable equipment must be checked and records of inspection and maintenance retained. Electricians employed must be competent.

**The Management of Health and Safety at Work Regulations, 1992 (SI. No. 2051)**

These Regulations set out broad duties for employers, which include a requirement that the health and safety of employees is assessed so that any necessary preventative and protective measures can be identified. Emergency procedures must be set up and employees must be given appropriate health and safety information and training.

**The Workplace (Health, Safety and Welfare) Regulations, 1992 (SI. No. 3004)**

Aspects covered include maintenance of workplaces and equipment, ventilation, temperatures, lighting, cleaning, room dimensions, workstations, seating and sanitary accommodation.

**The Health and Safety (Display Screen Equipment) Regulations, 1992 (SI. No. 2792)**
Covers the use of computers including the daily routine of users, eyesight tests, training and the provision of information.

**The Provision and Use of Work Equipment Regulations, 1992 (SI. No. 2932)**
General duties are placed on employers to ensure that equipment is suitable for its use, in good repair and, where necessary, guarded. Employees must be given adequate information, instruction and training to use equipment.

**The Manual Handling Operations Regulations, 1992 (SI. No. 2793)**
Include provisions relating to the avoidance of manual handling, assessment of risk, the reduction of risk of injury, training and information as to loads.

**The Personal Protective Equipment at Work Regulations, 1992 (SI. No. 2966)**
These Regulations require employers to provide and maintain suitable protective equipment following risk assessment. Equipment must be replaced when necessary and employees must be provided with appropriate information, instruction and training.

## SCOTTISH LEGISLATION

Scotland has a different legal system than England, being founded on principles originating from Roman law. In the event of any legal query, it is always best to consult someone conversant with the specifics of both the legal system and the subject matter in question.

### Scottish Legal Terms

*Licensing Board*
The statutory body made up of appointed councillors that meets every three months to grant licences to premises serving alcohol.

*Licensing Committee*
Part of a district council's committee structure that meets every committee cycle to grant licences to premises under the Civic Government (Scotland) Act. A major part of their time is taken in processing applications for licences not connected with the food trade, for example, taxi drivers.

*Procurator Fiscal* (sometimes abbreviated to either Procurator or Fiscal)
A full-time head of a department servicing each Sheriff Court. Officers of this department are responsible for the independent assessment of the validity of all cases which would be taken to a Sheriff Court or above. Members of this department are responsible for the presentation of prosecution evidence to the court. The staff who present evidence to a Sheriff Court are solicitors.

*Sheriff Court*

This court is the equivalent of the English Stipendiary Magistrates' Court. It is the usual location for all food cases to be heard.

*Sheriff*

A full-time paid official presiding alone over a Sheriff Court. They are usually QCs with considerable experience. The Sheriff Principal is the senior Sheriff for a Scottish region.

*High Court*

If a Sheriff feels that a case merits a greater sentence than he is empowered to impose, he can refer it to this Court for sentence. The Court moves around the country on circuit. It is presided over by a single Scottish Law Lord and has 15 jurors.

*Court of Session*

The highest Scottish Court - presided over by three Scottish Law Lords.

**Licensing (Scotland) Act, 1976 as amended by Law Reform (Miscellaneous Provisions) (Scotland) Act, 1990**

This Act requires that every new licensed premises (i.e. premises serving alcohol) must be in possession of a Food Hygiene Certificate, indicating compliance (or likely compliance in the case of a planned development) with the relevant food hygiene legislation. This certificate must be issued by the Environmental Health Department before a licence can be issued by the Licensing Board. Furthermore, the local authority is included as a statutory objector.

**Civic Government (Scotland) Act, 1982**

This Act requires the licensing of street traders, market stalls, places of public entertainment and late night caterers. These licences are issued by the Licensing Committee of the relevant local council.

**The Food Hygiene (Scotland) Regulations, 1959 (SI. No. 413) as amended 1959 (SI. No. 1153) and 1961 (SI. No. 662) and 1966 (SI. No. 967) and 1978 (SI. No. 173)**

These regulations which are cited together as the Food Hygiene (Scotland) Regulations, 1959 to 1978, were the main legislation regarding the detailed requirements for food hygiene in Scotland from 1959 to 1995. The Food Safety (General Food Hygiene) Regulations, 1995 revoked many of the above regulations, those requirements currently remaining are essentially concerned with temperature control and represent the differences between the Scottish food hygiene legislation and that in England and Wales. The main requirements now include:

(1) High risk foods must not be kept on food premises otherwise than in a refrigerator or refrigerated chamber or in a cool ventilated place, or at a temperature above 62.8°C. There are certain detailed exceptions to this.

(2) Re-heated food must be raised to a temperature of not less than 82.2° C.
(3) Gelatin used in the preparation of confectionery filling, meat or fish products must, immediately before use, be brought to the boil or brought to and kept at a temperature of not less than 71.1°C for 30 minutes.
(4) An adequate supply of wholesome water must be provided

Copies of the regulations may be purchased from HMSO and further information may also be available from the Royal Environmental Health Institute of Scotland.

## THE LAW AFFECTING MILK AND DAIRY PRODUCTS

**The Dairy Products (Hygiene) (Scotland) Regulations, 1995 (SI. No. 1372)**

These Regulations are broadly similar to those covering England and Wales and implement EC Directive 92/46/EEC, as amended. There purpose is to regulate the hygienic production, distribution and storage of raw milk, heat-treated milk and milk-based products.

**Ice-cream (Scotland) Regulations, 1948 as amended 1960 and 1963.**

These Regulations set out ingredients, conditions for registration of premises and vehicles, and permitted methods of manufacture. After freezing, all ice-cream must be kept below –2.2°C. If it rises above this temperature it must be reprocessed before sale.

**Memorandum on the Hygienic Control of Ice-cream, 1980**

This is the accepted code of practice dealing with ice-cream

## THE LAW AFFECTING MEAT AND POULTRY

**The Poultry Meat (Hygiene) (Scotland) Regulations, 1976 (SI. No. 1221) as amended 1979 (SI. No. 768) and 1981 (SI. No. 1169)**

The objective of these regulations is to bring Scotland into line with the EC as far as the slaughtering and storage of poultry meat intended for sale for human consumption. They are therefore similar to the corresponding English regulations.

**The Food (Preparation & Distribution of Meat) (Scotland) Regulations, 1963 (SI. No. 2001) as amended 1967 (SI. No. 1507)**

All parts relating to hygiene other than distribution have now been superseded.

## THE LAW RELATING TO FOOD POISONING & FOOD-BORNE ILLNESS IN SCOTLAND

**Notification of suspects or outbreaks**

*Ice-cream (Scotland) Regulations, 1948 Regulation 12*
*Slaughterhouse Hygiene (Scotland) Regulations, 1978 Regulation 54*

The above legislation requires food handlers who suspect they are suffering from food poisoning to tell their supervisor who must notify the Chief Administrative Medical Officer (CAMO).

**Examination of individuals**

*Ice-cream (Scotland) Regulations, 1948 Regulation 13*

The above legislation empowers the CAMO to examine individuals working with food when it is believed that they are associated with an outbreak of infectious disease.

*Health Services & Public Health Act, 1968 Section 72*

*Public Health (Infectious Disease) (Scotland) Regulations, 1975 Regulation 9*

The above legislation empowers a Sheriff, on written evidence, to order the medical examination of person(s) believed to be sufferers or carriers of an infectious disease. A person specified as a carrier should be treated as a continuing danger to others for a period specified (which can be up to three months).

**Discontinuation of an individual's employment**

*Public Health (Scotland) Acts, 1897 to 1907 Section 7*

*Ice-cream (Scotland) Regulations, 1948 Regulation 12*

*Poultry Meat (Hygiene) (Scotland) Regulations, 1976 Schedule 3 Part 1*

The above legislation prohibits persons suffering from infectious disease from continuing work.

*Health Services & Public Health Act, 1968 Section 71*

The designated medical officer may make a written request to an individual to discontinue his work with a view to preventing the spread of food poisoning.

*Social Security (Unemployment, Sickness & Invalidity Benefit) Regulations, 1975*

*Reg. 3.* Where a person is excluded from work on certification from the designated medical officer and is under medical observation by reason of being a carrier or having been in contact with a case of infectious disease, he may be deemed incapable of work for the purposes of benefit.

**Compensation for loss of employment**

*Health Services & Public Health Act, 1968 Section 71*

A person who has suffered loss in complying with a request to discontinue work shall be compensated by the local authority.

# Appendix I Food processing

These days there is not only a greater consumer demand for quality foods but also for foods that are convenient to prepare and serve. Many consumers are particularly concerned that the food is as "natural" as possible and free from food additives and contaminants. This is not always easy to achieve and virtually all foods that we consume are subjected to some form of preservation even if it is only chilling, packaging in a modified gas atmosphere or freezing. There is a demand for "fresh food" but usually to present such food to the consumer who might be miles away from the production point, requires the application of very sophisticated food technology. This may range from plant breeding to give the desired properties, for example, seedless grapes or potato varieties suitable for crisp making, to packaging in containers that will control the ripening rates of fruits.

The technology of food processing draws upon the principles of chemistry, physics and biology, along with those of engineering, to ensure safe food manufacture.

The general techniques of preservation used in food processing have been dealt with in Chapter 8 and this section is primarily concerned with specific processing techniques and foods.

## HEAT PRESERVED FOODS

These foods are made commercially sterile principally by the application of a predetermined amount of lethal heat. Various types of hermetically sealed containers are used such as cans, retortable plastic trays and pouches to prevent post-process contamination. The use of the term "canning" tends to be generic to all these types of packs. Unlike most other forms of preservation the food inside the can remains an ideal medium for bacterial growth. It is therefore imperative that:

(1) the heat process is adequate to destroy all pathogenic and spoilage organisms, capable of growth within the anaerobic conditions of the can;
(2) the closure of the can precludes the entry of microorganisms; and
(3) the post-process handling of the can prevents damage and subsequent contamination.

The most heat-resistant pathogenic organism is *Clostridium botulinum* and this bacterium will not grow below a pH of 4.5 (or an $a_w$ of 0.94). Consequently, when determining the heat process, regard must be had for the pH of the can contents. All foods with a pH of less than 4.5 are known as acid foods and those with a pH of more than 4.5 are termed low-acid foods.

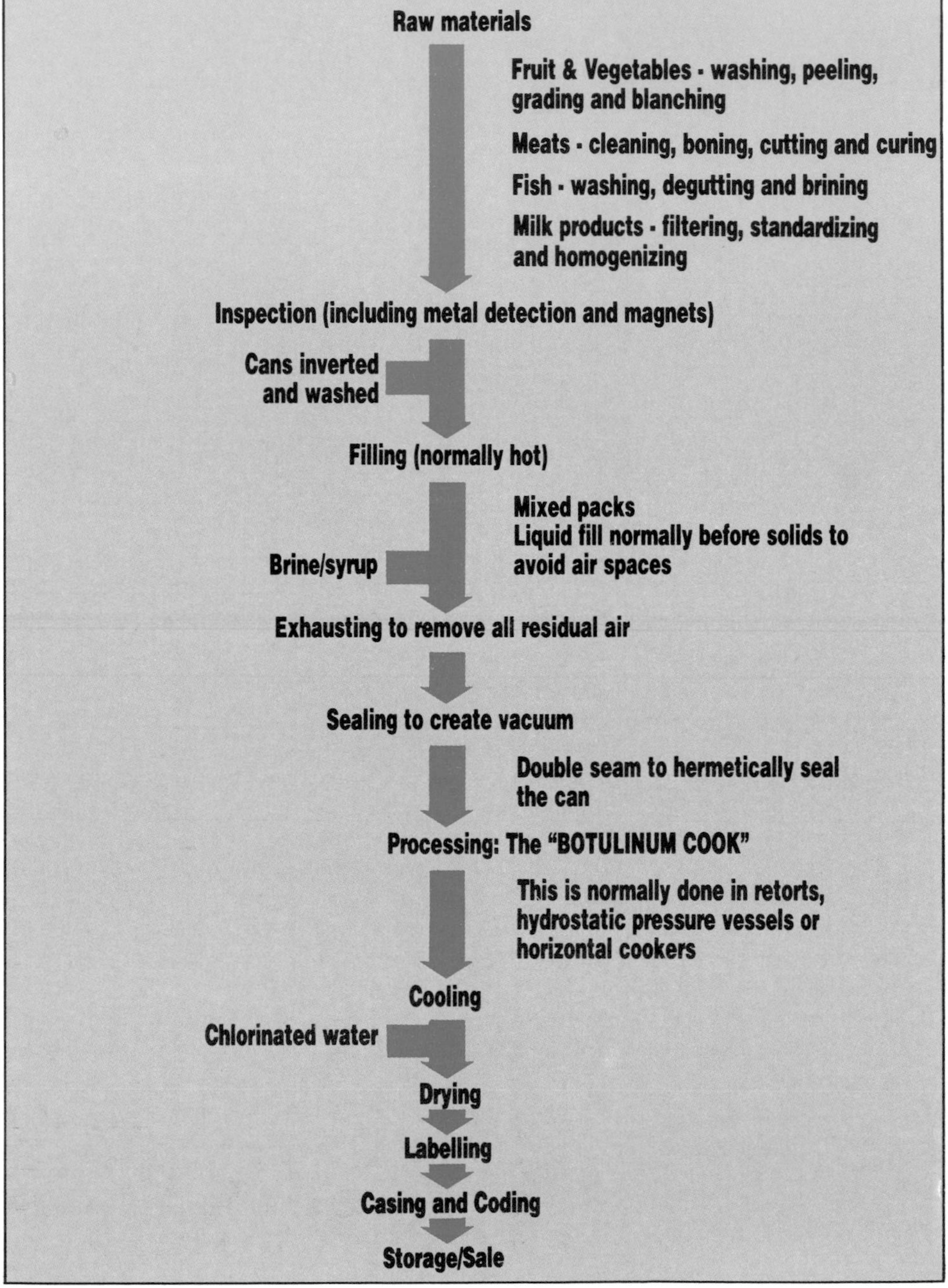


**A SCHEMATIC DIAGRAM OF CANNING OPERATIONS**

Fruits have a pH of less than 4.5 and consequently only receive a relatively low pasteurizing heat process. Vegetables and meats have pH's much higher than 4.5 and they are given a process known as a "botulinum cook" to render them commercially sterile.

Before canned food is heat processed it is normally prepared in some way. The actual process of preparation will vary depending on the food type but the above flow chart shows the usual processes involved.

## Exhausting

The exhausting process is usually done by blowing steam into the headspace (space above can contents at top of can). This has the effect of producing concave ends on the can after processing and cooling, due to the formation of a vacuum when the steam condenses. The removal of the oxygen from the can also reduces the risk of oxidative corrosion of the inner can surface and helps to maintain the nutritive quality of the food.

## Container seams and seals

The construction and size of the container seams are very important to ensure integrity and safety of the food. The issues of concern for plastic containers vary depending on type and are discussed elsewhere*. The diagram below shows the construction of a can seam.

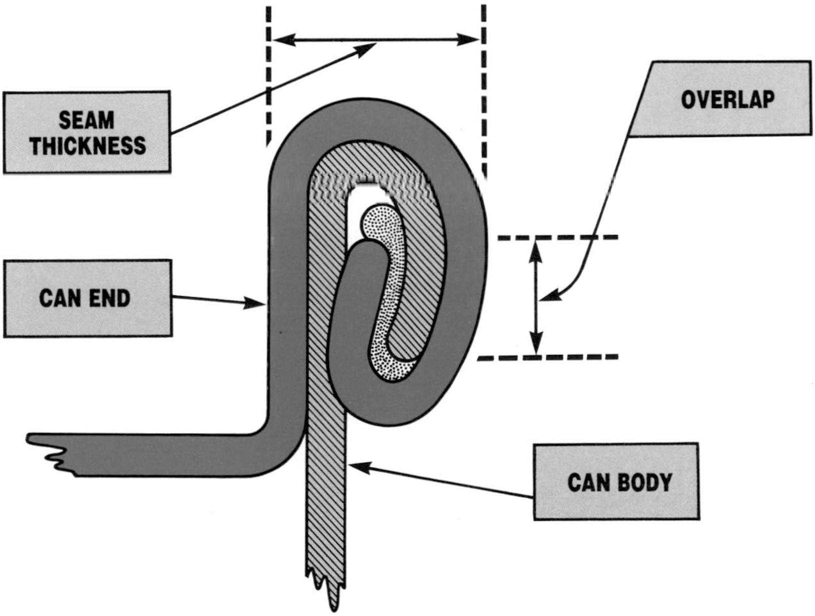


* Source: The shelf-stable packaging of thermally processed foods in semi-rigid plastic containers. A guideline to good manufacturing practice. Technical Manual No. 31, 1991. Campden Food and Drink Research Association.

**Processing**

The actual process time and temperature must be determined for each can size of low-acid food and will depend on such things as weight, composition, headspace, viscosity, presence of preservatives and intended storage conditions. Scheduled processes for all low-acid products have been established by the Campden Food and Drink Research Association, Chipping Campden, Gloucestershire GL55 6LD.

The minimum safe thermal process for a low-acid canned food is one which would reduce the chance of survival of one spore of *Clostridium botulinum* to less than one in $10^{12}$ (considered to be the equivalent of 121°C for three minutes, i.e. $F_O$ value of 3).

*$F_O$*

$F_O$ is the measure of the lethal effect of processing. It is the sum of the lethal effects of a heat process equated to minutes at 121°C. An $F_O$ of 6.0 is therefore equivalent to heating at 121°C for six minutes. The higher the temperature the shorter the time of heat processing necessary to achieve the same degree of microbial destruction.

To destroy the more heat-resistant food spoilage organisms, such as *Bacillus stearothermophilus,* a process in excess of an $F_O$ of 3.0 must be given.

Some typical examples of $F_O$ values are given in the Table* below:

| Product | $F_O$ |
|---|---|
| Canned salmon | 7.0 |
| Canned strawberries | 1.0 (high-acid product) |
| Beans in tomato sauce | 5.0 |
| Whole chicken in broth | 4.0 |
| Sterilized milk | 5.0 |
| Dog food | 14.0 |

Various types of retorts depend on different heating media including steam, hot water, steam-air mixtures, and "raining" hot water systems using recycled water. The use of microwaves has now been reported in Europe, but so far not in the UK. The validation and control of these heating systems is essential to the assured achievement of sterility.

**Cooling**

After the heating process the containers must be quickly cooled with chlorinated water. It is essential that cooling water is chlorinated before use to ensure its freedom from bacteria. A contact time of 20 minutes must be allowed to ensure complete disinfection. The level of chlorine in the water should be kept as low as possible to avoid corrosion of cans. A residual level of 0.5 ppm is normally the target. Regular samples, both chemical and bacteriological, should be taken from the cooling water. To avoid post-process contamination any handling of the hot cans must be prohibited.

---

* Source: Introduction to Food Technology, Open Learning Module, Humberside University, 1989. ISBN 0 903057 06 9.

The cooled and labelled cans must be completely dry before storage so as to prevent any rusting: cans which are made of sheet steel with only a thin layer of tin on each side may suffer damage which results in rusting of the iron.

### Underprocessing

Underprocessing may result in the production of gas, due to the action of the surviving microorganisms, which causes the can to swell, or the contents may undergo some other undesirable change without gas production. In the latter case, spoilage is only detected after opening and these cans are known as flat sours.

### Sources of contamination in canneries

Contamination may be either bacteriological, chemical or physical (see Chapter 5).

*Bacteriological contamination*

Contamination or spoilage in cans may occur because of:

(1) defects in the can such as unsatisfactory welding, pinholes in the plate or a damaged flange;
(2) coding on the can being too deep, causing fractures or pinholes;
(3) a change in raw materials with an increased loading of thermophilic organisms;
(4) poor hygiene prior to filling, which may result in a build-up of thermophiles in the blancher;
(5) underprocessing or uneven processing;
(6) post-process contamination, for example, because of a defective end-seam or infected cooling water;
(7) storage temperatures above 45°C, allowing the multiplication of thermophiles; or
(8) damage to the can in distribution, storage or retail.

If the examination of blown cans reveals the presence of one or two heat resistant thermophiles, then underprocessing is the likely cause. If a general flora of mesophiles is isolated, this usually indicates leaker spoilage. Apart from the moulds *Byssochlamys fulva and B. nivea*, which are occasionally responsible for the spoilage of canned fruit, yeasts and moulds are relatively easy to destroy by heat and are usually only present because of post-process contamination. Similar faults may occur with plastic containers.

### Post-process contamination

The greatest care must be taken after heat treatment, especially whilst the can is still warm and wet, and before the sealing compound has hardened. Bacteria are capable of being sucked into visually satisfactory cans through microscopic holes in the seams. If these bacteria are spoilage or pathogenic organisms, problems will occur.

Post-process contamination may arise because of:

(1) infected or unchlorinated cooling water;
(2) contaminated runways;
(3) operatives handling warm and wet cans; or

(4) damage to cans, especially while still warm.

It is recommended that cooling water contains less than 100 organisms per ml and that post-process conveying systems have less than 100 organisms per 500 square millimetres.

**COMMON THERMOPHILIC SPOILAGE BACTERIA OF CANNED FOODS**

| Bacterium | | Foods commonly spoiled | Remarks |
|---|---|---|---|
| Aerobic spore formers | *Bacillus stearothermophilus* | Low-acid foods such as vegetables | Can referred to as a flat-sour. Acid produced but no gas production and no swelling of the can |
| | *Bacillus coagulans* | Low and medium acid foods, especially foods such as tomato juice | |
| Anaerobic spore formers | *Clostridium thermosaccharolyticum* | Meat, fish and vegetables | Carbon dioxide and hydrogen produced, contents often have a cheesy odour |
| | *Clostridium nigrificans* | Meat, fish and vegetables | Hydrogen sulphide gas produced but is soluble and may be absorbed so preventing swelling. Rotten egg smell. Contents may go black as the hydrogen sulphide reacts with the iron of the container |
| | *Clostridium sporogenes* | Fish and meat | Gas production, contents foul smelling |

**Blown cans**

Cans may be blown, for example, because of carbon dioxide produced by microorganisms or because of hydrogen production. The vacuum created during processing normally ensures that the can ends are concave but the production of gas eventually destroys the vacuum and the can becomes blown. The first stage of this positive pressure is known as a flipper. This is a can with a slightly distended end which can be pressed back to the normal position with very light pressure. When the end is banged it flips out. The next stage is known as a springer. This is a can with one end distended which when pushed back to the normal position, causes the other end to spring out. A hard swell is the final stage of blowing when both ends of the can are permanently distended.

**Hydrogen swells**

This condition results from the action of the contents of the can on the internal surface of the can. It is a problem with acid foods such as canned tomatoes and fruits. Not only is there a build-up of hydrogen causing the can to pass through the flipper, springer and hard swell stages, but also lacquer stripping and a metallic taint of the contents occur, along with a high tin content of the food (maximum limit is 200 mg/kg). Hydrogen swells may be indistinguishable from a can damaged by microbial action and the cans must be discarded.

Certain cans containing foods rich in sulphur, for example, corned beef, sardines and legumes may show a dark staining of the inner surface of the can. This is due to the formation of hydrogen sulphide during processing which reacts with the tin lining to give tin sulphide. Whilst looking unpleasant it will normally present no danger to the consumer unless the can has become perforated.

**Over filling**

Due to the expansion of the contents during heating, the can becomes strained and distorted. These cans must be regarded with suspicion and can only be detected by physical or bacteriological checks of the contents.

**Damage**

Damage is caused by a variety of reasons including perforation by nails, sharp crates, dockers' hooks, knives used to open cardboard cartons in shops, and denting due to mishandling cases. Considerable bacteriological significance should be placed on damaged cans: leakage introduces an infection from the atmosphere and possibly subsequent bacterial spoilage and/or mould growth. Cans with badly damaged seams should be rejected. External wetting, for example, in flooding or fire-fighting, may re-introduce the risk of post-process contamination through seams, especially on handling.

**Incorrect storage**

Apart from thermophilic spoilage, high temperature storage may result in internal corrosion. Furthermore, if conditions are too humid, external rusting and eventual pinholing of the can may occur.

**Pasteurized canned foods**

As discussed earlier, most low-acid canned foods are processed to a minimum standard of the "botulinum cook". However, some foods if fully processed would be inedible. One example of this is canned cured ham. This product only receives a pasteurization process (a centre temperature of about 70°C). This means that other precautions are necessary to ensure that it does not become a source of *Clostridium botulinum* food poisoning. It is the presence of the curing salts (sodium or potassium nitrite and sodium chloride) that help to inhibit the growth of botulinum organisms and make canned cured ham a safe food. The combined inhibitory effect of curing salts and sodium chloride on spore germination is referred to as the **perigo** effect. A sufficient combination of heat process temperature and curing salt level may render the product ambient stable. Lesser treatments may necessitate the use of subsequent chilled storage. It is essential to first evaluate the stability of new products in order to establish if chilled storage is needed.

**Aseptic production technology**

This differs in that sterilization of the product is carried out as a separate operation from package sterilization, prior to filling aseptically. Various types of heat exchanger are used for these continuous flow processes. Recently ohmic heating has been used whereby heating is induced by passing a high-voltage electric current directly through the food material which is then packed under aseptic conditions into sterilized packaging containers, for example, multi-layered plastic film bags. The finished product has an extended shelf-life and is stable at ambient temperatures. In the future, ohmic heating may be combined with other forms of heating such as plate heat exchange systems.

## DAIRY PRODUCTS

**The processing and testing of milk**

In 1887 Anthony Hailwood produced sterilized milk and by 1920 pasteurized milk had been developed. From this time there has been a gradual improvement in the quality of milk and hygienic methods of production. The most important factor in securing improvements has been the introduction of refrigeration on the farm and the use of insulated tankers to transport milk to the dairy. However, better use of refrigeration and reducing contamination during packaging or bottling have extended the shelf-life of milk even more.

Most milk sold in this country is heat-treated by one of three methods:

(1) pasteurization;
(2) sterilization; or
(3) ultra heat-treated.

Pasteurization ensures the destruction of pathogens and most vegetative organisms. However, heat-resistant organisms and spores survive, which accounts for milk souring after a few days. Sterilization and UHT treatment destroy all organisms and this ensures a prolonged shelf-life, even without refrigeration. It is essential that the pathogenic contamination of heat-treated milk is prevented as the milk, devoid of its natural flora, is more likely to support the rapid multiplication of the pathogens.

**The production of pasteurized milk**

The heating process for producing pasteurized milk in the UK was based on the destruction of two potential pathogens, namely, *Mycobacterium tuberculosis/bovis* and *Brucella abortus*. Whilst destroying these organisms and many other pathogens and spoilage organisms, pasteurization is a relatively mild heat treatment and has a minimal effect on the flavour and nutritional value of milk. However, even with pasteurization up to 10% of many vitamins will be lost.

Pasteurized milk is usually produced by a heat treatment involving a high temperature for a short time (HTST process) (at least 71.7°C for 15 seconds or any equivalent combination) or a process using different time/temperature combinations to obtain an equivalent effect (e.g. the Holder Process involves 63°C for 30 minutes).

Pasteurized milk must:

(1) show a negative reaction to the phosphatase test and a positive reaction to the peroxidase test (in the case of high temperature pasteurization a negative reaction to both tests).

(2) meet certain microbiological standards in random sampling checks at the treatment establishment, including the absence of pathogens in 25g and only one out of five samples with a coliform (per ml) count of < 5.

Milk arriving at the dairy is weighed and checked for its quality, for example, added water, the presence of any blood and its microbiological load, and is placed in holding tanks where it will be mixed with milk from many other farms, so ensuring a consistent product. It is then filtered to remove gross contamination and pumped to a balance tank which maintains an even flow rate through the next part of the HTST plant where heat exchange takes place.

The cold milk entering the plant is preheated by the hot milk leaving the processing plant. It is finally heated to the required temperature of 72°C by using hot water at around 75°C. At no time do the water and milk come into direct contact. The heat exchange takes place through thin stainless steel plates. Regular checks of the unit, particularly the seals, must be made to ensure its integrity. The heated milk flows through a holding tube for 15 seconds before passing a flow diversion valve. If the milk is below 71.7°C a bell rings and the milk is diverted back to the balance tank and goes through the whole process again. If the temperature is at or above 71.7°C the milk passes out of the heat exchange, heating up incoming milk.

To preserve the cream line and reduce caramelization, dairies operate as close as possible to 72°C for 15 seconds. After heat treatment, the milk is cooled rapidly to below 10°C. This prevents the multiplication of heat-resistant organisms, maintains the cream line and improves the keeping quality. As a temperature of 72°C stimulates the germination of any *Bacillus cereus* spores that may be present, cold storage is particularly important to prevent the multiplication of the vegetative bacteria produced. After cooling, the milk is bottled or filled into cartons and stored under refrigeration. Strict stock rotation is essential to avoid complaints of souring, especially during the warm summer months. Regular tests are carried out to ensure that pasteurized milk: (i) has a reasonable shelf-life and (ii) has been given a satisfactory heat treatment.

*The methylene blue test*

This dye reduction test is a chemical method of assessing the microbiological quality of the milk. Methylene blue is added to the milk which is incubated at 37°C for 30 minutes. If the milk/methylene blue is decolourized in this time, it indicates that the level of microorganisms present is unacceptably high and the milk is rejected. The test does not differentiate the type of organism causing the contamination.

*The phosphatase test*

This test is used to determine whether or not the milk has been pasteurized satisfactorily and to ensure that raw milk has not been added after processing. Such contamination is likely to occur if the seals on the heat exchange units are defective. The test relies on the fact that the enzyme phosphatase, which is present in raw milk, is destroyed by effective pasteurization. The chemical di-sodium para nitro phenyl, which turns yellow if phosphatase is present, is added to the milk and the depth of colour is examined against a standard sample using a comparator. A figure of more than 10g represents a failure of the test.

**The production of sterilized milk**

The prolonged life of sterilized milk is obtained at the expense of flavour changes, due to the caramelization of lactose, and a loss in nutritional value (approximately 50% of vitamins are destroyed). Sterilized milk can be produced by heating milk at around 110ºC for 30 minutes in a hermetically sealed container, the seal of which must remain intact during such heat treatment, or by use of the continuous flow process.

*The turbidity test*

This test is to measure the degree of protein denaturation that has taken place. When heated to a sterilization level the proteins albumen and globulin are denatured and if ammonium sulphate is added, the protein casein is precipitated and can be filtered out. The filtrate will be clear and if this is further heated to boiling point will turn cloudy (turbid) if any protein has not been already precipitated. Thus, a turbid solution indicates that the original milk had not been adequately sterilized.

**Ultra heat treated milk**

UHT milk is produced by a continuous flow process with the application of a very high temperature for a short time (not less than 135ºC for not less than a second) so that all residual spoilage microorganisms and their spores are destroyed, but the chemical, physical and organoleptic changes to the milk are minimal. Immediately after heat treatment the milk is filled into opaque containers, or containers made opaque by the packaging. It will store for several months without refrigeration.

If the heat treatment involves direct contact with steam, it must be from potable water, must not adversely affect the milk, for example, by leaving foreign matter, and must not change the water content of the treated milk.

Sterilized (and UHT) milk must:

(1) not contain any unacceptable levels of any pharmacologically active substance;

(2) not contain any added water;

(3) after 15 days in a closed container at 30ºC (or seven days at 55ºC) be organoleptically normal, not show any sign of deterioration and have a plate count at 30ºC $\leq$ 100 per ml.

**Thermized milk**

Thermized milk is obtained by heating raw milk for at least 15 seconds between 57ºC and 68ºC so as to show a positive reaction to the phosphatase test.

**Raw milk tests at the dairy**

Raw milk must come from healthy animals on a registered production holding. Such animals must not show any disease symptoms, udder wounds or have recently been treated with dangerous substances. Herds must be tuberculosis and brucellosis free.

Raw milk must not contain added water or unacceptable antibiotic, hormonal, pesticide or detergent residues or other harmful substances. Raw cow's milk must have a plate count at 30ºC of ≤100,000 per ml and a somatic cell count of ≤ 400,000 per ml.

If raw milk is not heat treated at the dairy within four hours of acceptance it must be cooled to ≤ 6ºC. If not treated within 36 hours and the plate count at 30ºC exceeds 300,000 per ml, it must not be used for the production of heat-treated milk.

Milk is examined for the presence of taint, dirt, blood and antibiotics and several tests are carried out before processing. Unsatisfactory milk can then be rejected.

*Brucella abortus ring test*

An antigen is added to milk at 37°C and if the milk is positive for the organism, a blue ring rises to the top with the cream. This test is carried out at the Central Testing Laboratory of the Milk Marketing Board.

*Freezing point test*

This test is carried out to ascertain the addition of water to milk. The milk is frozen and if this occurs at between –0.53°C and –0.565°C it has not been adulterated. Freezing at higher temperatures indicates the addition of water.

*The Gerber test (fat content)*

The Gerber test is used to determine the fat content of milk. An electronic method involves using a milkotester and the result is obtained in 15 minutes.

*The hydrometer test*

The hydrometer test is used to check the density (total solids) of milk. If the fat content is known, the solids-not-fat can then be calculated by subtracting the fat per cent from the total solids per cent (approximately 87 % of milk is water).

*The resazurin test*

Resazurin is a violet dye which is decolourized by souring organisms. The resazurin is added to the milk and then left in a water bath at 37°C for ten minutes. The milk will first go pink and eventually colourless, depending on the number of organisms present. After ten minutes the colour is checked using a Lovibond comparator. A reading of 3.5 or less indicates the milk is unsatisfactory.

**Problems encountered with milk**

*Milkstone*

When milk is heated, phosphate and albumen are deposited as milkstone. This normally occurs above 72°C and is not a great problem in pasteurization. Milkstone harbours bacteria and causes cleaning problems. When it does occur, the plant should be given an acid clean, for example, with phosphoric acid.

*Milk taint*

Either odour or taste taint may be caused by:

(1) treatment of cows with particular medicines;
(2) certain types of animal feed such as turnips or kale;
(3) certain illnesses such as mastitis, which may produce bitterness;
(4) storage of uncovered milk near paint, manure or other strong-smelling substances;
(5) cows near the end of lactation producing a rancid taste;
(6) sunlight or contact with copper which may produce an oily taint; or
(7) phenol from cleaning chemicals at the farm, a rare but serious problem.

Taints of bacteriological origin increase with age; those due to feeding are strong, fresh from the udder. Taints may be retained by milk products.

*Blood*

May be introduced into milk because of animals suffering from clinical mastitis or from sore udders. Herds infected with mastitis produce a reduced yield and the compositional quality of the milk falls. The milk is tested for the presence of blood at the dairy.

*Ropey milk*

The milk is slimy which is caused by *Bacillus aerogenes*. It may be associated with faulty cleaning or disinfection. This is now rare due to improved cooling and cold storage.

*Leucocytes*

Occasionally, complaints are received of rusty droplets in bottles of homogenized milk. These deposits consist of milk fat, casein and large numbers of leucocytes, commonly referred to as milk slime. Leucocytes are a type of cell found in the udder, and the number present in milk increases if cows are suffering from mastitis. The presence of leucocytes in heat-treated milk is purely an aesthetic problem.

*Souring of milk*

Lactic acid bacteria break down lactose to produce lactic acid. Bacteria involved include *Staphylococcus* and *Streptococcus lactis*. *Bacillus proteus* forms whey.

**Cream**

The butterfat in milk is present as small globules which will gradually rise to the surface, as they are less dense than milk. This cream line can be seen in bottles of pasteurized milk which have not been homogenized. To speed up the process a mechanical separator, which acts like a centrifuge, is used. The stainless steel separator consists of an outer casing which encloses a stack of conical plates. Pre-warmed milk is fed into the separator which rotates at around 6,000 revolutions per minute. The lighter cream collects in the centre of the unit and is drawn off, heat treated and cooled. The heavier skimmed milk passes through the plates and is also drawn off, flash heated to around 80°C and then cooled to around 5°C. A valve may be used to control the fat content of the cream.

The cream may contain the same pathogens as milk and is normally pasteurized in an HTST plant at not less than 72°C (or the equivalent) for not less than 15 seconds and then cooled to less than 5°C. It is normally aged before filling into suitable cartons. Homogenization is sometimes used to thicken the cream.

*Sterilized cream*

Homogenized cream is canned or bottled and then sterilized, at a temperature of not less than 108°C for not less than 45 minutes (or the equivalent) and then cooled. Sterilized cream will keep for prolonged periods but obviously has a different flavour from pasteurized. The legislation relating to milk applies to cream. In addition, specific regulations lay down the appropriate compositional standards for particular types of cream; double cream must contain at least 48% milk fat; single cream must contain at least 18% milk fat.

*Imitation or non-dairy cream*

Is a substance which resembles cream and is produced by emulsifying edible oils or fats with water. Imitation cream is mainly used by bakeries for filling, in place of dairy cream. It is often prepared from palm kernel oils with egg yolk, water, sugar and milk powder.

## Yogurt

To manufacture yogurt, skimmed milk, sugar and water are mixed together and heated to approximately 95°C for around 30 minutes. The mix is then cooled to around 43°C, filled into incubation tanks, and a starter culture, for example, *Lactobacillus bulgaricus* and *Streptococcus thermophilus*, is added. These bacteria produce lactic acid, and the fermentation process is allowed to continue until a pH of approximately 4.0 is achieved and the yogurt has thickened considerably. The mix is then cooled to below 5°C. Unless plain yogurt is required, fruit is added and the mix is then filled into cartons and placed in cold storage.

## Yogurt spoilage

Bacterial spoilage is inhibited by the acidity of the yogurt and low storage temperatures. However, unless the mix is heat treated after fermentation, the starter culture will continue to produce acid and after approximately ten days the yogurt becomes unpalatable. Yeast and moulds are more likely to cause problems. Fermentation of sugar by yeast causes the production of carbon dioxide which results in a strained convex cap. Mould may be observed as a white or green clump on the surface.

**Butter**

Cream is held at 5°C in large, insulated, stainless steel tanks until required. It may be necessary to add lactic acid-producing bacteria (starters) and warm the cream to ensure the correct acidity. The temperature and pH are dictated by the flavour required. The cream is then pumped into a large, stainless steel churn which operates half full. The churn revolves for around 40 minutes which allows the fat globules to coalesce. The fat granules so formed are around the size of a grain of wheat. During churning the temperature is kept at around 7°C.

The buttermilk is then drawn off and the butter sprayed with chilled water to remove any traces of buttermilk. Excess water is drained off and salt may be added, depending on the flavour required. The churn is rotated slowly to disperse moisture and salt and to ensure a smooth finished product. This stage is known as working the butter. When the butter is removed, the moisture content must, by law, not exceed 16%. After packing, the butter should be stored away from chemicals or other food with strong odours. Modern manufacture is by continuous buttermakers which operate on the same principle but produce five tons per hour.

Defects in butter may be due to poor quality cream, production errors or post pasteurization contamination. The butter may be sour, rancid or cheesy, normally because of bacterial action. It is essential, therefore, to maintain high standards of factory hygiene and develop suitable quality control checks, including bacteriological examination of raw materials and finished product.

Growth of bacteria, yeast and moulds may occur rapidly if butter, especially unsalted, is stored above 16°C. The keeping quality depends on the bacterial load, type of organisms and storage temperature. Chilled or refrigerated storage is advisable. Growth of salmonellae has been recorded in butter kept at room temperatures (25°C).

**Margarine**

Margarine is produced from a blend of fat-free milk and vegetable, animal and marine oils or fats.

**Cheese**

Cheese may be made from:

(1) whole milk, for example, Cheddar;
(2) skimmed milk, for example, Dutch; or
(3) milk to which cream has been added, for example, Stilton.

There are three main types of cheese:

(1) *Hard cheeses*

Have relatively low-moisture content and possess excellent keeping qualities. Examples include Cheddar, Lancashire, Cheshire.

(2) *Soft cheeses*

Which are allowed to drain naturally as the curd is not pressed, such as, Camembert,

Limburger and Cambridge.

(3) *Blue-veined varieties*

Have a high-moisture content and soft curd. They are ripened by normal organisms and by the growth of specific moulds.

**Cheese manufacture**

Pasteurized milk is run into long stall troughs, and milk cultures of *Streptococcus lactis* are added to ensure the correct acidity. Rennet is then added and the milk-clots form a curd and a liquid whey which is drained off. The curd is cut into small cubes and then heated to expel moisture and assist in whey drainage. Higher temperatures are used to produce the drier, hard cheeses.

The cubes coalesce and the resultant mass is cut into slabs which are piled up to increase whey drainage. The dry, firm curd is then passed through a milling machine which tears it into small pieces, and salt is added. After salting, the cheese is filled into moulds or vacuum packs, pressed and then ripened at 10°C and 80 to 90% relative humidity. Ripening can take from three months to a year. Most types of cheese, once cut, should be stored in a refrigerator, provided that they are well-wrapped.

**Cheese faults**

Defects in cheese may occur because of:

(1) the use of unsatisfactory milk;
(2) the presence of foreign substances;
(3) the growth of abnormal bacteria; or
(4) production errors.

Bacterial faults include sliminess, bitterness, rancidity and pigmentation. Scrupulous attention must be paid to the quality of raw materials and to hygiene during production. Food poisoning incidents, including *Salmonella* and staphylococcal, have been traced back to contaminated cheese. In 1984 imported Camembert and Brie from France resulted in several cases of *E. coli* food poisoning.

Mycotoxin-producing moulds have been isolated from a number of cheeses including Cheddar.

**Condensed milk**

There are two types of condensed milk:

(1) sweetened condensed milk; and
(2) unsweetened evaporated milk.

*Sweetened condensed milk*

The milk is preheated, filtered and separated (separation is not carried out if full-cream condensed milk is to be produced). Further heating is carried out to destroy bacteria, moulds and enzymes. Sugar is added at a concentration which ensures preservation by producing a high osmotic pressure. The sweetened milk is pumped into an evaporator where approximately 60% of the water is boiled off under vacuum at around 55°C. The milk is cooled carefully, to prevent the formation of large lactose (milk sugar) crystals, and canned.

Thickening of condensed milk may be caused by micrococci and contamination by gas-producing yeast may cause the can to blow.

*Unsweetened evaporated milk*

The production of this milk is very similar to sweetened condensed milk apart from the fact that no sugar is added. After evaporation, the milk is homogenized to prevent the separation of fat and then cooled and filled into cans. The filled cans are heated to 115°C for 20 minutes to ensure their safety and shelf-life.

Underprocessing of evaporated milk may allow the survival of *Bacillus subtilis*, *Bacillus coagulans* or *Bacillus cereus*, which give the can contents a coagulated appearance.

**Dried milk**

The standardized raw milk is preheated and filtered before the removal of water. There are several methods available for the production of dried milk.

*Roller drying*

The milk is spread, as a very thin film, on an internally-heated, revolving, horizontal steel cylinder. The resultant dried milk is automatically scraped off.

*Spray drying*

After an initial boiling under vacuum, the concentrated milk is pumped into the top of a hot-air tower as a very fine spray. The resulting dried milk powder collects at the base of the tower and is cooled, burnt particles removed and it is then packed in air-tight containers.

*Accelerated freeze drying*

To improve reconstitution, this method may be used. The milk is frozen and then heated under vacuum so that the water is removed by sublimation. Salmonellae have been isolated from dried milk powder made from unpasteurized milk. There is also a possible risk if *Staphylococcus aureus* is present and allowed to multiply prior to drying as heat-resistant toxins may be produced.

**Ice-cream**

Ice-cream may be made with milk fat, sugar, eggs and cornflour, or vegetable fat, separated milk powder, sugar, gelatin, emulsifiers and water. Manufacture consists of mixing, pasteurizing, homogenizing, freezing and packaging. Alternatively, the mix may be sterilized and frozen, or dehydrated and sold as a complete cold mix which is reconstituted by the addition of water.

*Pasteurized ice-cream*

To comply with the Dairy Products (Hygiene) Regulations, 1995, pasteurization must be carried out by heating to not less than:

(1) 65.6°C for at least 30 minutes; or

(2) 71.1°C for at least ten minutes; or

(3) 79.4°C for at least 15 seconds.

After heating, the mixture is homogenized and cooled to below 7.2°C within one and a half hours and then frozen and packaged. The HTST plant must be provided with a flow diversion valve to redirect ice-cream that has not been heated to the correct temperature. Indicating and recording thermometers should be provided and records kept for at least one month.

*Sterilized ice-cream*

If the mixture is sterilized, it must be heated to not less than 148.9°C for at least two seconds and then cooled to below 7.2°C within one and a half hours, or alternatively canned under sterile conditions. If the can is opened, the ice-cream must be cooled to below 7.2°C and kept at this temperature until frozen.

*Soft ice-cream*

Soft ice-cream is freshly frozen ice-cream which is normally sold to the public direct from the freezer. When using a complete cold mix, it is essential that after reconstitution the mix is frozen in the soft ice-cream machine within one hour. (For cleaning a soft ice-cream machine, see Chapter 13.)

*Ice-cream spoilage*

Ice-cream may become either sour or rancid. Sour ice-cream is caused by prolonged storage before freezing or the use of sour milk. Rancid ice-cream is caused by the use of rancid fat.

*The methylene blue test*

This test is used to determine the bacteriological standard of ice-cream. The ice-cream is mixed with methylene blue and Ringer solution and then incubated in a water-bath at 20°C for 17 hours. It is then incubated at 37°C and inverted every 30 minutes until decolourized.

Interpretation of results.

| Grade | Time to decolourize (hrs) |
|---|---|
| 1 | 4.5 |
| 2 | 2.5 to 4 |
| 3 | 0.5 to 2 |
| 4 | 0 |

Most samples should be grade 1 or 2 and, although not legally binding, consistent grade 3 or 4 samples indicate poor hygiene at some stage of production or handling.

**Liquid egg**

The objective in pasteurizing liquid egg is to destroy pathogenic organisms, especially salmonellae, without affecting the physical and functional properties of the raw egg. Thus, the time and temperature used are critical to achieve this state of affairs. Liquid whole egg can be pasteurized at 60°C for three and a half minutes. The Egg Products Regulations, 1993 state a temperature of not less than 64.4°C for at least two and a half minutes, or another time and temperature that has the same lethal effect on vegetative, pathogenic organisms. Following the pasteurization process the treated egg must satisfy the alpha-amylase test. This is another enzyme test (similar to the phosphatase test for pasteurized milk). Absence of the enzyme signifies that the liquid egg has been adequately pasteurized.

# *Appendix II*

**EMPLOYEE MEDICAL QUESTIONNAIRE**

**NAME**..........................................................**OCCUPATION**.................................
**ADDRESS**......................................................**DEPARTMENT**.................................
.........................................................................
.........................................................................
.........................................................................

(1) Have you ever had or been a carrier of:

| | |
|---|---|
| A food-borne disease | **YES/NO** |
| Typhoid or paratyphoid | **YES/NO** |
| Tuberculosis | **YES/NO** |
| Parasitic infections | **YES/NO** |

(2) Has any close family contact suffered from any of the above? **YES/NO**

(3) Have you suffered from any of the following:

| | |
|---|---|
| Serious diarrhoea or vomiting | **YES/NO** |
| Skin trouble | **YES/NO** |
| Boils, styes or septic fingers | **YES/NO** |
| Discharge from the ears, eyes, gums/mouth | **YES/NO** |

(4) Please give details of any other medical problems which may affect your employment as a food handler, for example, recurring gastrointestinal disorder.

.............................................................................................
.............................................................................................
.............................................................................................
.............................................................................................

(5) Have you been abroad within the last two years? **YES/NO**
**WHERE?**.............................................................................................

(6) Should it be necessary, will you agree to provide such specimens that may be required by the company to ensure that you are not a carrier of any organism which may infect food? **YES/NO**

I declare that all the foregoing statements are true and complete to the best of my knowledge and belief.

Signed.....................................................................

# Appendix III Hygiene courses

## HYGIENE COURSES AND QUALIFICATIONS

Although food hygiene courses may form only a small part of hygiene training they can be extremely useful. Some large food organizations are able to provide excellent in-house courses but there are several advantages in attending certificated food hygiene courses run by a local college, a consultant or an Environmental Health Department.

(1) In-house courses will not receive national recognition and customers may not be convinced that staff are receiving the appropriate level of hygiene education.
(2) There will be less motivation for staff as they may perceive the course purely as an extension of company rules. They will not receive a nationally recognized qualification, which for many first-tier workers may be their first exam certificate.
(3) Staff will not have the opportunity to discuss hygiene with persons employed by other companies; an exchange of information and ideas will usually be beneficial.
(4) If an Environmental Health Officer is involved in the course, it will enable staff to discuss hygiene matters and ideas with him/her in an informal manner without the possible restrictions imposed during formal inspections of food premises.

*Organizations providing hygiene courses for food handlers*

(1) The Chartered Institute of Environmental Health, Chadwick Court, 15 Hatfields, London SE1 8DJ.
(2) The Royal Institute of Public Health and Hygiene, 28 Portland Place, London W1N 4DE.
(3) The Royal Society of Health, RSH House, 38A St. George's Drive, London SW1V 4BH.
(4) The Society of Food Hygiene Technology, PO Box 37, Lymington, Hampshire SO41 9WL.
(5) The Royal Environmental Health Institute of Scotland, Virginia House, 62 Virginia Street, Glasgow G1 1TX.

### Courses offered by the Chartered Institute of Environmental Health (CIEH)

*The CIEH Basic Food Hygiene Certificate Course*

This course is considered to be the minimum level of hygiene education required by food handlers involved in the preparation of high-risk food. The course length is a minimum of six hours, which is usually split into three sessions of two hours, six sessions of one hour or held over a full day. The short examination which concludes the course is available in a multiple-choice, tick-box format or as an oral examination. The pass mark is 60%. An alternative route to certification is a competence-based programme of training and continuous assessment in the workplace.

*The CIEH Intermediate Food Hygiene Certificate Course*

This course is intended for supervisors, students and those persons who wish to progress in stages from the Basic to the Advanced Course. The course length is a minimum of 18 hours, which may be offered as an intensive block or over a period of weeks. Candidates have to complete a one and a half hour written examination. The pass mark is 60%. Candidates gaining 80% or more are awarded a credit pass.

*The CIEH Advanced Food Hygiene Certificate Course*

This course is primarily intended for managers. The course length is a minimum of 36 hours and may be offered as an intensive block or over a period of weeks. There is particular emphasis on management responsibilities for food hygiene and the course is useful for personnel from all sectors of the food industry: catering, retailing and manufacturing. Candidates are assessed on the basis of two course assignments (40% of the final mark) and a two and a half hour written examination (60% of the final mark). The pass mark is 60%. Candidates gaining 80% or more are awarded a credit pass. Persons who successfully complete the Advanced Course, have an approved qualification in training and have adequate experience in the food industry, may seek approval from the CIEH to offer the Basic Food Hygiene Certificate Course.

There are over 4,000 centres in England, Wales and Northern Ireland registered as centres for CIEH certificated courses. These include environmental health departments, health authorities, public and private companies, training consultants and colleges.

**Basic Food Hygiene Certificate**

Bacteriology
Food poisoning
Prevention of contamination and food poisoning
Personal hygiene
Premises, equipment and pest control
Cleaning and disinfection
Legislation

**Intermediate Food Hygiene Certificate**

General introduction
Bacteriology
Non-bacterial food poisoning
Food poisoning and food-borne disease
Physical contamination of food and its prevention
Personal hygiene
Food storage and temperature control food preservation
Cleaning and disinfection
Pest control
Legislation
Design and construction of food premises and equipment
Supervisory management

**Advanced Food Hygiene Certificate**

General introduction
Non-bacterial food poisoning
Food poisoning and food-borne disease
Bacteriology
Physical contamination of food and its prevention
Personal hygiene
Training and education of food handlers
Food storage and temperature control
Food preservation
Design and construction of food premises
Design of equipment
Cleaning and disinfection
Legislation
Pest control
Management control techniques

**Courses offered by the Royal Institute of Public Health and Hygiene (RIPHH)**

*Primary Certificate in Food Hygiene*

This first stage qualification is designed for any person who is, or intends to be, a food handler. It is recognized by the Department of Health and the Ministry of Agriculture, Fisheries and Food as providing evidence of a standard of hygiene awareness appropriate to handlers of high-risk foods. Many candidates are catering or food industry workers who have attended an RIPHH accredited course provided by their own company, or by a specialist consultant, with an emphasis on practical and vocational application. A large number of colleges also offer accredited courses, either as part of a wider curriculum or as modules in their own right. Open learning courses are also available. The minimum length of time needed to cover the syllabus satisfactorily is seven hours of teaching or tutorials, but some institutions may find it necessary to extend the number of hours of tuition, according to the experience of the students. The examination consists of a written paper of 30 multiple-choice questions. The pass mark is 20 marks out of 30 (66%). Candidates achieving 25 marks (83%) are awarded a credit pass and those achieving 28 marks (93%) are awarded honours.

Sector specific examinations, covering the topics of the Primary Certificate syllabus but oriented to the needs of specific industry sectors, are also available.

*First Certificate in Food Safety*

An alternative to the Primary Certificate in Food Hygiene and takes into account the latest approach to food safety and consumer protection, i.e. elementary concepts of hazard identification and control. The examination consists of a written paper of 30 questions and the pass mark is 60%.

*Certificate in HACCP Principles* (Hazard Analysis Critical Control Point)

The RIPHH has recently developed a training standard for introductory courses in HACCP and an associated qualification. The Royal Institute offers accreditation of courses developed by food businesses and/or training organisations, which meet the HACCP Training Standard. The associated examination consists of two written papers which test knowledge of HACCP principles and their application in food businesses.

### *Certificate in Food Hygiene*

Candidates preparing for this qualification attend an RIPHH accredited course provided by their own company, by a consultant or by a college. Open learning courses are also available. The course lasts for a minimum of 16 hours and provides an acceptable level of hygiene education for students, skilled food handlers, supervisors and junior managers. The examination consists of a two hour written paper and an oral examination of approximately ten minutes. The pass mark is 50%. Candidates achieving 65% are awarded a credit pass and those achieving 80%, an honours pass.

### *Diploma in Food Hygiene*

The Diploma in Food Hygiene is an advanced level qualification designed for middle management and senior staff in food processing, catering, the retail trade and other food businesses, who have responsibility for the management of food hygiene and safety. Entrants to an accredited course leading to this qualification should already hold the Certificate in Food Hygiene, or possess knowledge of the subject to an equivalent standard. They should also have a good standard of general education. The minimum length of a course is 24 hours. The examination consists of two written papers, each of two hours, and an oral examination of approximately 15 minutes. The pass mark is 60% and candidates achieving marks of 70% and 80% are awarded credit and honours passes respectively.

### *Diploma in Hygiene Management*

This qualification is sufficiently flexible to allow it to be adapted to any work situation in which hygiene is a major concern. It is intended for middle managers and aims to develop management ability in promoting and maintaining hygiene at the workplace. Entrants should hold a Royal Institute Certificate in a hygiene related subject or an equivalent hygiene qualification. They are required to undertake a project on a given topic of hygiene management related to their own particular working environment which will form the basis of a 5,000 word dissertation to be produced within a one year period. Regular tutorials are arranged with appropriate experts to give advice on the management techniques to be employed and the method of presentation of information. A Diploma in Hygiene Management is awarded to each participant whose dissertation is assessed as satisfactory.

### **Primary Certificate in Food Hygiene**

Microbiology, food poisoning and food contamination
Principles of hygienic work practice
Personal standards
Maintenance and cleaning of premises and equipment
Food hygiene legislation
Control of pests

### **First Certificate in Food Safety**

Food poisoning and microorganisms
Maintenance and cleaning of premises and equipment

Temperature
Legal obligations
Hazards
Pests
The human body
Hazard Analysis Critical Control Point
Contamination and cross-contamination
Waste disposal
Personal standards
Storage and temperature control

**Certificate in Food Hygiene**

Introduction to microbiology
Hygiene principles
Preservation of food
Cleaning and disinfection
Food premises
Food poisoning/other food-borne diseases
Pest control in food premises
Law concerning food hygiene

**Certificate in HACCP Principles**

The need for a HACCP system.

The legal obligations to analyze hazards and identify critical steps, and how these obligations should be met in the appropriate industries.

The principles of HACCP and their importance.

The method by which hazard analysis may be carried out and appropriate control measures ascertained.

Identification of critical control points including critical limits to ensure their control, and overcoming implementation difficulties.

Development of suitable monitoring instructions for critical verification of the HACCP system by use of appropriate auditing steps needed to manage a fully operational HACCP system.

**Diploma in Food Hygiene**

Management of good food hygiene practice, including:

Microbiology and food poisoning
Canning
Refrigeration
Other methods of food preservation
Cleaning and disinfection
Control of pests
Complaints and how to deal with them
Education and health control of food handlers
Hygiene of bakery products
Hygiene of fish products
Hygiene of dairy products
Hygiene of meat and meat products
Mass catering
Retail food hygiene
Design of food premises and equipment, including legal requirements
Food legislation

**Courses offered by the Royal Society of Health (RSH)**

*The RSH Certificate in Essential Food Hygiene*

This course has a minimum duration of six hours and covers the basic principles of food hygiene in a simple and interesting manner. It is directed at those working in kitchens or who undertake first line duties in preparing, processing, serving or retailing food. The course is offered by many colleges and food hygiene consultancies and for in-house training. Students receive the RSH Handbook "Essential Food Hygiene". The examination (25 minutes) consists of 20 multiple-choice questions with a pass mark of 14 out of 20, subject to the candidate having correctly answered two specific questions. Successful candidates are awarded the Certificate in Essential Food Hygiene.

### *The RSH Certificate in Food Hygiene Awareness*

Introduced in 1995, the course has a minimum delivery time of three hours and is directed at those performing low-risk tasks The course covers much the same ground as the Essential Food Hygiene Course but in less detail and is less demanding. The examination (20 minutes) consists of 16 multiple-choice questions with a pass mark of 12 out of 16. Successful candidates are awarded the Certificate in Food Hygiene Awareness.

### *The RSH Certificate in Food Hygiene Management*

This course is pitched at a level between the Society's basic courses and the more advanced Diploma in Food Hygiene. It is aimed at supervisors and first line managers. The minimum duration is 22 hours. Formerly known as the Certificate in Hygiene of Food Retailing and Catering, the course maintains its previous thorough coverage of the elements of food hygiene and their application in practical situations but has been revised to reflect the needs of the wider food industry and to provide an introduction to the techniques of management. The examination paper consists of 50 questions requiring short answers (one and a half hours). Successful candidates are awarded the Certificate in Food Hygiene Management at pass or credit level and are eligible for election to the grade of Affiliate (Affil RSH) of the Society.

### *The RSH Diploma in Food Hygiene*

The course, of 40 hours (minimum) duration, is suitable for senior personnel in all sectors of the food industry and will also assist those preparing for a teaching role. The theory and practice of food hygiene are comprehensively covered as are those management aspects to meet legislative and other requirements. The examination consists of two papers, each of two hours duration (essay-type answers), and a viva-voce test of approximately 15 minutes. Successful candidates are awarded the Diploma in Food Hygiene Management at either pass or distinction level and are eligible for election to the grade of Associate Member (AMRSH) of the Society. Candidates who marginally fail the examination are considered for the award of the Certificate in Food Hygiene Management.

### **Certificate in Essential Food Hygiene**

Food poisoning, how it occurs, the symptoms and the consequences
Hygiene control
Pest control
Cleaning and disinfection
Bacteria and how they cause food poisoning
Personal hygiene
Temperature control
Legal requirements

**Certificate in Food Hygiene Management**

Introduction to food hygiene
Bacteria
Storage and transport of food
Food poisoning
Construction and layout of food premises/mobile vehicles/stalls
Cleansing techniques
Temperature control of food
Pest control
Choice of equipment in food premises/stalls
Personal hygiene
Law relating to food hygiene

**Diploma in Food Hygiene**

The management of food hygiene
Law relating to food hygiene
Food preservation, storage and fitness
General review of microorganisms
Construction and design of food premises/stalls/vehicles, etc.
Pest control
Ice cream and liquid egg
Eggs, fruit and vegetables
Hotels, fried fish shops, hospital kitchens, residential homes, railway and in-flight catering
Reasons for food hygiene
Cleaning and disinfection
Canning
Personal hygiene
Choice of equipment in food premises
Milk and milk products
Fish including shellfish
Meat and meat products
Bakery products, cereals, chocolates, etc.

**The Society of Food Hygiene Technology (SOFHT)**

*The SOFHT Hygiene Training Scheme for Food Handlers in Food Manufacturing and Supplying Industries*

This industry-specific, participative six hour food hygiene course is delivered by SOFHT authorized trainers who are subjected to regular moderation. All trainees are supplied with a passport at the start of the course and this is validated immediately following successful completion of the continuous multi-choice assessments. Full training records are held by the Society. The course consists of five modules:

(1) introduction, legislation and food handler's legal responsibilities;
(2) non-microbial contamination. Control of pests, foreign matter and chemicals;
(3) microbial contamination, simple microbiology, food spoilage, temperature control, shelf-life, food infection and food poisoning;
(4) cross-contamination, plant and equipment cleaning and disinfection and personal hygiene; and
(5) industry-specific, covering raw materials, production processes, packaging, storage and distribution.

**The SOFHT Food Hygiene Awareness Scheme**

This is a video and poster based package which has been developed to be used as part of an induction or refresher course. It is an eight section, one and a half hour course encouraging interaction between the trainer and trainees. Subjects include quality, pest control, foreign objects, cross-contamination, temperature control, cleaning and personal hygiene. As well as the video, it is supported by a range of posters, trainers' notes, exercises and a multi-choice pictorial assessment.

## The SOFHT Food Hygiene Microbiology Course

This course has been designed to provide the necessary practical skills and knowledge for non-microbiologists working in the food hygiene arena. It is a laboratory-based course, run over three days and covers an introduction to microbiology; microorganisms in food; growth of microorganisms, microbial spoilage of food; food related disease; food safety legislation; control of microorganisms in food; the application of quality control systems to food hygiene; and hygiene on food premises. An assessment is by a combined written/oral examination which is taken within three months from the end of the course.

## Courses offered by the Royal Environmental Health Institute of Scotland (REHIS)

### *The Elementary Food Hygiene Course*

This course, of six hours duration, is intended for people employed in all sectors of the food industry. The course has been structured to identify areas of major concern and to offer elementary guidance regarding good practice in the food industry.

A third question multiple-choice examination is used to test participants' understanding of the course material. Participants who pass the examination are awarded the Elementary Food Hygiene Certificate.

It is hoped that successful completion of this course will encourage participants to pursue further training in order to increase their awareness of food hygiene. It is recognized, however, that this course will remain a major source of elementary tuition on food hygiene principles and practices.

### *The Intermediate Food Hygiene Course*

This course, of a minimum of 16 hours duration, is intended to provide sound training in food hygiene for food handlers. The course represents an excellent progression for food handlers who have successfully completed the Elementary Food Hygiene Course. It is particularly appropriate for supervisors in the food industry.

A two hour written examination is used to test participants' understanding of the course material. Participants who pass the examination are awarded the Intermediate Food Hygiene Certificate. In appropriate circumstances, credit passes may be awarded with the certificate suitably endorsed.

### *The Diploma in Advanced Food Hygiene*

This course is of a minimum of 36 hours duration and is intended for managers, hygiene specialists, and for trainers who wish to present Elementary Food Hygiene Courses. The course covers in detail a wide variety of subjects relating to food hygiene.

Entry to the course is normally restricted to holders of an Intermediate Food Hygiene Certificate or equivalent qualification.

Successful completion of set course work permits entry to the examination which consists of a three hour written paper and an oral examination. Participants who are successful in the examination are awarded the Diploma in Advanced Food Hygiene. Credit passes with a suitably endorsed diploma may be awarded in appropriate circumstances.

**The Elementary Food Hygiene Course**

Introduction
Bacteria
Food poisoning and food-borne infections
Preventing food poisoning
Personal hygiene
Cleaning and disinfection
Food premises and equipment
Food pests
Food hygiene law

**The Intermediate Food Hygiene Course**

Introduction
Bacteriology
Bacterial food poisoning
Food-borne infections
Non-bacterial food poisoning
Food contamination and its prevention
Personal hygiene
Food storage and temperature control
Food preservation
Cleaning and disinfection
Pest control
Design, construction and maintenance of food premises and equipment
Legislation

**The Diploma in Advanced Food Hygiene**

Introduction
Bacteriology
Bacterial food poisoning
Food-borne infections
Non-bacterial food poisoning
Food contamination and its prevention
Hazard analysis and critical control points (HACCP)
Design, construction and maintenance of food premises
Food storage and temperature control
Legislation
Management control techniques
Cleaning and disinfection
Food preservation
Personal hygiene
Pest control
Design, construction and maintenance of equipment
The training and education of food handlers

# Glossary

| | |
|---|---|
| Acid | A chemical which forms hydrogen ions in solution, the hydrogen being replaceable by a metal to form a salt. Used for removing hard water scale. |
| Acute disease | A disease which develops rapidly and produces symptoms quickly after infection. Patients soon recover, or die. |
| Aerobic | Requiring oxygen. |
| Algae | Simple plants capable of photosynthesis and most commonly found in aquatic environments or damp soil, for example, seaweed and spirogyra (forms bright green slimy masses in ponds). |
| Alkali | A chemical which reacts with an acid to form a salt and water only. |
| Ambient temperature | The temperature of the surroundings. Usually refers to the room temperature. |
| Anaerobic | Requiring the absence of oxygen. |
| Antibiotic | A drug used to destroy pathogenic bacteria within human or animal bodies (some are only bacteriostatic). |
| Antiseptic | A substance that prevents the growth of bacteria and moulds, specifically on or in the human body. |
| Aseptic | Free from microorganisms. |
| Audit | A documented inspection performed to verify by examination and evaluation the effectiveness of a system. |
| $A_w$ (water activity) | $A_w = \frac{\text{Water vapour pressure of food}}{\text{Water vapour pressure of pure water}}$<br>$A_w \times 100$ = Equilibrium Relative Humidity. |
| Bactericide | A substance which destroys bacteria. |
| Bacteriostat | A substance that inhibits the multiplication of bacteria. |
| Binary fission | Asexual method of reproduction by the division of the nucleus into two daughter nuclei, followed by similar division of the cell body. The method of reproduction used by bacteria. |
| Biodegradable | Chemicals and materials which can be broken down by bacteria or other biological means (usually during sewage treatment). |
| Carrier | A person who harbours, and may transmit, pathogenic organisms without showing signs of illness. |

| | |
|---|---|
| Chronic disease | A disease which usually develops slowly and symptoms last for a prolonged period. |
| Chronic poison | A substance which is used at low concentration and relies on repeated intake by the target pest to ensure elimination. |
| Cleaning | The process of removing soil, food residues, dirt, grease and other objectionable matter. |
| Clean surface | A surface which is free from residual film or soil, has no objectionable odour, is not greasy to touch and will not discolour a white paper tissue wiped over it. |
| Compressor (refrigerator) | A mechanical pump which moves up and down in a cylinder which contains the refrigerant gas and pumps it round the system starting with the condenser. |
| Condenser (refrigerator) | A unit which looks like a car radiator with a fan in front of it. The fan draws air from the room across the surface of the condenser which cools the gaseous refrigerant, delivered from the compressor, and returns it to a liquid state. |
| Contamination | The occurrence of any objectionable matter in the product. |
| Controlled atmosphere packing | The packaging of food in an atmosphere that is different from the normal composition of air, the gases being precisely adjusted to specific concentration which are maintained throughout storage. |
| Critical control point (CCP) | A step in a process which, if controlled, will eliminate or reduce a hazard to an acceptable level. |
| Cuisine sous vide | A system of cooking (pasteurizing) raw or par-cooked food in a sealed pouch under vacuum. After pasteurization the pouch is cooled and stored below 3°C. Products have a shelf-life of up to 21 days (eight in the UK) and are regenerated using heat, immediately before consumption. |
| Danger zone of bacterial growth | The temperature range within which the greatest multiplication of pathogenic bacteria is possible, i.e. from 5°C to 63°C. |
| Detergent | A chemical or mixture of chemicals made of soap or synthetic substitutes; it facilitates the removal of grease and food particles from dishes and utensils and promotes cleanliness, so that all surfaces are readily accessible to the action of disinfectants. |
| Disinfectant | A chemical used for disinfection. |
| Disinfection | The reduction of microorganisms to a level that will not lead to harmful contamination nor spoilage of food. Chemical agents and/or physical methods which are used should not adversely affect the food. The term disinfection normally refers to the treatment of premises, surfaces and equipment, but may also be applied to the treatment of skin. |

| | |
|---|---|
| D value | The time, in minutes, required at a given temperature to reduce the number of viable cells or spores of a given microorganism to 10% of the initial number. |
| Epidemiology | The study of disease of people and animals, including causes, frequency, distribution and control. |
| Evaporator (refrigerator) | Consists of a long tube bent many times and passed through hundreds of aluminium fins. Air from the cabinet is drawn over the evaporator and heat is transferred to the liquid refrigerant, delivered from the condenser, which boils and reverts to a gas. |
| Faecal matter | Excreta. Stools. The indigestible residues voided from the alimentary canal after digestion and absorption of food and water. One third of the dry weight of human faeces is bacteria; mainly *Escherichia coli* and *Streptococcus faecalis*. |
| First aid materials | Suitable and sufficient bandages and dressings, including waterproof dressings and antiseptic. (All dressings to be individually wrapped.) |
| Food handling | Any operation in the production, preparation, processing, packaging, storage, transport, distribution and sale of food. |
| Food hygiene | All measures necessary to ensure the safety and wholesomeness of food during preparation, processing, manufacture, storage, transportation, distribution, handling and offering for sale or supply to the consumer. |
| Food poisoning | An acute illness of sudden onset caused by the recent consumption of contaminated or poisonous food. |
| Fungi | Plants unable to synthesize their own food and usually parasitic or saprophytic. Include single-celled microscopic yeasts, moulds, mildews and toadstools. Yeasts are used to produce alcohol, moulds cause food spoilage and ringworm is a fungal disease of animals. |
| Fungicide | A substance that kills fungi and mould. |
| Galvanized metal | Iron or steel which has been coated with zinc for protection against corrosion. |
| Gastroenteritis | An inflammation of the stomach and intestinal tract that normally results in diarrhoea. |
| Germicide | An agent used for killing microorganisms. |
| Grease trap | A device fitted into a drainage system to prevent fat and grease entering the sewer. |
| HACCP | Hazard analysis and critical control points. A structured and documented hazard analysis system based on specialist advice and applied to a standardized food production process with a view to ensuring cost-effective food safety. Critical control points are determined and then monitored. Specified remedial action is taken if any measurements deviate from safe limits. |

| | |
|---|---|
| Hazard | The potential to cause harm to the consumer (the safety aspect of the product) and can be microbiological, chemical or physical. |
| Hazard analysis and control | Any system which enables a food business to identify points in its activities which are critical to ensuring food safety and to identify and implement effective control and monitoring procedures, and periodically review these procedures to ensure food safety. |
| Health declaration | A medical questionnaire completed, for example, when applying for a job or on return to work after an illness, to determine fitness for food handling duties. |
| High-risk foods | Ready-to-eat foods which, under favourable conditions, support the multiplication of pathogenic bacteria and are intended for consumption without treatment which would destroy such organisms. |
| Immunocompromized | An individual who is unable to produce a normal immune response to an infection. |
| Incubation period | The period between infection and the first signs of illness. |
| Infective dose | The number of a particular microorganism required under normal circumstances to produce clinical signs of a disease. |
| Infestation | The presence of rats, mice, insects or mites in numbers or under conditions which involve an immediate or potential risk of contamination, loss or damage to food. The term usually implies the existence of a breeding population but may be used to denote the presence of individuals. |
| Larva | The immature stage of an insect that undergoes complete metamorphosis (Egg -larva- pupa- adult). |
| Mildew | A type of fungus similar to mould. |
| Moulds | Microscopic plants (fungi) that may appear as woolly patches on food. |
| Onset period | The period between consumption of the food and the first signs of illness. (Where incubation of microorganisms within the body does not take place.) |
| Optimum | Best. |
| Pathogen | Disease-producing organism. |
| Pest | Any living creature capable of directly or indirectly contaminating food. |
| Pesticide | A chemical used to kill pests. |
| pH | An index used as a measure of acidity or alkalinity. |
| Proteolytic | Having the ability to break down proteins. |
| Protozoa | Single-celled animals which form the basis of the food chain. Live in moist habitats such as oceans, rivers, soil and decaying matter. Some are pathogenic, for example, *Entamoeba histolytica*. |

| | |
|---|---|
| Pupa | The third stage of development of an insect that has complete metamorphosis. |
| Quats | A popular name for quaternary ammonium compounds. |
| Radicidation | The use of irradiation to destroy non-spore-forming pathogens, pests and parasites. |
| Radurization | The use of irradiation to destroy spoilage organisms, prolong shelf-life and reduce microorganisms to a safe level. |
| Residual insecticide | A long-lasting insecticide applied in such a way that it remains active for a considerable period of time. |
| Risk | The likelihood that the hazard will be realized. |
| Risk assessment | The process of identifying hazards, assessing risks and evaluating their significance. |
| Sanitizer | A chemical agent used for cleansing and disinfecting surfaces and equipment. |
| Spores | A resistant resting-phase of bacteria which protects them against adverse conditions. |
| Sterile | Free from all living organisms. |
| Sterilization | A process that destroys all living organisms. |
| Tap proportioner | A device fitted to a tap, which delivers the right amount of detergent or sanitizer to the water. |
| Terrazzo flooring | Coloured marble chips set in portland cement in a mosaic fashion. (May be attacked by acids and alkalis.) |
| Total viable count | The total number of living cells detectable in a sample. The number of cells is assessed from the number of colonies which develop on incubation of a suitable medium which has been inoculated with the sample of bacteria. |
| Toxins | Poisons produced by pathogens. |
| Viruses | Microscopic pathogens that multiply in living cells of their host. |
| Wholesome food | Sound food, fit for human consumption. |
| Yeast | A unicellular fungus which reproduces by budding and grows rapidly on certain food-stuffs, especially those containing sugar. Yeasts are the chief agents of fermentation. (Sugar converted to alcohol and carbon dioxide.) |
| Z value | The change in temperature in degrees celsius required for a ten-fold change in D value. |

# *Bibliography*


(1) Dillon M. and Griffith C. (1996) How to HACCP: M. D. Associates.

(2) Eley R. (Ed.) (1995). Microbial Food Poisoning. London: Chapman & Hall.

(3) Hersom A. C. and Hulland E. D. (1980). Canned Foods. London: Churchill Livingstone.

(4) Hobbs B. C. and Roberts D. (1995). Food Poisoning and Food Hygiene. London: Edward Arnold.

(5) Jay J. M. (1992) Modern Food Microbiology. New York: Van Nostrand Reinhold.

(6) LACOTS. (1995). Risk Assessment: Guidance to Local Authorities on the application of risk assessment principles to food hygiene inspections.

(7) Leaper S. (Ed.) (1992). Technical Manual No. 38. HACCP: A Practical Guide. Chipping Campden: Campden FDRA.

(8) MacDonald D. and Engel D. (1996). A Guide to HACCP: Highfield Publications.

(9) Mortimer S. and Wallace C. (1994). HACCP- A Practical Approach: London Chapman and Hall.

(10) North R.A.E. (1993). Guidelines for the Detailed Investigation of Salmonella Food Poisoning in Commercial Premises. Leeds: Leeds Metropolitan University.

(11) Sheard M. and Church I. (1992). Sous-Vide Cook-Chill. Leeds: Leeds Metropolitan University.

(12) Shapton D. A. & F. N. (1993). Principles and Practices for the Safe Processing of Foods: Butterworth-Heinemann.

# Index